POLYCENTRICITY AND
LOCAL PUBLIC ECONOMIES

INSTITUTIONAL ANALYSIS

Editors, Michael D. McGinnis and Elinor Ostrom

Institutions link political, economic, social, and biophysical processes. *Institutional Analysis* was established to encourage multi-disciplinary, multi-level, and multi-method research on institutions for collective action, public services, resource management, development, and governance. Each book in this series investigates the origins and operation of institutions in particular empirical contexts or their broader roles in the constitution of order in human societies.

Titles in the Series:

Polycentric Governance and Development:
Readings from the Workshop in Political Theory and Policy Analysis
Michael D. McGinnis, editor

Polycentricity and Local Public Economies:
Readings from the Workshop in Political Theory and Policy Analysis
Michael D. McGinnis, editor

Polycentric Games and Institutions:
Readings from the Workshop in Political Theory and Policy Analysis
Michael D. McGinnis, editor

Related Titles on the Analysis of Institutions:

The Meaning of Democracy and the Vulnerability of Democracies:
A Response to Tocqueville's Challenge
Vincent Ostrom

Rules, Games, and Common-Pool Resources
Elinor Ostrom, Roy Gardner, and James Walker,
with Arun Agrawal, William Blomquist, Edella Schlager, and Shui-Yan Tang

Trust, Ethnicity, and Identity: Beyond the New Institutional Economics
of Ethnic Trading Networks, Contract Law, and Gift-Exchange
Janet Tai Landa

Laboratory Research in Political Economy
Thomas R. Palfrey, editor

POLYCENTRICITY AND LOCAL PUBLIC ECONOMIES

Readings from the Workshop in Political Theory and Policy Analysis

Michael D. McGinnis, Editor

Ann Arbor

THE UNIVERSITY OF MICHIGAN PRESS

2002   2001   2000   1999   4   3   2   1

A CIP catalog record for this book is available from the British Library.

Library of Congress Cataloging-in-Publication Data

Polycentricity and local public economies : readings from the Workshop
in Political Theory and Policy Analysis / Michael D. McGinnis, editor.
    p. cm. — (Institutional analysis)
    Includes bibliographical references and index.
    ISBN 0-472-11038-1 (cloth : alk. paper) — ISBN 0-472-08622-7 (pbk. : alk. paper)
    1. Political science — Congresses.   2. Metropolitan government — Congresses.
I. McGinnis, Michael D. (Michael Dean)   II. Indiana University, Bloomington.
Workshop in Political Theory and Policy Analysis.   III. Series
JA71.P677   1999
320 — dc21   99-048673
                                           CIP

Contents

List of Figures   viii
List of Tables   x
Series Foreword   xiii
Acknowledgments   xviii

Introduction *by Michael D. McGinnis*   1

Part I. Conceptual Foundations of Institutional Analysis

Chapter 1.   The Organization of Government in Metropolitan Areas:
              A Theoretical Inquiry   31
              by Vincent Ostrom, Charles M. Tiebout, and Robert Warren

Chapter 2.   Polycentricity (Part 1)   52
              by Vincent Ostrom

Chapter 3.   Public Goods and Public Choices   75
              by Vincent Ostrom and Elinor Ostrom

Part II. Frameworks for the Study of Public Economies

Chapter 4.   A Behavioral Approach to the Study of Intergovernmental
              Relations   107
              by Vincent Ostrom and Elinor Ostrom

Chapter 5.   Polycentricity (Part 2)   119
              by Vincent Ostrom

Chapter 6.   Metropolitan Reform: Propositions Derived from Two Traditions   139
              by Elinor Ostrom

Part III. Empirical Research on Police Services

Chapter 7.   Why Do We Need Multiple Indicators of Public Service Outputs?   163
              by Elinor Ostrom

Chapter 8.   Does Local Community Control of Police Make a Difference?
              Some Preliminary Findings   176
              by Elinor Ostrom and Gordon P. Whitaker

Chapter 9.   Community Control and Governmental Responsiveness:
              The Case of Police in Black Neighborhoods   203
              by Elinor Ostrom and Gordon P. Whitaker

Chapter 10.   Size and Performance in a Federal System   232
              by Elinor Ostrom

Part IV. Implications for Metropolitan Governance

Chapter 11.   Defining and Measuring Structural Variations in
              Interorganizational Arrangements   265
              by Elinor Ostrom, Roger B. Parks, and Gordon P. Whitaker

Chapter 12.   Neither Gargantua nor the Land of Lilliputs: Conjectures
              on Mixed Systems of Metropolitan Organization   284
              by Elinor Ostrom and Roger B. Parks

Chapter 13.   Citizen Voice and Public Entrepreneurship: The Organizational
              Dynamic of a Complex Metropolitan County   306
              by Ronald J. Oakerson and Roger B. Parks

Chapter 14.   Fiscal, Service, and Political Impacts of Indianapolis-Marion
              County's Unigov   329
              by William Blomquist and Roger B. Parks

Chapter 15.   Do We Really Want to Consolidate Urban Areas? [It's Like
              Deja Vu All Over Again]   349
              by Roger B. Parks

Part V. Continuing Challenges for Research and Policy

Chapter 16.   Complex Models of Urban Service Systems   355
              by Roger B. Parks and Elinor Ostrom

Chapter 17.   Consumers as Coproducers of Public Services: Some
              Economic and Institutional Considerations   381
              by Roger B. Parks, Paula C. Baker, Larry L. Kiser,
              Ronald J. Oakerson, Elinor Ostrom, Vincent Ostrom,
              Stephen L. Percy, Martha Vandivort, Gordon P. Whitaker,
              and Rick K. Wilson

Suggested Further Readings   393
Contributors   397
Index   401

Figures

3.1   Types of Goods   78

6.1   Posited Relations Among Variables in the Metropolitan Reform
       Tradition   144
6.2   Posited Relations Among Variables in the Political Economy Tradition   150

8.1   Posited Relations of Small Size and Community Control with Intervening
       and Dependent Variables   179

10.1   The Theoretical Consolidation Model (Simplified Form)   232
10.2   The Operational Consolidation Model (Simplified Form)   233
10.3   The Alternative Operational Model (Simplified Form)   234
10.4   A Rival Methodological Model   235
10.5   The Independent Effects of Training Levels on Citizen Evaluations
       Controlling for Size of Police Department and Socioeconomic Status
       of Neighborhood   247

11.1   Fayetteville, North Carolina, SMSA   270

12.1   Frontier Production Possibility Curves   287
12.2   Graphical Representation of Relative Technical Efficiency   288

14.1   Marion County Townships and Pre-Unigov City of Indianapolis   333

16.1   Iso-Benefits Residuum Contours   368
16.2   Possibility and Utility Curves   369
16.3   Relationship Between Risk of Exposure to Citizen Monitoring Efforts
       and Multiplicity of Industry Structure   372
16.4   Bureau Chiefs' Indifference Curves in High and Low Multiplicity
       SMSAs   373
16.5   Frontier and Average Production Functions—Number of On-Street
       Cars   376
16.6   Frontier Production Possibility Curves   376

17.1   Production Relationships and Budget Functions   385

Tables

3.1	Public and Private Goods	80
3.2	Collective Consumption Units and Producer Units	86
3.3	Options for Obtaining Public Services	88
6.1	Empirical Studies of the Effect of Scale and Production on Average Unit Cost	152
7.1	Measures of Association between Citizen Perceptions of Roughness and Scores on Both the Quadrant and the Block Face Roughness Scales	170
8.1	Personal Background Characteristics of Respondents in the Two Types of Neighborhoods	183
8.2	Police Output as Measured by Direct Experiences	188
8.3	Police Output as Measured by Citizen Evaluation	192
8.4	Association between Type of Community Organization and Citizen Evaluation Controlling for Experience Variables	194
8.5	Comparative Output Levels	197
9.1	Rating of Police Services by Black Center-City Respondents, White Center-City Respondents, and White Incorporated Suburb Respondents Controlling for Income	206
9.2	Background Characteristics of Respondents in the Two Types of Neighborhoods	217
9.3	Comparison of Service Levels Received	220
9.4	Comparison of Citizen Evaluations of Police Services	221
9.5	Comparison of Citizen Evaluations of Local Government	223
10.1	Comparison of Citizen Experiences and Citizen Evaluations in Indianapolis, Grand Rapids, Nashville, and Chicago	237
10.2	The Correlation between Size of Police Department and Experiences, Evaluations, and Costs	244
10.3	Standardized Regression Coefficients and Variance Explained for Relationships between Size, Socioeconomic Variables and Experiences, Evaluations, and Costs	245
10.4	Independent Effects of Victimization and Assistance Rates When Combined with Training, Size of Department and Socioeconomic Status Variables on Evaluation Variables	249

10.5 Independent Effects of Percentage of Those Stopped in Neighborhood
      when Combined with Training, Size of Department and Socioeconomic
      Status Variables on Evaluation Variables   250
10.6 Independent Effects of Percentage of Those Who Know Someone
      Mistreated and Who Know One or More Policemen when Combined
      with Training, Size of Department and Socioeconomic Status Variables
      on Evaluation Variables   251
10.7 Percentage of Neighborhoods Served by Small, Medium or Large Police
      Departments with Higher than Mean Performance Levels   253

11.1 Patrol Services Matrix: Fayetteville, North Carolina, SMSA   271
11.2 Criminal Investigation Matrix: Fayetteville, North Carolina, SMSA   272
11.3 Adult Detention Matrix: Fayetteville, North Carolina, SMSA   273
11.4 Crime Lab Matrix: Fayetteville, North Carolina, SMSA   274
11.5 Structural Measures—Direct Services   278
11.6 Structural Measures—Intermediate Services   280

12.1 Relative Technical Efficiencies of Metropolitan Service Delivery
      Structures   289
12.2 Relative Efficiency and Industry Structure   291
12.3 Relative Efficiency and Industry Structure   291

14.1 Ratings of Local Government Services by Residents of Areas within
      Marion County, 1993   337
14.2 Total Percentage Employment Growth, 1970–1989   341
14.3 Municipal Election Outcomes in Indianapolis, 1951–1991   343
14.4 Voting Turnout in Marion County, Municipal and Presidential Election
      Years, 1951–1991   344

15.1 Evaluation of Neighborhood Police, 1970 and 1993   350

Series Foreword

Michael D. McGinnis

From its current location in a few scattered office buildings on the Bloomington campus of Indiana University, the Workshop in Political Theory
and Policy Analysis lies at the heart of a worldwide network of scholars
who use institutional analysis to understand and to strengthen the foundations of self-governance. Over the past twenty-five years the political scientists, policy analysts, economists, lawyers, anthropologists, sociologists, psy-
chologists, biologists, ecologists, and policymakers associated with the
Workshop have investigated diverse research topics. Results of these research programs have been published in books and journals from several dis-
ciplines. A portion of this work has been gathered in this volume; two related
volumes are scheduled to be published at approximately the same time.

Each of these edited volumes exemplifies what is special and distinctive
about *institutional analysis* as it has been developed and practiced by Workshop scholars. Institutions are ubiquitous in contemporary society, and the
fields of political science and economics have experienced a recent renais-
sance in the study of institutions. The Workshop approach is uniquely multi-
disciplinary, drawing on the complementary strengths of a wide range of social science methodologies: field studies, laboratory experiments, formal
models, comparative case studies, opinion surveys, archival research, philosophical investigations, physical measurements, computer simulations, and,
most recently, satellite imagery. Institutions affect all aspects of social life.
Major Workshop research programs have focused on (1) police services in
metropolitan centers in the United States; (2) the management of fisheries, irrigation systems, forests, and other common-pool resources from California
to Nepal (and many places in between); and (3) the macro structure of constitutional order from imperial China to the contemporary international system,
with particular emphasis given to the nature of American democracy.

Beneath this bewildering variety lies a core message, buttressed by reinforcing methodological and political foundations. Politically, the goal is to
establish and sustain capacities for *self-governance,* by which is meant the
structured ways communities organize themselves to solve collective problems, achieve common aspirations, and resolve conflicts. Methodologically,

the goal is to understand the institutional foundations of self-governance, that is, to determine which conditions strengthen and which conditions undermine community capacities for self-governance.

In practice these goals have inspired a series of careful, detailed studies of narrow ranges of empirical phenomena. Yet, since each study draws on a single framework of analysis, the overall product has import far beyond the confines of these particular settings. The aggregate lesson of these empirical analyses is clear: many, many self-governing communities thrive, in all parts of the world.

By focusing on community efforts to resolve local problems, the writings of Workshop scholars are sometimes misinterpreted as lending credence to the "small is beautiful" slogan. For many public purposes local community action will be effective, but other circumstances require coordinated policies at the regional, national, or international levels. It is important to remember that public officials at all levels of aggregation have important roles to play in helping communities provide for their own needs.

Shouting slogans about the desirability of decentralization or civil society contributes little toward the crucially important task of sustaining capacities for self-governance. The challenge of institutional analysis lies in producing solid research findings, based on rigorous empirical tests of hypotheses grounded in carefully articulated theories and models. Institutional analysts have a responsibility to combine policy relevance and scientific rigor.

A basic tenet of institutional analysis is that multiple arenas, or centers, of interaction and participation need to be considered simultaneously. Self-governance works best if the overall governance structure is *polycentric*. The word itself may be awkward, but it encapsulates a way of approaching the study of politics and policy analysis that stands in sharp contrast to standard modes of thought. Governance does not require a single center of power, and governments should not claim an exclusive responsibility for resolving political issues. Instead, politics should be envisioned as an activity that goes on in many arenas simultaneously, at many scales of aggregation. Implications of polycentric governance for particular empirical and theoretical contexts are detailed in the readings included in these volumes.

To illustrate the *coherence* of the theoretical approach that underlies applications to a wide array of empirical domains, a selection of previously published articles and book chapters have been collected into three books with similar titles: *Polycentric Governance and Development, Polycentricity and Local Public Economies,* and *Polycentric Games and Institutions.* Each book addresses a separate audience of scholars and policy analysts, but all of them will be of interest to anyone seeking to understand the institutional foundations of self-governance.

The essays in *Polycentric Governance and Development* demonstrate that empirical analyses of the management of irrigation systems, fisheries, groundwater basins, and other common-pool resources have important implications for development policy. Long before "sustainable development" became an over-used slogan, scholars associated with the Workshop were trying to understand the myriad ways self-governing communities had already achieved that goal in practice.

After an initial section on the general conceptual framework that has influenced research on the full array of Workshop research topics, *Polycentricity and Local Public Economies* presents essays published from the first major empirical project associated with the Workshop, a comparative study of the performance of police agencies in metropolitan areas of the United States. Although most of the research results included in this volume date from over a decade ago, they remain relevant today. Recent trends toward community policing, for example, reflect the continuing influence of factors identified in this research program.

In *Polycentric Games and Institutions* the general concepts that guided these empirical analyses themselves become the focus of analysis. Workshop scholars use game theory and laboratory experiments to understand how individuals behave in the context of diverse political and economic institutions. Results from laboratory experiments and field settings show that individuals draw upon an extensive repertoire of rules or strategies from which they select different strategies, given their understanding of the nature of the situation at hand.

By collecting readings on similar topics that were originally published in scattered outlets, we hope to highlight the contribution these research programs have made to their respective fields of study. Any evaluation of the scholarly contribution of *institutional analysis* as a whole, however, must be partial and incomplete, for the Workshop remains an active place. Each of these research themes is being pursued by scholars who have long been associated with the Workshop and by a new generation of scholars.

Each article or book chapter is reprinted without changes, except for a few minor corrections to the published versions. To avoid duplication of material and improve the flow of this presentation, textual deletions have been made in a few of the selections. Citations to forthcoming books and articles have been updated, and cross-references to essays included in the other volumes have been added. Otherwise, reference and footnote conventions used in the original sources have been left intact.

Selection of an appropriate set of readings was a daunting task, for the list of publications is long and diverse. I enjoyed digging through the extensive files of reprints, and I wish we could have included many more readings, but that would have defeated the purpose of compiling accessible surveys of selected Workshop research programs. I tried to minimize overlap with the most influential and widely available books that have emerged from these research programs. Each edited volume includes an integrative introductory essay, in which frequent references are made to the many other books and journals in which the results of these diverse research projects are reported. Each book also includes an annotated list of suggested readings.

One final caveat is in order. Elinor Ostrom and Vincent Ostrom are authors or coauthors of many of the readings in all three books. Both have served jointly as co-directors since its establishment in 1973. Without doubt, these two individuals have been absolutely crucial to the success of the Workshop. Even so, they would be the first to insist that they have *not* been the only reason for its success. Collaboration has always been a hallmark of the Workshop. Many individuals have made essential contributions, as will be apparent throughout the readings in these books. Yet it is impossible to imagine how the Workshop could have been established or sustained without the tireless efforts of Elinor and Vincent Ostrom. Their influence will continue to shape the future direction of the Workshop for years to come.

Acknowledgments

In an edited volume composed of papers written over a span of thirty years, the assistance of a many, many people and institutions deserves to be acknowledged. Fortunately, the contributors have already thanked those who assisted in the original preparation of each of the journal articles or book chapters reprinted here.

As editor, I am going to start my acknowledgments with Patty Dalecki. Her assistance has been invaluable for the preparation of all three of the volumes. Patty kept track of all the essays included in these volumes, arranging for copyright permissions and overseeing the process of translating them all into a single format. For this particular volume, however, most of the work was done by Anne Leinenbach, a relatively new addition to the Workshop staff. Anne ably guided this volume through several versions and typeset the final manuscript. It's clear Anne is off to a roaring start at the Workshop, and we hope she hangs around for many years to come.

I also want to thank all of the staff members who helped Patty, Anne, and me at various stages in this process. Amber Cleveland, Sara Colburn, Ray Eliason, Bob Lezotte, David Wilson, and Cynthia Yaudes all helped in scanning and proofreading the manuscripts or in posting drafts of the introduction and contents list on the Web. One of the strengths of the Workshop has always been our competent, hardworking, and friendly staff. Students also contribute in important ways. For example, Richard Hung prepared the comprehensive index for this volume.

At the other end of the publication process, I am deeply appreciative of the support and guidance offered by Colin Day, director of the University of Michigan Press. His comments and suggestions were crucial, all the way from initial planning of the volumes to preparation of the final manuscript. I would also like to thank two anonymous reviewers for their helpful comments and suggestions on drafts of the introduction and on the overall organization of the volume.

The research results published here emerged from a long series of overlapping research projects. Appropriate funding agencies are acknowledged in their respective essays. We also want to thank the Bradley Foundation for providing financial support for the preparation of this volume.

None of this activity would have been possible if the contributors to this volume had not written such excellent research reports in the first place. I thank each of the contributors for providing the foundational material out of which this book was constructed. They all returned corrections to the scanned versions in short order, helping us complete this book in a remarkably short period of time.

I particularly want to thank Roger Parks, who put up with my repeated inquiries to see if he'd allow us to include still another of his works in this volume. Roger kept me honest, correcting factual errors in the many drafts of my introductory essay. I hope we caught all of the errors, but I want to make it clear that any remaining mistakes are entirely my fault.

I also want to say a few words to those scholars associated with the Workshop whose work I was not able to include in this volume. I wish the book could have been twice as long, and I repeatedly found it necessary to restrain my enthusiasm for including more papers. I especially want to express my appreciation to those authors who were willing to proof papers that, for whatever reason, had to be cut from the final list.

Two of the contributors play uniquely pivotal roles. Elinor and Vincent Ostrom have inspired, encouraged, and supported all of the research included in this volume. Each has had a major impact on my own career, helping to broaden my interests and to sharpen my analytical skills. I can't thank them enough.

Introduction

Michael D. McGinnis

The Workshop in Political Theory and Policy Analysis was established at Indiana University in Bloomington in 1973 to coordinate several ongoing research projects. In the process of implementing this research, Workshop faculty and students began a long (and ongoing) series of discussions about broader conceptual questions and about how to organize multidisciplinary research on institutions. This volume of readings presents an overview of the results of the research program on police services and local public economies, as well as its enduring lessons for institutional analysis and public policy.

One basic presumption shared by the organizers of the Workshop is that theory has important ramifications for understanding practical policy problems. This close interaction between theoretical and empirical concerns is reflected in the basic organization of this book, which includes two distinctly different types of chapters: (1) conceptual discussions of federalism and other forms of constitutional order; and (2) empirical analyses of specific aspects of policing and other public services. Within the context of the conceptual framework developed here, even narrow analyses of seemingly mundane events can shed important new light on enduring dilemmas of governance.

Part I of this volume consists of summary statements of basic theoretical concepts and analytical distinctions that apply to the study of institutions generally. In part II the focus shifts to conceptual pieces that specifically address the nature of governance in metropolitan areas. Part III reports on a series of empirical studies of police performance. The essays included in part IV outline some of the broader implications of this research tradition for the organization of local public economies as a whole. Part V concludes with two essays summarizing conceptual advances that have continuing relevance for research and policy debates.

In some ways, this research was decades ahead of its time. More recently, scholars associated with the Workshop have documented the ability of self-governing communities to effectively manage common-pool resources (E. Ostrom 1990; E. Ostrom, Gardner, and Walker 1994; McGinnis 1999a,b). These projects now encompass research sites throughout the world, but the Workshop approach to institutional analysis was developed by scholars confronting the complexities of governance in metropolitan areas in the United States. Similar themes emerge from both areas of research, especially a deep appreciation for the merits of local self-government. Perhaps it is only now, in the current policy context of devolution and decentralization, that the import of this early Workshop research can be fully appreciated. By collecting essays originally published in a wide array of outlets, this volume should help scholars reassess the legacy of these interrelated research programs on the evaluation of police services and the organization of local public economies.

Part I. Conceptual Foundations of Institutional Analysis

Part I includes three statements of fundamental components of the Workshop approach to institutional analysis. The obvious place to begin is with a classic 1961 *American Political Science Review* article, "The Organization of Government in Metropolitan Areas: A Theoretical Inquiry," coauthored by Vincent Ostrom, Charles M. Tiebout, and Robert Warren. Although this article appeared in print more than 10 years before the establishment of the Workshop, it was essential to include it as the opening chapter of this volume of readings. The general concept of *polycentric order* elucidated in this essay is one cornerstone of institutional analysis. The notion that complex systems of overlapping jurisdictions might make more sense than a single center of power was quite novel then, and it still engenders resistance from many scholars more comfortable with simple governance structures.

The existence of multiple jurisdictions gives citizens more choices. In an earlier work, Charles Tiebout (1956) elaborated the implications of multiple jurisdictions for the ability of citizens to "vote with their feet" by moving to jurisdictions whose authorities offer a more desirable mix of public goods and services. Tiebout's conception remains a core concept of public choice theory (Mueller 1989). Even though the many costs associated with moving to new jurisdictions and the limited number of relevant jurisdictions may make physical movement impractical, this concept sheds light on important aspects of political economy at many levels of analysis. For example, the ability of private investors to move capital to jurisdictions with more favorable taxing policies limits the ability of political authorities to implement their desired economic policies. Lindblom (1977) decries this as a "market as prison" image, emphasizing the limitations market discipline imposes on the range of public policies that can be implemented. (If leaders impose policies that drive too many investors away, the local economy will suffer, and the officials would be likely to lose the next election.) From another perspective, this market discipline may limit the implementation of redistributive policies that would slow economic growth. Under either interpretation, a similar logic applies to interactions among separate municipalities in a metropolitan area, states in a federal system, or countries competing for foreign investment.

A polycentric order generalizes Tiebout's "voting-with-the-feet" model by enabling individuals or communities to choose among alternative producers of public services, without having to move from one jurisdiction to another. Polycentricity is a fundamental prerequisite of *self-governance,* that is, the ability of groups of individuals to work out problems for themselves. A community may decide to address some common problems directly. Alternatively, they may decide what they want and contract with some other organization to supply these services, or they may decide that some issues are best left up to more encompassing units of governments or to the creation of marketlike arrangements. In general, communities employ all of these options, selecting different means to achieve different ends. Without the full range of options, liberty is stunted.

Polycentric order is also supported by considerations of efficiency. As Ostrom, Tiebout, and Warren argue, different public goods can be most efficiently produced at different scales of organization, ranging from fire protection to national defense. In a polycentric order, communities can organize the production of different kinds of public goods at different scales of aggregation.

These authors introduce a distinction between the *production* of a public good or service and its *provision* by public authorities (or by the people themselves). Although these terms are used interchangeably in common discourse, this distinction between production and provision is crucial to this whole body of research. *Production* refers to the physical processes by which a public good or service comes into existence, while *provision* is the process by which this product is made available to consumers. Since we are dealing with public goods or services, the relevant consumption unit is a neighborhood, a community, or some other grouping of people.

The distinction between production and provision is unfamiliar because it plays such a minor role in markets for private goods. A consumer who buys, say, a television set at an electronics store is not dealing directly with the firm that built this product. The retail store acts as intermediary between the producer and the consumer, but this store is not *providing* the good, in the sense used here, because the ultimate decision concerning consumption is made by the individual purchaser. Since the individual consumer is, in effect, also the provider, little is gained by making this distinction.

For the case of public goods, however, the relationship between consumers and providers is steeped in political import. Citizens elect mayors, governors, and other officials in the clear expectation that they will make sure that the community enjoys certain public goods. Citizens will closely monitor the performance of public officials, especially with regard to tax burdens, crime rates, and other salient policy issues. If they are not satisfied, they may move elsewhere (as in Tiebout's model), they may vote to replace the offending officials, or they may find some way to pressure officials into providing a different policy mix. They may even decide to take matters into their own hands.

It is important to remember that groups of individuals can provide for the production of public goods themselves, without relying on the intercession of public authorities. For example, members of a housing association concerned about the poor condition of the medians of their common streets have options beyond petitioning the city for assistance. They could hire a professional groundskeeper; they could even roll up their sleeves and pick the weeds themselves. In either case, the neighborhood association is providing this public good. Political scientists and policy analysts are more familiar with an arrangement in which a public official provides for the production of some public good or service by seeing that all members of the appropriate groups receive or enjoy its benefits and that there are sufficient resources to pay for its production. But we cannot ignore the possibility that, in some instances, groups can do all this for themselves.

In sum, there are three types of actors involved in this process: (1) a collective consumption unit seeking some public good or service; (2) the entity that produces it; and (3) an intermediary who makes arrangements to connect producers to consumers. This intermediary may be an individual public entrepreneur or, more frequently, a government agency. In some cases, no intermediary is necessary. For example, when members of a new settlement jointly agree to dig and maintain a well for use by all, then this community has effectively fulfilled all three roles simultaneously. For analytical purposes, however, it is important to keep these distinctions in mind.

The details of the relationship between providers and producers may not always be easily observable by members of the collective consumption unit. Government officials can select from a wide array of options to arrange for the production of public goods and services. They may sign contracts with a private vendor or another public agency to produce the public good or service, or they may prefer to incorporate the production process within the scope of their own authority.

The important point here is that it is not necessary for a public good (or public service) to be produced by the same actors or organizations that make arrangements to provide that good or service to a community of individuals. Thus, there may not be a one-to-one correspondence between collective consumption units and provision units or between providers and producers. Polycentricity allows considerable mixing and matching of consumption, provision, and production units operating at different scales of aggregation.

One unfortunate consequence of the importance of this subtle distinction between production and provision is that confusion can easily arise when comparisons are made to works in which these terms are used inter-changeably. The phrase "service provider" is a good case in point. In common parlance, a church group that gives homeless people a place to sleep and some-thing to eat is a service provider, but in the technical language of polycentricity, these church groups are the producers of welfare services. Increasingly, gov-ernments provide for welfare services by contracting with nonprofit organi-zations. As Salamon (1995) puts it, governments and nonprofits are "partners," with governments providing the financing and making policy de-cisions but with nonprofit organizations actually doing the work. This makes government officials the service providers and nonprofit organizations the service producers, not providers.

Another level of complexity comes from the ability of concerned citi-zens to form an interest group that lobbies governmental officials on their behalf. Interest organizations seek to provide certain policy outcomes for their contributors, but in this case the production of public policy is carried out by public officials (legislators, executives, or bureaucrats). In polycentric systems, individuals and communities participate in the provision and pro-duction of public services in direct and indirect ways.

Clearly, polycentric orders are inherently complex. In its simplest form, a polycentric order must allow public officials or agencies (at various levels of a federal system) to make alternative arrangements for the provision of a public good for members of the collective consumption unit (typically a po-litical jurisdiction of some type) while production takes place at a larger or smaller scale of aggregation, depending on which scale is most efficient for that particular good. The term *polycentric* aptly encapsulates this vision of overlapping scales of production and multiple arenas of political interaction.

Although the word *polycentric* is cumbersome, Workshop scholars can take some comfort from the fact that it is considerably more attractive than "multinucleated political system," an alternative mentioned in the second endnote in Ostrom, Tiebout, and Warren's classic article, reprinted here as chapter 1. Chapter 2 is part 1 of "Polycentricity," a paper originally pre-sented by Vincent Ostrom at the American Political Science Association meeting in 1972. This conference paper was originally written as a critical review of the Ostrom, Tiebout, and Warren article 10 years after its publica-tion, but it was never published in that form. It remains the single best clarifi-cation of how polycentricity is related to several more familiar terms and concepts.

In this paper, Vincent Ostrom emphasizes that a polycentric order should not be dismissed as a simple market analogy. Obviously, markets per se cannot be expected to result in the production or provision of public goods, since markets are designed to take advantage of the special properties associated with private goods. The whole point of a public economy is that it must include some means by which public goods are produced and provided to collective consumption units. By allowing for the existence of multiple producers of public goods as well as alternative service providers, it becomes possible to approximate the benefits of market competition. However, polycentric orders have their own inherent properties and cannot be seen as exact analogues of private markets.

Ostrom clarifies how his usage differs from that of Polyani, who used *polycentric* as a synonym for *spontaneous*. In the current context, it is important to realize that polycentric orders are created by those who participate in them and they cannot be sustained as such unless the relevant actors continue to make use of their full range of alternatives. That is, if all authority and responsibility come to be concentrated in a single political entity, then the system can no longer be described as polycentric.

Another clarification is required, namely, that the mere existence of multiple centers of authority does not immediately convey the full connotations of the analytical term *polycentric*. The key point is not the number of jurisdictions but rather the concurrence of multiple opportunities by which participants can forge or dissolve links among different collective entities. In a system composed of many political units, each of which directly produces all the public goods for its own citizens, the full potential of polycentricity would not be realized. Instead, participants must be able to pick and choose those producers and providers that are most appropriate to each specific issue at hand.

Vincent Ostrom emphasizes that if the full potential of polycentricity is to be realized, it must be grounded in mutually supportive institutional arrangements in the economic, legal, constitutional, and political realms. Markets in private goods are needed to provide incentives for efficient production, and public entrepreneurs must have some assurance that their efforts to provide goods and services to various communities are legally recognized. Perhaps the most important factor is that political coalitions must be open to change and to compromise, with political leaders focusing attention on resolving problems rather than scoring partisan victories.

In chapter 3, "Public Goods and Public Choices," Vincent Ostrom and Elinor Ostrom develop several analytical distinctions that recur throughout the entire corpus of Workshop research. The first distinction concerns the *nature of the good* as a private good, public good, toll good, or common-pool resource. The authors argue that we cannot expect the same kinds of institutional arrangements to be appropriate for all kinds of goods or services. The "market" is an efficient institution for production and allocation of private goods (within the context of the existing distribution of resources and assuming the existence of secure property rights and reliable procedures for conflict resolution). However, market mechanisms fail in predictable manners when they are applied to the production or provision of public goods or the management of common-pool resources (see Weimer and Vining 1989; E. Ostrom 1990).

The Ostroms develop the concept of a "public economy" as analogous but not identical to a market economy. They discuss several examples of complex networks of service provision and the production of public goods. They emphasize the importance of formal and informal mechanisms of conflict resolution, through which conflicts of interest and responsibility among public authorities in overlapping jurisdictions are resolved. They pay particular attention to the important matter of financing. In order for a polycentric system to operate smoothly, there must be some correspondence, however inexact, between the beneficiaries of public goods and services and those who pay for them. If this provision process runs smoothly, the private production of public goods can be made economically efficient. The key element in all this is the ability of service providers to select producers operating at the most efficient scale of production.

Also included in this paper is a brief discussion of the concept of "coproduction." Chapter 17 develops this concept in detail, but the basic idea behind this important concept deserves mention here. The typical relationship between producer and consumer is one of exchange. That is, the consumer does not contribute in any direct manner to the quality of the good that is produced. (There will be an indirect effect in a competitive market setting, as consumers buy from those producers who offer higher quality products for a given price level.) However, for some kinds of goods and services, those consumers who adopt a passive attitude will not receive a high quality product. The Ostroms discuss education and health as examples of coproduction: in both cases the active involvement of students or patients is essential if they are to enjoy a quality education or good health. Coproduction denotes situations when the active involvement of the consumer is a requisite input for the production of a high quality good or service.

Coproduction is especially important in public economies. Members of a neighborhood seeking safer streets for all to enjoy would, for example, be well advised to take an active role in monitoring activities rather than passively relying on police patrols. Polycentricity provides an ideal setting for the coproduction of public goods and services. Communities should not be expected to passively await the largesse of political authorities but should instead take an active role in arranging for the coproduction (and coprovision) of desired public goods and services.

This insistence on the importance of the active involvement of citizens in their own governance is one of the ways in which the Workshop approach to institutional analysis differs, at least in emphasis, from the broader community of public choice scholars (see Mitchell 1988). Public choice is typically defined as the application of economic modes of analysis to the study of the behavior of political authorities, but institutional analysis casts a wider net. For example, although most of the same analytical presuppositions of rational choice can be applied to individuals, private corporations, or the office-seeking actions of public authorities, it is not appropriate to assume that markets exist in all arenas of interaction (see V. Ostrom 1993, 1998).

To a great extent, the concept of polycentricity emerges from a deep familiarity with the U.S. political system. In chapter 2 Vincent Ostrom shows how closely polycentricity is related to the political theory that lay behind the original design of the U.S. Constitution and especially to the defense of that Constitution in *The Federalist* (see V. Ostrom 1987). This theory of limited constitutions was exemplified in the plentiful examples of self-governance by voluntary associations that Tocqueville ([1835] 1969) observed in his journey through the United States of America in the early nineteenth century. In his most recent books, Vincent Ostrom (1991, 1997) stresses that self-governance is sustainable only if communities nurture the "habits of heart and mind" that Tocqueville considered the most important contributor to the success of American democracy. *Coproduction* and *polycentricity* are modern terms that capture important aspects of Tocqueville's insights into the proper organization of public affairs, and the Workshop approach to institutional analysis is an extended elaboration on the basic principles of the "art and science of association" that Tocqueville saw as critical to the continued success of democratic governance.

Part II. Frameworks for the Study of Public Economies

One of the enduring themes of Workshop research has been Vincent Ostrom's insistence that polycentricity be considered as a viable alternative to standard notions of sovereignty. In his first major book, *The Intellectual Crisis in American Public Administration* ([1973] 1989), he critiques the field of public administration for being dominated by a conception of centralized administration inconsistent with the foundational principles of American democracy. In particular, he contrasts the constitutional theory of the founders with that of Woodrow Wilson, whom he identifies as the central figure in the reform tradition in the first decades of the twentieth century. This influential tradition led to a widely shared consensus on the benefits that would accrue from consolidation of metropolitan areas into single, larger units of governance. The research programs reported in this volume present a fundamental challenge to this consensus.

In chapter 4, "A Behavioral Approach to the Study of Intergovernmental Relations," Vincent Ostrom and Elinor Ostrom conceptualize an area of public service provision and production as an "industry," akin to an industry in the private sector. They use examples from water supply, electric power, education, and police to illustrate complex patterns of interactions among the diverse actors involved in any single area of public services. A public industry constitutes, in effect, the polycentric order apparent in the specific contexts of public service provision and production.

Since this essay predates the establishment of the Workshop by about a decade, it serves as a useful overview of the Ostroms' general orientation to research. They insist on the need to understand both the physical nature of the good or service being produced and the social, political, and economic context of its provision. In subsequent research, scholars associated with the Workshop developed a broad analytical framework based on three sets of factors that jointly contribute to the nature of institutional arrangements. This institutional analysis and development (IAD) framework highlights interactions among (1) the nature of the goods being produced, provided, and consumed; (2) the content of "rules in use" in contrast to written laws and constitutions; and (3) overall attributes of the community (Kiser and E. Ostrom 1982; McGinnis 1999a,b). A central tenet of institutional analysis is that even detailed analyses of limited aspects of particular institutions must keep this broader range of factors in mind.

Any public service industry necessarily involves actors with common, complementary, and conflicting interests. Patterns of conflict resolution are shaped by the overall configuration of governance. The Gargantua approach critiqued by Ostrom, Tiebout, and Warren (chap. 1) seeks to resolve conflict by encompassing all of the parties within a single, comprehensive governance structure.

In chapter 5, part 2 of "Polycentricity," Vincent Ostrom elaborates further on the polycentric alternative for the governance of metropolitan areas. He begins by reviewing Tocqueville's observations concerning the existence of an underlying pattern of order beneath the confusing array of governing bodies in the United States of his day. Ostrom then addresses some difficult problems of language and conceptualization. Although widely used, the phrase "the government" is both imprecise and inappropriate. Since governments are complex networks of interrelated provision units, institutional analysts need to develop more sophisticated methods of analysis. He notes that any complete picture of polycentric governance would have to include consideration of the entire configuration of relevant individuals, their organizational roles, the rules that shape their interactions, and the empirical measures of outcomes that they use to evaluate policies. In subsequent research, Workshop scholars have devised conceptual frameworks that help institutional analysts make sense of these complex relationships (see especially Kiser and E. Ostrom 1982; E. Ostrom 1986; both reprinted in McGinnis 1999a). For present purposes, the important point is that no one person (whether sovereign, bureaucratic official, or policy analyst) is capable of seeing the whole picture at once.

Ostrom examines the negative consequences of fragmented authority that are most frequently decried in the policy reform literature: uneven service provision, pervasive racial segregation, increased costs, and an unequal distribution of financial burdens between suburbs and the inner city. He argues that analysts should have an open mind on these issues and that they should use the great natural laboratories of the diverse conditions of life in metropolitan areas throughout the United States as a means to test whether polycentricity actually has these negative effects.

Vincent's spouse and colleague Elinor Ostrom took the leading role in the empirical evaluation of polycentricity. In chapter 6, "Metropolitan Reform: Propositions Derived from Two Traditions," she details an exhaustive list of propositions concerning the contrasting implications of unitary and polycentric systems, when applied to the governance of metropolitan areas. This essay sets out an ambitious research agenda that was only partially fulfilled in the research projects summarized in the remainder of this book.

Scholars in the public administration or reform tradition emphasized the positive benefits of increasing the professionalization of public servants: more professional producers of public services could be expected to produce better public goods or services at a lower cost and with fuller concern for issues of equity and fair distribution of public resources. Since professionalization is easier to achieve in large jurisdictions, the seemingly obvious conclusion is that consolidation should lead to improved public service.

Elinor Ostrom lays out the contrasting views of scholars associated with what she called the "political economy" tradition in this essay but would now describe as "institutional analysis." In a related work, Bish and V. Ostrom (1973) contrast the "public choice" tradition with this reform tradition. Whichever label is used, Workshop scholars stress that the nature of the good or service is a crucial intervening variable in the relationship between scale of production and citizen evaluation of agency performance. Goods or services that are most efficiently produced at small scales would be hurt by consolidation, whereas larger-scale goods might still be efficiently produced if small jurisdictions were allowed to enter into contracts with larger-scale producers. For example, a small police force might produce better service in terms of patrolling or responding to reports of crimes than a large police force, but both might rely on the same crime lab or training facilities.

In this chapter Elinor Ostrom briefly surveys research findings that support the propositions implied by proponents of polycentric governance. The essays in part III report on an extensive series of empirical investigations carried out by scholars associated with the Workshop that directly address these issues.

Part III. Empirical Research on Police Services

After all this discussion of theories and concepts we finally get to the nitty-gritty of empirical analysis. In preparing this volume of readings it proved useful, for purposes of presentation, to collect theoretical conceptualizations and empirical analyses in separate sections. However, it is important to remember that the actual process of research is one in which conceptualizations and empirical investigations develop simultaneously and interact with each other in a dynamic fashion. For example, E. Ostrom, Parks, Whitaker, and Percy (1979) summarize interactions among inputs, organizational arrangements, activities, and outputs in figures that can be seen as precursors to the institutional analysis and development framework that later emerged as the organizing schema for Workshop research on common-pool resources (see Kiser and E. Ostrom 1982, reprinted in McGinnis 1999a).

The first step in the long series of empirical research programs summarized in this section was taken during a graduate seminar on the measurement of public goods. The specific area of application was selected by the students, after the instructor (Elinor Ostrom) vetoed anything to do with water management (which had been the subject of her own dissertation). The students selected police services, and they set out to answer such questions as: What services do police forces produce? How can one measure and evaluate the relative performance of different police forces?

None of the researchers associated with the Workshop began as experts in policing. Instead, they developed expertise in this area as a consequence of applying rigorous methods of social science to this particular area of concern. As suggested earlier, policing is also an area in which public jurisdictions at all levels of aggregation tend to interact in complex ways, in exactly the manner expected by scholars who think in terms of the polycentric ordering of public service industries.

The discussions begun in this seminar continued in the form of an externally funded "Measures Project." Participants in this research project demonstrated a remarkable ability to make effective use of the complementary strengths of surveys, participant observation, official data, and physical measures. In chapter 7, "Why Do We Need Multiple Indicators of Public Service Outputs?" Elinor Ostrom summarizes the many measures used in this project. Since this essay was published later in this project (1977), it also reflects the insights gathered from the other research programs summarized in subsequent readings.

Official police reports are notorious for being recorded so as to make police performance look good. Despite concerns about the self-serving nature of official reports, many policy studies of public service delivery rely heavily on such sources as the FBI crime index. Participants in this Workshop research team developed innovative means to measure actual conditions experienced by the public in their own neighborhoods. In regard to policing, they interviewed random samples of residents of matched neighborhoods, rode with police officers to observe activities directly, recorded calls for services, and used a variety of internal sources. In regard to lighting, rather than merely counting the number of streetlights, the project team used light meters to measure the ambient light at street level. Since this was a physical measure, values for different neighborhoods could be directly compared. The most memorable measuring instrument was a wheeled contraption called a "roughometer," used to measure the "bumpiness" of urban streets.

The research programs summarized in this volume were, to a great extent, inspired by matters of practical political concern. The Bloomington campus of Indiana University is located about an hour's drive south of the state capital of Indianapolis. After several years of public debate, Indianapolis city and Marion County governments were consolidated in 1970 to form a unitary governing authority popularly known as Unigov. Here, seemingly, was a clear manifestation of the reform tradition, ready to be tested.

There were some complications, however. This consolidation fell short of completeness because not all of the municipalities within Marion County decided to join this consolidated government. This conjunction of countywide consolidation with local exceptions provided a unique opportunity for social scientists to make direct comparisons between the performances of police forces with small or large scales of operation. Neighborhoods in Indianapolis serviced by the Indianapolis Police Department were matched up with independent communities that retained their own small police departments. Since these neighborhoods and communities were similar on all other demographic factors, any differences in performance measures could be directly attributed to the difference in the size of these production units.

In chapter 8, "Does Local Community Control of Police Make a Difference? Some Preliminary Findings," Elinor Ostrom and Gordon P. Whitaker summarize results from the study of police services in the Indianapolis metropolitan area. By comparing the performances of small and large police departments serving otherwise comparable middle-class, white neighborhoods directly adjacent to one another, it became clear that "bigger" was not necessarily "better." Instead, citizens in small communities expressed higher satisfaction with the police than did residents of demographically similar neighborhoods serviced by a larger police force.

It is worth noting that the researchers did not simply ask citizens to give their opinions about the police but also asked specific questions concerning the personal experiences of individual respondents. Had they ever been stopped by the police? How were they treated by the police officers in question? Questions of this sort enabled the researchers to go beyond vague measures of citizen satisfaction.

The issues of measurement discussed in the previous reading proved too difficult to solve in their entirety. For example, comparisons of the cost of providing services in small and large police departments were difficult to interpret, since they could be based on alternative means of allocating the expenditures of a large police force to specific neighborhoods (see E. Ostrom, Parks, and Whitaker 1973). The overall findings of the Indianapolis study of police performance are reported in more detail in E. Ostrom et al. (1973).

These researchers also addressed one criticism of this initial research, namely, concern that its findings might not apply to all types of communities. In particular, it has long been recognized that relationships between police forces and residents of primarily African-American communities are particularly strained. In chapter 9, "Community Control and Governmental Responsiveness: The Case of Police in Black Neighborhoods," Elinor Ostrom and Gordon P. Whitaker address the question of whether African-American communities can achieve similar successes by relying on smaller police forces.

For this project Ostrom and Whitaker compared two small independent villages in Cook County, Illinois, with three predominantly black neighborhoods in the city of Chicago that were similar to these villages in demographic terms. The results resembled those of the Indianapolis study in the general conclusion that, on most measures of evaluation, residents of the villages expressed more satisfaction with police performance than did residents of the Chicago neighborhoods selected for comparison. However, in this case the difference was attenuated, since overall levels of satisfaction were lower in both contexts than was the case for the predominantly white towns and neighborhoods in the Indianapolis study. Even so, the independent villages were able to provide slightly better policing services at a much lower per capita cost than was the more modern and professionalized Chicago Police Department. These differences in cost and performance evaluation stand in direct contrast to the expectations of the reform tradition.

In chapter 10, "Size and Performance in a Federal System," Elinor Ostrom summarizes the results of the next major empirical study, focused this time on St. Louis, Missouri. The St. Louis metropolitan area is particularly interesting for its large number of jurisdictions of widely varying sizes. This diversity enabled the researchers to select cases that differed in their racial composition (predominantly white, racially mixed, and predominantly African-American), income level, and size of police force (small, medium, and large). The larger number of cases also allowed the use of statistical methods to separate out the effects of these factors. The basic bivariate relationship between size and performance identified in the earlier studies held up for this broader context, but the strength of this relationship was weaker for predominantly African-American communities (for much the same reason as in the Chicago study). In this analysis medium-sized police forces proved to have some advantages over the smallest units, but in no instances did the largest units score the highest on measures of citizen satisfaction. The clear implication is that different scales of production are most appropriate for different aspects of the police service industry, exactly as one would expect in a polycentric order.

Part IV. Implications for the Study of Local Public Economies

Police services are but one aspect of the multifaceted range of public services provided or produced by local governments in the United States. Workshop scholars conducted detailed analyses of police services concurrently with broader investigations of the overall structure of metropolitan governance. Not surprisingly, the latter topic proved more difficult to master. The essays included in part IV can only illustrate selected aspects of this multifaceted body of research; readers interested in the complete picture are encouraged to consult the Suggested Further Readings.

Early statements of the Workshop perspective on urban political economies include Bish (1971) and Bish and V. Ostrom (1973). Bish (1971) surveys basic aspects of the public choice tradition that underlie the Workshop approach. Bish and V. Ostrom (1973) devote particular attention to transfer payments between authorities serving different-sized jurisdictions and other aspects of the financial arrangements needed to make polycentric governance work. The authors emphasize that conflicts among authorities at different levels are a natural component of such systems and thus that conflict resolution is an important component of polycentricity.

Much of the later work took the form of case studies, especially under the auspices of the United States Advisory Commission on Intergovernmental Relations (see ACIR 1988, 1992). Important overviews include ACIR (1987), Oakerson (1987), E. Ostrom (1983, 1997), and V. Ostrom, Bish, and E. Ostrom (1988). (This last book was originally prepared for publication by the Olivetti Foundation in Italy; see V. Ostrom, Bish, and E. Ostrom 1984.)

A major component of Workshop research on the organization of local public economies was a survey of the nature of police service delivery in a sample of 80 Standard Metropolitan Statistical Areas. This study investigated several measures of the networks of interrelationships among governmental authorities from different jurisdictions. This project began to explore the benefits (and the difficulties) of policing as a multilevel service industry. E. Ostrom, Parks, and Whitaker (1978) is a book-length treatment of this research project; a shorter overview was prepared as a report for the National

Science Foundation (E. Ostrom, Parks, and Whitaker 1977). The natural way in which the original police studies grew into this larger statistical project is best illustrated in E. Ostrom and Parks (1973), which combines brief discussions of a few matched case studies (including Indianapolis) with preliminary analysis of comparative measures of citizen evaluation of police performance in communities and departments of varying sizes.

Chapter 11, "Defining and Measuring Structural Variations in Interorganizational Arrangements," by Elinor Ostrom, Roger B. Parks, and Gordon P. Whitaker, gives a sample of the type of research conducted in this project. The authors discuss the characteristics of the case of Fayetteville, North Carolina, in some detail and briefly compare it to two other metropolitan areas. They define several measures of the overall structure of the police service industry. In effect, they interpret this public service industry as a network or system and apply aggregate measures to these conglomerations as a whole. Multiplicity, for example, is measured by the number of alternative producers for a particular service, whereas fragmentation refers to the number of consumption units in a given metropolitan area. As discussed earlier, there is no reason to expect a one-to-one correspondence in these two measures under conditions of polycentricity. The authors use a "service structure matrix" to graphically illustrate the complex relationships between consumption units and means of production. These examples of the diverse ways in which public officials in this one metropolitan area have arranged for the production of the full range of police services should bring some concreteness to the abstractions developed in previous chapters of this book.

In this project, attention shifted away from the evaluation of performance to focus instead on descriptive statistics applied to the networks of police service provision and production as found in U.S. metropolitan areas. Unfortunately, the remarkable diversity of modes of institutional arrangements that were identified in this study defies simple description. The capacity of self-governing communities to devise polycentric orders presents a daunting analytical challenge to anyone seeking to understand their properties and consequences.

One effort to bring the power of statistical analysis to bear on these issues is illustrated in chapter 12, "Neither Gargantua nor the Land of Lilliputs: Conjectures on Mixed Systems of Metropolitan Organization," an unpublished convention essay by Elinor Ostrom and Roger B. Parks. (Similar findings are discussed in Parks 1985; and Parks and E. Ostrom 1984.) The authors use data on activities of police forces of various sizes from the sample of 80 metropolitan areas to approximate the shape of the production possibility frontier for different-sized departments (see also chap. 16). They then separate the cases into those with larger or smaller than average values of the multiplicity and autonomy measures of the overall organization of that metropolitan area. They conclude that the most efficient metropolitan systems combine the production of some services by large-scale police agencies with the production of immediate response services by smaller departments.

This essay ends with a suggestive comparison of the historical development of governance structures that might occur in two hypothetical scenarios. Whether the initial state is one of complete consolidation or total fragmentation, they expect the ultimate result would be similar, namely, a complex arrangement in which the production and provision of public services occur simultaneously at multiple scales of aggregation. Officials in a consolidated region are likely to discover that some matters are best delegated to smaller scale organizations, whereas managers of initially small jurisdictions are likely to establish institutions operating at a larger scale that can best deal with matters of common concern. This discussion suggests that polycentricity may emerge naturally, provided communities and their agents are given the opportunity to change the scale of their operations when they feel it is appropriate.

The next two chapters evaluate how similar processes of historical development have worked out in practice. In chapter 13, "Citizen Voice and Public Entrepreneurship: The Organizational Dynamic of a Complex Metropolitan County," Ronald J. Oakerson and Roger B. Parks examine the overall structure of public service provision and production in the St. Louis metropolitan area. The mode of research used here is more informal than was the case in the earlier selections. Since it proved difficult to define summary measures of overall structures or networks of agency interactions, case studies were a more appropriate means to address these research questions. This particular essay is supplemented by a similar study applied to the Pittsburgh metropolitan area (Parks and Oakerson 1993). In both studies, the authors show that public officials of different jurisdictions are able to work together in a remarkably smooth fashion. (For a similar conclusion with reference to relations among agencies involved in policing in the St. Louis metropolitan area, see McDavid 1974.)

In the essay included here, Oakerson and Parks place this capacity within a broader framework. They examine the extent to which bureaucratic officials can be treated as entrepreneurs providing a service to their customers. They draw on Tiebout's (1956) model of voting with the feet, making explicit how polycentricity goes beyond that confining concept. Citizens' capacity to voice their concerns alleviates any need to explicitly move to new jurisdictions, provided that public officials have the right incentives to provide needed services to their communities. They also note that public entrepreneurs must find some way to coordinate their actions if they are to effectively address problems of wider concern.

In a related essay, Parks and Oakerson (1989) question the common perception that local governments are merely "creatures of the state," established at the discretion of state governments. They point out that nearly all local governing authorities have been initiated by the actions of local people. Far from being static and uninteresting, the boundaries of local jurisdictions change as a response to citizen action. Revisions in existing jurisdictions and creation of new municipalities all take place within a broader overarching system of rules and procedures. Interactions between citizens and public authorities are more dynamic than might be expected by the use of the term *constitutional*. Complex local economies are the norm, not the exception. In sum, these authors draw upon a detailed understanding of the diversity of local governing arrangements in the United States to reinforce arguments discussed earlier about the centrality of polycentric order to democratic governance.

In chapter 14, "Fiscal, Service, and Political Impacts of Indianapolis–Marion County's Unigov," William Blomquist and Roger B. Parks remind us that the organization and reorganization of local governance are inherently political processes. In their reexamination of the Unigov consolidation move that first inspired much of the research reported in this volume, they conclude that this reform was less comprehensive than is commonly believed. So many different administrative units continued to exist within Marion County that Unigov may best be interpreted as a political slogan, rather than an accurate representation of the structure of this local public economy. They also suggest purely political reasons for this reform effort. By incorporating suburban voters into city elections, Unigov has had the effect of perpetuating the control of the Republican party over elected offices in the combined city-county administration (see also Blomquist and Parks 1995).

However one interprets the political fallout from the Unigov reform, it remains clear that police departments in smaller jurisdictions continue to have significant advantages over the larger Indianapolis Police Department. In chapter 15, "Do We Really Want to Consolidate Urban Areas? [It's Like Deja Vu All Over Again]," Roger B. Parks briefly reports on a reexamination of this issue. The title of this essay, taken from the July 1995 edition of the Workshop newsletter *Polycentric Circles,* refers to one of the initial research reports on the Indianapolis police study (E. Ostrom, Parks, and Whitaker 1973). The tables included in this essay clearly demonstrate that citizens of smaller communities continue to express higher levels of satisfaction with the performance of their police forces than do citizens of comparable neighborhoods in Indianapolis. In sum, the findings of research originally conducted in the 1970s still hold true today.

Part V. Implications for Research and Policy

Not everyone is convinced that polycentricity is such a good thing. Some scholars still argue that consolidated government has significant advantages over fragmented governance arrangements. For example, in their systematic comparison of the (fragmented) Louisville and (consolidated) Lexington metropolitan areas, Lyons and Lowery (1989, 537) find that citizens in Louisville are, counter to the supposedly positive benefits of polycentricity, not very well informed about the "scope and nature of their service packages." They also fail to find any consistent difference between measures of citizen satisfaction with agency performance in these two metropolitan areas. (See also Lyons, Lowery, and DeHoog 1992.)

Despite initial appearances, these results do not directly contradict the earlier findings reported by scholars associated with the Workshop. After all, the latter focused specifically on public evaluation of police performance, whereas Lyons and Lowery paint on a broader canvas that encompasses a wide range of public services. Furthermore, there may be a potential common ground between these competing schools of thought. Lyons and Lowery (1989, 541–42) conclude that it is wrong to presume that consolidated governments "present individuals living in all areas and neighborhoods with a uniform tax-service package tailored to the median-voter preference of the entire urban population." Their analysis demonstrates that consolidated governments are capable of providing differentiated levels of service to different communities within a single large jurisdiction.

This observation is very much in line with the spirit of polycentricity, which acknowledges that integrating multiple scales of service provision and production is the key to increased levels of citizen satisfaction. A polycentric system cannot be completely fragmented, for there remain some services for which higher levels of aggregation are most appropriate.

Part of the problem may be that the contrast between polycentricity and consolidation has been overdrawn. A call for establishment of a polycentric order cannot be reduced to the slogan "small is beautiful." However, because of the widespread consensus on the benefits of consolidation that was current in the 1970s, scholars associated with the Workshop may have placed more emphasis on the benefits of smaller-scale agencies than would have been the case otherwise. In today's climate of decentralization and devolution of responsibilities to smaller units of government, advocates of polycentric order find it necessary to insist on the essential role played by larger-scale units! Despite this change in the overall framing of contemporary policy debates, the core ideas of polycentricity have remained the same.

Scholars associated with the Workshop continue to pursue studies of police services and other aspects of local public economies. For example, the Indianapolis Police Department has commissioned surveys of citizen evaluations that have been implemented by faculty and students affiliated with the Workshop and with the Center for Urban Policy and the Environment at the Indianapolis campus of Indiana University (Parks, Quinet, and Schmitt

1996). Visiting scholars have completed book projects while spending time at the Workshop. Books by Schneider (1989) and Stein (1990) are particularly noteworthy. These works connect to issues of major concern in the broader research community on urban politics, especially the deleterious effects of competition among municipalities to attract business investment. Stein, in particular, has been active in Houston, advising community leaders to find ways to take advantage of the opportunities inherent in polycentricity.

Although research on local public economies continues to be an active part of the Workshop tradition, the single most dominant focus in recent years has been on the study of common-pool resources in countries throughout the world (E. Ostrom 1990; McGinnis 1999a,b). The range of local governance structures investigated by scholars associated with the Workshop in Political Theory and Policy Analysis is equally broad-ranging, including Africa (Wunsch and Olowu 1995), Canada (Bish 1987, 1996; Sproule-Jones 1993), Italy (Sabetti 1984, forthcoming), the Netherlands (Toonen 1987), Nigeria (Olowu 1990), and Scandinavia (Bogason 1996). Still, no single book on metropolitan governance managed to capture the attention of the scholarly and policymaking communities in quite the same way that Elinor Ostrom's book *Governing the Commons* (1990) did for later research on the management of common-pool resources. Several contributing factors deserve mention.

First, working with complexity is never as appealing as simplicity. The policy issues of police forces turned out to be very complex and difficult to summarize. Books and essays from the later parts of these research programs show evident signs of the difficulties these scholars experienced in trying to come to grips with the complexity of polycentric governance of metropolitan areas.

Second, Workshop scholars have always been reluctant to "blow their own horn," so to speak, preferring instead to produce a steady stream of research results. This attitude stands as a refreshing contrast to the all-too-frequent tendency of research institutes or think tanks to trumpet their accomplishments. However, when it came time to sum it all up, under conditions of overwhelming complexity, the researchers were unable to do so in a sufficiently compelling manner. In collecting the essays for this volume, I have benefitted greatly from the clarity of hindsight, as well as my own personal distance from these research programs.

A third important factor is that two of the major players, Vincent Ostrom and Elinor Ostrom, eventually moved on to other research projects. Both had begun their professional careers with research on groundwater or natural resources, and Elinor Ostrom's later research, in particular, came to focus on a myriad of issues related to resource management.

In many ways, the study of the management of common-pool resources turned out to be a more productive empirical focus for exploration of the implications of polycentricity and self-governance. Anyone evaluating police performance in urban areas can scarcely avoid emotion-laden controversies over race relations and welfare policy. Also, one prominent issue concerns the appropriate role for the national government in the fight against urban blight. Needless to say, the management of fisheries, irrigation systems, and most common-pool resources typically evokes a considerably lower level of ideological salience. Furthermore, these resources are, in many cases, physically remote from urban centers or national capitals. In these more isolated communities, it is easier to identify the reasons why some communities manage to solve their own problems while other communities flounder or fail.

Perhaps the most fundamental reason, however, concerns the theme of the importance of local solutions to complex policy problems that recurs throughout the entire corpus of Workshop research. This attitude did not comport well with the prevailing inclination toward large-scale governmental intervention throughout society and in nearly all sectors of the economy. The relevant policymaking communities are now more open to a wider range of alternative approaches, partially as a response to the disappointing record of national policy initiatives. In short, the contrast between these two views of governance has taken on more prominence in contemporary debates over public policy. This volume of readings is intended as a contribution to these ongoing debates and as a spur toward more rigorous evaluation of the consequences of alternative institutional arrangements.

This volume concludes with two essays that present continuing challenges for research and policy. In chapter 16, "Complex Models of Urban Service Systems," Roger B. Parks and Elinor Ostrom stretch the standard mode of neoclassical economic theory to cover the behavior of public service producers. They argue that public bureaus, unlike firms, must be judged on multiple dimensions of outputs. That is, there is no single criterion equivalent to profits upon which bureau performance can be judged. They suggest that bureau managers might be modeled as if they maximize a two-component utility function that combines a measure of net community benefits (what they call the "benefits residuum") and personal gains in terms of status or budgetary discretion (measured by the number of specialized personnel in that agency). Managers of different bureaus would place different relative weights on these two considerations. For example, local service producers who actually reside in the area might put more emphasis on the net community benefits, since they themselves would share in these benefits.

In this way they generalize Niskanen's (1971) well-known model of bureau managers as budget maximizers. Competitive markets exert a strong selective pressure on firms that do not maximize their profits, but no similarly stringent selection process can be said to operate in the public sector. However, Parks and Ostrom argue that if a large number of alternative service producers are available for a given public industry (or if entry is relatively easy), then quasi-market competition can be said to exist. Under conditions of high multiplicity of service producers, bureau managers will put more weight on net community benefits as opposed to personal gain in those local public economies characterized by high values of multiplicity (as defined in earlier works also included in this volume). In effect, then, the existence of multiple service producers can closely approximate the positive benefits of competitive markets, as suggested in the classic *American Political Science Review* article leading off this set of readings.

This essay stands as a challenge to future researchers. Workshop scholars have made important contributions toward expanding the scope of game theory (McGinnis 1999a). For example, chapters in Kaufmann, Majone, and V. Ostrom (1986) explore alternative approaches to the formal analysis of rational behavior in the context of hierarchies or networks of interaction. Is it possible to represent the behavior of public service producers and providers as rational agents pursuing multiple objectives in a way that also takes account of the complex interrelationships among different public agencies and private organizations? This remains an open question.

Given the fundamentally collaborative nature of the research programs summarized in this volume, it seems particularly appropriate to conclude with an essay written by 10 coauthors. In chapter 17, "Consumers as Coproducers of Public Services: Some Economic and Institutional Considerations," this team of Workshop scholars emphasizes that certain public services (especially health, education, public safety) should be considered not as products produced by public authorities or professionals (physicians, teachers, police) but rather as the result of a process of interaction among these authorities or experts and the people themselves. The coauthors were participants in an informal seminar addressing citizen participation in community affairs. Similar interactions between faculty and students recur throughout the history of the Workshop, where instruction of graduate students is seen as a continual process of the coproduction of scholarly knowledge.

Coproduction has a close affinity to self-governance, and its importance for the evaluation of public policy deserves to be more widely appreciated. (That coproduction is equally important for development throughout the world is argued in Lam 1996; E. Ostrom 1996; both reprinted in McGinnis 1999b.) Unfortunately, as this essay demonstrates, analyses of coproduction may require the use of more complicated modes of formal analysis than is the case for single-source production. In this particular essay, the authors specify two forms of public goods production. One form is the standard sense in which "regular" producers exchange goods or services for monetary remuneration; the other is "consumer producers" in which citizen-customers directly participate in the production process. They use simple diagrams to illustrate situations in which trade-offs between these two kinds of production are useful. In some cases each form of production can be directly substituted for the other, but the more interesting cases are ones in which both forms of production interact in an interdependent manner.

Workshop scholars have published several other essays related to coproduction. Whitaker (1980) makes the important point that widespread use of the term *service delivery* conveys the misleading impression that the public must adopt an attitude of passive reception of goods and services produced by professional experts. Citizens can directly participate in the production of public services, and he emphasizes the extent to which such participation is crucial for the survival of a democratic, self-governing people. Voting and forming interest groups to lobby legislators may be important forms of political action, but if that is all we think of as political participation, then we are overlooking the important ways in which people can directly contribute to their own betterment. Sharp (1980) emphasizes the participatory attitude that the term *coproduction* conveys. Citizens of a democratic society need access to information that enables them to evaluate the performance of public officials, but citizens also need to actively engage in their own governance. She also argues that public officials need to see their role as creating the circumstances that encourage citizen participation and not just as providing public services in exchange for votes. Officials need to nurture citizens' capacity for self-governance and their experience at coproduction.

Many public officials have come to appreciate the benefits of actively involving communities in their own governance. For example, police departments throughout the country have implemented policies of "community policing" that reduce the distance between police officers and community members by encouraging informal contacts, removing patrol officers from their cars, and supporting community efforts to monitor and report suspicious behavior in their neighborhoods. At least some police officials realize that the public good of neighborhood safety is coproduced by communities and police acting together.

One prominent example of coproduction is the patrol-intensive and community-friendly "production strategy" that tends to be pursued by smaller police forces, primarily out of necessity. The long series of research programs summarized in the preceding demonstrated the relative effectiveness of this production strategy (see especially E. Ostrom et al. 1973). Community policing can be seen as an effort of large police forces to mimic the behavior of small forces in order to capitalize on the many advantages of this production strategy. However, the results reported by Roger Parks in chapter

15 of this volume demonstrate that this mimicry strategy has been less than completely successful, at least initially. Despite implementation of a community policing program in 1992, the Indianapolis police force still scored lower on measures of overall citizen satisfaction than did the smaller police forces servicing the nonconsolidated communities.

The conclusions and the methods of the interrelated research programs on the organization of local public economies in metropolitan areas of the United States continue to shape the Workshop approach to institutional analysis (see McGinnis 1999a,b). The methodological legacy of these metropolitan studies is a unique combination of insistence on scientific rigor and policy relevance, openness to multiple techniques of empirical and formal analysis, and sensitivity to nested levels of analysis.

The crux of this contribution is succinctly summarized in the following comment from Roger Parks, who has been associated with the Workshop from the very beginning, first as a graduate student and later as a faculty member at Indiana University's School of Public and Environmental Affairs.

The Workshop evolved from a collaboration among Elinor and Vincent Ostrom and their students that began in the late '60s in a small suite of offices in IU's Woodburn Hall. Although not formally designated as an Indiana University Research Center until 1973, most of the elements of the Workshop were in place by 1970. These included a strong commitment to theory-grounded empirical research, the inclusion of students as full colleagues in research and publication, and a rich intellectual experience anchored around regular colloquia where ideas were tabled and debated vigorously. The early Workshop built its reputation on a series of studies of police service delivery in neighborhoods served by small, medium, and large police departments. The results of these studies directly challenged the 'bigger is better' philosophy of would-be police reformers in the early and mid-'70s. Not only did they demonstrate that small- and medium-sized departments performed as well as or better than large departments when serving matched neighborhoods, they elucidated a logic grounded in polycentricity that explained why this outcome was to be expected. (Parks 1998)

The early Workshop research programs surveyed in this volume demonstrate that public services can be most efficiently provided under a system of multiple and overlapping jurisdictions, by enabling service producers to operate at the scale most efficient for particular activities. Related research programs have shown that polycentric orders prove equally effective for empirical contexts far removed from the provision of public safety in metropolitan areas of the United States.

REFERENCES

Bish, Robert L. 1971. *The Political Economy of Metropolitan Areas.* Chicago: Markham.

———. 1987. *Local Government in British Columbia.* Richmond, BC: Union of British Columbia Municipalities in cooperation with the University of Victoria School of Public Administration.

———. 1996. "Amalgamation: Is It the Solution?" Paper prepared for the Coming Revolution in Local Government conference, Atlantic Institute for Market Studies, Halifax, March 27–29, 1996.

Bish, Robert, and Vincent Ostrom. 1973. *Understanding Urban Government: Metropolitan Reform Reconsidered.* Washington, DC: American Enterprise Institute for Public Policy Research, Domestic Affairs Studies, vol. 20.

Blomquist, William, and Roger B. Parks. 1995. "Unigov: Local Government in Indianapolis and Marion County, Indiana." In *The Government of World Cities: The Future of the Metro Model,* ed. L. J. Sharpe, 77–89. New York: John Wiley.

Bogason, Peter, ed. 1996. *New Modes of Local Political Organizing: Local Government Fragmentation in Scandinavia.* Commack, NY: Nova Science Publishers.

Kaufmann, Franz-Xaver, Giandomenico Majone, and Vincent Ostrom, eds. 1986. *Guidance, Control, and Evaluation in the Public Sector.* Berlin and New York: Walter de Gruyter.

Kiser, Larry L., and Elinor Ostrom. 1982. "The Three Worlds of Action: A Metatheoretical Synthesis of Institutional Approaches." In *Strategies of Political Inquiry,* ed. Elinor Ostrom, 179–222. Beverly Hills, CA: Sage. Reprinted in McGinnis 1999a.

Lam, Wai Fung. 1996. "Institutional Design of Public Agencies and Coproduction: A Study of Irrigation Associations in Taiwan." *World Development* 24 (6): 1039–54. Reprinted in McGinnis 1999b.

Lindblom, Charles E. 1977. *Politics and Markets: The World's Political Economic Systems.* New York: Basic Books.

Lyons, William E., and David Lowery. 1989. "Governmental Fragmentation versus Consolidation: Five Public-Choice Myths about How to Create Informed, Involved, and Happy Citizens." *Public Administration Review* 49:533–43.

Lyons, William E., David Lowery, and Ruth Hoogland DeHoog. 1992. *The Politics of Dissatisfaction: Citizens, Services, and Urban Institutions.* Armonk, NY: M. E. Sharpe.

McDavid, James C. 1974. "Interjurisdictional Cooperation among Police Departments in the St. Louis Metropolitan Area." *Publius* 4 (4): 35–58.

McGinnis, Michael D., ed. 1999a. *Polycentric Games and Institutions.* Ann Arbor: University of Michigan Press.

———, ed. 1999b. *Polycentric Governance and Development.* Ann Arbor: University of Michigan Press.

Mitchell, William C. 1988. "Virginia, Rochester, and Bloomington: Twenty-Five Years of Public Choice and Political Science."*Public Choice* 56:101–19.

Mueller, Dennis C. 1989. *Public Choice II.* Cambridge: Cambridge University Press.

Niskanen, W. A., Jr. 1971. *Bureaucracy and Representative Government.* Chicago: AVC.

Oakerson, Ronald J. 1987. "Local Public Economies: Provision, Production, and Governance." *Intergovernmental Perspective* 13 (3/4): 20–25.

Oakerson, Ronald J., and Roger B. Parks. 1989. "Local Government Constitutions: A Different View of Metropolitan Governance." *American Review of Public Administration* 19 (4) (December): 279–94.

Olowu, Dele. 1990. *Lagos State: Governance, Society, and Economy.* Lagos: Malthouse Press.

Ostrom, Elinor. 1983. "A Public Service Industry Approach to the Study of Local Government Structure and Performance." *Policy and Politics* 11:313–41.

———. 1986. "An Agenda for the Study of Institutions." *Public Choice* 48:3–25. Reprinted in McGinnis 1999a.

———. 1990. *Governing the Commons: The Evolution of Institutions for Collective Action.* New York: Cambridge University Press.

———. 1996. "Crossing the Great Divide: Coproduction, Synergy, and Development." *World Development* 24 (6): 1073–87. Reprinted in McGinnis 1999b.

———. 1997. "The Comparative Study of Public Economies." Acceptance paper for the Frank E. Seidman Distinguished Award in Political Economy, presented at Rhodes College, Memphis, Tennessee, September 26, 1997.

Ostrom, Elinor, William H. Baugh, Richard Guarasci, Roger B. Parks, and Gordon P. Whitaker. 1973. *Community Organization and the Provision of Police Services.* Sage Professional Paper in Administrative and Policy Studies 03–001. Beverly Hills and London: Sage.

Ostrom, Elinor, Roy Gardner, and James Walker, with Arun Agrawal, William Blomquist, Edella Schlager, and Shui Yan Tang. 1994. *Rules, Games, and Common-Pool Resources.* Ann Arbor: University of Michigan Press.

Ostrom, Elinor, and Roger B. Parks. 1973. "Suburban Police Departments: Too Many and Too Small?" In *The Urbanization of the Suburbs*, ed. Louis H. Masotti and Jeffrey K. Hadden, 367–402. Urban Affairs Annual Reviews, vol. 7. Beverly Hills, CA: Sage.

Ostrom, Elinor, Roger B. Parks, and Gordon P. Whitaker. 1973. "Do We Really Want to Consolidate Urban Police Forces? A Reappraisal of Some Old Assertions." *Public Administration Review* 33 (September/October): 423–32.

———. 1977. *Policing Metropolitan America.* Washington, DC: U.S. Government Printing Office.

———. 1978. *Patterns of Metropolitan Policing.* Cambridge, MA: Ballinger.

Ostrom, Elinor, Roger B. Parks, Gordon P. Whitaker, and Stephen L. Percy. 1979. "The Public Service Provision Process: A Framework for Analyzing Police Services." In *Evaluating Alternative Law-Enforcement Policies*, ed. Ralph Baker and Fred A. Mayer, Jr., 65–73. Lexington, MA: Lexington Books.

Ostrom, Vincent. 1987. *The Political Theory of a Compound Republic: Designing the American Experiment.* 2d rev. ed. San Francisco: ICS Press.

———. 1989. *The Intellectual Crisis in American Public Administration.* 2d ed. Tuscaloosa: University of Alabama Press.

————. 1991. *The Meaning of American Federalism: Constituting a Self-Governing Society*. San Francisco: ICS Press.

————. 1993. "Epistemic Choice and Public Choice." *Public Choice* 77(1) (Sept.): 163–76.

————. 1997. *The Meaning of Democracy and the Vulnerability of Democracies: A Response to Tocqueville's Challenge*. Ann Arbor: University of Michigan Press.

————. 1998. "Some Developments in the Study of Market Choice, Public Choice, and Institutional Choice." In *Handbook of Public Administration*, ed. Jack Rabin, W. Bartley Hildreth, and Gerald J. Miller, 1,065–87. 2d ed. New York: Marcel Dekker.

Ostrom, Vincent, Robert Bish, and Elinor Ostrom. 1984. *Il governo locale negli Stati Uniti*. Milano, Italy: Fondazione Adriano Olivetti.

————. 1988. *Local Government in the United States*. San Francisco: ICS Press.

Parks, Roger B. 1985. "Metropolitan Structure and Systemic Performance: The Case of Police Service Delivery." In *Policy Implementation in Federal and Unitary Systems*, ed. Kenneth Hanf and Theo A. J. Toonen, 161–91. Dordrecht, the Netherlands: Martinus Nijhoff.

————. 1998. Personal communication with author.

Parks, Roger B., and Ronald J. Oakerson. 1989. "Metropolitan Organization and Governance: A Local Public Economy Approach." *Urban Affairs Quarterly* 25 (1) (September): 18–29.

————. 1993. "Comparative Metropolitan Organization: Service Production and Governance Structures in St. Louis (MO) and Allegheny County (PA)." *Publius* 23 (1) (winter): 19–39.

Parks, Roger B., and Elinor Ostrom. 1984. "Policing as a Multi-Firm Industry." In *Understanding Police Agency Performance*, ed. Gordon P. Whitaker, 7–22. Washington, DC: U.S. Department of Justice, National Institute of Justice.

Parks, Roger B., Kenna Davis Quinet, and Tamara Schmitt. 1996. *Indianapolis Police Department Community Policing: Citizen's Perspectives*. Indianapolis: Center for Urban Policy and the Environment, School of Public and Environmental Affairs.

Sabetti, Filippo. 1984. *Political Authority in a Sicilian Village*. New Brunswick, NJ: Rutgers University Press.

————. Forthcoming. *The Search for Good Government: Understanding Italian Democracy*. Montreal: McGill-Queen's University Press.

Salamon, Lester M. 1995. *Partners in Public Service: Government-Nonprofit Relations in the Modern Welfare State*. Baltimore: Johns Hopkins University Press.

Schneider, Mark. 1989. *The Competitive City: The Political Economy of Suburbia*. Pittsburgh: University of Pittsburgh Press.

Sharp, Elaine B. 1980. "Toward a New Understanding of Urban Services and Citizen Participation: The Coproduction Concept." *Midwest Review of Public Administration* 14 (2) (June): 105–18.

Sproule-Jones, Mark. 1993. *Governments at Work: Canadian Parliamentary Federalism and Its Public Policy Effects*. Toronto: University of Toronto Press.

Stein, Robert. 1990. *Urban Alternatives: Public and Private Markets in the Provi-*

sion of Local Services. Pittsburgh: University of Pittsburgh Press.

Tiebout, Charles M. 1956. "A Pure Theory of Local Expenditures." *Journal of Political Economy* 64 (October): 416–24.

Tocqueville, Alexis de. [1835] 1969. *Democracy in America*. Ed. J. P. Mayer, trans. George Lawrence. Garden City, NY: Anchor Books.

Toonen, Theo A. J. 1987. "Denken over Binnenlands Bestuur: Theorieë van de gedecentraliseerde eenheidsstaat bestuurskundig beschouwd" (Conceptual analysis of intergovernmental relations: A public administration perspective on theories of the decentralized unitary state). Ph.D. diss., Erasmus Universiteit, Rotterdam.

United States Advisory Commission on Intergovernmental Relations (ACIR). 1987. *The Organization of Local Public Economies*. ACIR Report A-109. Washington, DC. (Author: Ronald J. Oakerson)

———. 1988. *Metropolitan Organization: The St. Louis Case*. ACIR Report M-158. Washington, DC. (Coauthored by Ronald J. Oakerson and Roger B. Parks with the assistance of Henry A. Bell).

———. 1992. *Metropolitan Organization: The Allegheny County Case*. ACIR Report M-181. Washington, DC. (Coauthored by Roger B. Parks and Ronald J. Oakerson.)

Weimer, David L., and Aidan R. Vining. 1989. *Policy Analysis: Concepts and Practice*. 2d ed. Englewood Cliffs, NJ: Prentice-Hall.

Whitaker, Gordon P. 1980. "Coproduction: Citizen Participation in Service Delivery." *Public Administration Review* 40 (3): 240–46.

Wunsch, James S., and Dele Olowu, ed. 1995. *The Failure of the Centralized State: Institutions and Self-Governance in Africa*. 2d ed. San Francisco: ICS Press.

Part I
Conceptual Foundations
of Institutional Analysis

CHAPTER 1

The Organization of Government in Metropolitan Areas: A Theoretical Inquiry

Vincent Ostrom, Charles M. Tiebout, and Robert Warren

Allusions to the "problem of metropolitan government" are often made in characterizing the difficulties supposed to arise because a metropolitan region is a legal nonentity. From this point of view, the people of a metropolitan region have no general instrumentality of government available to deal directly with the range of problems that they share in common. Rather, there is a multiplicity of federal and state governmental agencies, counties, cities, and special districts that govern within a metropolitan region.

This view assumes that the multiplicity of political units in a metropolitan area is essentially a pathological phenomenon. The diagnosis asserts that there are too many governments and not enough government. The symptoms are described as "duplication of functions" and "overlapping jurisdictions." Autonomous units of government, acting in their own behalf, are considered incapable of resolving the diverse problems of the wider metropolitan community. The political topography of the metropolis is called a "crazy-quilt pattern," and its organization is said to be an "organized chaos." The prescription is reorganization into larger units—to provide "a general metropolitan framework" for gathering up the various functions of government. A political system with a single dominant center for making decisions is viewed as the ideal model for the organization of metropolitan government. "Gargantua" is one name for it.[1]

The assumption that each unit of local government acts independently without regard for other public interests in the metropolitan community has only a limited validity. The traditional pattern of government in a metropolitan area with its multiplicity of political jurisdictions may more appropriately be conceived as a "polycentric political system."[2] "Polycentric" con-

Originally published in *American Political Science Review* 55 (December 1961): 831–42. Reprinted by permission of the American Political Science Association and the authors.

Authors' note: Ostrom and Warren wish to acknowledge the early support of their work by the Bureau of Governmental Research at U.C.L.A. Background for discussion of the final section on "conflict and conflict resolution" was derived from research supported by the Water Resources Center of the University of California, help that Ostrom wishes to acknowledge.

notes many centers of decision making that are formally independent of each other. Whether they actually function independently, or instead constitute an interdependent system of relations, is an empirical question in particular cases. To the extent that they take each other into account in competitive relationships, enter into various contractual and cooperative undertakings or have recourse to central mechanisms to resolve conflicts, the various political jurisdictions in a metropolitan area may function in a coherent manner with consistent and predictable patterns of interacting behavior. To the extent that this is so, they may be said to function as a "system."

The study of government in metropolitan areas conceived as a polycentric political system should precede any judgment that it is pathological. Both the structure and the behavior of the system need analysis before any reasonable estimate can be made of its performance in dealing with the various public problems arising in a metropolitan community. Better analysis of how a metropolitan area is governed can lead in turn to more appropriate measures of reorganization and reform.[3]

This essay is an initial effort to explore some of the potentialities of a polycentric political system in providing for the government of metropolitan areas. We view the "business" of governments in metropolitan areas as providing "public goods and services." The first section of the essay will examine the special character of these public goods and services.

We shall then turn to an analysis of the problems of scale in constituting the public organizations that provide them. This discussion seems relevant to an analysis of any political structure in a metropolitan area and equally applicable to gargantua or to a polycentric political system. A brief reference will then be made to the problems of public organization in gargantua. Finally, patterns of organization in a polycentric political system will be analyzed with particular regard to the experience of the Los Angeles metropolitan area.

The Nature of Public Goods and Services

The conditions that give rise to public rather than private provision of certain goods and services are examined in this section. Three views of these conditions can usefully be distinguished: (1) public goods arising from efforts to control indirect consequences, externalities, or spillover effects; (2) public goods provided because some goods and services cannot be packaged; and (3) public goods consisting of the maintenance of preferred states of community affairs.

The Control of Indirect Consequences as Public Goods

The basic criterion traditionally offered for distinguishing between public and private affairs was formulated some years ago by John Dewey: "the line between private and public is to be drawn on the basis of the extent and scope of the consequences of facts which are so important as to need control whether by inhibition or by promotion" (Dewey 1927, 15). The indirect consequences of a transaction, which affect others than those directly concerned, can also be described as "externalities" or "spillover effects." Those indirectly affected are viewed as being external to the immediate transaction. Some externalities are of a favorable or beneficial nature; others are adverse or detrimental.

Favorable externalities can frequently be recaptured by the economic unit that creates them. The builder of a large supermarket, for example, may create externalities for the location of a nearby drugstore. If the builder of the supermarket also controls the adjacent land, he can capture the externalities accruing to the drugstore through higher rents or by common ownership of the two enterprises. From the builder's point of view he has "internalized"[4] the externalities.[5]

Where favorable externalities cannot be internalized by private parties, a sufficient mechanism to proceed may be lacking, and public agencies may be called upon to provide a good or service. A privately owned park, even with an admission charge, may not be able to cover costs. If the externalities in the form of the dollar value of a better neighborhood could be captured, such a park might be profitable.

Unfavorable spillovers or externalities are another matter. The management of a refinery that belches out smoke has little incentive to install costly equipment to eliminate the smoke. Control or internalization of diseconomies usually falls upon public agencies. A function of government, then, is to internalize the externalities—positive and negative—for those goods which the producers and consumers are unable or unwilling to internalize for themselves, and this process of internalization is identified with the "public goods."

Not all public goods are of the same scale. Scale implies both the geographic domain and the intensity or weight of the externality. A playground creates externalities that are neighborhood wide in scope, while national defense activities benefit a whole nation—and affect many outside it. Thus, for each public good there corresponds some "public." As John Dewey has formulated the definition, "The public consists of all those who are affected by the indirect consequences of transactions to such an extent that it is deemed necessary to have those consequences systematically provided for" (Dewey 1927, 15–16). The concept of the public is important to later considerations in determining the criteria of scale appropriate to public organizations.

Packageability

Public goods and services and, in turn, the functions of governments in metropolitan areas can be distinguished from private goods by a criterion commonly used by economists. A private good must be "packageable," that is, susceptible to being differentiated as a commodity or service before it can be readily purchased and sold in the private market. Those who do not pay for a private good can then be excluded from enjoying its benefits. This notion is formulated by economists as the "exclusion principle" (Musgrave 1959, esp. chap. 1). In contrast with Dewey's formulation of the nature of public goods, the exclusion principle focuses attention on the practicability of denying benefits. National defense, for example, will not be provided by private firms because, among other reasons, the citizen who did not pay would still enjoy the benefits. Furthermore, if citizens understate their preferences for defense—as by failing to build bomb shelters—on the assumption that it will be paid for by others, the result will be inadequate provision for defense.

Most municipal public goods such as fire and police protection, or the abatement of air pollution, are not easily packageable, either; they cannot be sold only to those individuals who are willing to pay (Tiebout 1956). This suggests two problems for public organizations.

First, private goods, because they are easily packageable, are readily subject to measurement and quantification. Public goods, by contrast, are generally not so measurable. If more police are added to the force, output will presumably increase. But how much, is a question without an exact answer. Moreover, when factors of production can be quantified in measurable units of output, the production process can be subject to more rigorous controls. A more rational pricing policy is also possible. With quantifiable data about both input and output, any production process can be analyzed, and the performance of different modes of production can be compared for their efficiency. Rational control over the production and provision of public goods and services therefore depends, among other things, upon the development of effective standards of measurement; this gets into the allocation of joint costs as well as of joint benefits.

A second, closely related, problem arises in the assessment of costs upon persons who can benefit without paying directly for the good. Only public agencies with their taxing powers can seek to apportion the costs of public goods among the various beneficiaries. The scale criterion of political representation, discussed subesquently, takes account of how this difference between private and public goods affects the organization of public agencies.

Public Goods as the Maintenance of Preferred States
of Community Affairs

The exclusion principle provides a criterion for distinguishing most public goods from private, but it does not, as commonly stated, clarify or specify the conditions that determine the patterns of organization in the public service economy. However, by viewing public goods as "the maintenance of preferred states of community affairs," we may introduce a modified concept of packageability, one that is amenable to some measurement and quantification and that therefore may be more helpful in clarifying criteria for the organization of public services in metropolitan areas. The modification consists of extending the exclusion principle from an individual consumer to all the inhabitants of an area within designated boundaries.

The concept can be illustrated on a small scale in the operation of a household heating system that uses conveniently measurable units of inputs. However, the household temperature it maintains is a joint benefit to the family, and a marginal change in family size will have no material effect upon the costs of maintaining this public good for the family. Yet since the family good derived from it is effectively confined to the household, outsiders are excluded, and there are no substantial spillover effects or externalities for them. The family good is not a public good in the larger community. So household heating is treated as a private good in most communities. Similarly, a public good on a neighborhood or community scale can be viewed as "packaged" within appropriate boundaries so that others outside the boundaries may be excluded from its use. In this way, in some communities adjacent to New York City, for example, the use of parks and beaches is restricted to local residents whose taxes presumably support these recreation facilities.

Wherever this is practicable, the analogy of a household as a "package" for an atmosphere with a controlled temperature may be generalized and applied to the maintenance of a desired state of affairs within particular local government boundaries. Just as the temperature and the cost of heating can be measured, so it may be possible to develop direct or closely approximate measures both of a given state of community affairs resulting from the production of many public goods and services and also of the costs of furnishing them. An air pollution abatement program, for example, may be measured by an index of quantities of various pollutants found in air samples. Given costs of abatement, some preferred tolerance levels may then be specified.

Similarly, any community has a "fire loss potential," defined as the losses to be expected if no provision for fire protection is made. The difference between this potential and the actual fire losses is then the output or "production" of the fire protection service, and the net fire loss can be termed the "state of affairs" in that community with respect to fire losses. Fire protection, of course, does not eliminate but only reduces fire losses. Any effort at complete elimination would probably be so expensive that the costs would greatly exceed the benefits. The "preferred" state of affairs is some optimal level of performance where benefits exceed costs. The provision of a community fire department as a public good can thus be viewed as the maintenance of a preferred state of affairs in fire protection for that community, and the benefits can ordinarily be confined to its residents.

Police protection can be regarded in the same way. The traffic patrol, for example, operates to optimize the flow of traffic while reducing the losses to property and injury to persons. Even if perfect control were possible, the costs would be so great that the preferred state of affairs in police protection would be something less.

It must be acknowledged, however, that in the case of police protection and many other public services, in contrast, say, with garbage collection or air pollution abatement, the performance level or net payoff is much more difficult to measure and to quantify. Proximate measures such as the gross number of arrests for different types of offenses per month or per 10,000 population annually have little meaning unless considered in relation to various conditions existing in the community. Decision makers consequently may be forced, for want of better measurements, to assume that the preferred state of affairs is defined as a balance between the demands for public services and the complaints from taxpayers.

While the output of a public good may not be packaged, this does not of course mean that its material inputs cannot be. The preferred state of affairs produced by mosquito spraying is enjoyed by the whole community, while spraying supplies and equipment are readily packageable. Mosquito spraying, that is to say, can be produced by a private vendor under contract to a public agency.

This illustrates an important point, that the *production* of goods and services needs to be distinguished from their *provision* at public expense. Government provision need not involve public production—indeed, at some stage in the sequence from raw materials to finished products virtually every public good, not already a natural resource, is of private origin. So, a public agency by contractual arrangements with private firms—or with other public agencies—can provide the local community with public services without going into the business of producing them itself.

When the desired performance level or the net payoff can be specified by a measurable index, an element of rigor can be introduced to assure substantial production controls in providing a public good, even where the production itself is the function of a separate agency or entrepreneur. The producer can be held accountable for maintaining affairs within certain tolerances, and the agency responsible for providing the service can ascertain the adequacy of performance. Advances in the measurement and quantification of performance levels in the public service economy will consequently permit much greater flexibility in the patterns of organization for the production and provision of public goods and services.

If Dewey's definition is extended to include "events" generally rather than being limited to "acts" or to "transactions" among actors, his formulation is consistent with the conception of public goods as the maintenance of preferred states of affairs.[7] Public control seeks to internalize those events, viewed as consequences that impinge directly and indirectly upon diverse elements in a community, in such a way that adverse consequences will be inhibited and favorable consequences will be promoted.

In the final analysis, distinctions between private and public goods cannot be as sharply made in the world of human experience as this analysis might imply. In part, the technical character of specific goods influences the degree of differentiation or isolability that characterizes their distribution and utilization. Vegetables and landscapes cannot be handled in the same way. Many private goods have spillover effects such that other members of the community bear some portion of the benefits and losses, whatever the degree of public regulation. In every large community most people philosophically accept some of the costs of bigness—air pollution, traffic congestion, noise, and a variety of inconveniences—on the assumption that these are inevitable concomitants of the benefits that derive from living in a metropolis.

Scale Problems in Public Organization

Viewing the boundaries of a local unit of government as the "package" in which its public goods are provided,[8] so that those outside the boundaries are excluded from their use, we may say that where a public good is adequately packaged within appropriate boundaries, it has been successfully internalized. Where externalities spill over upon neighboring communities, the public good has not been fully internalized.

In designing the appropriate "package" for the production and provision of public goods several criteria should be considered. Among these are control, efficiency, political representation, and self-determination. Needless to say, they are sometimes in conflict.

The Criterion of Control

The first standard applicable to the scale of public organization for the production of public services requires that the boundary conditions[9] of a political jurisdiction include the relevant set of events to be controlled. Events are not uniformly distributed in space; rather, they occur as sets under conditions such that boundaries can be defined with more or less precision. Rivers flow in watershed basins, for example. Patterns of social interaction are also differentially distributed in space, and boundaries can generally be defined for them too. In other words, all phenomena can be described in relation to specifiable boundary conditions, and the criterion of control requires that these be taken into account in determining the scale of a public organization.

Otherwise the public agency is disabled in regulating a set of events in order to realize some preferred state of affairs. If the boundaries cannot be suitably adjusted, the likely result is a transfer of the governmental function to a unit scaled to meet the criterion of control more adequately.

Pasadena, for example, is subject to severe smog attacks, but the city's boundary conditions do not cover an area sufficient to assure effective control of the appropriate meteorological and social space that would include the essential variables constituting the "smogisphere" of southern California. None of the separate cities of southern California, in fact, can encompass the problem. Instead, county air pollution control districts were organized for the Los Angeles metropolitan community. The failure even of these counties to meet adequately the criterion of effective control has led the California state government to assume an increasingly important role in smog control.

The Criterion of Efficiency

The most efficient solution would require the modification of boundary conditions so as to assure a producer of public goods and services the most favorable economy of scale, as well as effective control. Two streams with different hydrologic characteristics, for example, might be effectively controlled separately; but, by being managed together, the potentialities of one may complement the other. This has certainly been the case in Los Angeles's joint management of the Owens River and the Los Angeles River by making one the tributary of the other through the 300–mile Los Angeles Aqueduct, skirting the Sierras. Joint management permits a greater joint payoff in recreational facilities and water and power production.

Other factors such as technological developments and the skill or proficiency of a labor force can bear upon efficiency as a criterion of the scale of organization needed. If machinery for painting center stripes on city streets can only be efficiently used on a large scale, special arrangements may be required to enable several small cities to act jointly in providing such a service. The same may be true in the utilization of uncommon and expensive professional skills; and it accounts for the fact that mental institutions and prisons are apt to be state rather than municipal undertakings.

The Criterion of Political Representation

Another criterion for the scale of public organization requires the inclusion of the appropriate political interests within its decision-making arrangements. The direct participants in a transaction are apt to negotiate only their own interests, leaving the indirect consequences or spillover effects to impinge upon others. Third-party interests may be ignored. Public organizations seek to take account of third-party effects by internalizing the various interests in rendering public decisions and in controlling public affairs. Specification of the boundary or scale conditions of any political jurisdiction is important in determining the set of interests that is to be internalized within the organization.

In considering the political design of a public organization three elements of scale require consideration. The *scale of formal organization* indicates the size of the governmental unit that provides a public good. The *public,* as noted above, consists of those who are affected by its provision. The *political community* can be defined as those who are actually taken into account in deciding whether and how to provide it. Those who are affected by such a decision may be different from those who influence its making. An ideal solution, assuming criteria of responsibility and accountability consonant with democratic theory, would require that these three boundaries be coterminous. Where in fact the boundary conditions differ, scale problems arise.

If both the direct and indirect beneficiaries of a public transaction are included within the domain of a public organization, the means are in principle available for assessment of the cost of public control upon the beneficiaries. Except where a redistribution of income is sought as a matter of public policy, an efficient allocation of economic resources is assured by the capacity to charge the costs of providing public goods and services to the beneficiaries.[10]

The public implicated in different sets of transactions varies with each set: the relevant public for one set is confined to a neighborhood, while for another the relevant public may be most of the population of the globe. Between these two extremes are a vast number of potential scales of public organizations. Given certain levels of information, technology, communication, and certain patterns of identification, a scheme might be imagined that has an appropriate scale of public organization for each different public good. As these conditions and circumstances change, the scale of the public for any set of transactions should be altered correspondingly. If it is not, what then?

Where the political community does not contain the whole public, some interests may be disregarded. A city, for instance, may decide to discharge its sewage below its boundaries, and the affected public there may have no voice in the decision. On the other hand, where the political community contains the whole public and, in addition, people unaffected by a transaction, the unaffected are given a voice when none may be desired. Capricious actions can result. The total political community in a city of three million population may not be an appropriate decision-making mechanism in planning a local playground.

Nevertheless, the statement that a government is "too large (or too small) to deal with a problem" often overlooks the possibility that the scale of the public and the political community need not coincide with that of the formal boundaries of a public organization. Informal arrangements between public organizations may create a political community large enough to deal with any particular public's problem. Similarly, a public organization may also be able to constitute political communities within its boundaries to deal with problems that affect only a subset of the population. It would be a mistake to conclude that public organizations are of an inappropriate size until the informal mechanisms, which might permit larger or smaller political communities, are investigated.

Seen in relation to the political community, the scale of formal public organizations merely specifies the formal boundaries. Since the feasible number of governmental units is limited when compared to the number of public goods to be provided, a one-to-one mapping of the public, the political community, and the formal public organization is impracticable. Moreover, the relevant public changes. Even if, at one time, formal public organizations, political communities, and the publics were coterminous, over time, they would become dislocated. As a result, public organizations may (1) reconstitute themselves; (2) voluntarily cooperate, or, failing cooperation; (3) turn to other levels of government in a quest for an appropriate fit among the interests affecting and affected by public transactions.

The Criterion of Local Self-Determination

The criteria of effective control, of efficiency, and of the inclusion of appropriate political interests can be formulated on general theoretical grounds, but their application in any political system depends upon the particular institutions empowered to decide questions of scale. The conditions attending the organization of local governments in the United States usually require that these criteria be controlled by the decisions of the citizenry in the local community, that is, subordinated to considerations of self-determination.

The patterns of local self-determination manifest in incorporation proceedings usually require a petition of local citizens to institute incorporation proceedings and an affirmative vote of the local electorate to approve. Commitments to local consent and local control may also involve substantial home rule in determining which interests of the community its local officials will attend to and how these officials will be organized and held responsible for their discharge of public functions.

Local self-government of municipal affairs assumes that public goods can be successfully internalized. The purely "municipal" affairs of a local jurisdiction, presumably, do not create problems for other political communities. Where internalization is not possible and where control, consequently, cannot be maintained, the local unit of government becomes another "interest" group in quest of public goods or potential public goods that spill over upon others beyond its borders.

The choice of local public services implicit in any system of self-government presumes that substantial variety will exist in patterns of public organization and in the public goods provided among the different local communities in a metropolis. Patterns of local autonomy and home rule constitute substantial commitments to a polycentric system.

Public Organization in Gargantua

Since all patterns of organization are less than perfectly efficient, responsive or representative, some consideration should be given to the problem of organizing for different types of public services in gargantua, in contrast to the problems in a polycentric political system. This brief discussion will only touch on theoretical considerations involved in organizing diverse public services in the big system.

Gargantua unquestionably provides an appropriate scale of organization for many huge public services. The provision of harbor and airport facilities, mass transit, sanitary facilities, and imported water supplies may be most appropriately organized in gargantua. By definition, gargantua should be best able to deal with metropolitan-wide problems at the metropolitan level.

However, gargantua with its single dominant center of decision making, is apt to become a victim of the complexity of its own hierarchical or bureaucratic structure. Its complex channels of communication may make its administration unresponsive to many of the more localized public interests in the community. The costs of maintaining control in gargantua's public service may be so great that its production of public goods becomes grossly inefficient.

Gargantua, as a result, may become insensitive and clumsy in meeting the demands of local citizens for the public goods required in their daily life. Two to three years may be required to secure street or sidewalk improvements, for example, even where local residents bear the cost of the improvement. Modifications in traffic control at a local intersection may take an unconscionable amount of time. Some decision makers will be more successful in pursuing their interests than others. The lack of effective organization for these others may result in policies with highly predictable biases. Bureaucratic unresponsiveness in gargantua may produce frustration and cynicism on the part of the local citizen who finds no point of access for remedying local problems of a public character. Municipal reform may become simply a matter of "throwing the rascals out." The citizen may not have access to sufficient information to render an informed judgment at the polls. Lack of effective communication in the large public organization may indeed lead to the eclipse of the public and to the blight of the community.

The problem of gargantua, then, is to recognize the variety of smaller sets of publics that may exist within its boundaries. Many of the interests of smaller publics might be properly negotiated within the confines of a smaller political community without requiring the attention of centralized decision makers concerned with the big system. This task of recognizing the smaller publics is a problem of "field" or "area" organization. The persistence of bureaucratic unresponsiveness in the big system, however, indicates it is not easily resolved. Large-scale, metropolitan-wide organization is unquestionably appropriate for a limited number of public services, but it is not the most appropriate scale of organization for the provision of all public services required in a metropolis.

Public Organization in a Polycentric Political System

No a priori judgment can be made about the adequacy of a polycentric system of government as against the single jurisdiction. The multiplicity of interests in various public goods sought by people in a metropolitan region can only be handled in the context of many different levels of organization. The polycentric system is confronted with the problem of realizing the needs of wider community interests or publics beyond the functional or territorial bounds of each of the formal entities within the broader metropolitan region. The single jurisdiction, in turn, confronts the problem of recognizing and organizing the various subsidiary sets of interests within the big system. It is doubtful that suboptimization in gargantua is any easier to accomplish than supraoptimization in a polycentric political system.

The performance of a polycentric political system can only be understood and evaluated by reference to the patterns of cooperation, competition, and conflict that may exist among its various units. Cooperative arrangements pose no difficulty when joint activities produce a greater return to all parties concerned, if the appropriate set of public interests is adequately represented among the negotiators. A contractual arrangement will suffice. As a result, this discussion of the behavior of a polycentric political system will focus upon the more difficult problems of competition, of conflict, and its resolution. If a polycentric political system can resolve conflict and maintain competition within appropriate bounds, it can be a viable arrangement for dealing with a variety of public problems in a metropolitan area.

Competition[11]

Where the provision of public goods and services has been successfully internalized within a public jurisdiction, there are no substantial spillover effects, by definition. In such circumstances there need be no detrimental consequences from competition in the municipal services economy. Patterns of competition among producers of public services in a metropolitan area, just as among firms in the market, may produce substantial benefits by inducing self-regulating tendencies with pressure for the more efficient solution in the operation of the whole system.

Variety in service levels among various independent local government agencies within a larger metropolitan community may give rise to a quasi-market choice for local residents in permitting them to select the particular community in the metropolitan area that most closely approximates the public service levels they desire. Public service agencies then may be forced to compete over the service levels offered in relation to the taxes charged. Such competition, however, would only be appropriate for those public goods that are adequately internalized within the boundaries of a given political jurisdiction.

Conditions amenable to competition normally exist among local units of government where a number of units are located in close proximity to each other and where information about each other's performance is publicly available. Information can lead to comparison, and comparison can lead to pressure for performances to approximate the operations of the more efficient units. Where more than one public jurisdiction is capable of rendering service in a single area, further competitive tendencies may develop. Contractual arrangements among public jurisdictions for the provision of specific public services have long provided a competitive alternative to each jurisdiction that might otherwise produce its own services.

The separation of the *provision* of public goods and services from their *production* opens up the greatest possibility of redefining economic functions in a public service economy. Public control can be maintained in relation to performance criteria in the provision of services, while allowing an increasing amount of competition to develop among the agencies that produce them.

With the incorporation of the city of Lakewood in 1954, Los Angeles County, for example, expanded its system of contracting for the production of municipal services to a point approaching quasi-market conditions. Newly incorporated cities, operating under the so-called Lakewood Plan, contract with the county or other appropriate agencies to produce the general range of municipal services needed in the local community.

Each city contracts for municipal services for the city as a whole. Services beyond the general level of performance by county administration in unincorporated areas are subject to negotiation for most service functions. Each city also has the option of producing municipal services for itself. Private contractors too have undertaken such services as street sweeping, engineering, street maintenance and repair, and related public works. Some contracts have been negotiated with neighboring cities. As the number of vendors increases, competition brings pressures toward greater responsiveness and efficiency.

By separating the production from the provision of public goods it may be possible to differentiate, unitize, and measure the production while continuing to provide undifferentiated public goods to the citizen-consumer. Thus Los Angeles County has, under the Lakewood Plan, unitized the production of police services into packages, each consisting of a police car on continuous patrol with associated auxiliary services. A price is placed on this police-car-on-continuous-patrol package, and a municipality may contract for police service on that basis. Within the local community, police service is still provided as a public good for the community as a whole.

Problems of scale arising from possible conflicts between criteria of production and criteria of political representation may be effectively resolved in this way. Efficient scales of organization for the production of different public goods may be quite independent of the scales required to recognize appropriate publics for their consumption of public goods and services. But competition among vendors may allow the most efficient organization to be utilized in the production, while an entirely different community of interest and scale of organization controls the provision of services in a local community.

The separation of production from provision may also have the consequence of turning local governments into the equivalents of associations of consumers. While Sidney and Beatrice Webb viewed local governments as associations of consumers, the dominance of production criteria in U.S. municipal administration has largely led to the subordination of consumer interests (Webb and Webb 1922, 437ff.). However, cities organized to provide the local citizenry with public services produced by other agencies may be expected to give stronger representation to consumer interests. Among the so-called Lakewood Plan cities in Los Angeles County, for example, the local chief administrative officer has increasingly become a spokesman or bargainer for local consumer interests.

In this role, the chief administrative officer is similar to a buyer in a large corporation. Recognizing that the greater the number of vendors of public services, the greater the competition, the local chief administrative officer may seek to expand the number of his potential suppliers. As competition increases, vendors become more sensitive to the consumer demands he negotiates.

The production of public goods under the contract system in Los Angeles County has also placed considerable pressure upon the county administration to become more responsive to demands of the public service clientele organized through their local cities. Important changes in operating procedures and organizational arrangements have been introduced into the county's administration of police protection, fire protection, library services, street maintenance, building inspection, and engineering services in order to increase efficiency and responsiveness.

Under these circumstances, a polycentric political system can be viable in supplying a variety of public goods with many different scales of organization and in providing optimal arrangements for the production and consumption of public goods. With the development of quasi-market conditions in production, much of the flexibility and responsiveness of market organization can be realized in the public service economy.

Several difficulties in the regulation of a competitive public service economy can be anticipated. Economic pricing and cost allocation are dependent upon the development of effective measurement of municipal services. Since the preferred states of affairs in a community cannot be converted to a single scale of values such as dollar profits in a private enterprise, it may be more difficult to sustain an objective competitive relationship in a public service economy. Although costs of contract services from different vendors of a public good may be the same, objective standards for determining the value of the benefits are needed and may be hard to come by; otherwise the latitude of discretion available to the negotiators may limit the competitive vitality of the system and shift the competition to side payoffs.

Without careful control of cost allocations and pricing arrangements, funds from noncompetitive welfare functions might be used to subsidize the more competitive service areas. In Los Angeles County, close scrutiny of cost accounting practices and pricing policies by the grand jury has helped to prevent funds from being so transferred.

Any long-term reliance upon quasi-market mechanisms in the production of public goods and services no doubt will require more of such careful scrutiny, control, and regulation than has been applied toward maintaining the competitive structure of the private market economy. The measurement of cost and output performance may become an essential public function of the state in the administration of metropolitan affairs if continued reliance is placed primarily upon a polycentric system in the government of metropolitan areas.

Reliance upon outside vendors to produce public services may also reduce the degree of local political control exercised. The employee is subject to the control of the vendor and not directly to the control of the municipality. In contrast to the more immediate lines of responsibility and communication between local municipal employees and city officials, reliance upon vendors to provide municipal services may also restrict the quality and quantity of information about community affairs that are provided to the city's decision makers. This constraint on information might reduce the degree of their control over public affairs.

This discussion merely indicates some of the considerations to be examined in an analysis of the effects of competitive arrangements in providing public services. As long as the particular contracting agencies encompass the appropriate sets of public interests, no absolute impediment to their use need exist. With appropriate public control, competitive arrangements may afford great flexibility in taking advantage of some of the economies of scale for the production of public services in a metropolitan area, while, at the same time, allowing substantial diversity in their provision for the more immediate communities, based upon political responsibility within local patterns of community identification.

Conflict and Conflict Resolution

More difficult problems for a polycentric political system are created when the provision of public goods cannot be confined to the boundaries of the existing units of government. These situations involving serious spillover effects are apt to provoke conflict between the various units in the system. Arrangements must be available for the resolution of such conflicts if a polycentric political system is to solve its problems. Otherwise, competition and conflict are apt to become acute.

No community, on its own initiative, has much incentive to assume the full costs of controlling adverse consequences that are shared by a wider public. The competitive disadvantage of enforcing pollution abatement regulations, for example, against individuals and firms within a single community, when competitors in neighboring communities are not required to bear such costs, leads each community to excuse its failure to act by the failure of other similarly situated communities to act. In a polycentric system this is especially serious where many of the public "goods" involve the costly abatement of public nuisances.

Concerted action by the various units of government in a metropolitan area is easier to organize when costs and benefits are fairly uniformly distributed throughout the area. By way of example, this has been done under contractual agreements for mutual aid to assure the mobilization of greater fire-fighting capability in case of serious conflagrations. The random and unpredictable nature of such fires cause them to be treated as a uniform risk that might occur to any community in the larger metropolitan area.

Similar considerations apply to efforts to control mosquito infestations or air pollution. Leagues of cities, chambers of commerce, and other civic associations have frequently become the agencies for negotiating legislative proposals for the creation of mosquito abatement districts, air pollution control districts, and the like.

More difficult problems for the polycentric political system arise when the benefits and the costs are not uniformly distributed. Communities may differ in their perception of the benefits they receive from the provision of a common public good. In turn, a community may be unwilling to "pay its fair share" for providing that good simply because its demands for provision are less than in neighboring communities. These situations call for effective governmental mechanisms that can internalize the problem. If necessary, sanctions must be available for the enforcement of decisions.

The conflicting claims of municipal water supply systems pumping water from the same underground basins in southern California, for example, have uniformly been resolved by recourse to legal actions in the state courts. The courts have thereby become the primary authorities for resolving conflicts among water supply agencies in southern California; and their decisions have come to provide many of the basic policies of water administration in the Southern California metropolitan region. The state's judiciary has played a comparable role in conflicts among other local government agencies in such diverse fields as public health, incorporation and annexation proceedings, law enforcement, and urban planning.

The heavy reliance upon courts for the resolution of conflicts among local units of government unquestionably reflects an effort to minimize the risks of external control by a superior decision maker. Court decisions are taken on a case-by-case basis. The adversaries usually define the issues and consequently limit the areas of judicial discretion. This method also minimizes the degree of control exercised following a judgment. California courts, in particular, have accepted the basic doctrines of home rule and are thus favorably disposed to the interests of local units of government in dealing with problems of municipal affairs.

The example of municipal water administration may be pursued further to illustrate other decision-making arrangements and their consequences which bear upon the resolution of conflict in a polycentric political system.[12]

While litigation may be an appropriate means for resolving conflicts over a given supply of water, local water administrators in southern California have long recognized that lawsuits never produced any additional water. Organization for the importation of new water supplies was recognized as the only means for solving the long-term problem.

Los Angeles built the first major aqueduct to import water into the area on its own initiative. This water supply was used to force adjoining areas to annex or consolidate to the city of Los Angeles if they wished to gain access to the new supply. The condition for the provision of water required adjoining areas to sacrifice their identities as separate political communities. To get that one public good they were forced to give up other public goods. This provoked sufficient opposition to block any new developments that were not based upon consent and cooperation. The mechanisms for the resolution of subsequent conflicts were required to take on new forms.

The importation of Colorado River water was later undertaken by a coalition of communities in southern California formed through the agency of the southern section of the League of California Cities. The League afforded a neutral ground for the negotiation of the common interests of the city of Los Angeles and the other cities in the metropolitan area which shared common water problems. After satisfactory arrangements had been negotiated, including provision for the formation of a new metropolitan water district and endorsement of the Boulder Canyon project, a Boulder Dam Association was formed to realize these objectives. In due course a new agency, the Metropolitan Water District of Southern California, was formed; and the Colorado River aqueduct was constructed and put into operation by this new district.

More recently, the Southern California Water Coordinating Conference, meeting under the auspices of the Los Angeles Chamber of Commerce, has been the agency for negotiating regional interests in the development of the California Water Program. The Metropolitan Water District was not able to represent areas in southern California that did not belong to that district; and the rise of a variety of special municipal water districts precluded the League of California Cities, which represents cities only, from again serving as the agency for the negotiation of metropolitan interests in municipal water supply.

These illustrations suggest that a variety of informal arrangements may be available for negotiating basic policies among local government agencies in a metropolitan area. Such arrangements are vital in negotiating common interests among them. The larger public is taken into account in an informally constituted political community. These arrangements work effectively only so long as substantial unanimity can be reached, for formal implementation of such decisions must be ratified by each of the appropriate official agencies, including the state government when changes in state law or administrative policies are involved.

Higher levels of government may also be invoked in seeking the resolution of conflict among local governments in metropolitan areas. Again recourse is sought to a more inclusive political community. Under these circumstances, conflict tends to centralize decision making and control. The danger is that the more inclusive political community will not give appropriate recognition to the particular public interests at issue and tend to inject a variety of other interests into settlements of local controversies.

Appeal to central authorities runs the risk of placing greater control over local metropolitan affairs in agencies such as the state legislature, while at the same time reducing the capability of local governments for dealing with their problems in the local context. Sensitivity over the maintenance of local control may produce great pressure for the subordination of differences while conflicting parties seek a common position approximating unanimity. A substantial investment in informal negotiating and decision-making arrangements can be justified from the perspective of the local authorities if such arrangements can prevent the loss of local autonomy to higher levels of government.

Ironically but logically, this effort to avoid recourse to conflict and the consequent centralization of decision making tends also to reduce the local autonomy or degree of independence exercised by the local governing boards. Pressure for agreement on a common approach to some metropolitan problem limits the choices available to any particular local government. However, this range of choice may still be greater than that which would result from a settlement by a central authority. Negotiation among independent agencies allows the use of a veto against any unacceptable position. Agreement must be negotiated within the limits of the various veto positions if the alternative of recourse to an external authority at a higher level of political jurisdiction is to be avoided.

To minimize the costs of conflict to their power positions, administrators of local government agencies in metropolitan areas have tended to develop an extensive system of communication about each other's experience and to negotiate standards of performance applicable to various types of public services. Professional administrative standards may, thus, operate to constrain the variety of experience in local government agencies. Information about areas of difference and of potential conflict tends to be repressed under these circumstances. The negotiations about common problems through informal agencies are apt to be conducted in secrecy, and careful control may be developed over sensitive information.

These pressures to avoid the costs of conflict and seek agreement about metropolitan problems reflect the importance to local governments of resolving general public problems by negotiation at the local level in a metropolitan community. To the extent that these pressures are effective, the patterns of local government in a metropolitan area can only be understood by attention to the variety of formal and informal arrangements that may exist for settling areawide problems.

Contrary to the frequent assertion about the lack of a "metropolitan framework" for dealing with metropolitan problems, most metropolitan areas have a very rich and intricate "framework" for negotiating, adjudicating, and deciding questions that affect their diverse public interests. Much more careful attention needs to be given to the study of this framework.

NOTES

1. The term is taken from Wood 1958. Wood defines gargantua as "the invention of a single metropolitan government or at least the establishment of a regional super-

structure which points in that direction." We do not argue the case for big units vs. small units as Wood does in his discussion of gargantua vs. grass roots. Rather, we argue that various scales of organization may be appropriate for different public services in a metropolitan area.

2. We use this term for want of a better one. An alternative term might be *multinucleated political system*. We do not use *pluralism* because it has been preempted as a broader term referring to society generally and not to a political system in particular.

Polycentric political systems are not limited to the field of metropolitan government. The concept is equally applicable to regional administration of water resources, to regional administration of international affairs, and to a variety of other situations.

3. By analogy, the formal units of government in a metropolitan area might be viewed as organizations similar to individual firms in an industry. Individual firms may constitute the basic legal entities in an industry, but their conduct in relation to one another may be conceived as having a particular structure and behavior as an industry. Collaboration among the separate units of local government may be such that their activities supplement or complement each other, as in the automobile industry's patent pool. Competition among them may produce desirable self-regulating tendencies similar in effect to the "invisible hand" of the market. Collaboration and competition among governmental units may also, of course, have detrimental effects, and require some form of central decision making to consider the interests of the area as a whole. For a comprehensive review of the theory of industrial organization see Bain 1959.

4. Krutilla and Eckstein 1958, 69ff. Krutilla and Eckstein develop the concept of "internalizing" external economies as a criterion for determining scale of a management unit in the administration of water resources.

5. In practice, shopping centers may also give favorable rents to large supermarkets as "traffic generators." This recognizes the externalities they create.

6. Dewey 1927, 4–5. Dewey's use of the terms *acts* and *transactions* implies that only social behavior is contemplated in public action. But physical events, for example, floods, may also become objects of public control.

7. See the discussion of "district boundaries and the incidence of benefits" in Smith 1956.

8. The boundary conditions of a local unit of government are not limited to the legally determined physical boundaries but should include reference to extraterritorial powers, joint powers, and so on.

9. This factor might be separately characterized as a criterion of equitable distribution of costs and benefits, but we have chosen to consider it here in the context of political representation.

10. This analysis is confined to competition between units of government and makes no reference to competitive forces within a unit of government. Competition among pressure groups, factions, and political parties is a fundamental feature of the democratic political process but is not within the primary focus of this essay and its concern with the polycentric system.

11. For further detail see Ostrom 1953, esp. chaps. 3, 6, and 7.

REFERENCES

Bain, Joe S. 1959. *Industrial Organization.* New York: Wiley.
Dewey, John. 1927. *The Public and Its Problems.* New York: H. Holt.
Krutilla, John V., and Otto Eckstein. 1958. *Multiple Purpose River Development: Studies in Applied Economic Analysis.* Baltimore, MD: Johns Hopkins University Press.
Musgrave, Richard. 1959. *The Theory of Public Finance.* New York: McGraw-Hill.
Ostrom, Vincent. 1953. *Water and Politics.* Los Angeles, CA: Haynes Foundation.
Smith, Stephen C. 1956. "Problems in the Use of the Public District for Ground Water Management." *Land Economics* 32 (August): 259–69.
Tiebout, Charles M. 1956. "A Pure Theory of Local Expenditures." *Journal of Political Economy* 64 (October): 416–24.
Webb, Sydney, and Beatrice Webb. 1922. *English Local Government: Statutory Authorities for Special Purposes.* London: Longmans, Green.
Wood, Robert C. 1958. "The New Metropolis: Green Belts, Grass Roots or Gargantua." *American Political Science Review* 52 (March): 108–22.

CHAPTER 2

Polycentricity (Part 1)

Vincent Ostrom

A decade ago, Charles Tiebout, Robert Warren, and I proposed that patterns of governance in metropolitan areas might be viewed as polycentric political systems (Ostrom, Tiebout, and Warren 1961 [chap. 1 in this volume]). We identified a polycentric political system as having many centers of decision making that were formally independent of each other. We used the term *political* as synonymous with *government.* We indicated that the "business" of governments was the production (and provision) of various public goods and services. A "system" was viewed as a set of ordered relationships that persists through time.

By conceptualizing metropolitan areas as polycentric political systems, we were suggesting that a system of ordered relationships underlies the fragmentation of authority and overlapping jurisdictions that had frequently been identified as "chaotic" and as the principal source of institutional failure in the government of metropolitan areas. If an appropriate theory were developed, it should explain the patterns of behavior observed in an urban area and predict behavioral tendencies.

Given a theoretical understanding of the behavior of polycentric systems, we argued that no prima facie grounds existed for expecting less efficient performance from polycentric arrangements than from a fully integrated system with one governmental unit having exclusive jurisdiction over any particular metropolitan area. Individuals associated with the "efficiency and economy" reform movement had urged on grounds of efficiency that many local jurisdictions be consolidated or merged into a single overall unit of government for any particular metropolitan region. They inferred that overlapping jurisdictions created a duplication of services or functions. A dupli-

Originally prepared for delivery at the 1972 annual meeting of the American Political Science Association, Washington Hilton Hotel, Washington, DC, September 5–9. Published by permission of the author. Comments by Robert Bish, Phillip Gregg, John Hamilton, Norton Long, Brian Loveman, James McDavid, Nancy Neubert, Elinor Ostrom, Roger Parks, Dennis Smith, Mark Sproule-Jones, and Donald Zauderer have stimulated substantial revisions in this essay from the earlier draft circulated in late June 1972.

This essay has been divided into two parts for publication in this volume. References for both parts are listed at the end of part 2 (chap. 5).

cation of services was presumed on prima facie grounds to be wasteful or inefficient. We challenged that presumption. Such inferences need not hold if agencies are offering similar but differentiated services that impinge upon diverse communities of interest. The FBI, for example, does not necessarily duplicate the services of state and local police forces.

We did not, however, assume that all polycentric systems were necessarily efficient. The efficiency of any particular polycentric system would depend upon how well operational relationships corresponded to the theoretically specified conditions for efficient performance. These necessary conditions for efficient performance were: (1) the correspondence of different units of government to the scales of effects for diverse public goods; (2) the development of cooperative arrangements among governmental units to undertake joint activities of mutual benefit; and (3) the availability of other decision-making arrangements for processing and resolving conflicts among units of government.

The prevailing theoretical orientation had construed the existence of fragmentation of authority and overlapping jurisdictions as generating a state of affairs often described as "chaotic." The characterization of some state of affairs as "chaotic" implies the absence of an explanatory theory to account for that state of affairs. Presumably, a truly chaotic state of affairs would not persist over time unless a grand randomizer were available to "maintain" a chaotic "order." Furthermore, a truly chaotic state can hardly be evaluated by performance criteria such as efficiency or responsiveness. For a polycentric political system to exist and persist through time, a structure of ordered relationships would have to prevail, perhaps, under an illusion of chaos. If such a structure of ordered relationships exists one might assume that specifiable structural conditions will evoke predictable patterns of conduct. Only if predictable patterns of ordered relationships could be established would it be possible to evaluate the performance of a polycentric system *and* anticipate its future performance as against some other structure of ordered relationships. The development of an explanatory theory must precede the evaluation of alternative patterns of organization in relation to normative criteria.

The thesis advanced in Ostrom, Tiebout, and Warren evoked a response among scholars that cast some doubt upon that formulation. The most consistent response was to identify the approach as a "market model." Once it had been so named, some scholars dismissed it as an inappropriate analogy. Others used the reference to "market model" as an occasion for free association about atomistic individualism and other attributes of classical economic theory. If Ostrom, Tiebout, and Warren were a simple market model, derived from classical economic theory, then every reason would exist for rejecting that formulation. From economic theory, we would predict that efforts to provide *public* goods and services to individuals under market conditions will *fail*.

However, we never intended to develop a strict market model for the supply of public goods and services to individual buyers. Nor did we intend to present an economic analogy based upon classical economic theory. On the other hand, we thought an indication that quasi-market mechanisms were operable in a public service economy would imply important new dimensions for a theory of public administration.

Another response was to identify the formulation in Ostrom, Tiebout, and Warren as a rationalization or defense of the status quo. A theory that accounts for an order under an illusion of chaos and explains the status quo has attained some small measure of success as positive theory. Presumably, any explanatory theory, if it is successful, will rationalize the status quo in the sense that relationships between conditions and consequences can be explained. However, a theory should also enable predictions to be made about different hypothetical outcomes under varying conditions. In this sense, a political theory should, also, enable political decision makers to *alter* structural arrangements and modify outcomes in a predictable manner. Thus, an adequate knowledge of the regularities present in an existing system, and the consequences likely to flow from changes in that system, is a necessary prerequisite for successful reform. An explanatory theory should, however, be consistent with normative solutions other than the status quo.

A theory of polycentric organization should be no more of a rationalization of the status quo in the contemporary United States than a theory of bureaucratic organization is a rationalization of the status quo in the ancien regimes of France or Russia. Any given political system is amenable to a larger range of alternative policy solutions than the existing set of policy solutions that evoke the status quo within any given time horizon. Indeed, a polycentric system should be amenable to a greater variety of policy solutions than a monocentric system.

These responses indicated some serious weaknesses in Ostrom, Tiebout, and Warren. The task we undertook was more difficult than we had realized. Polycentricity must be applicable to a large range of social tasks if the *governance* of metropolitan areas is to be subject to a polycentric ordering. Quasi-market structures in a public service economy will be generated only if conditions of polycentricity are applicable to various aspects of political organization.

Polycentricity poses fundamental issues in political theory that have broader ramifications than the governance of metropolitan areas. A resolution of these issues is, however, necessary to an understanding of the structural and behavioral characteristics of polycentric systems of government in metropolitan areas. In turn, such an understanding is also essential to anyone who is interested in the normative problems of designing alternative institutional arrangements for the governance of metropolitan areas.

The possibility that a polycentric political system *can* exist does not preclude the possibility that a monocentric political system *can* exist. Each possibility depends upon conceptualizing the essential defining characteristics for each system and indicating the logically necessary conditions that must be met for the maintenance of a system having those defining characteristics. Furthermore, a predominantly monocentric political system need not preclude the possibility that elements of polycentricity may exist in the organization of such a system. Conversely, the existence of a predominantly polycentric political system need not preclude elements of monocentricity from existing in such a system.

Political relationships always exist as a set of possibilities within a much larger domain of all sets of possibilities inherent in the *potential variety* of human behavior. Social organization occurs when the *potential variety* in human behavior is *constrained* so as to exclude some possibilities and permit other possibilities. Decision rules or laws serve as a means for partitioning the set of all possibilities into authorized and proscribed relationships. However, proscribed relationships or unlawful actions are still technically or empirically *possible*.

The operation of legal constraints depends upon the actions taken by some decision makers (i.e., governmental officials) to determine, enforce, and alter legal relationships. Laws themselves are never self-generating, self-determining or self-enforcing. The maintenance of any pattern of social organization depends upon the potential use of sanctions by some decision makers to enforce legal relationships among other decision makers. Thus, *an unequal distribution of decision-making capabilities must necessarily exist in any political system* (V. Ostrom 1971a).

The essential defining characteristic for a monocentric political system is one where the governmental prerogatives for determining, enforcing and altering legal relationships are vested in some single office or decision structure that has an ultimate monopoly over the legitimate exercise of coercive capabilities in some particular society. In a monocentric political system the inequalities in decision-making capabilities between those vested with "ultimate authority" and those who are subject to that authority assume extreme proportions. The essential defining characteristic of a polycentric political system is one where many officials and decision structures are assigned limited and relatively autonomous prerogatives to determine, enforce and alter legal relationships. No one office or decision structure has an ultimate monopoly over the legitimate use of force in a polycentric political system. Inequalities in the authority of "rulers" and the "ruled" are purposely constrained and limited so that "rulers" can also be *subject* to a "rule" of law and be required to *serve* the "ruled."

The basic structure of a polycentric political system will depend upon the feasibility of polycentric arrangements that are appropriate to the governance of different types of human relationships. Polycentricity in the structure of formal governmental arrangements will in itself be inadequate for the maintenance of polycentricity in the conduct of political and social relationships. In the discussion that follows, I shall refer to polycentricity in market organization as a means for governing a wide variety of human transactions. I shall then turn to polycentricity in judicial decision making as a means for enforcing legal relationships. I shall go on to consider polycentricity in constitutional rule as a means for enforcing provisions of constitutional law in relation to those who exercise the extraordinary prerogatives of government. I shall then examine polycentricity in the selection of political leadership and in the formation of political coalitions.

Finally, I shall examine the application of polycentricity to the provision and production of public goods and services in a public service economy. If polycentricity can be maintained in the structure of each of these sets of political relationships, then polycentricity in the *government* of metropolitan areas is both a theoretically and technically feasible possibility. In political theory the necessary *and* sufficient conditions can *never* be specified without resorting to highly arbitrary law and order assumptions that obviate essential problems by assuming them away.

I shall also be interested in the normative implications that follow as a consequence of utilizing polycentric forms of organization in structuring political relationships. A broad dispersion of decision-making capabilities that allows for substantial discretion or freedom to individuals and for effective and regular constraint upon the actions of governmental officials is an essential characteristic of democratic societies. Lasswell and Kaplan (1950), for example, define democracy in those terms. From a normative point of view, the viability of democratic societies will depend upon the existence of substantial elements of polycentricity in the governance of such societies. Polycentricity allows for autonomy among individual decision makers in reference to publicly formulated rules of law. Individual liberties and constraints upon the actions of officials depend upon constitutional "guarantees." The enforcement of constitutional "guarantees" depends critically upon the juridical status of constitutional law. The maintenance of an enforceable system of constitutional law would appear to be a theoretically necessary but insufficient condition for the realization of such values as "liberty," "freedom," and "justice."

To clarify the application of polycentricity to each of the elements in the governance of human societies, I shall draw upon the work of Michael Polanyi, who adds an essential element in the definition of a polycentric order. Polanyi also indicates the relevance of the concept of polycentricity for understanding patterns of behavior in market organization and judicial decision making. However, Polanyi does not resolve the problem of whether the government of a political system can be organized in a polycentric manner. The solution to that problem was formulated much earlier by Alexander Hamilton and James Madison in *The Federalist*. Hamilton and Madison do not use the term *polycentricity* but their conception of the principles of federalism and separation of powers within a system of limited constitutions meets the defining conditions for polycentricity. Fragmentation of authority in many centers of decision making will *necessarily* exist in a federal system of government with a separation of powers among different decision structures in each unit of government. Where a constitutional structure is designed as a polycentric arrangement, the maintenance of polycentricity in practice will depend upon whether conditions of polycentric organization prevail in the selection of political leadership and in the formation of political coalitions. Such conditions were anticipated by Madison and have been considered by Ostrogorski. There, then, remains the question of whether polycentricity can apply to the provision and production of public goods and services in a public service economy.

The Concept of Polycentricity

The term *polycentricity* so far as I know was first used by Michael Polanyi in essays that were eventually published as *The Logic of Liberty* (1951). Polanyi distinguishes between two different methods for the organization of social tasks or two kinds of order. One is a *deliberate* or *directed order* that is coordinated by an ultimate authority exercising control through a unified command structure. In a deliberate or directed order, a superior-subordinate relationship exists where a superior A may direct subordinate B_1, B_2, B_3 . . . B_n to perform specific tasks or to accomplish particular missions. In an extreme case, superior A might command subordinate B_2 to destroy subordinate B_3. Such an order might also be conceptualized as a unitary or monocentric order.

The other type of order for organizing social tasks is identified by Polanyi as a *spontaneous* or *polycentric* order. A spontaneous or polycentric order is one where many elements are capable of making mutual adjustments for ordering their relationships with one another within a general system of rules where each element acts with independence of other elements. Within a set of rules, individual decision makers will be free to pursue their own interests subject to the constraints inherent in the enforcement of those decision rules.

In a theory of polycentric orders, individuals are the basic unit of analysis. Individuals are assumed to be interested decision makers who can calculate potential benefits and costs subject to elements of risk and uncertainty. Individuals will select those strategies that are anticipated to enhance their net welfare potential. Individuals may occupy positions where decisions are taken on behalf of the interests of others. All such cases will involve a choice from among strategic opportunities in light of potential payoffs derived in part from the calculation of power and liability contingencies where each choice is a move in a series of simultaneous games. Business firms, legislatures, political parties, public agencies, or nation-states may also be used as units of analysis where structural conditions expose the sets of individual decision makers involved to similar strategic calculations.

Business firms can be used as units of analysis where the set of individual decision makers in each firm is exposed to similar strategic calculations established by the arena of market competition or rivalry. Nation-states can be used as units of analysis where each nation is exposed to similar strategic calculations in the international arena. In turn, political parties can be used as units of analysis where each party is exposed to similar strategic calculations in winning elections or in organizing governing coalitions. However, markets, elections and international relations may involve such different strategic calculations that *predictive inferences cannot be made in general, regarding all units of analysis across all decision-making arenas*. Predictive inferences can be made only in relation to units of analysis where arenas can be specified or where multiple arenas can be conceptualized as a series of simultaneous or concurrent games. A polycentric political system is one where each actor participates in a series of simultaneous games and where each act has the potential for being a move in simultaneous games.

Polanyi's emphasis upon a general system of rules as providing a framework for ordering relationships in a polycentric system is an issue that was seriously neglected in Ostrom, Tiebout, and Warren. Our implicit identification of the term *political* with *government* and our identification of the "business" of government with the production and provision of public goods and services led us to gloss over the essential relationship of rules to the structure of political systems. The task of formulating a general system of rules applicable to the conduct of governmental units in metropolitan areas and of maintaining institutional facilities appropriate to enforce such rules of law is a problem that we failed to treat. *Whether the governance of metropolitan areas can be organized as a polycentric system will depend upon whether various aspects of rule making and rule enforcing can be performed in polycentric structures.*

The organization of a single unit of government to have general jurisdiction or political authority over an entire metropolitan region reduces the magnitude of juridical relationships involved. Rules of law in such cases would presumably apply to private individuals and private associations. The question of whether general rules of law would apply to various units of government within a metropolitan area is removed by eliminating all units of government except one. Within that unit of government a directed order establishing relationships between superiors and subordinates can be substituted for a juridical order that is applicable to the conduct of numerous public agencies capable of acting with substantial independence.

A directed order where subordinates are subject to the command of superiors will be subject to serious theoretical limits unless ultimate authority is exercised by an omniscient observer and all subordinates are perfectly obedient. If all individuals have limited knowledge and limited capabilities, central decision makers will become overloaded. Subordinates will bias information that they transmit in order to please their superiors. Loss of information and the communication of biased information will lead to loss of control and a disparity between expectations and performance.

Patterns of organization analogous to a polycentric ordering may, thus, arise from system failure in a directed order. In such circumstances, polycentricity accrues more from a logic of political corruption (Loveman 1969) than from a conscious effort to design a polycentric order based upon principles of independence, self-determination or self-government. Our concern here will be with specifying the conditions that must be taken into account if the design of a system of government in metropolitan areas is to be consciously organized in a polycentric manner.

A critical element entering into the design of a polycentric system is the matter of spontaneity. Polanyi's use of the term *spontaneous* as synonymous with *polycentric* suggests that the attribute of spontaneity might be viewed as an additional defining characteristic of polycentricity. Spontaneity implies that patterns of organization within a polycentric system will be self-generating or self-organizing in the sense that *individuals* will have incentives to create or institute appropriate patterns of ordered relationships. For a polycentric *system* to manifest "spontaneity" in the development of ordered relationships, self-organizing tendencies will have to occur at several different levels of conduct.

One level in a pattern of ordered relationships applies to the *conditions of entry and exit* in a particular polycentric ordering. In the case of a relatively simple market, individual persons may be free to enter or exit as either buyers or sellers. However, in the case of an advanced technology, individual persons may not be viable market participants. If such were the case, the viability of the market as a polycentric ordering will depend upon whether individuals have incentives to organize firms that will be effective participants in such a market. Thus, the maintenance of market arrangements will depend upon whether individuals will be led to organize firms and whether such firms are free to enter the market and engage in trade.

This condition is especially important in the case of *public* goods and services where we would *not* expect individuals acting alone to be capable of producing public goods and services of any substantial proportions. Such individuals would succeed only if they were able to organize an appropriately structured public enterprise where potential beneficiaries could be coerced to pay for the cost of the service. The principle of spontaneity, in this case, can be met only if individuals will be led to undertake the task of public entrepreneurship in the creation of appropriately structured public enterprises to supply public goods and services.

A second level of organization applies to the *enforcement* of general rules of conduct that provide the legal framework for a polycentric order. If individuals or units operating in a polycentric order have incentives to take actions to enforce general rules of conduct, then polycentricity will become an increasingly viable form of organization.

Still a third level of organization pertains to the *formulation and revision* of the basic rules of conduct that provide the framework any particular polycentric order. If individuals can know the relationship between particular rules and the social consequences that those rules tend to evoke under specifiable conditions, then specific polycentric orders can be created as a matter of conscious design. If conditions were to change and a particular set of rules failed to evoke an appropriate set of responses, rules could then be altered to evoke appropriate responses. These assumptions imply that if individuals have access to a warrantable political science, they would be able to design political structures that will conform to general rules of conduct and be appropriate to advance their own welfare. Such conditions must be met before an explicitly designed polycentric political system becomes a technically feasible, empirical possibility.

Polycentricity in the Organization of Various Decision-Making Arenas

Polycentricity in Market Systems

Since Adam Smith, market systems have been identified as spontaneous or polycentric orders where the conduct of any one person or firm is determined by a mutual adjustment to the activities of other persons and firms participating in any particular market. The ordering of market relationships occurs by mutual adjustment, and a market system behaves as though it were governed by an invisible or hidden hand. While each individual seeks to gain his own advantage, the market adjusts to variations in supply and demand so that each participant in the market tends to behave in a way that is consistent with the welfare of the larger community of persons.

Polanyi emphasizes that participants in a market system are not subject to *specific* commands by some superior authority but are free to pursue their individual advantage subject to general rules of law that are impersonal in nature. "No marketing system can function without a legal framework which guarantees adequate proprietary powers and enforces contracts" (Polanyi 1951, 185). Individuals will have no incentive to trade if all goods are free goods and if no one can distinguish between mine and thine. Goods acquire a *public* value only by reference to a right to use, control and dispose of goods as property. Property rights depend upon a distinction between mine and thine, between ours and yours.

The pervasiveness of property and trade relationships in many different societies under varying political conditions would indicate that the essential legal relationships for the creation of market arrangements are not difficult to conceptualize. However, the maintenance of market arrangements depends critically upon the enforcement of property rights and contractual obligations. An essential question is whether the enforcement of legal relationships for a market system can also be conceptualized as a polycentric task subject to general rules of law applicable to persons who are assigned prerogatives of enforcement.

Polycentricity in Judicial Decision Making

Polanyi conceives of courts of law and the larger legal community who participate in the settlement of conflicts under common rules of law to be organized as a polycentric order. The judiciary and members of the legal profession are viewed as rendering judgments and resolving conflicts under conditions where each participant exercises substantial independence in relation to other participants subject to common rules of legal process and legal procedure.

The possibility of conceptualizing the judiciary and the legal profession as a polycentric ordering will depend upon the development of (1) legal concepts and terms that can be *known* in a *public* interpersonal context; (2) legal criteria that can be used as bases for judgment; and (3) methods of legal reasoning that can be used to organize thought and to array evidence as a basis for judgment. Unless a community of agreement (i.e., substantial unanimity) can exist regarding basic legal concepts, criteria for choice or judgment and methods of legal reasoning then the basis *cannot* exist for a polycentric ordering.

The sophisticated lawyer or political scientist will find many objections to an assumption that legal processes occur in a polycentric order. They will point to the existence of contradictions in legal judgments and inconsistencies in legal reasoning. Such conditions imply disagreement. If areas of disagreement can be confined to a few specific issues, a community of agreement can still be preserved for reaching reasoned solutions to ambiguous or undetermined problems.

Reasoned solutions are more likely to be evoked through open conten-

tion among autonomous colleagues who are learned in the law than by under-
lings in a unified command structure. If legal judgments turn only upon the
discretion of superiors who are capable of directing persons as legal subordinates, then persons will have no security in their legal rights. Persons in a
market economy who cannot have confidence about the enforcement of property rights and contractual obligations will stand legally exposed. Proprietors
would have little incentive for taking economic risks when they stand legally
exposed and have no confidence in their ability to enforce legal rights. Entrepreneurial initiative and the integrity of market structures depend upon the
integrity of legal relationships. And integrity of legal relationships would, in
turn, appear to depend upon a substantial degree of polycentricity in the legal
community.

The fairness of the judicial process turns upon the principles of any fair
game: that each participant have a fair chance. A fair chance depends upon
the existence of known rules that give each participant an equal opportunity
to pursue his interest. A fair judge is one who renders reasoned decisions that
are considered to be reasonable by the various parties involved. A judge in a
polycentric order is required to support his judgments both by findings of
fact and critical reasoning about the implications of legal relationships. Such
judgments are subject to critical scrutiny by appellate judges and by the
members of the larger legal profession. Law evolves by adversary contention,
consultation, reasoned argumentation and reasoned judgment among members of a learned profession. The large degree of political independence in
such a judiciary is accompanied by a commensurate degree of intellectual
discipline in rendering reasoned judgments within an organized system of
thought.

If spontaneity is to apply to adjudicatory arrangements, traders in an established market who maintain trade relationships with one another over a
period of time would be led to develop adjudicatory relationships in order to
minimize the costs of conflict while maintaining their own prerogatives as
proprietors and traders. Gordon Tullock in *The Logic of the Law* (1971) con-
ceptualizes the conditions under which traders will be led to *contract* with
one another for the *enforcement* of *contracts*. By specifying such conditions,
Tullock has indicated where judicial arrangements will arise spontaneously
among communities of traders.

If individuals have incentives to develop adjudicatory arrangements for
the settlement of recurrent disputes, we would predict that specialized adjudicatory arrangements will be organized wherever such arrangements are less
costly to use than official courts. Third party mediation and arbitration arrangements would be evidence of such possibilities. The prevalence of such
arrangements in many different commercial settings, in professional societies, and in voluntary associations, including organized crime, indicates a

substantial propensity for self-organizing capabilities in creating adjudicatory arrangements to minimize the costs of recurrent conflict. The practice of most lawyers involves more mediation and arbitration of interests and the development of instrumentalities for the governance of human relationships than pleading before courts of law.

Polanyi does not extend his analysis of polycentricity beyond the structure of judicial decision making. In concluding *The Logic of Liberty,* Polanyi indicates that, "the tasks which can be achieved only by independent mutual adjustments demand an institutional framework which will uphold independent positions" (Polanyi 1951, 199). Polanyi implies that there are limits to polycentricity in the organization of government and that any society will depend upon the services of some oligarchy to exercise the ultimate authority of government. Governments, according to such a presumption, can provide an appropriate institutional framework for the maintenance of polycentricity in various sectors of society, but "an institutional framework which can uphold independent positions" does not apply to the organization of government itself.

Polycentricity in Constitutional Rule

Alexander Hamilton and James Madison writing in *The Federalist* were explicitly concerned with "an institutional framework which can be used to uphold independent positions" in the organization of a system of government. Such an institutional framework was conceptualized in terms of a constitution that specified a set of general decision rules that applied to those who participate in the conduct of government.

Solving the problem of constitutional rule is more difficult than designating some agency or office to exercise the prerogatives of government. For a constitution to provide a meaningful framework for the conduct of government, that constitution cannot be mere words or "a mere demarkation on parchment" (*Federalist,* 48) to use Madison's expression. If a constitution is to provide for a general institutional framework applicable to the conduct of government, then the terms of a constitution must be *enforceable* as against those who exercise the prerogatives of government.

But to specify a condition of enforceability when applied to a constitution would appear to create a contradiction. Institutions of government are precisely those that are assigned decision-making capabilities for determining, enforcing, and altering legal relationships. If legal relationships are to be operable in human conduct, institutions must exist for the enforcement of those legal relationships. How, then, can those who exercise governmental prerogatives be used to enforce the provisions of a constitution as against those who exercise governmental prerogatives? Such authorities would be expected to enforce promises against themselves. This is equivalent to expecting an individual to enforce a contract that he entered into with himself (Rousseau, *The Social Contract,* bk. I, chap. 7).

Polycentricity in the general structure of governmental institutions is the necessary condition for resolving the seeming paradox inherent in the problem of constitutional rule (V. Ostrom 1971a; Vile 1967). The U.S. effort to solve the problem of constitutional rule included the following conditions.

First, the U.S. theory of the "limited" constitution conceives a "constitution," in contrast to a "law," to be a set of general enforceable decision rules assigning the prerogatives of government among diverse decision structures or decision-making authorities.

Second, processes of constitutional decision making are organized apart from ordinary processes of legislation so that the terms of a constitution can *not* be altered by a government acting upon its own authority. Alterations in the provision of a constitution require recourse to extraordinary processes of constitutional decision making (V. Ostrom 1971a, chap. 3).

Third, decision-making capabilities are assigned among the diverse decision structures of a government so that each decision structure can exercise essential prerogatives with independence of other decision structures (*Federalist,* 47–51). At the same time each decision structure can interpose limits or potential *veto capabilities* in relation to other decision structures. In short, constitutional government demands "an institutional structure that will uphold *independent* positions," and independence depends upon the exercise of veto capabilities.

Fourth, recourse to concurrent regimes with overlapping jurisdiction inherent in the federal principle is a means for reinforcing the principle of constitutional rule by creating diverse units of government that are subject to limited jurisdiction. Each person gains access to legal, political, administrative, and constitutional remedies afforded by different units of government. When "the system of each State within that State" (*Federalist,* 36; V. Ostrom 1971a, chap. 6) is taken into account the federal principle *can* be extended to several concurrent regimes.

Fifth, the placing of constitutional limitations upon governmental authorities is accompanied by an assignment of constitutional prerogatives to individual persons (V. Ostrom 1971a, chap. 7). Persons are, thus, entitled to assert claims for judicial remedies based upon their constitutional prerogatives as against governmental officials who threaten to impair those prerogatives. The maintenance of polycentricity in the organization of government, thus, depends upon the maintenance of polycentricity in the organization of the judiciary and in the conduct of the legal profession (*Federalist,* 78). Those who exercise governmental prerogatives can be used to enforce provisions of a constitution against those who exercise governmental prerogatives only if governmental decision making is allocated among diverse decision structures where each is capable of imposing constitutional limits upon others. Ambition can be used to counter ambition; and each set of decision makers will be constrained by the decisions exercised by each other set of *independent* decision makers. Shifting coalitions that form under varying decision rules and veto positions in a polycentric political system are highly unstable coalitions. Such coalitions are unlikely to exercise long-term dominance over the prerogatives of government and acquire a monopoly over the authoritative allocation of values in a society.

Finally, an enforceable system of constitutional rule will, also, depend upon citizens who are prepared to pay the price of civil disobedience. Such citizens when they are persuaded that constitutional rules have been violated must be willing to challenge the constitutional validity of any law or official action and face punishment and official displeasure if their cause is not affirmed. The constitutional office of *persons* assumes substantial significance in the maintenance of a lawful constitutional order. Individuals occupying the office of persons can exercise their essential prerogatives only if provisions of constitutional law are a common body of law knowable to members of a political community and enforceable by the actions of persons as against officials.

The possibility of devising an enforceable system of constitutional rule carries the further implication that constitutional decision makers can use an "existing system of thought" to formulate a set of decision rules for inclusion within a constitution that will evoke appropriate consequences. Such a system of thought would presumably include the essential elements of a political science and would imply that "societies of men are really capable . . . of establishing good government from reflection and choice" (*Federalist,* 1).

Not any set of decision rules nor any constitution will induce an appropriate "rig" to the game of politics in order to facilitate the maintenance of a system of positive constitutional law. Only a constitution that allows for independence among diverse decision-making units with a broad dispersion of authority among persons can be a self-enforcing constitution. No one has yet conceptualized a system of government where a constitution can be enforced by a specialized enforcer.

The relationship of polycentricity to constitutional rule assumes special significance when it is recognized that Thomas Hobbes and John Austin both contend that an enforceable system of constitutional law is not possible in a unitary commonwealth where the prerogatives of government are vested with some single, ultimate center of authority. Hobbes argues that law as a human artifact depends upon arrangements for some person or set of persons to exercise ultimate authority to promulgate, enforce and alter rules of law if there is to be one system of law in a commonwealth. Those who exercise sovereign prerogatives are the source of law, are above the law, and thus cannot be held accountable to the law. The human condition in a Hobbesian theory of sovereignty necessarily implies that some monarch or set of oligarchs will exercise the ultimate authority of government; and such a sovereign body cannot itself be subject to the rule of law.

John Austin in his *Province of Jurisprudence* ([1832] 1955) follows a similar line of reasoning to conclude that constitutional law can only be positive morality, not positive (i.e., enforceable) law. The provisions of a constitution can be an expression of moral sentiments, but they cannot be enforceable rules of law. Thus, a unitary commonwealth with a fully integrated structure of authority will foreclose the possibility of maintaining an enforceable system of constitutional rule. In that case those who are responsible for making, enforcing, and altering laws are above the law and are *not* themselves subject to enforceable rules of constitutional law.

If reformers transform a polycentric political system into a highly integrated monocentric system, we would infer from this analysis that one of the costs of such reforms would be to forego the maintenance of an enforceable system of constitutional law. Once an enforceable system of constitutional law is foregone, concepts like "freedom," "liberty," and "justice" may be no more than pious platitudes and meaningless rhetoric. The possibility of conceptualizing justice, for example, as a meaningful criterion for rendering judgments and taking decisions about alternative possibilities depends critically upon the establishment of requirements for due process of law that can be enforced as against those who exercise governmental prerogatives.

The design of a polycentric political system, thus, depends upon an explicit political theory where constitutional decision makers know what they are doing. The alteration or modification of such a system in order to realize new capabilities under radically changing social conditions should be equally well grounded in a political theory where reformers know what they are doing. An absence of such knowledge would imply that men may be seized by a maelstrom of crises without knowing the causes of their miseries nor their remedies (V. Ostrom 1973).

Polycentricity in the Selection of Political Leadership and in the Organization of Political Coalitions

Polycentricity in the essential structure of government is a necessary but insufficient condition for the maintenance of an enforceable system of constitutional law. Madison's concern about the dangers of majority faction and Tocqueville's consideration of majority tyranny point to the possibility that a single dominant coalition will be able to control all essential decision structures for its advantage and the detriment of others in the society. Under such circumstances, the powers of government can be usurped by political entrepreneurs who are able to form a machine or an organization to dominate the various processes for collective choice. The machine or organization will then be able to superimpose a directed order upon a formally established polycentric order and mobilize the coercive capabilities exercised by various governmental authorities to dominate the allocation of values in a society for its own advantage and to the disadvantage of the society as a whole.

In examining the structure of different political machines, Ostrogorski explicitly recognizes that the costs of appealing to constituencies in excess of 100,000 population give an advantage to those who can make a regular *business* of organizing slates of candidates and conducting political campaigns to win elections. An entrepreneur engaged in such a business will, in the long run, be required to cover costs by payments for services rendered. Such an entrepreneur will be confronted with the problems inherent in the organization of collective enterprises supplying public goods and services. This problem can be surmounted if the coercive capabilities inherent in governmental authority can be utilized to the advantage of a machine or an organization. But this advantage can be gained only if those who exercise the prerogatives of government will render decisions in response to commands from the boss as a political entrepreneur.

If a boss is able to acquire control over all centers of governmental decision making, then effective patterns of polycentricity can be foreclosed. The boss who has acquired effective monopoly power to dominate all decision structures has transformed a formally constituted polycentric system into a monocentric system. Political bosses in the late nineteenth century were able to put together strong organizations in several cities and in several states. However, no political machine ever developed that was capable of dominating all decision centers in the United States. Ample latitudes of polycentricity continued to exist so that even the most successful bosses were still exposed to decisions beyond their control.

If the essential integrity of electoral laws and electoral machinery can be maintained, and if other political entrepreneurs are free to contest elections, then the success of each such entrepreneur will depend upon his appeal to the electorate. So long as voters have a choice among candidates, severe constraints will be placed upon the discretion that politicians can exercise over the conduct of government. Basic election laws and electoral machinery provide an institutional structure where politicians can pursue independent strategies in competition with other politicians. To the extent that such conditions prevail, elements of polycentricity will exist in the selection of political leadership.

A recurrent debate has persisted among U.S. political scientists over the course of the last century regarding the desirability of instituting reforms that would establish a system of *responsible party government*. Following the

British tradition, a system of responsible party government would mean that control over the executive establishment would be vested with an executive committee composed of the leadership of the party capable of procuring majority support in the representative assembly of the national legislature. The government—that is, the executive apparatus—is organized by that party that is able to form a majority coalition in a win-the-government game apart from popular elections.

The U.S. political system with its constitutional separation of powers is organized by reference to a variety of different electoral constituencies, terms of office and voting rules. Government occurs in a *public* context with open deliberation where varying coalitions may be required depending upon the relevant constitutional decision rule. A different coalition of interests is required for the passage of legislation through the House of Representatives, for example, than is required for its passage through the Senate. The intervention of a presidential veto requires a radically different coalition to be formed than is required for the initial passage of legislation by Congress.

As a consequence of varying constitutional decision rules, *shifting* coalitions formed in *an open public* context have characterized the U.S. system of government in contrast to the British tradition of *party* government. The British tradition of party government occurs in a context of strong party discipline reinforced by strong provisions for secrecy in government affairs. Members of cabinets are *privy* councillors whose oath of office is essentially a *secrecy* oath. This is reinforced by an Official Secrets Act that makes it unlawful (i.e., a criminal offense) to publish internal government documents or information derived from internal government sources. Such secrecy makes British governments virtually immune to public scandals. British governments are party governments; and open public deliberation is largely confined to those issues placed upon the agenda for debate by the government party.

The existence of concurrent regimes in a highly federalized political system adds a significant dimension to polycentricity in the selection of political leadership and in the organization of political coalitions. The probability that a political boss can successfully organize a machine to dominate all centers of decision making in a political system with as much fragmentation of authority and overlap among jurisdictions as the American political system is very small. In nearly 200 years, no one has succeeded in putting together such a political machine. Bosses have succeeded in organizing limited machines in the short run; but they have been exposed to high risks of defeat. As a consequence, most successful bosses have adjusted their own strategies to take account of their potential adversaries in appealing to the electorate and in responding to popular demand.

The success of political entrepreneurs in putting together limited political machines for short periods of time has meant that substantial political corruption has existed in the United States. The enforcement of public law has suffered as a consequence. Yet, the inability of political entrepreneurs to maintain party control over the different instrumentalities of government has meant that constitutional and other types of reform have been available to the American people as a means for coping with political corruption and the tyranny of those who exercise governmental prerogatives.

A substantial reduction in the amount of polycentricity in the U.S. political system as recommended by those who urge a "responsible party system" can be expected to reduce the costs of political entrepreneurship and increase the probability that a single coalition can be formed to dominate all essential decision structures. If such a dominant coalition were formed, the possibility of maintaining an enforceable system of constitutional law would be forgone. Fundamental political reforms would become infeasible. Coups d'etat and revolutionary action would become methods of basic political change. Basic *reforms* that are contrary to the interests of established authorities can occur *only where political stalemates are possible.* Polycentricity in the selection of political leadership and in the organization of political coalitions is thus a further condition for the maintenance of an enforceable system of constitutional law and for the maintenance of a lawful *public* order.

Polycentricity in a Public Service Economy

The development of a polycentric order in a public service economy can, I believe, be conceptualized as occurring under special conditions. Polycentricity in the organization of (1) market arrangements; (2) the legal community; (3) constitutional rule; and (4) political coalitions is a necessary precondition for the existence of polycentricity in a public service economy. Market structures provide the necessary conditions for the generation of prices to provide a *public* measure of value. Some public measure of value for most goods and services is necessary if individuals are to calculate the terms on which alternative possibilities will be available to them. A polycentrically ordered legal system is necessary if entrepreneurial independence is to exist within general rules of law and if criteria for judicial decision making and methods of legal reasoning are to be established in meaningful terms that are knowable in a public interpersonal context. Meaningful terms that are knowable in a public interpersonal context must exist if authority is to be challenged by methods that rely upon reason. Otherwise, law is no more than a mystery of high priests.

Polycentricity is also necessary in the operation of a system of government if the services of governmental authorities are to be available *upon demand* to serve the lawful interests of individuals living in such a society. The maintenance of an enforceable system of public law, including constitutional law, and the maintenance of an open rivalry for political leadership and in the formation of political coalitions are necessary conditions before citizens will be able to enforce lawful demands as against officials.

Where these conditions of polycentricity exist, we might further imagine the existence of a general set of laws whereby individuals can initiate proceedings for the organization of various municipal corporations, quasi-municipal corporations and other forms of public enterprise to undertake the provision of public good or service. Such general rules of law might provide for incorporation, annexation, merger, separation and disincorporation proceedings. Other provisions of law might establish general rules for the organization and operation of any such enterprise. Such laws would, in effect, constitute general charters for public enterprises. Alternatively, individuals acting to incorporate a public enterprise might be assigned prerogatives to prepare their own charter under specifiable rules of constitutional decision making. In that case a community of individuals could prepare a home-rule charter for the governance of a public enterprise.

Such general rules of law will, in effect, provide a constitutional allocation of authority among the community of persons forming a public enterprise. Provisions for elections, representation, referenda, initiative, recall, authority to sue and be sued, and special provisions bearing upon the prerogatives of individuals vis-à-vis those exercising corporate prerogatives can be included in charters for public enterprises.

Under such conditions individuals will have an incentive to function as public entrepreneurs when they can conceptualize circumstances where common actions can be taken to realize a public benefit for a discrete community of people. If the projected benefits will exceed costs by a margin that is recognizable by any reasonable person, then individuals will have an incentive to risk an expenditure of some time, effort and money provided that known institutional facilities are available to bind each member of the community of beneficiaries to pay his proportion of the costs.

If such a community of individuals were essentially coterminous with an existing unit of government, individuals assuming the costs of entrepreneurship would have an incentive to use that existing unit of government as a sponsor for the new enterprise. If the public good to be provided were not coterminous with any existing unit of government, then the community of individuals would be confronted with the task of determining whether some alternative structure could be used to provide the service at a lesser cost.

We might further expect rational entrepreneurs associated with such public enterprises to develop mechanisms for the resolution of conflict that would enhance their net welfare. If other values remained constant we would expect such individuals to search out mechanisms for the resolution of conflict that would least jeopardize their autonomy. If opportunities arose where economies of scale could be realized through a larger production unit, we would not be surprised to see merger movements occur. Nor would we be surprised to see cooperative arrangements or overlapping organizations develop as alternative means to facilitate joint efforts for mutual gain.

The difficulty in measuring the output of a public enterprise poses serious obstacles for users of public services or their representatives to acquire information for evaluating the performance of those who are commissioned to produce a public good or service. As a consequence, managers of public enterprises will not be highly responsive to changes in user preferences and will have little incentive to search out the most efficient modes of production. The larger the enterprise, the greater its mix of services, the less voice any one user will have in articulating demands for his preferred bundle of public goods and services.

So long as these conditions prevail a public enterprise *system* supplying a diverse mix of public goods and services will be responsive to user preferences only so long as some public enterprises are organized on a small scale capable of responding to immediate neighborhood demands. If such small-scale enterprises have bargaining capabilities in dealing with larger-scale enterprises then there is *an increased probability* that an appropriate mix of public goods and services will be forthcoming. Where multiple public agencies or enterprises concurrently participate in rendering particular types of public goods or services, such agencies will take on the characteristics of public-service industries. Patterns of government in different metropolitan areas might be viewed as public service economies composed of many public service industries including a police industry, an education industry, a transportation industry, and so on. A fully integrated monopoly is among the structural variations that might exist either in a public service economy or in a particular public service industry. Other patterns of industrial organization will have reference to increasing measures of polycentricity.

Ostrom, Tiebout, and Warren proposed that the theory of public goods be used to conceptualize the task of governance as the maintenance of preferred states of community affairs. The existence of public goods of diverse sizes and shapes implies the maintenance of diversely sized and shaped states of community affairs. We further suggested that criteria of (1) control; (2) efficiency; (3) political representation; and (4) self-determination could be used in determining how to "package" or bound diversely sized and shaped states of community affairs as governmental jurisdictions.

The criterion of control implies that choice of appropriate boundary conditions would include the relevant field of effects. Some fields of effects such as play spaces for children might be quite small; others such as the airshed over a metropolitan region might be quite large. The criterion of efficiency implies that patterns of organization would be selected so as to maximize the aggregate net benefit. The criterion of political representation implies that those who are affected by the maintenance of some public good or service will be organized as a political community and be represented by common council in collective decision making. The criterion of self-determination implies that the government of a public enterprise will be controlled by the decisions of its constituents.

We further suggested that the *production* of a public good or service can be distinguished from the *provision* of a public good or service. Provision pertains to arrangements for financing and using or consuming a public good or service as distinguished from production as combining various factors or inputs to generate outputs. If sufficient redundancy were to exist among the units of government serving any particular metropolitan area then communities of people could take advantage of that redundancy or overlap by using one unit of government as a buyer's cooperative to contract with other units of government and/or private vendors to produce different public goods and services.

Thus, competitive rivalry and quasi-market conditions are artifacts of polycentricity and can be induced in a polycentrically organized public service economy. Efforts to supply public goods and services directly to individual users through market arrangements will *fail*. The provision of public goods and services must be collectively organized *before* quasi-market mechanisms can be generated in a public service economy. A polycentric political system is not a market; and a theory of polycentric organization is not a metaphor for a market model. Polycentric systems can be organized so as to induce elements of market organization *among* public enterprises. Such conditions can exist only if advantage can be taken of a rich structure of overlapping jurisdictions and fragmentation of authority.

Competitive rivalry among public enterprises can generate adverse social consequences as well as beneficial effects. Cooperative arrangements among public entrepreneurs can also degenerate into collusive efforts to raid the public treasury. These circumstances call for obvious remedies. The extension of full monopoly power over the production of all public goods and services would appear to diminish the prospect for attaining appropriate remedies. The alternative is to rely upon the likelihood that a polycentric system will lead those who may be injured to articulate their grievances and demand remedies from other governmental officials.

Finally, we suggested that the larger units of government provided a structure of institutional arrangements for the resolution of conflicts that cannot otherwise be resolved by mutual adjustment and mutual agreement. Individuals in a metropolitan community can exercise their constitutional prerogatives as persons and secure the services of other governmental officials in procuring remedies where the actions of some cause injuries for others. The pursuit of strategic opportunity in a series of simultaneous political games provides the basis for reordering and reconstituting political relationships in metropolitan areas when individuals know the appropriate grammar of polycentric political forms.

The reliance upon multiorganizational arrangements for the provision and production of public goods and services need not be confined to metropolitan areas. Bain, Caves, and Margolis, for example, have used the approach of industrial organization to analyze the comparative efficiency of diverse public enterprises in the water industry operation described in their book *Northern California's Water Industry* (1966). A similar analysis of the legal and political structure of the California water industry was made in my *Institutional Arrangements for Water Resource Development* (V. Ostrom 1971b). Multiple jurisdictions provide opportunities to realize diverse economies of scale and to articulate the preferences of diverse communities of interests. Concurrent use of processes of popular control in different jurisdictions allows for the amplification of democratic powers (Gregg 1972). The availability of the judiciary to resolve interjurisdictional conflicts can be used to develop a rule of law as among public jurisdictions. A system of public administration operating through a multiplicity of jurisdictions subject to strong democratic controls, to adjudication of interjurisdictional conflicts and to competitive rivalry under quasi-market conditions engenders patterns of democratic administration that have radically different characteristics from those of bureaucratic administration (V. Ostrom 1973).

Conclusion

A polycentric organization has been defined as a pattern of organization where many independent elements are capable of mutual adjustment for ordering their relationships with one another within a general system of rules. The occurrence of polycentricity in market systems, judicial decision making, constitutional rule, coalition formation and the operation of a public service economy has been considered. Each of these structures of relationships has reference to decision-making arenas where many elements are capable of mutual adjustment with one another within a general system of rules where each element can act with independence of each other element. The existence of polycentricity in each of these decision-making arenas suggests that the governance of metropolitan areas *can* occur in a *polycentric political system* so long as no single set of decision makers is able to gain dominance over all decision-making structures. Polycentricity is not confined to market structures but can be extended to the organization of diverse political processes and by implication can apply to the political process in general.

Having explored the relationship of polycentricity to different aspects of political decision making, I shall turn [in part 2] to some implications that polycentricity has for organizing research in the governance of metropolitan areas. Polycentricity implies quite different configurations of political relationships in metropolitan areas than would exist in a monocentric order. We can expect scholars from the two traditions to use different approaches, different concepts and languages and different methods. However, if these differences can be focused upon contradictory conclusions that derive from different theoretical analyses, then empirical research can be used to sort out the competing contentions.

CHAPTER 3

Public Goods and Public Choices

Vincent Ostrom and Elinor Ostrom

Until recently, the private sector and the public sector have been viewed as two mutually exclusive parts of the economy. The private sector is generally viewed as organized through market transactions. The public sector is generally viewed as being organized only through governmental institutions where services are delivered through a system of public administration. Principles of public administration traditionally called for the organization of services through an integrated command structure where all personnel are accountable to a single chief executive. Coordination in the private sector is attained by the market system that governs economic relationships through competitive buying and selling. Coordination in the public sector presumably is attained, by contrast, through a bureaucratic system in which superiors control subordinates in an integrated command structure that holds each public employee accountable to a chief executive as an elective public official.

During the last two decades, traditional presumptions about public sector organization have been subject to serious challenge. Economists studying public sector investment and expenditure decisions have observed that institutions designed to overcome problems of market failure often manifest serious deficiencies of their own. Market failures are not necessarily corrected by recourse to public sector solutions.

This section analyzes the basic characteristics of public services and the important role for diverse organizations, including private enterprises, in the delivery of such services. The public economy need not be an exclusive government monopoly. It can be a mixed economy with substantial private participation in the delivery of public services. Such a possibility offers impor-

Originally published in E. S. Savas, ed., *Alternatives for Delivering Public Services. Toward Improved Performance* (Boulder, CO: Westview Press, 1977), 7–49. Reprinted with permission of the publishers and authors.

The support of Indiana University for the Workshop in Political Theory and Policy Analysis and the RANN Division of the National Science Foundation in the form of Grant No. GI–43949 is gratefully acknowledged, but the opinions expressed herein are those of the authors and not necessarily those of Indiana University or the National Science Foundation. Helpful comments have been made by Spencer Ballard, John Baden, Frances Bish, Robert Bish, Alfred Diamant, Norman Furniss, Roger Parks, and E. S. Savas, who contributed to the revision of this essay.

tant prospects for overcoming some public sector inefficiencies and providing taxpayers with an increased return for their tax dollars.

Public economies, however, are quite different from market economies. A private entrepreneur who decides to engage in the delivery of a public service by relying upon traditional market mechanisms is destined to failure. He must instead understand the logic of a public economy and learn to pursue his opportunities within those constraints. The *private* delivery of *public* services is a different ball game from the *private* delivery of *private* goods and services.

In clarifying the logic of a public economy, we shall first consider the nature of public goods as distinguished from private goods. We shall then explore the organizational possibilities for the public sector, including the development of marketlike arrangements. Such arrangements suggest an industry approach to public services with quite different implications for public administration.

The Nature of Public Goods

People have long been aware that the nature of goods has a bearing upon human welfare. Aristotle, for example, observed: "That which is common to the greatest number has the least care bestowed upon it." Within the last two decades an extensive literature has developed on the characteristics that distinguish public or collective goods from private or individual goods. In this discussion we shall consider exclusion and jointness of use or consumption as two essential defining characteristics in distinguishing between private and public goods. We shall also examine basic differences in measurement and degree of choice that have a significant bearing upon the organization of public services. Implications will then be drawn about some inherent problems of organizing economic relationships that involve public goods.

Exclusion

Exclusion has long been identified as a necessary characteristic for goods and services to be supplied under market conditions. Exclusion occurs when potential users can be denied goods or services unless they meet the terms and conditions of the vendor. If both agree, goods or services are supplied at a price. A quid pro quo exchange occurs. The buyer acquires the good, and the seller acquires the value specified.

Where exclusion is infeasible, anyone can derive benefits from the good so long as nature or the efforts of others supply it. The air we breathe can be viewed as a good supplied by nature, so exclusion is difficult to attain. A view of a building—whether seen as a "good" or a "bad"—is supplied by the efforts of others and is not subject to exclusion in normal circumstances. Air, noise, and water pollution are "bads" that an individual cannot exclude or avoid except at a cost; conversely, an individual cannot be excluded from receiving a good when the pollution level is reduced.

Jointness of Use or Consumption

Another attribute of goods or services pertains to jointness of use or consumption. No jointness of consumption exists when consumption by one person precludes use or consumption by another person. In that case consumption is completely subtractible. A loaf of bread consumed by one person is not available for consumption by another: it is subtracted from the total that was originally available. A good *having no jointness* of consumption and with which exclusion *is* feasible is defined as a purely private good. Jointness of consumption, on the other hand, implies that the use or enjoyment of a good by one person does not foreclose its use or enjoyment by others; despite its use by one person, it remains available for use by others in undiminished quantity and quality. A weather forecast is an example of a joint consumption good.

Few, if any, joint consumption goods are perfectly nonsubtractible. The use and enjoyment of gravity as a force that firmly keeps our feet on the ground may illustrate the case of perfect *nonsubtractibility*, but most joint consumption goods are instead subject to *partial subtractibility*. At certain thresholds of supply, one person's use of a good subtracts *in part* from its use and enjoyment by others. Congestion begins to occur. Each further increase in use impairs the use of the good for each other person in the community of users. Highways, for example, become subject to congestion when the addition of more users causes delays and inconveniences for others. Fire protection, another joint consumption good, may deteriorate when a finite force experiences a high rate of demand. Such goods are then subject to degradation or erosion in their quality unless supply is modified to meet the new demand.

Both exclusion and jointness of consumption are characteristics that vary in degree rather than being all-or-none characteristics. The two extreme cases of jointness of consumption—complete subtractibility and complete nonsubtractibility—give logical clarity in distinguishing *purely* private from *purely* public goods. Whenever use by one user subtracts *in part* from the use and enjoyment of a good by other users we have partial subtractibility. In the same way we can think of exclusion as applying in degrees. A walled city can attain a high degree of exclusion by controlling admission to those who wish to reside, enter, and do business with the city. Even in the unwalled city, jurisdictional boundaries may be a way for distinguishing between residents and nonresidents where some public goods and services are primarily for the joint benefit of persons living within those boundaries. A weak form of partial exclusion may exist in such circumstances.

Exclusion and jointness of consumption are independent attributes. Both characteristics can be arrayed in relation to one another. The jointness characteristic can be arrayed into two classes: *alternative uses,* which are highly subtractible and *joint uses,* which are nonsubtractible. Exclusion can also be arrayed into two classes, in which exclusion is either *feasible* or *infeasible.* Exclusion is technically infeasible where no practical technique exists for either packaging a good or controlling access by a potential user. Exclusion may also be economically infeasible where the costs of exclusion are too high. If these defining characteristics are then arrayed in a simple matrix, four logical types of goods are revealed as indicated in figure 3.1.

Jointness of Use or Consumption

		Alternative Use	Joint Use
E X C L U S I O N	Feasible	Private Goods: Bread, shoes, automobiles, haircuts, books, etc.	Toll Goods: Theaters, night clubs, telephone service, toll roads, cable TV, electric power, library, etc.
	Infeasible	Common-Pool Resources: Water pumped from a groundwater basin, fish taken from an ocean, crude oil extracted from an oil pool	Public Goods: Peace and security of a community, national defense, mosquito abatement, air pollution control, fire protection, streets, weather forecasts, public TV, etc.

Fig. 3.1. Types of goods

Market arrangements can be used to deliver either private goods or toll goods, that is, where exclusion is feasible. In the case of toll goods a price is charged for access or use, but the good is enjoyed in common. Special problems arise, as in a theater, where the conduct of one user may detract from the enjoyment of other users. The value of the good depends both upon the quality of the good produced *and* upon the way it is used by others.

In the case of a common-pool resource, exclusion may be infeasible in the sense that many users cannot be denied access. But, use by any one user precludes use of some fixed quantity of a good by other users. Each pumper in a groundwater basin, for example, makes a use of water that is alternative to its use by each other pumper. Each fish or ton of fish taken by any one fisherman prevents any other fisherman from taking those same fish. Yet no basis exists for excluding fishermen from access to fish in the ocean. Once appropriated from a natural supply, water can be dealt with as a toll good to be supplied to those who have access to a distribution system; similarly, once taken from the ocean, fish can be dealt with as a private good. Water management problems, typifying common-pool resources, are likely to be subject to market failure while water distribution problems typifying toll goods are likely to manifest market weaknesses associated with monopoly supply.

The broad range of services rendered by governmental agencies may cover all different types of goods and services. The food supplied to school-children under surplus commodity programs is an example of purely private goods. Most governmental services, however, are of the public good, toll good, or common-pool resource types. These variations may, for example, have significant implications for the development of user charges as substitutes for taxes and other marketlike mechanisms in the operation of governmental service activities. In this discussion we shall focus more upon the type characterized as public goods because they pose the more difficult problems in the operation of a public economy.

Before pursuing some of the implications that follow from joint consumption in the absence of exclusion, we shall consider two other characteristics of public goods and services. These relate to measurement and degree of choice. These characteristics also have important implications for the organization and delivery of public services.

Measurement

Since public goods are difficult to package or unitize they are also difficult to measure. Quantitative measures cannot be calculated like bushels of wheat or tons of steel. Qualitative measures such as the amount of dissolved oxygen in water, victimization rates, and traffic delay can be used to measure important characteristics of goods subject to joint consumption, but such measures cannot be aggregated in the same way that gross production can be calculated for a steel factory or for the steel industry as a whole.

The task of measuring performance in the production of public goods will not yield to simple calculations. Performance measurement depends instead upon estimates in which indicators or proxy measures are used as estimates of performance. By utilizing multiple indicators, weak measures of performance can be developed even though direct measures of output are not feasible. Private goods are easier to measure, account for, and relate to cost-accounting procedures and management controls.

Degree of Choice

Where a good is characterized by jointness of consumption and nonexclusion, a user is generally unable to exercise an option and has little choice whether or not to consume. The quality of a good or service is available under existing terms and conditions, and one's preference will not materially affect the quality of such a good. Furthermore, individuals may be forced to consume public goods that have a negative value for them. Streets, for exam-

ple, may become congested thoroughfares restricting the convenience of local residents and shoppers who are required to cope with the traffic whether
they like it or not.

Yet, the structure of institutional arrangements may have some effect on
the degree of choice that individuals have. Councilmen representing local
wards would, for example, be more sensitive to protests by local residents
about how streets are used in those wards than councilmen elected at large.
Voucher systems, where individual use of a pro rata share of tax funds to
procure services from alternative vendors of educational services, for example, may allow for a much greater degree of choice on the part of individual
users. Educational services, however, have less the characteristics of a public
good and more the characteristics of a toll good. Other forms of local option
might exist in organizing public services. Table 3.1 summarizes several of
the key characteristics associated with public and private goods.

TABLE 3.1. Public and Private Goods

Private Goods	Public Goods
Relatively easy to measure quantity and quality	Relatively difficult to measure quantity and quality
Can be consumed by only a single person	Consumed jointly and simultaneously by many people
Easy to exclude someone who doesn't pay	Difficult to exclude someone who doesn't pay
Individual generally has a choice of consuming or not	Individual generally has no choice as to consuming or not
Individual generally has a choice as to kind and quality of goods	Individual generally has little or no choice as to kind and quality of goods
Payment for goods is closely related to demand and consumption	Payment for goods is not closely related to demand or consumption
Allocation decisions are made primarily by market mechanism	Allocation decisions are made primarily by political process

Source: Authors and E. S. Savas. The tables in this chapter were worked out jointly with Savas, editor
of the volume in which the essay was originally published.

Some Implications for Organization

Public goods—defined as goods subject to joint consumption where exclusion is difficult to attain—present serious problems in human organization. If
a public good is supplied by nature or the efforts of other individuals, each
individual will be free to take advantage of the good since he cannot be excluded from its use or enjoyment. A cost-minimizing individual has an incentive to take advantage of whatever is freely available without paying a price

or contributing a proportionate share of the effort to supply a public good. So long as rules of voluntary choice apply, some individuals will have an incentive to "hold out" or act as "free riders," taking advantage of whatever is freely available. If some are successful in pursuing a holdout strategy, others will have an incentive to follow suit. The likely short-run consequence is that voluntary efforts will *fail* to supply a satisfactory level of public goods. Individuals furthering their own interests will fail to take sufficient account of the interests of others, and the joint good will inexorably deteriorate.

Market institutions will fail to supply satisfactory levels of public goods and services. Exclusion is infeasible. Therefore, to supply many public goods and services, it is necessary to have recourse to some form of collective action in which sanctions can be used to foreclose the holdout problem and to compel each individual to pay his share of the burden. In small groups, individuals may be successful in keeping account of each other's efforts and applying social coercion so that each person assumes a share of the burden to procure jointly used goods. But large groups are less successful in coping with the provision of public goods shared by a whole community of people. Each individual is more anonymous. Each person's share of the total good may seem insignificantly small. Each can function as a holdout with greater impunity. Potential recourse to coercion in levying taxes and preventing holdouts will be more important. This is the reasoning behind Aristotle's contention that the good or property shared in common by "the greatest number has the least care bestowed upon it."

Patterns of organization that can mobilize coercive sanctions are necessary for the operation of a public economy. This is why people seek recourse to governmental institutions. The provision of law and order is simply one of many public goods that are important to the welfare of human societies. Market institutions will fail to supply such goods and services because markets require exclusion, exchange, and voluntary transactions.

But recourse to coercive sanctions and governmental organization does not provide both the necessary and sufficient conditions for the delivery of public goods and services under relatively optimal conditions. Instruments of coercion can be used to deprive others and make them worse off rather than better off. Governmental institutions permit those who mobilize majority support to impose deprivations upon those in the minority. Governmental institutions can become instruments of tyranny when some dominate the allocation of goods in a society to the detriment of others.

Furthermore, difficulties in measuring the output of public goods and services imply that governmental officials also will have difficulties in monitoring the performance of public employees. Management of public enterprises will be subject to even less effective control than the management of private enterprises where outputs can be measured in quantifiable units.

Where citizens have little choice about the quality of public services supplied to them they will also have little incentive to do anything about it. The costs of attempting to do anything about the services they receive are likely to exceed any tangible benefit that they themselves will receive. As a result, individuals face situations in which anticipated costs exceed anticipated benefits. The rational rule of action in such cases is to forgo the "opportunity" to accrue net losses.

The Organization of a Public Economy

The characteristics of nonexclusion, joint consumption, lack of unitization and direct measurability, and the small degree of individual choice pose substantial problems for the organization of a public economy. Recognizing that the world is composed of many different goods and services that have these characteristics, and that such goods come in many different forms, we are confronted with the task of thinking through what patterns of organization might be used to accommodate these difficulties and yield reasonably satisfactory results. Just as we can expect market weakness and failure to occur as a consequence of certain characteristics inherent in a good or service, we can also expect problems of institutional weakness and failure in governmental operations as a consequence of the characteristics of certain goods and services.

Furthermore, no solution will work by itself. Markets have important self-regulating or self-governing characteristics; but all market systems depend on nonmarket decision-making arrangements to establish and maintain property rights, to authorize and enforce contracts, and to provide other joint facilities including a common medium of exchange, common weights and measures, roads, and so forth, that are used by all market participants.

In considering the organization of a public economy, we shall reason through a number of the problems involved. First, we shall consider some basic elements in a public economy. There we indicate some basic assumptions and terms and characterize the function of collective consumption units and production units. The organization of both consumption and production requires explicit attention in a public economy. Multiple collective consumption units and multiple production units acting jointly to procure and supply particular types of goods or services that are jointly consumed by a community of people can, in turn, be viewed as elements in public service industries.

Second, we shall then examine some difficulties in the nature of public goods that pose special problems in the relationship of collective consumption units to production units in any particular public service industry. These problems include (1) financing; (2) regulating patterns of use; and (3) coproduction where service users are essential to producers.

Third, we shall then examine some opportunities for enhancing efficiency and creating self-regulating tendencies in public service industries. Economies of scale can be realized among multiple units. Relationships among collective consumption units and production units can assume marketlike characteristics where competitive pressures enhance efficiency. Mechanisms for conflict resolution, however, must be available if conflicts, which are not amenable to voluntary agreement, are to be resolved effectively.

Some Basic Assumptions and Terms

It is useful to consider individuals as the basic unit of analysis, and to assume that goods are scarce and that individuals attach values to goods and services. We can stipulate a decision-making framework that structures opportunities and constraints for individuals to act in relation to one another. Then we can analyze the consequences when people choose strategies to enhance their well-being.

A public good, as defined in the preceding, is a good or service subject to joint use or consumption where exclusion is difficult or costly to attain. The essential difficulty in organizing public economies, thus, is on the consumption side of economic relationships. Governments, like households, might be viewed first as *collective consumption units.* Once the collective consumption aspects of governmental organization have been identified, we can then turn to the production side. Governmental agencies and private enterprises can be viewed as potential production units concerned with the supply and delivery of public goods and services. We shall distinguish between these two aspects by referring to "collective consumption units" and "production units." A single unit of government may include both types of organizations within its internal structure. Or, a governmental unit operating as a collective consumption unit may contract with another governmental agency or a private enterprise to produce public services for its constituents.

Collective Consumption Units

In the organization of collective consumption units the holdout problem must be avoided. Arrangements must be made for levying assessments, taxes, or user charges on beneficiaries. Strictly voluntary efforts to supply public goods and services will fail to yield satisfactory results. Authority to levy taxes or assessments or to coerce user charges is necessary to avert holdouts and to supply funds for jointly used goods or services.

Some forms of private organization have the authority to levy compulsory assessments upon members. Homeowners' improvement associations and condominiums may be organized under terms of deed restrictions so that all individuals buying a house in a subdivision or a unit in an apartment complex are required to become and remain members so long as they continue to own the house or apartment. Bylaws of homeowners' improvement associations or condominiums provide for the election of officers to act on behalf of members and authorize the levy of assessments as the equivalent of a tax for the provision of joint services and facilities to be used in common by the residents of the subdivision or the apartment complex.

Each person acquiring property in such a subdivision or condominium voluntarily agrees to pay assessments and be bound by the terms of the by-laws as a part of the purchase contract. All other purchasers are required to do so as well. With unanimity about the appropriateness of the bylaws and their taxing authority assured, no single resident can function as a holdout and derive benefits from joint endeavors without paying a proportionate share of the costs. When effectively organized, homeowners' improvement associations and condominiums can undertake the provision of police protection services, recreation services, public works, and other efforts for the joint benefit of members.

Where property rights have already been vested and people want to procure services for their joint benefit, the problem of dealing with potential holdouts usually requires some form of governmental organization established through majority vote as a substitute for the unanimous consent of all property owners or residents. Various forms of municipal corporations and public service districts can be organized under such arrangements. An alternative option sometimes available is to create a special assessment or improvement district within an established unit of government to finance a special service for a particular neighborhood. Each of these public instrumentalities has authority, under the terms of its charter, to exercise governmental prerogatives to tax and to use criminal sanctions to enforce its rules and regulations.

Whereas the income received for providing a private good conveys information about the demand for that good, taxes collected under the threat of coercion say little about the demand for a public good or service. Payment of taxes indicates only that taxpayers prefer paying taxes to going to jail. Little or no information is revealed about user preferences for goods procured with tax-supported expenditures. As a consequence, the organization of collective consumption units will need to create alternative mechanisms to prices for articulating and aggregating demands into collective choices reflecting individuals' preferences for a quantity and/or quality of public goods or services.

An appropriately constituted collective consumption unit would include within its jurisdictional boundary the relevant beneficiaries who share a common interest in the joint good or service and would exclude those who do not benefit. The collective consumption unit would be empowered to make operational decisions without requiring unanimity: this is necessary to foreclose holdouts. It would hold a limited monopoly position on the consumption side. It would have authority to exercise coercive sanctions, but it need not meet the criterion sometimes used to define a government as exercising a monopoly over the legitimate use of force for a society as a whole.

The choice of particular voting rules, modes of representation and rules applicable to making operational decisions about taxes, expenditures and levels of service needs to be viewed from a constitutional perspective where the consequences of such rules are estimated in choosing a particular structure of organization. The set of rules most likely to produce decisions that take account of citizen-consumer interests is preferred. Citizens are presumed to be the best judges of their own interests. Such rules provide mechanisms for articulating and aggregating demand in the absence of market prices and for translating demand into decisions about the level of service to be procured.

If action can be taken under a set of decision rules where the benefits for each individual can be expected to exceed costs, and costs can be fairly proportioned among beneficiaries, each individual would have an incentive to agree to such a form of collective organization, forgo holdout strategies and procure the joint consumption good. Substantial unanimity would exist among such a community to undertake collective action to procure a public good or service.

Production Units

A production unit, by contrast, would be one that can aggregate technical factors of production to yield goods and services meeting the requirements of a collective consumption unit. The organization of an appropriate production unit will require a manager who can assume entrepreneurial responsibility for aggregating factors of production and organizing and monitoring performance of a production team that would supply the appropriate level of a good or service.

A collective consumption unit may supply a public good or service through its own production unit. In that case, the collective consumption unit and the production unit would serve the same population. Yet, the constitution of the two units may be essentially separable. The chief executive or city council representing the collective consumption unit, for example, may bargain with managers of production units to secure an appropriate supply and delivery of public goods and services. The headlines in many local newspapers are filled with accounts of such negotiations. They frequently stress the conflict of interest between production units and those who represent the interests of citizens as consumers. Nevertheless, this is a very common organization pattern, typified by a municipality with its own police, fire, or street maintenance department.

As an alternative to organizing its own production unit, a collective consumption unit might decide to contract with a private vendor to supply a public good or service. In that case, public officials would translate decisions about the quantity or quality of public goods or services into specifications used to secure bids from potential vendors, state the terms and conditions for contractual arrangements, and establish standards for assessing performance. The collective consumption unit would also need to employ its own manager who would function as a purchasing agent to receive information about costs and production possibilities from potential vendors, negotiate and contract with vendors, receive service complaints from users, and monitor vendors' performance in delivering services. The collective consumption unit would operate as a "provider" or "arranger" of the service and the private vendor as the "producer" or "supplier." Organizing the consumption functions in a public economy can be distinguished from organizing the production functions. We refer to the one as *provision,* the other as *production.* Some general characteristics of collective consumption units and production units are summarized in table 3.2. A variety of municipal services in the United States, including street sweeping, snow removal, solid waste collection and disposal, fire and police protection, engineering services, planning services, and construction of public works, among many others, is supplied by private vendors.

TABLE 3.2. Collective Consumption Units and Producer Units

Collective-Consumption Unit	Producer Unit
Generally, a government that aggregates and articulates the demands of its constituents	May be a unit of government, a private, profit-making firm, a not-for-profit institution, or a voluntary association
Has coercive power to obtain funds to pay for public services and to regulate consumption patterns	Aggregates factors of production and produces goods to the specification of a collective consumption unit
Pays producer units for delivering public goods	Receives payment from collective consumption unit for delivering public goods
Receives complaints and monitors performance of production unit	Supplies information to collective consumption unit about costs and production possibilities

Source: See table 3.1.

A third option is to establish standards of service that apply to all residents of a community and leave to each household the decision concerning what private vendor should supply service to that household. Multiple vendors may be franchised, or anyone wishing to do business under the terms and conditions specified by the collective consumption unit for such a service may do so. Solid waste collection is a service often supplied under such conditions. Such services are highly individualized with only a limited degree of joint use or consumption. The limited degree of jointness can be taken care of by applying common standards to all households and vendors.

A fourth option is to collect taxes, assuring that each contributes his proportionate share of the burden, and then make available a voucher to each household so that it can decide among alternative producers and service packages. If applied to educational services for example, a voucher would be issued for each child or person eligible for educational services. The decision of the type of school and curriculum to be selected would be left to the family rather than to school authorities. Services amenable to voucher arrangements have characteristics associated with toll goods where consumption benefits others as well. The community at large benefits from an individual's education apart from the separable benefit derived by each individual. Community contributions to each individual's education are then justified. If those benefits were as great or greater when expenditure decisions are made by the family unit rather than by educational authorities, then a voucher system would be justified. Vouchers have been used for housing (rent supplement vouchers), health services (Medicaid can be considered a form of health voucher), and even for food (food stamps). The last, while usually considered a private good, is like education in that everyone benefits by having no one starve.

A fifth possibility is for a collective consumption unit to contract with a production unit that is organized by a different unit of government. Many municipalities acting as collective consumption units contract with other municipalities, or some other unit of government, to supply police services, fire services, water storage and transmission services, educational services, library services, and a wide range of other public services.

A sixth way of organizing production occurs when a collective consumption unit decides to rely upon its own production unit to supply some components of a service but to rely upon other consumption and production units to arrange for other components of a service. Its own production unit may draw upon other producers to supply it with factors of production, serve as a purchasing agent to procure and monitor the delivery of supplemental services, or function as a joint producer supplying a mix of services rendered by the joint effort of multiple production teams. Any given collective consumption unit may rely upon the joint production efforts of several different producers in supplying and delivering a particular bundle of goods and services that is subject to joint consumption. It may also act in cooperation with other joint consumption units that are willing to contribute supplemental funds to procure a particular level of services. Options for obtaining public services are summarized in table 3.3.

Public Service Industries

As soon as we begin to array some of these options for organizing collective consumption units and production units, a wide variety of possibilities be-

TABLE 3.3. Options for Obtaining Public Services

A government that serves as a collective consumption unit may obtain the desired public goods by

1. Operating its own production unit
Example: A city with its own fire or police department

2. Contracting with a private firm
Example: A city that contracts with a private firm for snow removal, street repair, or traffic-light maintenance

3. Establishing standards of service and leaving it up to each consumer to select a private vendor and to purchase service
Example: A city that licenses taxis to provide service, refuse collection firms to remove trash

4. Issuing vouchers to families and permitting them to purchase service from any authorized supplier
Example: A jurisdiction that issues food stamps, rent vouchers, or education vouchers, or operates a Medicaid program

5. Contracting with another government unit
Example: A city which purchases tax assessment and collection services from a county government unit, sewage treatment from a special sanitary district, and special vocational education services from a school board in an adjacent city

6. Producing some services with its own unit, and purchasing other services from other jurisdictions and from private firms
Example: A city with its own police patrol force that purchases laboratory services from the county sheriff, joins with several adjacent communities to pay for a joint dispatching service, and pays a private ambulance firm to provide emergency medical transportation

Source: See table 3.1.

comes apparent. Such a system may have large numbers of autonomous units of government with substantial degrees of overlap among multiple levels of government. Many private enterprises and voluntary associations may function as integral parts of such a public service economy. Substantial separation of powers within each unit of government may exist where all decision makers are constrained by enforceable legal or constitutional limits upon their authority. Each citizen participates in multiple consumption units organized around diverse communities of interest through overlapping levels of government and is served by an array of different public and private producing units supplying any particular bundle of public goods or services.

Each citizen, in such circumstances, is served not by "the" government, but by a variety of different *public service industries.* Each public service industry is composed of the collective consumption units serving as providers and production units serving as suppliers of some types of closely related public goods or services that are jointly consumed by discrete communities of individuals.

We can then think of the public sector as being composed of many public service industries including the police industry, the education industry, the water industry, the fire protection industry, the welfare industry, the health services industry, the transportation industry, and so on. The governmental component in some industries, such as the police industry, will be proportionately larger than other industries, such as the health services or the transportation industry. But most public service industries will have important private components.

Each industry will be characterized by distinctive production technologies and types of services rendered. These facilitate coordination of operational arrangements within an industry and allow for substantial independence between industries. The water industry, for example, is based upon technologies that facilitate collaboration among many agencies operating at different levels of government and among both public and private interests. These technologies in the water industry are easily distinguishable from the police industry or the education industry. The water industry serving any particular area will normally include large-scale water production agencies like the U.S. Corps of Engineers, which operates dams and large water storage facilities, intermediate producers like metropolitan water districts and county water authorities that operate large aqueducts and intermediate storage facilities, and municipal water departments, water service districts, mutual water companies, or private water utility companies that operate terminal storage facilities and retail distribution systems. The quality and cost of water delivered at the tap and the facilities available for recreation, navigation, flood control, and related uses will depend upon the joint operation of many different governments, agencies, and firms functioning in a water industry.

Some Problems Affecting Relationships among Collective Consumption Units and Production Units in Public Service Industries

The special characteristics of public goods generate a number of difficulties that affect relationships within public service industries. These difficulties create problems especially in the relationship of collective consumption units with production units. Marketing arrangements in the private sector usually involve financial arrangements as an incidental feature of each transaction. The public sector, by contrast, usually disassociates financial arrangements from service delivery. This disassociation of financing from service delivery further implies that service delivery may occur without satisfactory information about demand or user preference. Where jointness of consumption is accompanied by partial subtractibility, special problems may also arise in regulating patterns of use among diverse users. One use or pattern of use may, in the absence of regulation, seriously impair the value of the good or service for other users. Many public services—like some private services—depend critically upon service users to function as essential coproducers. Each of these problems—(1) financing; (2) regulating patterns of use; and (3) coproduction—poses difficulties in the relationship between collective consumption units and production units. Satisfactory performance in public service industries will depend upon finding constructive resolution to these problems.

Finance

In market relationships, the decision to buy any particular good or service automatically entails a consideration of forgone opportunities. The price expressed in money terms is the equivalent of all other goods and services that could be purchased with the same amount of money. A decision to buy a particular good or service reflects a willingness to forgo all other opportunities for which that money could have been used. An expression of demand in a market system always includes reference to what is forgone as well as what is purchased.

The articulation of preferences in the public sector often fails to take account of forgone opportunities. The service is available for the taking. Unless collective consumption units are properly constituted to give voice to user preferences, much essential information may be lost in the system. The mode of taxation may have little or no relationship to the service being supplied. Furthermore, individuals may function in many different communities of users. Residents of local neighborhoods may, for example, have different demands for police services involving different communities of interest when they commute from an area of residence to work in a different location.

Because most public goods and services are financed through a process of taxation involving no choice, optimal levels of expenditure are difficult to establish. The provision of public goods can be easily overfinanced or underfinanced. Public officials and professionals may have higher preferences for some public goods than the citizens they serve. Thus they may allocate more tax monies to these services than the citizens being served would allocate if they had an effective voice in the process. Underfinancing can occur where many of the beneficiaries of a public good are not included in the collective consumption units financing the good. Thus they do not help to finance the provision of that good even though they would be willing to help pay their fair share.

Financial arrangements are also the means by which redistribution is accomplished. Many of the proposals for large-scale consolidation of governmental units serving metropolitan areas are based on an assumption that increased equity will result by expanding the tax base. A broader tax base, it is thought, will ensure that wealthy suburbanites pay for essential services needed by the poor. No evidence is available to indicate that this actually happens in large cities. Poor neighborhoods receiving "services" that are not tailored to their needs may not be better off when increased resources are allocated to their neighborhood. In large collective consumption units, residents of poor neighborhoods may have even less voice about levels and types of services desired than they do in smaller-sized collective consumption units. Increasing the size of the smallest collective consumption unit to which citizens belong may not help solve problems of redistribution.

The financing of any particular public good or service may require contributions from more than a single collective consumption unit because beneficiaries from the production of that good may not be isolated in a single unit. Public education, for example, is of primary benefit to the family units whose children are being educated. However, substantial external benefits to others located within the same state and within the nation may accrue as a result of having a good educational system in each locality. Thus, the financing of education may best be achieved through a combination of resources coming from local, state, and national sources. However, the funding of a school system directly from several tax sources may make the school system less sensitive to the diverse interests of the different family units that directly receive educational services. The use of a voucher system for at least a major portion of the financing of public education would increase the relative voice of the family units that would choose the school or schools to supply educational services for their children.

The working out of financial arrangements between collective consumption units and production units is one of the most difficult problems faced by entrepreneurs in the public economy. Without market prices and market transactions, the act of paying for a good generally occurs at a time and place far from the act of consuming the good; individual costs are widely separated from individual benefits. Yet a principle of fiscal equivalence—that those receiving the benefits from a service pay the costs for that service—must apply in the public economy just as it applies in a market economy. Costs must be proportioned to benefits if people are to have any sense of economic reality. Otherwise beneficiaries may assume that public goods are free goods, that money in the public treasury is "the government's money," and that no opportunities are forgone in spending that money. When this happens the foundations of a democratic society are threatened. The alternative is to adhere as closely as possible to the principle of fiscal equivalence and to proportion taxes as closely as possible to benefits received.

Where charges can be appropriately levied on individual beneficiaries, user charges or use taxes can substantially alleviate the problems associated with rationing the use of a joint good when partial subtractibility results in potential congestion costs. Highway construction and maintenance services, highway police patrols and other services for motorists could, for example, be charged against gasoline taxes rather than other forms of general taxation. User charges or use taxes lead beneficiaries to calculate the cost of a service as against the value of a marginal use. Criminal sanctions need not be the principal means to regulate the use of a public good or service that is freely available to all users, if user charges can more appropriately proportion use to supply.

Regulating Patterns of Use

The characteristics of partial subtractibility of consumption imply that increased use at any given threshold of supply may impair the value of a good or service for other users. As congestion occurs, parks or streets decline in value to each individual user as more users take advantage of available facilities. Where multiple uses occur, one pattern of use may drive out other patterns of use. The use of a waterway to discharge wastes, for example, may exclude its use for recreational purposes. As some uses drive out other uses a serious erosion in the qualities of public life can occur. Jointness of use under conditions of partial subtractibility may require rules for ordering patterns of use so as to reduce potential conflict among the different uses made by any community of users. If rules are to be effective, mechanisms for their enforcement must be available. The delivery of public goods and services under these conditions depends upon the proportioning of supply to demand by way of a system of rules that takes account both of the conditions of supply and the patterns of use. Unless those rules take account of varying patterns of use and supply conditions in discrete circumstances, they are likely to become serious impediments to joint well-being. Heavy use of city streets for through traffic may, for example, impair their use by local residents in patronizing local businesses and tending to local problems.

These conditions may require an especially close coordination between production and consumption units. The delivery of service by a producer needs to occur where patterns of use are regulated to gain optimal advantage of the services and facilities made available. The construction and maintenance of rural farm-to-market roads is not compatible, for example, with their use to transport coal from mines to major transport terminals. Heavy coal hauls will destroy roads that are not constructed and maintained for those loads. Vendors, in such circumstances, are not producing for anonymous buyers. Vendors, instead, are supplying a tailor-made service subject to particular terms and conditions of use by discrete communities of users.

The regulation of patterns of use becomes one of the critical consumption functions performed by collective consumption units. This is why authority to enforce rules and regulations by recourse to criminal sanctions is usually assigned to governmental instrumentalities responsible for procuring a public good or service. Collective consumption units must assume primary responsibility for regulating and enforcing patterns of use. Yet, those regulations are meaningful only in light of discrete demand and supply conditions. Modifying supply conditions may alter the regulation and enforcement problems.

Even among governmental agencies, production of a service is frequently separated from regulating and enforcing patterns of use. Agencies responsible for policing the use of streets and highways, for example, are separate from those responsible for constructing and maintaining those streets and roads. Nevertheless, producers in a public service industry need to be aware that services subject to joint use involve sensitive problems in proportioning supply to use and in regulating patterns of use. Otherwise, problems of congestion and conflicts among users can lead to the erosion of public services and a degradation of community life.

Coproduction

Another problem in proportioning supply to patterns of use arises when users of services also function as essential coproducers. Without the intelligent and motivated efforts of service users, the service may deteriorate into an indifferent product with insignificant value. The quality of an educational product, for example, is critically affected by the productive efforts of students as users of educational services. Unless educational services are delivered under conditions that treat students as essential coproducers, the quality of the product is likely to be of little value. The health of a community depends as much on the informed efforts of individual citizens to maintain good health as it does upon professional personnel in health care institutions. The efforts of citizens to prevent fires and to provide early warning services when fires do break out are essential factors in the supply of fire protection services. The peace and security of a community are produced by the efforts of citizens as well its professional policemen. Collaboration between those who supply a service and those who use a service is essential if most public services are to yield the desired results.

These problems arise in all service industries in both the private and public sectors. The private doctor is confronted with the same problem as the public school teacher. When professional personnel presume to know what is good for people rather than providing people with opportunities to express their own preferences, we should not be surprised to find that increasing professionalization of public services is accompanied by a serious erosion in the quality of those services. High expenditures for public services supplied exclusively by highly trained cadres of professional personnel may be a factor contributing to a service paradox. The better services are, as defined by professional criteria, the less satisfied citizens are with those services. An efficient public service delivery system will depend upon service personnel working under conditions where they have incentives to assist citizens in functioning as essential coproducers.

Intelligent and efficient strategies of consumption are as essential to the welfare of human communities as intelligent and efficient strategies of production. Coproduction requires that both go hand in hand to yield optimal results. The organization of a public economy that gives consideration to economies of consumption as well as of production and provides for the coordination of the two is most likely to attain the best results.

Opportunities in Public Service Industries

Where multiple consumption and production units have served communities of people in both procuring and supplying public goods and services, conventional wisdom has alleged that duplication of functions occurs as a consequence of overlapping jurisdictions. Duplication of functions is assumed to be wasteful and inefficient. Presumably efficiency can be increased by eliminating "duplication of services" and "overlapping jurisdictions." Yet we know that efficiency can be realized in a market economy only if multiple firms serve the same market. Overlapping service areas and duplicate facilities are necessary conditions for the maintenance of competition in a market economy.

Can we expect similar forces to operate in a public economy? If we can, relationships among the governmental units, public agencies, and private businesses functioning in a public economy can be coordinated through patterns of interorganizational arrangements. Interorganizational arrangements, in that case, would manifest marketlike characteristics and display both efficiency-inducing and error-correcting behavior. Coordination in the public sector need not, in those circumstances, rely exclusively upon bureaucratic command structures controlled by chief executives. Instead, the structure of interorganizational arrangements may create important economic opportunities and evoke self-regulating tendencies. Some of these opportunities are examined.

Proportioning Consumption and Production Possibilities

In a world where goods subject to joint consumption vary from household size to global proportions, the availability of an array of differently sized collective consumption and production units will provide opportunities to realize diverse economies of scale. Where heterogeneous preferences for public services exist, advantage can be gained by having relatively small collective consumption units. As long as a collective consumption unit can articulate preferences for its own constituency and has access to a reasonably equitable distribution of income, the collective consumption unit can specify the mix of services preferred, procure an appropriate supply of those services, and pay for them. In this case a small collective consumption unit might contract with a large production unit, and each might take advantage of diverse scale considerations in both the consumption and production of a public good or service.

Another circumstance may exist where the collective consumption unit is large but efficient production is realized on a smaller scale. The appropriate consumption unit for users of interstate highways in the United States, for example, is probably a national unit. This national unit functions as a "provisioner" by developing appropriate specifications and financial arrangements for procuring interstate highway services. However, variability in climatic and geographic conditions over a large continental area is such that the production and maintenance services can be more efficiently supplied by smaller organizations. Thus, the U.S. Department of Transportation acts as a buyer of interstate highway services from state highway departments and private contractors that act as the principal production units.

The proportioning of diverse consumption and production possibilities in a complex public economy will not occur automatically but requires a conscious pursuit of relative advantages. An awareness that bigger is not necessarily better must precede a search for the combinations that generate the highest level of user satisfaction for given expenditures of efforts. Substantial improvements might be made.

Competition, Bargaining, and Cooperative Efforts

If each collective consumption unit has potential access to several production units and is prepared to consider alternative options in arranging for the supply of a good or service, the relationships between collective consumption units and production units will take on the characteristics of a quasi-market relationship. The market in this case is *not* between producers and *individual consumers.* We would expect such market structures to fail. The quasi market, instead, arises in the relationships among collective consumption units and production units.

If the potential producers include an array of private vendors and public agencies, an opportunity exists for bargaining to procure public goods or services at least cost. The opportunity for bargaining among collective consumption units and production units also creates incentives on the part of the bargaining parties to increase levels of information and to develop indicators of performance.

Bargaining may also occur in a noncompetitive situation in which multiple production units may be able to gain a joint benefit by coordinating their actions with one another. Various police agencies may, for example, have mutual aid or joint operating agreements to provide backup service whenever emergencies arise and all personnel are otherwise committed. Peak-load capabilities may be maintained by drawing upon reserves in other departments rather than requiring all departments to meet their own separate peak-load demands from their own reserves.

These joint efforts may be extended to organizing supplemental public or private enterprises to supply a variety of indirect services such as crime laboratories, police training academies, and joint dispatching services. Where high levels of interdependency have developed through cooperative arrangements, collective consumption and production units can be expected to develop routine organizational arrangements to reduce bargaining costs. These arrangements often take the form of a voluntary association with regularly scheduled meetings, with officials to set meeting agendas and to arrange for the organization and presentation of pertinent information. Many of these voluntary associations of collective consumption and production units may be formally organized with bylaws and membership fees or assessments to cover the cost of a small permanent secretariat that organizes information, implements decisions, and engages in entrepreneurial activities on behalf of the association.

Conflict and Conflict Resolution

Cooperative arrangements maintained under a rule of unanimity can always be threatened by the presence of a holdout where multiple collective consumption and production units are creating significant externalities for one another. If those externalities have the characteristics of a public good in a large domain that impinges upon several collectivities, one collectivity may find it advantageous to hold out and enjoy the benefits it can derive from the joint actions of others without assuming its proportionate share of the costs. If some holdouts are successful in their strategy, others will follow suit. Cooperative arrangements will fail, and there will be an erosion in welfare for everyone concerned. The maintenance of a holdout strategy and the impending threat of tragedy may lead some to respond to holdouts with threats or counterthreats. Unless constrained by the availability of institutions for adjudicating and resolving conflicts, threats and counterthreats can escalate into violence and warfare.

A highly fragmented political system *without* substantial overlap among the many jurisdictions is especially vulnerable to this form of institutional failure. Americans refer to this as "balkanization." With overlapping units of government, conflicts among governments at any one level may be resolved by recourse to the decision-making arrangements existing at a higher level of government. Such arrangements are inherent in federal systems of government. The critical feature is the availability of legal, political, and constitutional remedies to the parties injured as a consequence of negative externalities that are generated by governmental action.

Courts have played an especially important role in resolving conflicts among independent agencies and firms operating in a public economy. They are competent to decide an issue without dominating all channels of control and allocations of resources. In contrast, when a chief executive in an integrated command structure resolves conflicts among his subordinate public agencies, the impact is rarely confined to discrete issues. It is likely to affect future budgetary allocations, career opportunities for public employees, and the organizational status of operating agencies.

In California, where contracting for public services has the greatest competitive pressure, county grand juries have assumed a continuing responsibility for monitoring the operation of intergovernmental contracts. Inappropriate use of tax funds by public agencies functioning as contract producers would transfer service costs to the public treasury of the producing agency rather than paying for them from the treasury of the benefiting community. Inappropriate use of tax funds might also constitute subsidies to public producers. Such subsidies would drive private enterprises out of the business of producing public services even though private enterprises might be more efficient in rendering a comparable quality of service. Grand juries with jurisdiction to inquire into the discharge of public trust by state and local agencies can perform an important function in maintaining the integrity of marketlike relationships and encouraging competitive pressure in a public economy.

Without appropriate mechanisms for processing conflicts and monitoring the operation of a public service economy, contracting can be used as an instrument for the grossest forms of political corruption. Contracts with firms that are the chosen instruments of political bosses have long been used as a means of milking public treasuries, supplying the coffers of political machines, and creating private fortunes. (The Indiana Department of Motor Vehicles, for example, contracts out its licensing operation to the county chairmen or other party officials of the political party that is successful in controlling the office of governor. The party official derives fees from this contract service to finance political operations. In the absence of competitive pressure from other vendors, it is most doubtful that this form of contracting enhances efficiency.) No system of economic relationships will perform well without appropriate public policies and institutions to enforce these policies.

Conflict arises when someone believes he is being harmed by another's action. If the situation is remedied so that no one is harmed, a net improvement in welfare will occur. Thus, conflict is as important an indicator of potential economic losses as the red ink on a balance sheet. Mechanisms for conflict resolution contribute to economic welfare when they formulate solutions that right wrongs and restructure arrangements so that everyone is either left better off or no one is harmed or left worse off.

But to maintain a system that is open to conflict and conflict resolution, the participating parties in the system must have autonomous legal status with authority to sue and be sued and to take independent decisions in advancing a set of interests. If public economies are to gain the advantage of quasi-market competition and voluntary cooperation in producing and consuming public goods, they must be able to maintain arms-length relationships and they must have available to them institutions that can adjudicate conflicts among parties with equal standing in law. Adjudication does not occur in the absence of equal legal standing. Subordinates obey rather than cooperate.

Alternatives and Choices

Alternative possibilities can be conceptualized for the organization of public sector activities. One possibility is a bureaucratic system of public administration in which all relationships are coordinated through a command structure culminating in a single center of authority. This possibility treats the public and private sectors as mutually exclusive. No place exists for private enterprise in the organization of such a system of public administration.

Another possibility is to conceive of units of government as being collective consumption units whose first order of business is to articulate and aggregate demands for those goods that are subject to joint consumption where exclusion is difficult to attain. Demands are effectively articulated when decisions reflecting user preferences about services are reached and funds are committed. Several options are available for organizing production including that of contracting with private vendors to produce specified goods or services. Relationships are coordinated among collective consumption and production units by contractual agreements, cooperative arrangements, competitive rivalry, and mechanisms of conflict resolution. No single center of authority is responsible for coordinating all relationships in a public economy. Marketlike mechanisms can develop competitive pressures that tend to generate higher efficiency than can be gained by enterprises organized as exclusive monopolies and managed by elaborate hierarchies of officials.

This new mode of analysis that applies economic reasoning to nonmarket decision making should be used to reconsider the basic structure of a public economy. Changes that offer the prospect of advancing the net wellbeing of everyone concerned should be experimented with as being economically justified. The exercise of political power is economically justified only when benefits exceed costs; it is not justified as a means for the powerful to benefit themselves at the cost of the powerless.

The critical factor in this approach is to begin with the nature of the goods involved, in terms of exclusion, partial subtractibility, and measurability. To the extent that such characteristics exist, elements of public choice, in increasing degrees, can be introduced.

If the community of beneficiaries can be identified, then a principle of fiscal equivalence can be relied upon to design a collective consumption unit so that beneficiaries bear the cost and exercise the dominant voice in determining the quantity and/or quality of service to be made available. Wherever user charges or use taxes can be established, they can be used to advantage in giving users a sense of reality about the costs inherent in alternative choices.

The particular forms of organization used in establishing collective consumption units—consumer cooperatives, municipal corporations, public service districts, or other forms of governmental organization—are choices that can be taken by the relevant community of people so long as they bear the costs of the enterprise. The community of beneficiaries can, so long as they bear the costs, also be assigned substantial constitutional authority to establish and modify the terms and conditions that apply to the future governance of the collective consumption unit.

The selection of appropriate arrangements for the supply and delivery of a public service is open to several potential options. The wider the range of these options, the greater the degree of competitive pressure that will exist in any particular public service industry. It is precisely this competitive pressure that offers prospects for the best performance both in the sense of being responsive to user demands and in the sense of minimizing costs in doing so. In a well-developed public economy, many collective consumption units may find a mixed strategy advisable in which they rely, in part, upon their own production agencies but maintain extensive contractual arrangements with private enterprises and other public agencies to produce the mix of services preferred by their constituents.

Competitive pressures are the key factors in maintaining the viability of a democratic system of public administration. Substantial incentives will exist among established businesses and governmental agencies to protect their own interests by restricting the entry of competitive alternatives. If such efforts are successful, competitive rivalry loses its capacity to enhance efficiency and deteriorates into collusive efforts by some to gain dominance over others. This risk is carried to the greatest extreme in the case of a fully integrated monopoly solution. The traditional principles of public administration imply monopoly organization applied to the entire public sector. Private enterprises as producers of public goods and services can significantly improve the efficiency of the public sector so long as competitive pressures can be openly and publicly maintained.

REFERENCES

Altshuler, Alan A. 1970. *Community Control: The Black Demand for Participation in Large American Cities.* Indianapolis, IN: Pegasus.

Barzel, Yoram. 1969. "Two Propositions on the Optimal Level of Producing Public Goods." *Public Choice* 6 (spring): 31–37.

Bish, Robert L., and Hugh O. Nourse. 1975. *Urban Economics and Policy Analysis.* New York: McGraw-Hill Book Co.

Bish, Robert L., and Robert Warren. 1972. "Scale and Monopoly in Urban Government Services." *Urban Affairs Quarterly* 8 (September): 97–120.

Boskin, M. J. 1973. "Local Government Tax and Product Competition: The Optimal Provision of Public Goods." *Journal of Political Economy* 78 (January/February): 203–10.

Breton, Albert. 1974. *The Economic Theory of Representative Government.* Chicago: Aldine.

Buchanan, James M. 1970. "Public Goods and Public Bads." In *Financing the Metropolis,* ed. John P. Crecine, 51–71. Beverly Hills, CA: Sage.

Buchanan, James M., and Gordon Tullock. 1962. *The Calculus of Consent: Logical Foundations of Constitutional Democracy.* Ann Arbor: University of Michigan Press.

California Governor's Task Force on Local Government Reform. 1974. *Public Benefits from Public Choice.* Sacramento: Governor's Office.

Crozier, Michel. 1964. *The Bureaucratic Phenomenon.* Chicago: University of Chicago Press, Phoenix Books.

Dales, J. H. 1968. *Pollution, Property and Prices.* Toronto: University of Toronto Press.

Elazar, Daniel J. 1971. "Community Self-Government and the Crisis of American Politics." *Ethics* 81 (January): 91–106.

Gregg, Phillip M. 1974. "Units and Levels of Analysis: A Problem of Policy Analysis in Federal Systems." *Publius* 4 (fall): 59–86.

———. 1975. *Problems of Theory in Policy Analysis.* Lexington, MA: D. C. Heath.

Hamilton, Alexander, John Jay, and James Madison. [1788] n.d. *The Federalist.* New York: Modern Library.

Hirsch, Werner. 1964. "Local versus Areawide Urban Government Services." *National Tax Journal* 17 (December): 331–39.

———. 1968. "The Supply of Urban Public Services." In *Issues in Urban Economics,* ed. Harvey S. Perloff and Lowden Wingo, Jr., 435–75. Baltimore, MD: Johns Hopkins University Press.

Hochman, Harold M., ed. 1976. *The Urban Economy.* New York: W. W. Norton Co.

Kotler, Milton. 1969. *Neighborhood Government: The Local Foundations of Community Life.* Indianapolis, IN: Bobbs-Merrill Co.

Landau, Martin. 1969. "Redundance, Rationality, and the Problem of Duplication and Overlap." *Public Administration Review* 29 (July/August): 346–58.

Lindblom, Charles E. 1955. "Bargaining: The Hidden Hand in Government." Research Memorandum RM-1434-RC. Santa Monica, CA: RAND Corporation.

————. 1965. *The Intelligence of Democracy: Decision Making through Mutual Adjustment.* New York: Free Press.

Long, Norton E. 1970. "Rigging the Market for Public Goods." In *Organizations and Clients: Essays in the Sociology of Service,* eds. William R. Rosengren and Mark Lefton. Columbus, Ohio: Charles E. Merrill.

Martin, Dolores Tremewan. N.d. "The Institutional Framework of Community Formation: The Law and Economics of Municipal Incorporation in California." Ph.D. diss., Virginia Polytechnic Institute and State University.

McKean, Roland N. 1965. "The Unseen Hand in Government." *American Economic Review* 55 (June): 496–506.

Mishan, E. J. 1969. "The Relationship between Joint Products, Collective Goods, and External Effects." *Journal of Political Economy* 77 (May/June): 329–48.

Mushkin, Selma, ed. 1972. *Public Prices for Public Products.* Washington, DC: Urban Institute.

Niskanen, William A., Jr. 1971. *Bureaucracy and Representative Government.* Chicago: Aldine.

Olson, Mancur. 1969. "The Principle of 'Fiscal Equivalence': The Division of Responsibility among Different Levels of Government." *American Economic Review* 59 (May): 479–87.

Ostrom, Elinor. 1971. "Institutional Arrangements and the Measurement of Policy Consequences in Urban Areas." *Urban Affairs Quarterly* 6 (June): 447–75.

————. 1972. "Metropolitan Reform: Propositions Derived from Two Traditions." *Social Science Quarterly* 53 (December): 474–93. (Chapter 6 in this volume.)

————. 1975. "On Righteousness, Evidence, and Reform: The Police Story." *Urban Affairs Quarterly* 10 (June): 464–86.

Ostrom, Elinor, and Roger B. Parks. 1973. "Suburban Police Departments: Too Many and Too Small?" In *The Urbanization of the Suburbs,* ed. Louis H. Masotti and Jeffrey K. Hadden, 367–402. Urban Affairs Annual Reviews, vol. 7. Beverly Hills, CA: Sage.

Ostrom, Elinor, Roger B. Parks, and Gordon P. Whitaker. 1973. "Do We Really Want to Consolidate Urban Police Forces? A Reappraisal of Some Old Assertions." *Public Administration Review* 33 (September/October): 423–33.

————. 1974. "Defining and Measuring Structural Variations in Interorganizational Arrangements." *Publius* 4 (fall): 87–108. (Chapter 11 in this volume.)

Ostrom, Elinor, and Dennis C. Smith. 1976. "On the Fate of 'Lilliputs' in Metropolitan Policing." *Public Administration Review* 36 (March/April): 192–200.

Ostrom, Elinor, and Gordon P. Whitaker. 1974. "Community Control and Governmental Responsiveness: The Case of Police in Black Communities." In *Improving the Quality of Urban Management,* ed. David Rogers and Willis Hawley, 303–34. Urban Affairs Annual Reviews, vol. 8. Beverly Hills, CA: Sage. (Chapter 9 in this volume.)

Ostrom, Vincent. 1968. "Water Resource Development: Some Problems in Economic and Political Analysis of Public Policy." In *Political Science and Public Policy,* ed. Austin Ranney, 123–150. Chicago: Markham.

————. 1969. "Operational Federalism: Organization for the Provision of Public

Services in the American Federal System." *Public Choice* 6 (spring): 1–17.

———. 1971. "Institutional Arrangements for Water Resource Development." PB 207 314. Springfield, VA: National Technical Information Service.

———. 1973. "Can Federalism Make a Difference?" *Publius* 3 (fall): 197–237.

———. 1987. *The Political Theory of a Compound Republic: Designing the American Experiment.* 2d rev. ed. San Francisco, CA: ICS Press.

Ostrom, Vincent, and Elinor Ostrom. 1965. "A Behavioral Approach to the Study of Intergovernmental Relations." *Annals of the American Academy of Political and Social Science* 359 (May): 137–46. (Chapter 4 in this volume.)

———. 1971. "Public Choice: A Different Approach to the Study of Public Administration." *Public Administration Review* 31 (March/April): 203–16. (Reprinted in Michael D. McGinnis, ed., *Polycentric Games and Institutions* [Ann Arbor: University of Michigan Press, 1999].)

Ostrom, Vincent, Charles M. Tiebout, and Robert Warren. 1961. "The Organization of Government in Metropolitan Areas: A Theoretical Inquiry." *American Political Science Review* 55 (December): 831–42. (Chapter 1 in this volume).

Pennock, J. Roland. 1959. "Federal and Unitary Government: Disharmony and Frustration." *Behavioral Science* 4 (April): 147–57.

Polanyi, Michael. 1951. *The Logic of Liberty: Reflections and Rejoinders.* Chicago: University of Chicago Press.

Savas, E. S. 1974. "Municipal Monopolies versus Competition in Delivering Urban Services." In *Improving the Quality of Urban Management,* ed. Willis Hawley and David Rogers, 473–500. Urban Affairs Annual Review, vol. 8. Beverly Hills, CA: Sage.

Savas, E. S., and S. Ginsburg. 1973. "The Civil Service: A Meritless System?" *The Public Interest* 32 (summer): 70–85.

Shields, Currin V. 1952. "The American Tradition of Empirical Collectivism." *American Political Science Review* 46 (March): 104–20.

Stigler, George S. 1962. "The Tenable Range of Functions of Local Government." In *Private Wants and Public Needs: Issues Surrounding the Size and Scope of Government Expenditures,* ed. Edmund S. Phelps. New York: W. W. Norton.

Tiebout, Charles M. 1956. "A Pure Theory of Local Expenditures." *Journal of Political Economy* 64 (October): 416–24.

Tolley, G. S. 1969. *The Welfare Economics of City Bigness.* Urban Economics Report No. 31. Chicago: University of Chicago Press.

Tullock, Gordon. 1965. *The Politics of Bureaucracy.* Washington, DC: Public Affairs Press.

———. 1969. "Federalism: The Problem of Scale." *Public Choice* 6 (spring): 19–29.

———. 1970. *Private Wants, Public Means: An Economic Analysis of the Desirable Scope of Government.* New York: Basic Books.

Warren, Robert O. 1964. "A Municipal Services Market Model of Metropolitan Organization." *Journal of the American Institute of Planners* 30 (August): 193–204.

———. 1966. *Government in Metropolitan Regions: A Reappraisal of Fractionated Political Organization.* Davis, CA: Institute of Governmental Affairs, University of California.

————. 1970. "Federal-Local Development Planning: Scale Effects in Representation and Policy Making." *Public Administration Review* 30 (November/December): 584–95.

Weschler, Louis F., and Robert Warren. 1970. "Consumption Costs and Production Costs in the Provision of Antipoverty Goods." Paper delivered at the sixty-sixth annual meeting of the American Political Science Association, Los Angeles, California, September 8–12.

Wildavsky, Aaron. 1966. "The Political Economy of Efficiency." *Public Administration Review* 26 (December): 292–310.

————. 1976. "A Bias toward Federalism: Confronting the Conventional Wisdom on the Delivery of Governmental Services." *Publius* 6 (spring): 95–120.

Part II
Frameworks for the Study
of Public Economies

CHAPTER 4

A Behavioral Approach to the Study of Intergovernmental Relations

Vincent Ostrom and Elinor Ostrom

If the study of intergovernmental relations is to advance beyond the point of listing and describing relationships among governmental units, the focus of concern must be upon the systemic character of intergovernmental relations.[1] The study of the systemic character of intergovernmental relations requires that we begin to search for the nature of the order that exists in the complex of relationships among governmental units and abandon the assumption that all of these relationships are unique or random. This requires a shift in orientation from a belief that a system of government composed of numerous, independent, specialized units of government is necessarily fragmented and ineffective to an analysis of how the system works.[2] Seeking to understand how a system composed of a multitude of autonomous units manages to function as a system does not constitute a commitment to a moral justification of events as they are. Rather, a scholar undertaking such a search assumes the obligation to understand the patterns of behavior in systems composed of many governmental units before predicting their imminent failure and recommending the creation of alternative structures.

Scholarly inquiry into the systemic character of interorganizational relationships has long been the principal focus of concern in the study of economics.[3] Our discussion will be based primarily upon the application of findings and concepts from economics to the study of intergovernmental relationships. In this essay we propose to give consideration first to the concept of an industry as an effort to characterize a set of interrelated enterprises that uses a common body of knowledge and methods in the production of similar goods and services. Second, we shall give consideration to the disparity of interests within an industry and the implication of this disparity for organization of enterprises in the public sector of the U.S. economy. Finally, we shall explore some aspects of the problem of regulating the interrelationships among numerous independent public agencies functioning in public industries.

Originally published in *Annals of the American Academy of Political and Social Science* 359 (May 1965): 137–46. Copyright © 1965 by Sage Publications. Reprinted by permission of Sage Publications and the authors.

The Concept of an Industry

A basic assumption in modern economics is that organizational structures and production methods will vary depending upon the nature of the product being produced.[4] The similarities in production methods required to produce a particular product lead to an identification of the different enterprises concerned with the production, distribution, and utilization of such goods as being in a particular industry. Those in the same industry share a common body of information and knowledge about the nature of the products, their production, and their uses. Intelligent decisions, whether by a producer, a distributor, or a consumer in the same industry, require access to a similar body of knowledge. The similarities in production methods, technology, and information lead to considerable similarities among firms in the same industry and to the development of a characteristic structure of interrelationships among the firms in an industry.

The conception of an industry is crude, but even a crude concept may be a useful tool for exploring the systemic character of a gross structure of events lying somewhere between individual units of government and a general system of government. The industry concept is one way of considering an intermediate level of organization where many separate enterprises have developed interdependent patterns of organization based upon a complementarity of functions in producing and using a similar type of product or service.

Both the usefulness and the limitations of this concept can be illustrated by reference to industries in the private sector of the economy. The lumber industry is based upon the manipulation, control, or transformation of quite a different set of events than the oil industry, the electric power industry, or the automobile industry, as some obvious examples. The importance that knowledge derived from particular fields in the biological sciences, the earth sciences, and the physical sciences assumes in each of these industries is of quite different proportions as one shifts his focus from forest products, to petroleum products, to electricity, or to automotive products.

The relationship of production technology to organizational structure is also quite evident from a commonplace knowledge of these industries. The electric power industry, which depends upon a distribution system with direct electrical connections to each consumer, is not amenable to a pattern of economic organization that enables consumers to choose their source of electricity from alternative distributors. The electric power industry, as a result, is an industry composed largely of producers occupying monopoly positions in their respective service areas. In the automobile industry, consumers have a choice among the products of different producers, but the very high capital costs required to finance production substantially restrict the number of producers able to enter the industry. When timber reserves were large and rough-saw lumber was the preponderant product, the lumber industry was composed of many highly competitive firms. As the capital costs of production have increased with technological changes, and as the range of forest products has become more diverse, the structure of the industry is becoming more highly specialized, with a smaller number of larger firms.

The concept of an industry is subject to a limitation that derives from the inability to specify precise boundaries to any particular industry. What was a relatively simple lumber industry at one period may become a relatively complex forest-products industry at another point in time. The precise boundaries between the oil industry, the automobile industry, and the electric power industry may also be somewhat obscure. The absence of precision in being able to specify exact boundary conditions, however, does not constitute a serious impediment to the use of the concept of an industry for examining the regularities that occur in the behavior of the many organizations that perform closely interrelated activities in the production of similar goods or services. If boundary conditions are adjusted to include the essential structural elements to account for the conduct of an industry as a whole, meaningful generalizations can be made about an industry as a social system composed of many interacting organizations.

When applied to the public sector, the concept of an industry is useful in being able to identify areas of productive activity involving interrelationships among many different agencies and units of government concerned with the provision of similar public services. The traditional approach among some political scientists has been to classify all public instrumentalities as governments or governmental agencies and, consequently, to expect that all public instrumentalities behave similarly without regard to the product being produced and without regard to structural variations in interagency relationships in particular public industries. Different industries in the public sector are subject to as a great variation in patterns of organization, in technology, and in production methods as are industries in the private sector.

The water industry, for example, is composed of a very large number of highly independent federal, state, and local governmental agencies operating side by side with large numbers of private utility companies, cooperative associations, and individual proprietorships.[5] All of these agencies carry on activities relating to a similar form of phenomenon, which is the subject of a common body of knowledge and can be controlled by the use of similar facilities and production methods. The U.S. educational system can be conceptualized as an industry composed predominantly of many independent public enterprises and nonprofit private enterprises ranging from kindergarten and elementary schools through universities specializing in professional training and graduate studies (see Machlup 1962). Again, similar production methods prevailing within the education industry would enable one to draw relatively effective boundaries concerning the essential enterprises to include within the industry. A relatively low order of discrimination is required to distinguish between public enterprises functioning in the water industry as against those functioning in the education industry.

The concept of an industry can also be applied to the provision of police services by the many local, state, and federal agencies who use closely related production methods to attempt to control similar sets of events in relation to similar objectives or intended outcomes. The concept of an industry can, in the same way, be applied to any other set of closely related public services using similar methods to control selective sets of events in relation to the production of certain values or preferred consequences. The variety of different types of goods and services produced in the public sector is reflected in a highly differentiated complex of public industries, each of which has its own characteristic production methods and is organized to take account of its own particular production problems.

The use of the industry concept is amenable to systematic analysis of the sets of events being regulated and transformed by certain control and production methods performed by the several agencies operating in a single public industry. In the same way that the hydraulic behavior of a river system can be simulated on a computer, the production of any given water industry can also be subject to systems analysis. Comparative studies of different production strategies have already been made to determine conditions of optimal development in patterns of water resource management (see Maass and Hufschmidt et al. 1962).

Comparative study of alternative structural arrangements for the organization of a public water industry is amenable to similar methods of inquiry.

The Diversity of Interests in an Industry

The organization of any particular industry always reflects certain common characteristics related to its technology, its production methods, and the type of product it produces. These common characteristics distinguish any one industry from other industries. Any particular industry, also, reflects a diversity of interests in the organization of different elements within that industry. Closely related production functions in any particular industry may give rise to differentiated products affecting different scales of organization and different sets of community interests. In addition, the interests of consumers of goods and services in an industry may not be identical with producer interests.

The diversity of interests involved in providing closely related but differentiable services can be readily illustrated by reference to different public service industries. In the California water industry, for example, the interests of a community of farmers irrigating desert benchlands may be quite independent of the interests of the residents of the floodplain who are subject to recurrent flooding, fishermen who are concerned with the maintenance of a salmon fishery, or shippers who use the main channel of a river for navigation purposes. If the irrigation district acts solely on behalf of its own water users, its water production facilities would be inadequate to take account of the other set of interests. On the other hand, a large-scale water production agency such as the Bureau of Reclamation, the Corps of Engineers, or the California Department of Water Resources can undertake the construction of appropriately sized projects to take account of the various demands of irrigation districts, flood control districts, and other interests of water-user groups. Interests among the different large-scale producers can also be organized so that the Corps of Engineers, for example, can use Bureau of Reclamation and Department of Water Resource storage reservoirs in scheduling the storage and release of flood flows so that efficient use can be made of the many different storage projects to reduce flood damages. Among the western states, Bureau of Reclamation projects, for example, provide more flood control storage than Corps of Engineers projects, but the Corps of Engineers schedules the use of Bureau storage for flood control purposes.

When all of these interests are taken together, the water industries in different regions of the United States are apt to be organized in a structure composed of one or more large-scale water production agencies, several intermediate producers and wholesalers, and a very large number of local distribution agencies that produce at least a portion of their own water supply from local sources. The California water industry is notable for its reliance upon several large-scale water production agencies in contrast to the water industry in the Tennessee Valley, which relies largely upon a single major producer.

Wholesale agencies, such as the Metropolitan Water District of Southern California, and local distributors are invariably organized as independent agencies that maintain a variety of contractual and operating arrangements with the large-scale production agencies. These local agencies are capable of driving an arm's-length bargain on behalf of the interests of the local water users while the large-scale production agencies are able to organize their production functions to take account of large-scale, multiple-purpose development of a river system.

Similar structural variations are found in other public industries including the public education industry and the police industry. The police industry, for example, has a complex structure including municipal, county, state, and federal police forces. Most municipal police forces depend upon essential police services rendered by federal, state, and county agencies in conducting their day-by-day police operations at the local level. In turn, the Federal Bureau of Investigation depends upon services rendered by local police agencies in the conduct of its national police services.

In the absence of competitive market arrangements, the organization of public entities has usually been based upon the assumption that consumer or user interests are to be reflected in the internal decision-making structure of a public enterprise.[6] Voters are supposed to reflect their demands by selecting decision makers who are responsible for making production decisions concerning the supply of public services to be produced. When public service users and voters constitute identical populations, and their decisions are made regarding the operation of a single enterprise producing a single type of public service, the task of harmonizing producer decisions with consumer decisions is relatively simple.

The trend toward the development of more complex structures of highly differentiated and relatively autonomous public agencies in the different public industries of our public economy may be more understandable, however, if the assumption of disparity between producer and consumer interests is accepted (see Thompson 1963, esp. chap. 7). The concept of the single self-sufficient public firm producing all of the public goods and services for its resident population is no longer a tenable concept for understanding the structure and conduct of the public service economy. The horizontal coordination afforded through any general units of government simply reflects one dimension in a public service economy that has an equally significant counterpart in the vertical differentiation of the public economy to reflect its diversified industrial structure.

The lack of a quid pro quo relationship between producers and consumers in many public service industries may require independent organization of financial arrangements both with reference to revenues derived from general forms of taxation and to expenditures made from general funds (see Downs 1960). A quid pro quo relationship between buyers and sellers in the private market permits the financial aspect of a private transaction to be organized in an economic exchange, and the costs of production can be covered in the price charged for goods and services. Wherever user service charges can be made by a public enterprise in the provision of its services, a public industry may also take advantage of the quid pro quo relationship in pricing its services to take account of costs of production and in allocating services.[8] Public agencies performing services subject to user charges can operate with substantial autonomy if economic return provided by user charges is based upon the formulation of an efficient pricing policy.

Public industries concerned with the production of the more purely public goods and services that are not amenable to the economic use of user charges are confronted with the necessity of organizing their operations in relation to other forms of public finance. As the financing of government services is subject to an increasing amount of intergovernmental and interagency transfers independent of direct quid pro quo transactions, there will be increased pressure to organize public revenue, public investment, and public-expenditure decisions in the management of public funds in a way that will have strong parallels to the operation of a public banking and investment industry.

The Regulation of Relationships among Agencies in Public Industries

In economics and in political science, scholars have given substantial attention to modes for regulating public behavior as a function of the political process and for regulating private economic behavior through the operation of market arrangements. Considerable attention has also been given to the problem of regulating economic behavior of private enterprises through public regulation when markets fail to provide satisfactory solutions. A number of private industries that operate with substantial elements of monopoly power are considered to be public utilities, and their investment decisions, pricing policies, and consumer service policies are subject to detailed regulation by federal and state public regulatory agencies under established standards of public policy.

Relatively less attention has been given to problems of regulating the conduct of the legally independent but functionally interdependent public agencies operating in a public industry. The U.S. system of government is deliberately designed to provide for the division of governmental power among territorial jurisdictions and among different decision structures within any particular governmental jurisdiction. Public enterprises, consequently, enjoy substantial measures of independence in their vertical relationships with each other from one level of government to another. At the same time, public enterprises operating at any given level of government also occupy positions of substantial political independence. Operational independence is a condition of survival in a government organized with independent legislative and executive establishments, each of which is separately subject to changing patterns of political control. An operating agency must reach an independent political accommodation to any and all changes in political conditions in relation to the executive and legislative establishments that control the allocation of its resources if its survival is to be assured.

The political process, as a consequence of these basic divisions of authority, is not available to provide for a single source of regulation applicable to all operations of all public enterprises. The political processes afforded by different governmental jurisdictions do provide significant means for partially ordering the conduct of public enterprises in their relationships with one another. Any form of political control, thus, is necessarily limited by the constitutional conditions of the U.S. system of government to a partial ordering of relationships in any particular public industry. In addition, other methods of regulation by mutual accommodation are being developed to regulate the relationships among different governmental agencies functioning in a particular public industry.

The degree of vertical independence exercised by agencies of different levels of government performing related functions in the same public industry has been an important source of regulation through the exercise of countervailing power (Galbraith 1952). The arm's-length bargaining among agencies in the water industry, for example, is simply one illustration of the exercise of countervailing power in a public industry. Different sets of agencies may seek to alter the balance of power at the bargaining table by forming coalitions to pool information on one side of the table, by encouraging the entry of new agencies on the other side of the table, and by generally seeking to alter the patterns of supply and demand. While the exercise of countervailing power is apt to have a significant influence upon the nature of the economic bargain that can be struck, it also has a significant influence upon the articulation of any political issues that may arise in any unresolved conflict between public agencies. All forms of public decision making have the structure of a contest to facilitate the articulation of information and the consideration of alternative solutions in the course of reaching a public decision.

The regulation of interrelationships among public enterprises by arm's-length bargaining between vertically independent agencies can be rapidly transformed into a collusive game against a treasury wherever public funds are made available to produce public services without requiring beneficiaries directly to bear the costs of the services. As a result, the analysis of criteria appropriate to public expenditure decisions has become a matter of significant concern among scholars examining the operation of public enterprises (see Krutilla and Eckstein 1958; McKean 1958; Hirshleifer, DeHaven, and Milliman 1960; Eckstein 1961). Consideration of the cost of public funds and of appropriate interest rates to charge on public investments is also being examined.[9]

Some attention has been given to the development of quasi-market arrangements among independent public agencies operating in different public industries (see Ostrom, Tiebout, and Warren 1961; Warren 1964a,b). In Los Angeles County, for example, many governmental services are arranged by short-term contracts between governmental agencies legally capable of producing the same services. Some agencies function as producers and other agencies operate as buyers in arranging the provision of such municipal services as police services, library services, planning services, public works services, and many others. The exercise of countervailing power has been used to such an extent in the development of the so-called Lakewood Plan that the structure of the across-the-table relationships has been transformed into a quasi-market arrangement involving competition among producers and competition among buyers. Grand jury scrutiny of this contract-service system has maintained the competition within appropriate boundaries, and the force of competition appears to be a positive force toward efficient performance.

Deliberate pseudoprice and pseudomarket arrangements are also being examined for their applicability to public industries (see Vickrey 1963). The pricing of private fire insurance policies to take account of public fire protection services has had a powerful influence in regulating the conduct of the various public agencies providing fire protection services in a local community. The operation of a municipal water service, a municipal fire department, cooperative arrangements among fire agencies, and other such matters are taken into account in determining ratings that affect the price of fire insurance. It may be possible to use flood insurance in juxtaposition to the operation of public flood control agencies and to establish a system of insurance or compensatory payments vis-a-vis the operation of police protection agencies.

The function of service charges to create an incentive for more efficient and responsible behavior by stream polluters has been explored as a means of establishing deliberate public pricing policies to affect behavior among agencies operating in the water industry (see Kneese 1964). Fishing and hunting licenses offer opportunities to pursue pricing policies that can affect the allocation of water resources among competing users rather than simply providing a minimum-cost charge to cover the traditional operations of fish and game agencies. Free provision or minimum-cost pricing of scarce public resources such as water supplies may simply increase the economic value of the political stakes, place a premium upon political maneuvering, and result in overinvestment in large-scale water transfer schemes. The creation of appropriate pricelike charges to reflect the value of water for different joint and alternative uses would create incentives to avoid excessive investment in water facilities and encourage the economic use and reuse of the available supplies of water among competing water users.

To the extent that mechanisms can be designed to regulate the economic relationships among independent public enterprises functioning within any particular public industry, the burdens for regulation through the political process can be reduced proportionately. Public enterprises will always have to depend upon the political process to make adjustments in the self-regulating mechanisms within a public industry and to exercise a substantial burden in supplementing the regulatory force provided by mutual accommodations within a public industry. Without the availability of self-regulating mechanisms within particular public industries, there can be little confidence that a viable and efficient public economy can be maintained.

Some Conclusions

The absence of an efficient market arrangement for the private provision of goods and services does not necessarily mean that public provision of goods and services under nonmarket conditions will assure efficient solutions. More efficient and more responsible performance in the public sector may be attainable if selective consideration is given to the formulation of user service charges to reflect deliberate public pricing policies, to the development of general criteria for public expenditure and public investment decisions, and to the development of quasi-market and pseudomarket arrangements to regulate the conduct of public agencies functioning in particular public service industries.

As the demand for public services tends to accelerate in an expanding national economy, relationships among diverse public enterprises will assume an increasing importance in U.S. public life. Students of intergovernmental relationships have an important opportunity to extend our understanding of some of the basic patterns of behavior that exist among the complex variety of governmental agencies responsible for producing, financing, and arranging for the provision of public goods and services. The concept of an industry can afford a useful approach for analyzing the interrelationships that exist among separate agencies using similar methods to deal with closely related events in order to provide a similar type of public service. The operation of a public enterprise system composed of diverse public industries will require a knowledge of both political and economic processes. Scholars in economics, political science, and related behavioral sciences have much to contribute toward an understanding of the structure, conduct, and performance of the different public industries that form a part of the U.S. public enterprise system.

NOTES

1. There are too many studies of intergovernmental relations that list the variety of relationships that various units of government maintain with each other to cite. An example of the opposite approach is the article by Wheaton (1963, 225), in which he urges metropolitan planners to come "to grips with the nature of the systems which comprise metropolitan areas."

2. The traditional view that relations among governments in metropolitan areas cannot be rationally analyzed because of their chaotic nature is expressed in each of the following: Wood 1963; Gulick 1957, 58; Herman 1963, 21.

3. Sociology has little to offer in the study of interorganizational relationships per se as indicated by the following observation: "One major lacuna in current sociological study is research on interorganization relations—studies which use organizations as their unit of analysis" (Litwak and Hylton 1962).

Other fields of inquiry including those concerned with game theory and systems analysis have also been concerned with efforts to generalize about interorganizational relationships, but this work is less directly applicable than work in economics to the study of intergovernmental relationships within the nation-state.

4. See Bain 1959 for the most general exposition of the concept of industry and of the analytical problems associated with the study of industrial organization. See also

Caves 1964. The emphasis in economic studies tends to be upon the substitutability of final products that gives rise to market competition in defining an industry. Since competitive markets per se do not exist among public enterprises providing public goods and services, the use of the industry concept in the public sector needs to emphasize similarities in production methods, common knowledge, and similar technology among enterprises coordinating their activities in the provision of related services.

5. See Ostrom 1962. A study of the California water industry was completed by a team of economists and political scientists including Joe S. Bain, Richard E. Caves, Julius Margolis, and Vincent Ostrom as the senior investigators.

6. For the traditional statement of this position see Maxey 1922; Studenski 1930; Jones 1942.

7. Fitch (1957) discusses the criteria that should be applied in determining whether it is appropriate to charge for a public service rather than funding it through general taxes.

8. See Krutilla and Eckstein 1958 for a discussion of the opportunity costs of money and the appropriate rate of interest to take account of the value of money.

REFERENCES

Bain, Joe S. 1959. *Industrial Organization.* New York: John Wiley & Sons.

Caves, Richard E. 1964. *American Industry: Structure, Conduct, Performance.* Englewood Cliffs, NJ: Prentice-Hall.

Downs, Anthony. 1960. "Why the Government Budget Is Too Small in a Democracy." *World Politics* 12 (July): 541–64.

Eckstein, Otto. 1961. *Water Resource Development.* Cambridge, MA: Harvard University Press.

Fitch, Lyle C. 1957. "Metropolitan Financial Problems." *Annals of the American Academy of Political and Social Science* 314 (November): 66–73.

Galbraith, John K. 1952. *American Capitalism: The Concept of Countervailing Power.* Boston: Houghton Mifflin.

Gulick, Luther. 1957. "Metropolitan Organization." *Annals of the American Academy of Political and Social Science* 314 (November): 57–65.

Herman, Harold. 1963. *New York State and the Metropolitan Problem.* Philadelphia, PA: University of Pennsylvania Press.

Hirshleifer, Jack, James C. DeHaven, and Jerome W. Milliman. 1960. *Water Supply: Economics, Technology and Policy.* Chicago: University of Chicago Press.

Jones, Victor. 1942. *Metropolitan Government.* Chicago: University of Chicago Press.

Kneese, Allen V. 1964. *The Economics of Regional Water Quality Management.* Baltimore: Johns Hopkins University Press.

Krutilla, John V., and Otto Eckstein. 1958. *Multiple Purpose River Development.* Baltimore: Johns Hopkins University Press.

Litwak, Eugene, and Lydia F. Hylton. 1962. "Interorganizational Analysis: A Hypothesis on Coordinating Agencies." *Administrative Science Quarterly* 6 (March): 395–420.

Maass, Arthur, and Maynard M. Hufschmidt et al. 1962. *Design of Water-Resources Systems.* Cambridge, MA: Harvard University Press.

Machlup, Fritz. 1962. *The Production and Distribution of Knowledge in the United States.* Princeton, NJ: Princeton University Press.

Maxey, Chester C. 1922. "The Political Integration of Metropolitan Communities." *National Municipal Review* 11 (August): 220–53.

McKean, Roland N. 1958. *Efficiency in Government through Systems Analysis.* New York: John Wiley & Sons.

Ostrom, Vincent. 1962. "The Water Economy and Its Organization." *Natural Resources Journal* 2 (April): 55–73.

Ostrom, Vincent, Charles M. Tiebout, and Robert Warren. 1961. "The Organization of Government in Metropolitan Areas: A Theoretical Inquiry." *American Political Science Review* 55 (December): 831–42. (Chapter 1 in this volume.)

Studenski, Paul. 1930. *The Government of Metropolitan Areas in the United States.* New York: National Municipal League.

Thompson, Wilbur R. 1963. *A Preface to Urban Economics. Preliminary.* Washington, DC: Resources for the Future.

Vickrey, William W. 1963. "General and Specific Financing of Urban Services." In *Public Expenditure Decisions in the Urban Community,* ed. Howard G. Schaller, 62–90. Washington, DC: Resources for the Future.

Warren, Robert. 1964a. "A Municipal Services Market Model of Metropolitan Organization." *Journal of the American Institute of Planners* 30 (August): 193–203.

———. 1964b. "Changing Patterns of Governmental Organization in the Los Angeles Metropolitan Area." Ph.D. diss., University of California, Los Angeles.

Wheaton, William L. C. 1963. "Operations Research for Metropolitan Planning." *Journal of the American Institute of Planners* 29 (November): 250–59.

Wood, Robert. 1963. "The Contribution of Political Science to Urban Form." In *Urban Life and Form,* ed. Werner Z. Hirsch, 99–128. New York: Holt, Rinehart and Winston.

CHAPTER 5

Polycentricity (Part 2)

Vincent Ostrom

Some Implications for Research on the Governance of Metropolitan Areas

The illusion of chaos or the appearance of disorder is a phenomenon that has characterized U.S. public life for a very long time. Tocqueville recognized this condition in the 1830s when he observed:

> The appearance of disorder which prevails on the surface leads one at first to imagine that society is in a state of anarchy; nor does one perceive one's mistake till one has gone deeper into the subject. (Tocqueville 1835, 1:89)

Tocqueville's effort to go deeper into the subject led him to juxtapose a circumstance where "the government can administer the affairs of each locality" as against one where "the citizens do it for themselves" (Tocqueville 1835, 1:89). In comparing the two circumstances, Tocqueville concludes that, "the collective strength of the citizens will always conduce more efficaciously to the public welfare than the authority of the government" (Tocqueville 1835, 1:89). He goes on to observe further that

> In no country in the world [other than the United States] do the citizens make such exertions for the common wealth. I know of no people who have established schools so numerous and efficacious, places of public worship better suited to the wants of the inhabitants, or roads kept in

Originally prepared for delivery at the 1972 annual meeting of the American Political Science Association, Washington Hilton Hotel, Washington, DC, September 5–9. Published by permission of the author. Comments by Robert Bish, Phillip Gregg, John Hamilton, Norton Long, Brian Loveman, James McDavid, Nancy Neubert, Elinor Ostrom, Roger Parks, Dennis Smith, Mark Sproule-Jones, and Donald Zauderer have stimulated substantial revisions in this essay from the earlier draft circulated in late June 1972.

This essay has been divided into two parts for publication in this volume. References for both parts are listed at the end of this chapter.

119

better repair. Uniformity or permanence of design, the minute arrangement of detail, and the perfection in administrative system must not be
sought for in the United States; what we find there is the presence of a
power which, if it is somewhat wild, is at least robust, and an existence
checkered with accidents, indeed, but full of animation and effort.
(Tocqueville 1835, I:91–92)

Tocqueville's distinction between the one circumstance where "the government can administer the affairs of each locality" and the other where "the
citizens do it for themselves" points to basic differences between a monocentric structure in France and a polycentric structure in the United States.
Tocqueville quite explicitly recognized that Americans had recourse to diverse foci of authority and relied upon methods of election and adjudication
to resolve conflicts among public authorities rather than a single hierarchy of
command. He observed that

> Nothing is more striking to a European traveler in the United States than
> the absence of what we [the French] term the government, or the admini-
> stration. Written laws exist in America, and one sees the daily execution
> of them; but although everything moves regularly, the mover can no-
> where be discovered. *The hand that directs the social machinery is in-
> visible.* Nevertheless, as all persons must have recourse to certain gram-
> matical forms, which are the foundation of human language, in order to
> express their thoughts; so all communities are obliged to secure their ex-
> istence by submitting to a certain amount of authority, without which
> they fall into anarchy. This authority may be distributed in several ways,
> but it must always exist somewhere. (Tocqueville 1835, 1:70; my emphasis)

Some Problems of Language

Penetrating an illusion of chaos and discerning regularities that appear to be
created by an "invisible hand" imply that the tasks of scholarship in metropolitan governance will be presented with serious difficulties. Relevant
events may occur without the appropriate *proper* names being attached to
them. Presumably events implicated by definitions used in scholarship may
deviate from conventions that apply to the use of proper names. Patterns and
regularities which occur under an illusion of chaos may involve an order of
complexity that is counterintuitive.

The elementary task of specifying what we mean when we refer to the
governance of metropolitan areas remains ambiguous. How is the domain of
a "metropolitan area" to be specified? The conventions of the U.S. Bureau of
the Census in designating Standard Metropolitan Statistical Areas are clearly

unsatisfactory. Any county with an incorporated city of 50,000 population can qualify as a Standard Metropolitan Statistical Area. Whether or not several counties are grouped in a single SMSA is a highly arbitrary decision. Each county in the southern California coastal region, except for San Bernardino and Riverside Counties, is, for example, designated as a separate SMSA. Few would contend that six distinct metropolitan areas can be identified in southern California apart from the arbitrary conventions of the Census Bureau.

A similar problem exists in the designation of the units of government within a metropolitan area. Is a privately incorporated mutual land company rendering the usual range of municipal service for local inhabitants a "unit of government" or not? What about a fully urbanized area procuring municipal services through the instrumentality of an irrigation district? Is it a "municipality" or not?

Are the units of government participating in the "governance of metropolitan areas" limited to units of "local" government? If state police provide highway patrol services throughout a metropolitan area, are those state police forces an element in the governance of that metropolitan area? If a state highway department is responsible for planning, engineering, constructing, and maintaining state, U.S., and Interstate highways as the principal thoroughfares in a metropolitan area, is it a unit of government in a metropolitan area?

Similarly, are agencies of the federal government units in the government of metropolitan areas? Does the U.S. Postal Service, for example, render a public service in metropolitan areas? Does the U.S. Postal Service provide as satisfactory service *within* metropolitan areas as *among* metropolitan areas? If mail dispatched from Palo Alto, California, for example, is delivered more quickly to Cambridge, Massachusetts, than to Berkeley, California, we should be able to evaluate the performance of the Postal Service within a metropolitan area apart from its service to national users in different metropolitan centers. Does the organization of the Independent Postal Service indicate shortcomings in the intrametropolitan postal services performed by the U.S. Postal Service? Does the Independent Postal Service render a *public* service in metropolitan areas? Is it a unit of government in a metropolitan area? These questions can be reiterated for every type of service rendered by federal agencies for citizens who reside within metropolitan areas and for private and other public agencies that render equivalent services.

When we speak of councils of governments, do we mean only those agencies that are organized in reference to specific Federal statutes and that have proper names that can be appropriately capitalized as Councils of Governments? Is a "league of cities" or an "association of counties" the equivalent by definition of a council of governments? If not, how does a "council" differ from a "league" or an "association"? Is the Southern California Section of the League of California Cities a council of governments for the southern California metropolitan region? Is the Municipal Water Districts Section of the California Irrigation Districts Association or the Southern California Water Coordinating Conference a council of governments? Is the St. Louis County Association of Police Chiefs a council of governments? Need there be only *one* council of governments in each metropolitan area?

Nearly 50 years ago, the Southern California Section of the League of California Cities provided the organizational context in which numerous civic leaders in southern California initiated efforts to sponsor the Boulder Canyon project as a means for supplying water and electrical energy for various southern California municipalities. Legislation eventually enacted as the Metropolitan Water District Act was originally drafted by a committee of city attorneys sponsored by the Southern California Section of the League of California Cities. No single set of decisions has been more influential in shaping the growth of the southern California metropolitan region than those sponsored by the Southern California Section of the League of California Cities. Was this a part of "the political process" involved in the "governance" of the southern California metropolitan region? Were they participating in a "council" of governments?

This series of questions indicates that fundamental issues of language remain unresolved in the study of metropolitan governance. Presumably the language of scientific inquiry depends upon definitions that have reference to equivalent sets of events. Proper names rarely serve as appropriate proxies for definitions unless the act of naming is based upon a classification scheme devised for the purposes of arranging events into theoretically equivalent classes. The conventions of the Bureau of the Census are clearly unsatisfactory for defining metropolitan areas and for specifying units of government in metropolitan areas. The naming of federally financed and sponsored forums for consideration of interjurisdictional problems as Councils of Governments does not mean that these institutions are definitionally different from the hundreds of such forums that have existed on the U.S. local scene for many decades without federal sponsorship.

I doubt that these issues of language and points of reference will be resolved by stipulation in a workshop on metropolitan governance. Instead, we may be able to clarify why scholars pursue basically different approaches as they engage in inquiry into problems of metropolitan governance. If we can understand the basic differences in approach and the basic differences in the language that go with different theoretical orientations we may be in a position to identify critical points of disagreement. Where critical points of disagreement reflect conflicting or contradictory explanations regarding causal relationships between conditions and consequences, we have opportunities to clarify which approach offers the better explanation. Such clarification requires that considerable attention be paid to an *explicit* development of the theoretical orientations underlying the analysis of metropolitan problems. With the conscious use of explicitly derived theoretical inferences and carefully designed empirical studies, reforms can also be utilized as political experiments. The rejection of hypotheses based on methodologically sound research and carefully monitored reforms will eventually enable us to sort out some of the kernels of warrantable knowledge from the chaff of rhetoric and slogans.

Differences in Approach

Scholars who approach a complex subject from the vantage of different theoretical orientations will take hold of their subject in different ways. Scholars in the monocentric tradition, for example, have followed Woodrow Wilson to presume that the essential concern of a political scientist is to reveal the real depositories and essential machinery of power. They follow Wilson further in presuming that "There is always a centre of power . . . within any system of government." The task of a scholar then is to identify the following: (1) "Where in this system is that centre?"; (2) "In whose hands is [this] self-sufficient authority lodged?"; and (3) "Through what agency does that authority speak and act?" (Wilson 1885, 30). The formal repository of authority need not be identical with the effective center of power. Thus, the task of the scholar is to penetrate behind the facade of authority to find the essential machinery of power.

A scholar who relies upon the monocentrist presumption engages in a search for "a center of power." If he finds a candidate he can then explore the "opportunities" and "potentialities" for his candidate to become a "reality." If he finds none, he can express his despair at having found only chaos amid the fragmentation of authority and overlapping jurisdictions.

Once a monocentric presumption is abandoned a scholar is confronted with some serious difficulties in deciding how to take hold of this subject matter. A scholar who begins with a polycentric presumption cannot rely upon the expedient of using a government as his unit of analysis. He cannot presume that there will be "a center of power" in any system of government. Nor can he presume that the Bureau of the Census has identified the relevant "units of government" or other categories pertaining to his study.

Ultimately he is forced to use the individual as a basic unit of analysis. However, he need not presume that individuals are atomistic and fail to take account of interdependent relationships with other individuals. Instead, he can assume that individuals find themselves in situations or environmental conditions where they confront different structures of events.

Structures of events might be viewed as having the attributes of "goods" and/or "bads" when evaluated in terms of individual preferences. Such events might also be characterized by their divisibility or indivisibility when measured in terms of the capabilities of individual persons to exercise exclusive possession, control, or use of such events. Events that are highly divisible and are subject to exclusive possession, control, and use by individuals are the equivalent of private goods (and bads) in classical economics. Theories of externalities, common-pool resources, and public goods enable him to differentiate other structures of events that will confront individuals as they cope with the difficulties and opportunities in life.

A scholar in the polycentric tradition can further assume that any individual living in an organized society will also be confronted by specifiable sets of decision rules or decision structures. Decision rules assign both capabilities and constraints regarding an individual's choice of strategy in the pursuit of opportunities inherent in different structures of events or environmental conditions. A choice of strategy combined with the choice of others in relation to a specified state of affairs will "determine" outcomes. Outcomes can be viewed as the set of consequences that follows from the choice of strategies given (1) individuals; (2) structures of events; and (3) decision rules.

Outcomes can then be evaluated in relation to various criteria or standards of evaluation to measure performance. Efficiency can be used as one criterion or standard of evaluation to measure performance. The responsiveness of some specifiable sets of decision makers to the demands of other specifiable sets of decision makers can also be used as a measure of performance. Propensity for error might be another measure of performance. The "equity" or "justness" of the outcome might be developed into other criteria for evaluation (see Rawls 1971). If evaluative criteria can be developed into general measures of performance, then different patterns of organization or different institutional arrangements can be measured in relation to common standards of measurement or yardsticks.

Thus, the critical variables of concern to scholars in the polycentric tradition include (1) individuals; (2) decision rules; (3) sets of events; (4) outcomes; and (5) measures of performance. Each set of these five variables may include subsets of variables so that all possible combinations of structure relationships will require reference to a multidimensional matrix.

Various theories of social organization should enable scholars to draw upon a substantial structure of inferential reasoning about the consequences that will follow when individuals pursue strategies consistent with their interests in light of different types of decision structures in order to realize opportunities inherent in differently structured sets of events. Economic theory, for example, enables us to infer that individuals in market structures can pursue their individual advantage and enhance social welfare in relation to some events (private goods) with a high degree of success but will experience serious frustrations and failures in dealing with other sets of events (externalities, common-pool resources, and public goods). The theoretical analyses of a number of economists, political scientists, and sociologists enables us to use a theory of bureaucracy in much the same way to derive quite different results.

Once we can conceptualize how individuals will choose strategies in light of the opportunities available to them in differently structured events with reference to different sets of decision rules, we can begin to specify the consequences for each set of permutations. We then have the necessary foundation for specifying the behavioral characteristics for aggregations of individuals who are organized into different types of collectivities. Collectivities can then be used as units of analysis in the context of a different arena where diverse collectivities of individuals will again pursue opportunities in the context of differently structured events and in reference to different sets of decision rules. We would expect individuals organized as "political parties" under different electoral rules to associate together in different ways, and we would expect those parties to behave differently under different sets of rules for "win-the-government games." We would also expect patterns of coalition formation for political parties seeking to win elections to be different than patterns of coalition formation for business firms seeking to dominate markets. This mode of analysis can be extended to patterns of governance in metropolitan areas, to international affairs, or to any other pattern of human relationship if we can conceptualize circumstances where individuals are confronted with a choice of strategy where each course of action becomes a potential move in a series of simultaneous games. The first variable—individuals—can now be extended to a much larger set of units at different levels of analysis.

The complexity of relationships involved in the government of metropolitan areas is such that mortal human beings can never observe the "whole picture." Anyone who attempts to "see" the "whole picture" will "see" only what is in the "eyes" or the "mind" of the beholder. In such circumstances, we would expect different scholars to paint different word pictures about metropolitan government. Such scholarship is an art form reflecting the images and fantasies of the beholder rather than the world of events that manifests itself in the discrete affairs of people comprising the populations of metropolitan areas. The world of events cannot be known in its finite detail.

As a consequence, research that is worth doing will depend upon limited probes that seek to clarify specific theoretical issues. Findings from such research will be trivial unless there has been an effort to array evidence so that a hypothesis can be rejected. Arraying evidence that can be used to reject a hypothesis is much easier if a scholar can have reference to different explanatory theories and can find circumstances that provide a critical test of the contradictions inherent in different theoretical explanations. It is this circumstance that provides a challenging opportunity for the generation of empirical research being undertaken in the 1970s. We may well be on the threshold where political science becomes an intellectual discipline grounded in analytical theory and when empirical research can be used to mobilize evidence for rejecting some of the propositions that now pass for political science. If nothing can be rejected the aggregate accumulation can only be trash. Theory can be improved only when erroneous conceptions can be abandoned and when weak conceptions can be replaced by stronger conceptions.

Arraying Evidence on Critical Issues

With basic differences in theoretical perspectives, scholars will adopt quite different orientations to their subject matter, will use different concepts and languages, and will pursue their inquiries in quite different ways. These differences will not be resolved by discussion and deliberation alone. Instead, efforts should be made to take advantage of differences in approaches to clarify essential issues. By arraying alternative explanations and expectations, we can then attempt to undertake critical tests where divergent theories imply contradictory conclusions. The theory that has the weaker explanatory capability presumably would give way in the course of time to the theory with the stronger explanatory capability.

Given the circumstance that great structural diversity exists within and among metropolitan areas, we have rich "laboratories" for the conduct of carefully designed comparative urban research. In many metropolitan areas, the center city is a highly integrated political jurisdiction providing numerous services for city residents. The center city approximates a monocentric solution for all residents within its jurisdiction. Within the same metropolitan area, citizens living in the suburbs may be served by large numbers of jurisdictions with some aspects of overlap among jurisdictions. Such areas manifest substantial polycentricity. Given neighborhoods of similar density, spatial location, and socioeconomic status served by different types of institutional arrangements, evidence can be arrayed regarding a range of critical issues. Some examples might include research to array evidence regarding the following propositions.

1. *A high degree of polycentricity or fragmentation will be associated with a wide range in the quality of services and service levels in different parts of a metropolitan area.* As it happens, scholars working in both the monocentric and polycentric traditions might adopt this proposition as a working hypothesis. However, a monocentrist would expect to find variation in service levels *among* jurisdictions within a metropolitan area but not *within* a particular jurisdiction. A polycentrist would expect to find variation in service levels *among* jurisdictions where individuals have distinct preferences for different types or styles of service and where they can move to those

jurisdictions that most closely approximate their preferred mix of public goods and services (Tiebout 1956). A polycentrist would also expect that the magnitude of these variations would be dampened by competitive rivalry among jurisdictions regarding levels of taxation and acquisition of financial base.

A polycentrist would further expect wide variation in service levels *within* large jurisdictions due to the effective capability of wealthy and well-educated citizens to articulate demands to central decision makers and the failure of the poor and uneducated to do so. Large bureaucratic establishments will also contribute serious institutional weaknesses in loss of information and control over street-level services. Radical variations in service levels and the quality of services will, as a consequence, exist among different neighborhoods *within* a single large centralized city. By placing both theoretical traditions side by side, a much stronger research design can be constructed and used to compare differences in service levels *among and within* different jurisdictions serving the same metropolitan area for different types of services.

Since most students of metropolitan governance have had occasions to observe diverse neighborhoods in large cities as well as suburban communities, they should have some crude impressions whether unification of authority into a single unit of government will yield uniformity in the quality of service and in the level of service among all neighborhoods within a large city. Or, will there be radical variations in the quality of service and in service levels among different neighborhoods of the large city? From my own casual observations, I assume that the answer is obvious. I am, however, puzzled by my failure to explain the persistence of beliefs that are contrary to readily available evidence and casual observation.

2. *A high degree of polycentricity or fragmentation is positively associated with racial segregation and segregation by social class.* Monocentrists would expect to find the degree of racial and economic segregation to be greater in suburban areas than in the center city. From the Tiebout hypothesis, polycentrists would expect individuals to express their preferences by voting with their feet when diverse jurisdictions exist in a metropolitan area (Tiebout 1956). If preferences are affected by racial biases, polycentrists would expect these biases to be expressed in a polycentric system. However, a polycentrist would also look at the possibility that other arenas are more crucial in affecting segregation than the existence of political jurisdictions per se. A critical question is whether housing and realty markets are not the relevant arenas affecting segregation. If such were the case, one would expect to find as much racial and social class segregation among neighborhoods in large cities as among suburban jurisdictions unless appropriate actions had been taken to exercise control over relevant housing and realty transactions.

Unfortunately, the Census Bureau does not have data organized by neighborhoods for large cities. However, if neighborhoods can be identified, data can be aggregated from census blocks and cross-jurisdictional comparisons can be made between communities in suburban areas and neighborhoods within central cities. Again, casual observation leads me to note substantial racial and social class segregation in center cities and to wonder whether more intense segregation exists in suburban areas.

3. *A high degree of polycentricity or fragmentation will lead to increased costs in public services rendered.* An early tradition among students of public administration directly associated efficiency with hierarchy so that perfection in hierarchical organization was assumed to be the basis for building efficiency into the administrative structure of government. Scholars in this tradition would expect a high degree of polycentricity to lead to increasing costs for services rendered. Studies by a number of political economists have challenged that presumption and have advanced the thesis that economies of scale will vary with factors of production, with type of good or services produced, and with factors of consumption. As a consequence they would not expect that a high degree of polycentricity will necessarily lead to increased costs in rendering public services. . . .

4. *A high degree of polycentricity or fragmentation evokes an unequal distribution of financial resources and burdens between central cities and suburbs.* An unequal distribution of financial resources would be expected among diverse sets of local jurisdictions. Whether a net inequality exists between central cities and suburban communities to the disadvantage of the central city is an empirical question subject to findings of fact so long as comparable standards of evaluation and assessment exist. The *Serrano* case, for example, arose in Baldwin Park, a poor suburban community in eastern Los Angeles County. The assessed valuation backing each student in the city of Los Angeles is equivalent to the average for the State of California as a whole and substantially greater than that in Baldwin Park. The center city of Los Angeles presumably will not benefit if the guidelines in the *Serrano* decision were implemented. The assessed valuation per student in the city and county of San Francisco is roughly equivalent to that in Beverly Hills—the epitome of wealthy suburbia. The redistribution effect of *Serrano* will mean a loss of revenue for San Francisco to the benefit of poor suburban and rural areas.

High levels of expenditure are, however, not necessarily associated with high levels or qualities of service or with a high level of citizen satisfaction. Expenditures for police services in the city of Chicago, for example, are relatively high even in poor neighborhoods within the city. Equalization of financial resources in the city of Chicago has increased expenditures on police services in black neighborhoods, but the services rendered are no better when measured by victimization rates or citizen satisfaction than those rendered in the most impoverished black suburban communities. These black suburban communities spend less than 10 cents on police services for every dollar spent by the city of Chicago in comparable black neighborhoods (E. Ostrom and Whitaker 1971).

Reference to evidence and to observation through comparative studies conducted within structurally differentiated metropolitan areas can be used to reject a number of widely held beliefs about life in large urban areas. Suburbs are not populated exclusively by affluent white bigots. Segregation by race, ethnic groupings, and wealth does occur among neighborhoods within central cities. Radical variations in service levels and in qualities of service do occur among neighborhoods within central cities. The redistribution of tax resources within central cities has not eliminated radical variations in the quality of public services or in the conditions of life among different neighborhoods within central cities.

Reforms as Political Experiments

Empirical research organized to reject hypotheses, and incidentally to dispel popular myths and impressions, will contribute toward policy analysis by challenging some of the presumptions inherent in proposals to solve "the urban crisis" by organizing each metropolitan area into one overarching regional unit of government. However, much more substantial analytical capabilities need to be mobilized both in diagnosing the conditions that have generated the current discontent and in considering alternative possibilities as a basis for alleviating that discontent.

Since any diagnosis of a problematical situation is based upon a body of knowledge that associates causal conditions with resultant consequences, we would expect policy analysts drawing upon different theories of organization to make different diagnostic assessments and to prescribe different policy solutions. It is these circumstances that make important demands upon the intellectual capabilities of policy analysts and create an opportunity to use reforms as political experiments.

While any one analyst can attempt to use diverse forms of theoretical analysis, he will probably have greater skill in applying one form of analysis. In such circumstances, the analytical skills of different scholars need to be mobilized so that their diagnostic assessments and the predictive inferences following from their policy recommendations can be compared.

For example, a high degree of unanimity exists among students of urban affairs that serious "ills" afflict *large* center cities. However, this situation gives rise to immediate disagreement regarding different diagnostic assessments and different policy solutions based upon radically different *explanations* of causal relationships.

One approach to the problem is to identify the ills of the center city with growing black populations in central cities and to the conditions of extreme poverty existing among urban blacks. The existence of many suburban areas, this explanation alleges, has enabled the well-to-do to "escape" to the suburbs and to disassociate themselves from "responsibility" for the ills of the center city. The resources of the wealthy suburbs do not contribute to the solution of center city problems that affect the society as a whole. Regionalization of metropolitan government so that the prerogatives of government can be exercised over the whole metropolitan area is viewed as a necessary condition for removing the "ills" of center cities and restoring health to the urban scene.

An alternative approach that I would take in analyzing this problem would identify serious social pathologies as existing in center cities. The ills are associated with ghetto areas populated by blacks and other impoverished groups. However, my diagnostic assessment of these conditions would identify the problems of institutional failure with the political structure of very large urban centers. Where populations of a million or more persons are governed by reference to a single unit of government, the voice exercised by any one individual becomes irrelevant to an expression of preferences for an appropriate mix of public goods and services and to an articulation of demands to procure the services of officials for coping with problems of social interdependency. The most impoverished and least educated populations will have the least voice in relation to these political authorities. Bureaucracies will be dominated by career "professionals" who assume that they minister to the needs of "laymen." The discrepancy between public rhetoric and public performance will, under these conditions, assume radical dimensions. In short, many of the critical problems in core cities derive from institutional weaknesses and institutional failures that are internal to the governmental structure of center cities themselves.

Students in this tradition of analysis will, as a consequence of their diagnostic assessments, look to remedies that bear upon the organization of neighborhoods and communities within large cities. Organizing voluntary enterprises to provide public goods and services will involve very high costs to entrepreneurs unless some form of coercive sanction can be mobilized. When communities are tyrannized and victimized by public authorities and professional administrators, patterns of "voluntary" organization may arise where sanctions are mobilized outside the law and outlaw societies emerge. Struggles between outlaw societies and police will evoke a crisis of "law and order."

In this circumstance, an institutional arrangement that would enable communities and neighborhoods to organize public instrumentalities for collective action is an alternative to the escalation of latent warfare between police forces and the soldier societies of ghetto communities. Community control, neighborhood government, or the organization of urban villages downtown afford potential remedies. In short, the ills of core cities require more polycentricity for their solution, not less (see Altschuler 1970; Dahl 1967; Elazar 1971; Horowitz 1970; Jacobs 1961; Kotler 1969; Press 1963; Waskow 1970).

However, the architecture of polycentric political arrangements does *not* imply that "balkanization" be carried to the neighborhood level in disregard for essential interdependencies among diverse communities of interest. The modern phenomenon of poverty in affluent societies is not a product of social interdependencies confined to particular neighborhoods, to particular cities, or to particular metropolitan areas.

Since the Full Employment Act of 1946, conditions of "economic prosperity" and "full employment" have become the objects of macroeconomic regulation undertaken by the federal or national government in the United States. As early as 1949, Joseph A. Schumpeter called attention to difficulties that would necessarily follow from efforts to maintain "full employment" (Schumpeter 1950). Conditions of full employment will be accompanied by a high level of demand for labor. If the economy were rigged to sustain a high demand for labor, the bargaining power of organized labor will be increased. Organized labor will have an opportunity to drive wages up. Where large corporations exercised power over product markets, wage increases can occur that exceed increases in the productivity of labor. Costs will then be passed on to consumers in the form of higher prices. Such price increases will generate a strong factor of inflation into the national economy.

This inflationary factor unsupported by commensurate increases in productivity does not enhance efficiency. Rather, this type of inflation is a generator of economic redistribution from those who have little or no market or bargaining power to those who have substantial market or bargaining power. Some of the population including elements of organized labor will prosper at the expense of other elements of the population who experience a serious decline in economic welfare. They have experienced increasing poverty amid growing affluence.

If we assume that Schumpeter's warning is correct, it does not follow that either regional metropolitan governments, city governments, or neighborhood or village governments can successfully cope with these problems of poverty in an affluent society. Nor does Schumpeter's warning imply that macroeconomic controls should necessarily be abandoned. If we assume that efforts at macroeconomic regulation have realized a *net* advantage for economic prosperity or aggregate social welfare, we may still be confronted with a circumstance where those who have been the primary beneficiaries should be expected to cover the costs of deprivations imposed upon those who have suffered from the redistributive consequences of inflation.

Presumably, current distribution of income is a crude indicator of who is participating in the new prosperity. The federal government by its preponderant position as a taxer of incomes is in a position to derive a significant share of the new prosperity that has been created as a consequence of its own macro-economic policies. It follows from this analysis that the federal government is the appropriate instrumentality for taking corrective measures to compensate for the costs of inflation that its policies have engendered. Transferring these burdens to the level of local governments within metropolitan areas to be borne by property-tax payers is an inappropriate solution.

Those who propose regionalization of government in metropolitan areas as a means of alleviating the ills of the large center cities do so on the basis of an explanatory theory that associates causal conditions with resultant consequences. Where the unification of government occurs in a metropolitan region an opportunity is created to estimate the consequences of such an experiment. Such experimental situations can be compared with other areas not so organized.

Those who propose to increase substantially the degree of polycentricity within large cities would predict that a monocentric solution will only exacerbate the urban crisis. However, they would also argue that increased polycentricity in large cities will not directly alleviate the phenomenon of poverty in affluent societies. Economic regulatory programs of the federal government have served the interests of the powerful to exploit the powerless. Programs to compensate for the deprivations suffered by the poor can be feasibly undertaken by the federal government and not local units of government. Few would contend that local units of government are the appropriate instrumentalities to undertake macroeconomic regulatory programs to realize prosperity and full employment. Local units of government, by the same reasoning, are not the appropriate instrumentalities to *correct institutional weaknesses* inherent in *federal* efforts at macroeconomic regulation. Local units of government will be no more successful in combating poverty than individual union leaders or individual businessmen will be successful in fighting inflation.

If reform is approached as a problem in political experimentation, then advantage can be taken of differing diagnostic assessments and differing policy prescriptions. Where any given policy prescription has been pursued as a remedy, the course of reform can be observed as a test of the conception being acted upon. If reforms are carefully monitored, we may then be in a position to reach a tentative evaluation of the explanatory theory used to guide reform efforts. Such observations can be best organized and conducted when there is an awareness of alternative possibilities and of different inferential hypotheses that can be derived from different theoretical analyses. In time, we may be able to penetrate the veil created by the illusion of chaos and comprehend the regularities produced by the "invisible hand." These opportunities will be forgone if reform is viewed as a struggle where analysts attempt to mobilize forces and seek recourse to the slogans and rhetoric of warfare.

REFERENCES

This list includes a few of the references that are relevant to polycentricity in different realms of organization.

Alexander, Christopher. 1964. *Notes on the Synthesis of Form.* Cambridge, MA: Harvard University Press.

———. 1965. "A City Is Not a Tree." *Architectural Forum* 122 (April/May): 58–62.

Altschuler, Alan A. 1970. *Community Control: The Black Demand for Participation in Large American Cities.* New York: Pegasus.

Ashby, W. Ross. 1960. *Design for a Brain: The Origin of Adaptive Behavior.* 2d ed. New York: John Wiley and Sons.

———. 1962. "Principles of the Self-Organizing System." In *Principles of Self-Organization,* ed. H. Von Foerster and G. W. Zopf, 255–78. New York: Macmillan.

Austin, John. [1832] 1955. *The Province of Jurisprudence Determined,* ed. H. L. A. Hart. London: Weidenfeld and Nicolson.

Ayres, Robert U., and Allen V. Kneese. 1969. "Production, Consumption and Externalities." *American Economic Review* 59 (June): 282–97.

Bain, Joe S., Richard E. Caves, and Julius Margolis. 1966. *Northern California's Water Industry: The Comparative Efficiency of Public Enterprise in Developing a Scarce Resource.* Baltimore: Johns Hopkins University Press for Resources for the Future, Inc.

Beck, Henry. 1970. "The Rationality of Redundancy." *Comparative Politics,* 3 (January): 469–78.

Bish, Robert L. 1968. "A Comment on V. P. Duggal's 'Is There an Unseen Hand in Government?' " *Annals of Public and Co-operative Economy* 39 (January-March): 89–94.

———. 1969. "The American Public Economy as a Single Firm: Reply to Duggal." *Annals of Public and Co-operative Economy* 40 (July/September): 361–65.

———. 1971. *The Public Economy of Metropolitan Areas.* Chicago: Markham Publishing Company.

Bish, Robert, and Robert Warren. 1972. "Scale and Monopoly Problems in Urban Government Services." *Urban Affairs Quarterly* 8 (September): 97–122.

Buchanan, James M. 1960. *Fiscal Theory and Political Economy.* Chapel Hill, NC: University of North Carolina Press.

———. 1967. *Public Finance in Democratic Process: Fiscal Institutions and Individual Choice.* Chapel Hill, NC: University of North Carolina Press.

———. 1968. *The Demand and Supply of Public Goods.* Chicago: Rand McNally.

———. 1969. *Cost and Choice: An Inquiry in Economic Theory.* Chicago: Markham.

———. 1970. "Public Goods and Public Bads." In *Financing the Metropolis,* ed. John P. Crecine, 51–71. Beverly Hills, CA: Sage.

Buchanan, James M., and Gordon Tullock. 1962. *The Calculus of Consent: Logical Foundations of Constitutional Democracy.* Ann Arbor, MI: University of Michigan Press.

Campbell, Donald T. 1969. "Reforms as Experiments." *American Psychologist* 24

(April): 409–29.

Committee for Economic Development. 1966. *Modernizing Local Government.* New York: Committee for Economic Development.

———. 1970. *Reshaping Government in Metropolitan Areas.* New York: Committee for Economic Development.

Crouch, Winston, and Beatrice Dinerman. 1964. *Southern California Metropolis: A Study in Development of Government for a Metropolitan Area.* Berkeley: University of California Press.

Dahl, Robert A. 1967. "The City in the Future of Democracy." *American Political Science Review* 61 (December): 953–70.

Dales, J. H. 1968. *Pollution, Property and Prices.* Toronto: University of Toronto Press.

Duggal, V. P. 1966. "Is There an Unseen Hand in Government?" *Annals of Public and Cooperative Economy* 37 (April/June): 145-50.

Elazar, Daniel J. 1966. *American Federalism: A View from the States.* New York: Thomas Y. Crowell.

———. 1971. "Community Self-Government and the Crisis in American Politics." *Ethics* 81 (January): 91–106.

Follett, M. P. [1924] 1951. *Creative Experience.* New York: Peter Smith.

Friesema, H. Paul. 1966. "The Metropolis and the Maze of Local Government." *Urban Affairs Quarterly* 2 (December): 68–90.

———. 1971. *Metropolitan Political Structure: Intergovernmental Relations and Political Integration in the Quad-Cities.* Iowa City: University of Iowa Press.

Gregg, Phillip M. 1972. "Reformulation of Theory in Policy Study." Ph.D. diss., Indiana University.

Grodzins, Morton. 1966. *The American System,* ed. Daniel J. Elazar. Chicago: Rand McNally.

Hamilton, Alexander, John Jay, and James Madison. [1788] n.d. *The Federalist.* New York: Modern Library.

Hawley, Amos H., and Basil G. Zimmer. 1970. *The Metropolitan Community: Its People and Government.* Beverly Hills, CA: Sage.

Hayek, F. A. 1960. *The Constitution of Liberty.* Chicago: University of Chicago Press.

———. 1966. "The Principles of a Liberal Order." *Il Politico* 31 (December): 601–17.

———. 1967. "The Constitution of a Liberal State." *Il Politico* 32 (September): 455–60.

Hirsch, Werner. 1964. "Local Versus Areawide Urban Government Services." *National Tax Journal* 17 (December): 331–39.

———. 1968. "The Supply of Urban Public Services." In *Issues in Urban Economics,* ed. Harvey S. Perloff and Lowden Wingo, Jr., 435–76. Baltimore: Johns Hopkins University Press.

Hobbes, Thomas. [1651] 1960. *Leviathan or the Matter, Forme and Power of a Commonwealth Eccliesiasticall and Civil,* ed. Michael Oakeshott. Oxford: Basil Blackwell.

Holden, Matthew, Jr. 1964. "The Governance of the Metropolis as a Problem in Diplomacy." *Journal of Politics* 26 (August): 627–47.

Horowitz, Irving Louis. 1970. "'Separate but Equal': Revolution and Counter-Revolution in the American City." *Social Problems* 17 (winter): 294–312.

IsHak, Samir. 1972. "Consumers' Perception of Police Performance. Consolidation vs. Deconcentration: The Case of Grand Rapids, Michigan Metropolitan Area." Ph.D. diss., Indiana University.

Jacob, Philip E., and James V. Toscano. 1964. *The Integration of Political Communities.* Philadelphia: J. B. Lippincott.

Jacobs, Jane. 1961. *The Death and Life of Great American Cities.* New York: Vintage Books.

Kotler, Milton. 1969. *Neighborhood Government: The Local Foundations of Community Life.* Indianapolis: Bobbs-Merrill.

Landau, Martin. 1969. "Redundance, Rationality and the Problem of Duplication and Overlap." *Public Administration Review* 29 (July/August): 346–58.

Lasswell, Harold D., and Abraham Kaplan. 1950. *Power and Society. A Framework for Political Inquiry.* New Haven: Yale University Press.

Lindblom, Charles E. 1955. "Bargaining: The Hidden Hand in Government." Research Memorandum RM-1434-RC. Santa Monica, CA: RAND Corporation.

———. 1965. *The Intelligence of Democracy: Decision Making through Mutual Adjustment.* New York: Free Press.

Long, Norton E. 1958. "The Local Community as an Ecology of Games." *American Journal of Sociology* 44 (November): 251–61.

———. 1962. *The Polity.* Chicago: Rand McNally.

———. 1970. "Rigging the Market for Public Goods." In *Organizations and Clients: Essays in the Sociology of Service,* ed. William R. Rosengren and Mark Lefton. Columbus, OH: Charles E. Merrill.

Loveman, Brian. 1969. *The Logic of Political Corruption.* Bloomington: Indiana University, Department of Political Science, Studies in Political Theory and Policy Analysis.

McKean, Roland N. 1965. "The Unseen Hand in Government." *American Economic Review* 55 (June): 496–506.

Niskanen, William A., Jr. 1971. *Bureaucracy and Representative Government.* Chicago: Aldine-Atherton.

Olson, Mancur. 1965. *The Logic of Collective Action.* Cambridge, MA: Harvard University Press.

———. 1969. "The Principle of 'Fiscal Equivalence': The Division of Responsibility among Different Levels of Government." *American Economic Review* 59 (May): 479–87.

Ostrom, Elinor. 1968. "Some Postulated Effects of Learning on Constitutional Behavior." *Public Choice* 5 (Fall): 87–104.

———. 1971. "Institutional Arrangements and the Measurement of Policy Consequences: Applications to Evaluating Police Performance." *Urban Affairs Quarterly* 6 (June): 447–75.

Ostrom, Elinor, William Baugh, Richard Guarasci, Roger Parks, and Gordon P. Whitaker. 1971. *Community Organization and the Provision of Police Services.*

Bloomington: Indiana University, Department of Political Science, Studies in Political Theory and Policy Analysis.

Ostrom, Elinor, Roger B. Parks, and Gordon P. Whitaker. 1973. "Do We Really Want to Consolidate Urban Police Forces? A Reappraisal of Some Old Assumptions." *Public Administration Review* 33 (September/October): 423–33.

Ostrom, Elinor, and Gordon P. Whitaker. 1971. "Black Citizens and the Police: Some Effects of Community Control." Paper prepared for presentation at the annual meeting of the American Political Science Association, Chicago, September 7–11.

———. 1973. "Does Local Community Control of Police Make a Difference? Some Preliminary Findings." *American Journal of Political Science* 17 (1) (February): 48–76. (Chapter 8 in this volume.)

Ostrom, Vincent. 1968. "Water Resource Development: Some Problems in Economic and Political Analysis of Public Policy." In *Political Science and Public Policy,* ed. Austin Ranney, 123-50. Chicago: Markham.

———. 1969. "Operational Federalism: Organization for the Provision of Public Services in the American Federal System." *Public Choice* 6 (spring): 1–17.

———. 1971. "Institutional Arrangements for Water Resource Development." Prepared for the National Water Commission. Springfield, VA: National Technical Information Service, Accession No. PB207314.

———. 1987. *The Political Theory of a Compound Republic: Designing the American Experiment.* 2d rev. ed. San Francisco, CA: ICS Press.

———. 1989. *The Intellectual Crisis in American Public Administration.* 2nd ed. Tuscaloosa: University of Alabama Press.

Ostrom, Vincent, and Elinor Ostrom. 1965. "A Behavioral Approach to the Study of Intergovernmental Relations." *Annals of the American Academy of Political and Social Science* 359 (May): 137–46. (Chapter 4 in this volume.)

———. 1970. "Conditions of Legal and Political Feasibility." In *Natural Resource Systems Models in Decision Making,* ed. Gerrit H. Toebes, 191–208. Lafayette, IN: Purdue University, Water Resources Research Center.

———. 1971. "Public Choice: A Different Approach to the Study of Public Administration." *Public Administration Review* 31 (March/April): 203–16. (Reprinted in Michael D. McGinnis, ed., *Polycentric Games and Institutions* [Ann Arbor: University of Michigan Press, 1999].)

Ostrom, Vincent, Charles M. Tiebout, and Robert Warren. 1961. "The Organization of Government in Metropolitan Areas: A Theoretical Inquiry." *American Political Science Review* 55 (December): 831–42. (Chapter 1 in this volume.)

Polanyi, Michael. 1951. *The Logic of Liberty: Reflections and Rejoinders.* Chicago: University of Chicago Press.

Press, Charles. 1963. "The Cities within a Great City: A Decentralist Approach to Centralization." *Centennial Review* 7: 113–30.

Rawls, John. 1963. "Constitutional Liberty and the Concept of Justice." In *Nomos VI: Justice,* ed. Carl J. Friedrich and John W. Chapman, 98–125. New York: Atherton Press.

———. 1971. *A Theory of Justice.* Cambridge, MA: Harvard University Press.

Schumpeter, Joseph A. 1950. *Capitalism, Socialism and Democracy.* 3d ed. New York: Harper and Row.

Smith, Paul. 1965. "The Games of Community Politics." *Midwest Journal of Political Science* 9 (February): 37–60.

Sproule-Jones, Mark. 1972. "Strategic Tensions in the Scale of Political Analysis: An Essay for Philomphalasceptics." *British Journal of Political Science* 1: 173–91.

Stigler, George S. 1962. "The Tenable Range of Functions of Local Government." In *Private Wants and Public Needs: Issues Surrounding the Size and Scope of Government Expenditure,* ed. Edmund S. Phelps. New York: W. W. Norton.

Thompson, James D. 1967. *Organization in Action.* New York: McGraw-Hill.

Tiebout, Charles M. 1956. "A Pure Theory of Local Expenditure." *Journal of Political Economy* 44 (October): 416–24.

Tocqueville, Alexis de. [1835 and 1840] 1945. *Democracy in America.* 2 vols. Ed. Phillip Bradley. New York: Alfred A. Knopf.

———. [1856] 1955. *The Old Regime and the French Revolution.* Garden City, NJ: Doubleday, Anchor Books.

Tolley, G. S. 1969. *The Welfare Economics of City Bigness.* Urban Economics Report No. 31. Chicago: University of Chicago Press.

Tullock, Gordon. 1965. *The Politics of Bureaucracy.* Washington, DC: Public Affairs Press.

———. 1969. "Federalism: The Problem of Scale." *Public Choice* 6 (spring): 19–29.

———. 1970. *Private Wants, Public Means: An Economic Analysis of the Desirable Scope of Government.* New York: Basic Books.

———. 1971. *The Logic of the Law.* New York: Basic Books.

U.S. Congress, Joint Economic Committee, Subcommittee on Economy in Government. 1969. *A Compendium of Papers on the Analysis and Evaluation of Public Expenditures: The PPB System.* 3 vols. Washington, DC: U.S. Government Printing Office.

Vile, M. J. C. 1967. *Constitutionalism and the Separation of Powers.* Oxford: Oxford University Press.

Wagner, Richard E. 1971. *The Fiscal Organization of American Federalism: Description, Analysis, Reform.* Chicago: Markham.

Warren, Robert O. 1964. "A Municipal Services Market Model of Metropolitan Organization." *Journal of the American Institute of Planners* 30 (August): 193–204.

———. 1966. *Government in Metropolitan Regions: A Reappraisal of Fractionated Political Organization.* Davis, CA: Institute of Governmental Affairs, University of California.

Waskow, Arthur I. 1970. *Running Riot.* New York: Herder and Herder.

Weschler, Louis F. 1968. *Water Resource Management: The Orange County Experience.* Davis, CA: University of California, Institute of Public Affairs.

Weschler, Louis F., and Robert Warren. 1970. "Consumption Costs and Production Costs in the Provision of Antipoverty Goods." Paper delivered at the sixty-sixth annual meeting of the American Political Science Association, Los Angeles, California, September 8–12.

Wildavsky, Aaron. 1966. "The Political Economy of Efficiency." *Public Administra-*

tion Review 26 (December): 292–310.

Williams, Oliver P., Herold Herman, Charles S. Liebman, and Thomas R. Dye. 1965. *Suburban Differences and Metropolitan Politics*. Philadelphia: University of Pennsylvania Press.

Wilson, Woodrow. 1885. *Congressional Government: A Study in American Politics*. Boston: Houghton, Mifflin.

Wood, Robert C. 1961. *1400 Governments*. Garden City, NJ: Doubleday, Anchor Books.

CHAPTER 6

Metropolitan Reform: Propositions Derived from Two Traditions

Elinor Ostrom

Cries for reform and change are frequently heard concerning problems occurring in U.S. urban areas. While the existence of grave problems tells us
that reform is needed, it does not tell us what kind of reform will lead to
amelioration of problems. Reforms can make things worse as well as making
them better.[1] One purpose of this essay is to attempt to isolate the theoretical
structure implicit in the traditional metropolitan reform movement so that
empirical research can be organized to examine the warrantability of the
propositions contained therein. A second purpose of the essay is to pose an alternative theoretical structure derived from the work of political economists.

The elucidation of alternative theoretical structures may help guide future research efforts toward ascertaining which of these theoretical structures
(or possibly others) provides a better explanation for the relationship among
variables such as the size of governmental units and their multiplicity in a
metropolitan area, and variables such as output, efficiency, equal distribution
of costs, responsibility of public officials, and citizen participation. With a
warrantable explanation for changes in these variables, reforms can be devised that will produce desired, rather than undesired, outcomes.[2] In addition
to the preceding, this essay will also (1) discuss the need for developing
agreed-upon definitions of terms and their operationalizations; and (2) present findings from a few studies that challenge the empirical warrantability of
some of the propositions elucidated in the first section.

Originally published in *Social Science Quarterly* 53 (December 1972): 474–93. Reprinted
by permission of the University of Texas Press and the author.

Author's note: Revision of a paper presented at the annual meeting of the Society for the
Study of Social Problems, August 1971. The author gratefully acknowledges support from the
National Science Foundation, Grant No. GS-27383, and from the Center for Studies of Metro-
politan Problems of the National Institute of Mental Health, Grant No. 5 ROI MH19911. I am
deeply appreciative of the comments and suggestions made by William Baugh, Vincent
Ostrom, Nancy Neubert, Roger Parks, Dennis Smith, and Gordon Whitaker.

The Traditional Conception of "the" Urban Problem

For more than a half century, most political scientists, urban planners, and many other social scientists writing about urban areas have agreed that "the" urban problem is the existence of a large number of independent public jurisdictions within a single metropolitan area. A metropolitan region has been viewed as one large community tied together by many economic and social relationships but artificially divided by imposed governmental units (see, e.g., Hawley and Zimmer 1970, 2; Institute for Local Self Government 1970; see also Friesema 1966, 69). The basic textbook on U.S. city government during the 1940s and 1950s describes the development of local governments as being woven "piecemeal and without general plan by local groups to meet transient needs; the web of local boundaries spreads unevenly and most chaotically over the land" (Anderson and Weidner 1950, 169). In a report released in February 1970, the Committee for Economic Development argued that

> the present arrangement of overlapping local units is not serving the people well. Citizens in metropolitan areas are confronted by a confusing maze of many—possibly a dozen—jurisdictions, each with its own bureaucratic labyrinth. This baffling array of local units had made it difficult for citizens—the disadvantaged particularly—to gain access to public services and to acquire a voice in decision making.[3]

Since the turn of the century, many scholars have participated in a reform movement that has attempted to build a different type of governmental structure in large metropolitan areas. Participants in this tradition have not always agreed on all aspects of their description of and prescriptions for "the" metropolitan problem (i.e., too many governmental units). However, enough consistency in their recommendations for change exists to talk about a single tradition.[4] In their attempts to reform institutional arrangements so as to achieve their objectives, metropolitan reformers also share a relatively consistent, although implicit, underlying theoretical structure. In a discussion of the efforts of one team of social scientists to prepare a reform proposal for the greater St. Louis area, Scott Greer summarizes the working hypotheses of that group. In his words:

> It was . . . hypothesized that this congery of heterogeneous and overlapping governmental units would produce these results:
>
> 1) great variation in output, or service levels, among the different units,
> 2) great variations in the efficiency, or cost benefit ratio, among the units,
> 3) a generally low level of some services throughout the area, due to

the deleterious effects of poor services in one governmental unit upon the services in other, interdependent units. . . .

Finally, it was hypothesized that size of governmental units would have no relationship to the vitality of the local political process" (Greer 1961, 193).

Greer indicates that the propositions sketched in above "were not initially stated as hypotheses; *their validity was assumed, for they were part of the over-all ideology of the movement to save the cities"* (ibid., my emphasis).

Based upon similar working hypotheses, proponents of the metropolitan reform tradition have consistently recommended basic institutional changes in metropolitan areas. Most metropolitan reformers have recommended that

as far as possible in each major urban area *there should be only one local government.* . . . A second point upon which agreement is almost complete is that *the voters should elect only the important, policy-making officers* and that these should be few in number. . . . Most reformers are also anxious to see *the complete abolition* of the separation of powers in local government. . . . At the same time, however, . . . the functions of legislation and control on the one hand are so distinct from that of administration . . . that *those who do the work of administration should* be a separate group of men and women, especially trained and adequately compensated for their work . . . Furthermore, the *administration should be organized as a single integrated system* upon the hierarchical principle, tapering upward and culminating in a single chief executive officer. . . .[5]

Another theme of considerable importance in the work of metropolitan reformers is a concern for a more equal distribution of the costs of urban services throughout a metropolitan area. Jurisdictional lines are considered to be arbitrary boundaries that protect rich suburban residents from the necessity of paying for the costs of services provided by the center city. Since residents of suburban communities surrounding a center city live in the metropolitan area, it is assumed that services provided by the center city spill over and benefit all who live within the area. Consequently, reformers have argued that all residents in the metropolitan area should bear an equal share of these costs (see Lineberry 1970).

Thousands of books, reports, and articles have been written in this tradition. Specific proposals for metropolitan "reform" by consolidation or similar means have been placed before the voters in city after city (Press 1963, 113). When presented to the residents of an area, such proposals have usually met a rousing defeat at the polls.[6] The number of local units in metropolitan areas has, in fact, been increasing. "Metropolitan areas are leading the rest of the country in municipal incorporations and establishment of special districts, and lagging behind in the reduction of school districts" (Advisory Commission on Intergovernmental Relations 1966, 22).

The lack of success at the polls has not reduced the reformers' zeal. Rather, voters have been blamed for their inconsistency (Hawley and Zimmer 1970, 140) or for being "influenced more by arguments promising to keep the tax rate low, and the government close to the people and free of corruption, than by arguments stressing the correction of service inadequacies and the economical and efficient provisions of services" (Zimmerman 1970, 531).

Another possible explanation for these failures is that the metropolitan reform proposals have been based upon theoretical presumptions that are not warranted in light of experience. The theory underlying the major reform proposals is a collection of implicit presuppositions that are largely unsupported by specific research designed to ascertain their warrantability. The basic working hypotheses of the metropolitan reform proposals have rarely been clearly formulated and subjected to empirical research by those who recommend drastic change.[7] The changes recommended are presumed to lead to the postulated consequences without need for empirical investigation of the relationships involved. Without empirical examination of the postulated relationships implicit in the reform tradition, it is possible that different consequences than those predicted flow from adopting the recommendations made by metropolitan reform advocates. If this is the case, voters may have had a better intuitive understanding of the relationship among structural variables in metropolitan areas than the social scientists who have consistently made, and are still making, the same recommendations. Empirical research investigating the warrantability of the postulated relationships may be long overdue.

Propositions Derived from the Metropolitan Reform Tradition

A first step in the process of ascertaining the warrantability of the theoretical structure implicit in the metropolitan reform movement is to make the structure explicit and organize it in propositional form. An attempt to do this is presented in this section. A set of seven propositions is stated that has been derived from the literature cited in the preceding. This is not a complete listing of all the logical statements that could be derived from the reform tradition. Rather, it represents a beginning effort directed at isolating the most general theoretical structure implicit in the work of the metropolitan reformers. Further effort will be needed to extend these propositions in order to complete a description of the theoretical structure of the metropolitan reform tradition.

P₁ Increasing the size of urban governmental units will be associated with higher output per capita, more efficient provision of services, more equal distribution of costs to beneficiaries, increased responsibility of local officials, and increased participation by citizens.[8]

P₂ Increasing the size of urban governmental units will be associated with more professionalization of the public service and a greater reliance upon hierarchy as an organizing principle.

P₃ Reducing the number of public agencies within a metropolitan area will be associated with more output per capita, more efficient provision of services, more equal distribution of costs to beneficiaries, more responsibility of local officials, and more participation by citizens.

P₄ Reducing the number of public agencies within a metropolitan area will increase the reliance upon hierarchy as an organizing principle and will decrease the number of locally elected public officials within the metropolitan area.

P₅ Increasing the professionalization of public employees will be associated with a higher level of output per capita, more efficient provision of services, and increased responsibility of local officials.

P₆ Increasing the reliance upon hierarchy as an organizing principle within a metropolitan area will be associated with higher output per capita, more efficient provision of services, more equal distribution of costs to beneficiaries, and increased responsibility of local officials.

P₇ Increasing the number of locally elected officials within a metropolitan area will be associated with less responsibility on the part of public officials and less participation by citizens.

The theoretical structure outlined here contains two independent variables: size of urban governmental units and multiplicity of agencies within a metropolitan area. Three intervening variables are also posited: professionalization, reliance upon hierarchy, and number of elected officials. Five dependent variables are included in the system: output per capita, efficient provision of services, equal distribution of costs to beneficiaries, responsibility of local officials, and participation by citizens. The posited relationships among this set of variables are represented schematically in figure 6.1.

An Alternative Conception of Urban Problems

While political scientists, urban planners, and other social scientists associated with the traditional reform movement have repeatedly reaffirmed propositions similar to the set specified previously, a group of political economists have analyzed urban problems from a different perspective. Little communi-

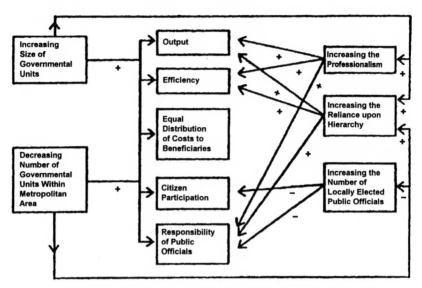

Fig. 6.1. Posited relations among variables in the metropolitan reform tradition

cation has occurred between these two groups. Political economists have studied urban problems rather than *the* urban problem. The conclusions of political economists differ radically from the traditional "reform" oriented scholars. The extent of the difference in approach can be seen from the following conclusion reached by Stigler.

> If we give each governmental activity *to the smallest governmental unit* which can efficiently perform it, there will be a vast resurgence and revitalization of local government in America. A vast reservoir of ability and imagination can be found in the increasing leisure time of the population, and both public functions and private citizens would benefit from the increased participation of citizens in political life. An eminent and powerful structure of local government is a basic ingredient of a society which seeks to give to the individual the fullest possible freedom and responsibility. (Stigler 1962, 146)

How can conclusions be so different? They differ, in part, because working assumptions of the two schools of thought vary significantly.[9] Most political economists begin with an assumption that the individual is the basic unit of analysis. Next, they assume that any individual, if given full information, will make decisions so as to maximize his own welfare. Third, they assume that some goods and services are most efficiently produced and distributed through the workings of private market arrangements. Fourth, they assume that some other goods and services, once provided, generate extensive spillovers beyond those individuals who are directly involved in a transaction. Sometimes these spillovers are of benefit to others affected and are referred to as external economies; otherwise, spillovers are costly to those affected and are called external diseconomies.[10] Goods that involve either extensive external economies or diseconomies may need to be provided by public agencies of some form. Most urban public goods and services, public health, and education would be included in this group. A fifth assumption is frequently made that the provision of goods involving extensive externalities affects a clearly delineated group or area. Such a group or area "can be as large as the entire population of the earth, or as small as the population of the smallest community" (Olson 1969).

Analysts of metropolitan problems who have been trained in political economy are quite familiar with the analysis of complex private industries involving many hundreds or thousands of enterprises, large and small, interacting in such a way as to produce and distribute vast quantities of goods in a reasonably efficient way. Consequently, the large number of public enterprises operating in a metropolitan area does not seem unusual. Stigler, for example, has noted that the student of industrial organization is surprised by repeated references to a presumed optimum scale of performance by large units of government. He comments that he is "accustomed to finding that the activity in an industry with a complex technology is usually efficiently conducted by a firm smaller by almost any measure than the government of a town of 25,000" (Stigler 1962, 144–45). He goes on to ask: "Is there some special characteristic of governmental functions that makes large units necessary to efficiency?" He responds by observing that efficiency depends upon the type of service that a governmental agency produces.

> Some of these functions can be performed efficiently on a very small scale. Many of the most distinguished private schools and colleges are much smaller than the school system of a town of 5,000 people. Others are more varied. A police department can efficiently control local traffic on a small scale; in one sense it must be worldwide to have an efficient 'missing persons bureau.' (Ibid. 145)

Political economists tend to assume that the optimum scale of production is not the same for all urban public goods and services. Some services are produced "more efficiently on a large scale than on a small scale. In a few instances the opposite can be true, while in others scale of operation is unimportant" (Hirsch 1964, 332). It is frequently felt that scale economies are not as prevalent in the public sector as in the private, since most governmental goods and services are "user oriented" and cannot be "rendered efficiently over large distances."[11] Examples of such services include police and fire protection and education. Because these are services and user oriented, they are labor intensive rather than capital intensive. Normal economies of scale accrue when a capital intensive firm can spread the high cost of a capital over a large number of customers. Political economists will usually agree that major economies of scale are likely to occur in the production of the following services: air pollution control, sewage disposal, public transportation, power production and distribution, water supply, public health services, hospitals, and public works planning.

In addition to examining the effect of scale economies for a single agency, political economists are also interested in the efficiencies that can result from the exchange and utilization by one enterprise of goods and services produced by other agencies. Stigler has noted that

> Every enterprise must use goods and services, or produce goods and services, which must be produced or sold on a much wider scale than the enterprise itself can undertake. Even a huge department store is not large enough to make its own delivery trucks, or to print the newspapers in which it advertises. Just as cooperation in these matters is brought about by the price system, so cooperation among governmental units has been developed—and could be carried much further—to avoid the determination and execution of all public functions by the governmental unit which is most efficient in conducting the functions with the largest scale of operation. (Stigler 1962, 145)

The existence of multiple agencies with some overlap may enable some aspects of services to be performed at a small scale while other aspects can be performed at a large scale. If there were no overlap between municipal, county, state, and national police agencies, for example, all aspects of police service would have to be performed by one agency alone even though some aspects of police services can be provided efficiently on a small scale while other aspects require a much larger scale for efficient provision (Hirsch 1964, 332; see also Netzer 1968, 435–76).

The recognition that most private enterprises purchase many of the goods and services that they need from other enterprises leads the political economist to consider the *production* (physical rendering) of urban government services separately from the *provision* of such services (i.e., the decision to provide and possibly the billing and/or other financing) (see V. Ostrom and E. Ostrom 1965). Thus, questions such as scale and efficiency, concerned mainly with production, can be considered separately from questions of the distribution of the costs of such services. In their normative analysis, most political economists will use as a first maxim that those individuals who receive services should pay for them. Whenever the boundaries of political jurisdictions correspond to the group of individuals receiving benefits from their provision, and all costs are borne by the residents, this maxim is followed. Whenever a political jurisdiction is larger than the group receiving benefits, some individuals may pay for benefits that they do not receive. On the other hand, whenever a political jurisdiction is smaller than the group receiving benefits, some individuals may receive benefits and not pay. Either of the last two situations can occur easily in a metropolitan area particularly if restrictions are placed on the number and size of political jurisdictions that may be established within the area. When the most efficient scale of production is a large political unit, then the establishment of a large jurisdiction in the area will have the dual effect of providing goods at least cost and forcing individuals who receive benefits to pay for them. However, if the most efficient scale of production is small, but there are spillovers to other jurisdictions, the political economist as policy analyst would recommend that production be undertaken by small units and that larger units of government provide grants-in-aid to cover the marginal cost of the production that benefits the larger units. If the policy concern is primarily that of redistribution, the political economist is apt to recommend that grants-in-aid be provided by larger units of government to smaller units of government without concern to marginal cost (Olson 1969, 329). With such a program, one gains a redistribution of resources from a large economic base to help support service levels in poorer areas. Thus, the posited relationship between the size of governmental units and the number of governmental units within an area on the distribution of costs within the area is a far more complex relationship for the political economist than for the metropolitan reformer.

To further understand the differences between these two approaches, it is necessary to examine the political economist's orientation toward competition. In the political economist's view, competition among numerous producers and sellers of goods and services enables the market to be an efficient decision structure for producing and distributing goods not subject to externalities. Consequently, when political economists turn to the analysis of nonmarket decision structures, they do not assume a priori that competition among public agencies is necessarily inefficient (see V. Ostrom, Tiebout, and Warren 1961; Bish 1971). Competition among public agencies within an urban area does *not* take the same form as market competition and would not always be beneficial. The presence of multiple producers within the same geographic region may have an effect on the relationship between citizens and public agencies as well as on the relationship between elected and appointed public officials and the producers of public services. The presence of more than a single producer of urban public goods within a metropolitan area may enable citizens to make more effective choices about the mix of services they prefer to receive than reliance upon voting mechanisms and a single producer. Multiple governments existing within a metropolitan area enable citizens to "vote with their feet" (Tiebout 1956; see also Ellickson 1971; Oates 1969). The presence of multiple producers within one metropolitan area may also reduce the cost for citizens of comparing the levels of output provided by different jurisdictions. Public officials who are representing one constituency in a bargaining process with other public officials over cooperative arrangements (such as contracting for services to be performed) may be able to bargain more effectively if alternative public producers are present in the area (Niskanen 1971, 155–68). However, it is also possible that multiple producers of some urban public goods may nullify each other's actions and lead to a reduction in the net output of urban public goods. The political economist will consider the effect of competition among public agencies as an empirical question. The effect may be positive or negative depending upon the type of urban public good being considered.

To political economists, the market is an efficient decision-making structure for some purposes and grossly inefficient for others. Likewise, hierarchy is considered to be a potentially efficient decision structure for some purposes and inefficient for others. However, political economists are apt to argue that most large bureaucracies are less efficient in solving problems than either smaller bureaucracies or a multiplicity of independent agencies coordinating their efforts through competition or bargaining.[12] Tullock has argued that a significant loss of information and control occurs between those at the bottom of a large hierarchy and those at the top.[13] Schlesinger has posited that "large organizations find it hard to anticipate, to recognize, or to adjust to change" (Schlesinger 1966, 19). McKean and Anshen have suggested that large centralized public agencies frequently neglect the variety of choices available and may underestimate the degree of uncertainty involved in a problem (McKean and Anshen 1965).

Propositions Derived from the Political Economist's Tradition

In an attempt to compare the theoretical structure underlying the work of those associated with the metropolitan reform movement and those associated with the political economy tradition, a group of alternative propositions derived from the work of political economists is presented subsequently. No attempt has been made to present the complete theoretical structure of the political economists. Rather, an attempt has been made to examine posited relationships among the same variables utilized in the propositions derived from the work of the metropolitan reform tradition. This is possible for the two independent variables and the five dependent variables posited previously. However, the intervening variables of professionalization and number of locally elected officials are rarely considered in the political economy tradition and have consequently been omitted from the following propositions. A new intervening variable, type of public good or service, has been included in the following propositions.

Alternative P_{1A} Whether increasing the size of urban governmental units will be associated with a higher output per capita, more efficient provision of services, more equal distribution of costs to beneficiaries depends upon the type of public good or service being considered.

Alternative P_{1B} Increasing the size of urban governmental units will be associated with decreased responsibility of local officials and decreased participation by citizens.[14]

Alternative P_2 Increasing the size of urban governmental units will be associated with a greater utilization of hierarchy as an organizing principle.

Alternative P_{3A} Whether reducing the number of public agencies within a metropolitan area will be associated with more output per capita, more efficient provision of service, and more equal distribution of costs to beneficiaries depends upon the type of public good or service being considered.

Alternative P_{3B} Reducing the number of public agencies within a metropolitan area will be associated with less responsibility of public officials.

Alternative P_4 Reducing the number of public agencies within a metropolitan area will increase the reliance upon hierarchy as an organizing principle within the metropolitan area.

Alternative P_{6A} Whether increasing the reliance upon hierarchy as an organizing principle within a metropolitan area will be associated with higher output per capita and more efficient provision of services depends upon the type of public good or service being considered.

Alternative P_{6B} Increasing the reliance upon hierarchy as an organizing principle within a metropolitan area will be associated with decreased participation by citizens and decreased responsibility of local officials.

The posited relationships among this set of variables are represented schematically in figure 6.2.

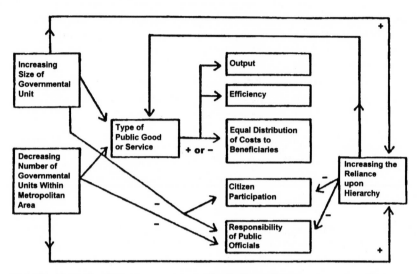

Fig. 6.2. Posited relations among variables in the political economy tradition

The Need for Research to Examine Alternative
Theoretical Structures

Utilizing one or the other of the theoretical structures outlined previously as the foundation for recommending reform of the institutions serving metropolitan areas leads to drastically different types of proposals.[15] Given the different recommendations for reform that would be derived from these two traditions, considerable need exists for research to increase the warrantability of one or the other approach. Until a warrantable explanation has been established, recommendations for reform may produce more harm than good.

The development of an explanation will also require the careful and consistent definition of all concepts included in the theoretical structures. Frequently, terms used in one tradition do not quite mean the same as when used in another tradition. For example, the term *efficiency* is used as a dependent variable in both of the theoretical structures posed in the preceding. However, as used by the metropolitan reformers, the term *efficiency* is usually conceptualized as a ratio of benefits *produced* to the cost of *producing* them (Simon 1957, 172–97). Social costs are rarely included within this definition of efficiency. In analyzing the efficiency of public agencies, political economists are apt to define efficiency so as to include the social costs or the resources required to produce and consume the public good valued in terms of alternative uses forgone (see Coase 1960). Social costs "may not equal the costs borne by the urban government that provides the service" (Hirsch

1968, 493). That portion of the total costs represented in the budget of a government agency may be called "agency costs." But, in addition, other parties, both public and private, may incur costs that are not explicitly charged to the agency in question nor considered in that agency's efficiency and financial deliberations (ibid.).

Equally perplexing problems exist with such concepts as "output," "equal distribution of costs," "responsibility of local leaders," and "citizen participation." Not only will scholars define these concepts differently, but the indicators that are utilized for operationalizing variables are frequently open to serious questions of validity. One of the most perplexing problems facing those interested in quantitative, comparative urban research is the development of valid measures of output. Many of the pioneering efforts have relied upon expenditure figures (input or "effort" measures) as indicators of output (see Gastil 1970). However, since the amount expended by a government may not always be transformed on a one-to-one basis into benefits for the citizens of the jurisdiction, we need to be developing other measures of output that indicate the level of output received by citizens.

Some Evidence Related to Alternative Propositions

The primary purpose of this essay is to elucidate alternate theoretical structures and not to evaluate the warrantability of either. However, since so many reform proposals are based on the metropolitan reform structure and its *warrantability is assumed to be established* by so many scholars, it is important to briefly present findings from a few studies that raise questions about the warrantability of this theoretical structure.

A number of studies have examined the effect of the size of the governmental agency on its output and are consequently of relevance to P_1 and Alternative P_{1A}. A summary of the results of these studies adapted from the work of Werner Hirsch is presented in table 6.1.[16] Hirsch has interpreted the results of these studies in terms of the Average Unit Cost (AUC) of providing a service. The conclusion one would reach based upon the series of studies reviewed by Hirsch is that economies of scale are *not* uniformly present in the public sector. The output of public agencies does not appear from these studies to be positively associated with the size of an agency. Consistent with this finding is a recent bulletin issued by the ACIR that concluded that

> Size does not seem to matter in cities of 25,000 to 250,000—neither economies nor diseconomies of scale were of significant number. But in cities over 250,000 population, size *does* make a difference—the law of diminishing returns sets in and there are significant *diseconomies* of scale. (Advisory Commission on Intergovernmental Relations 1970, 2)

TABLE 6.1. Empirical Studies of the Effect of Scale of Production on Average Unit Cost

Name of Investigator	Type of Urban Public Service	Type of Data Used[a]	Result[b]
Riew (1966)	Secondary Education	S	AUC is U-shaped with a trough at about 1,700 pupils.
Kiesling (1966)	Primary & Secondary Education	S	AUC is about horizontal.
Hirsch (1959)	Primary & Secondary Education	S	AUC is about horizontal.
Schmandt-Stevens (1960)	Police Protection	S&Q	AUC is about horizontal.
Hirsch (1960)	Police Protection	S&Q	AUC is about horizontal.
Will (1965)	Fire Protection	E	AUC is declining with major economies reached at 300,000 population.
Hirsch (1959)	Fire Protection	S	AUC is U-shaped with a trough at about 110,000 population.
Hirsch (1965)	Refuse Collection	S	AUC is about horizontal.
Hirsch (1959)	School Administration	S	AUC is U-shaped with trough at about 44,000 pupils.
Nerlove (1961)	Electricity	S	AUC is declining.
Isard-Coughlin (1957)	Sewage Plants	S	AUC is declining.
Lomax (1951)	Gas	S	AUC is declining.
Johnston (1960)	Electricity	S	AUC is declining.

[a] S = statistical data; Q = questionnaire data; E = engineering data.
[b] AUC = average unit cost.

Kirkpatrick and Morgan recently interviewed 87 public officials in 21 cities in the Oklahoma City metropolitan area. Each official was asked to evaluate the services performed by his city. The authors expected city size and growth rate to affect these evaluations since "larger cities are often thought to provide better services" (Kirkpatrick and Morgan 1971, 660).

However, they found no such relationship. These officials were also asked to rank services according to whether they favored their provision on an areawide basis. Officials most supported the provision of services including health, libraries, transportation/traffic planning, water, refuse, and parks/recreation on an areawide basis. They least supported areawide provision of planning/zoning, fire, urban renewal, education, and police (669).

Several research projects have been initiated at Indiana University to examine the empirical warrantability of P_1 and Alternative P_{1A} concerning the effect of size of governmental agencies on their output. [See the essays in Part III of this volume.] The findings from a variety of studies, thus, seem to reduce the warrantability of P_1.

Hawkins and Dye have reported findings that relate to P_3 and Alternative P_{3A}. In particular, they were interested in examining "one of the assumptions of the reform literature on metropolitan 'problems' [which] is that fragmentation adversely affects the level of governmental services. Fragmentation is said to increase the costs of municipal services and lower the quality and/or quantity of services provided" (Hawkins and Dye 1971, 497). Hawkins and Dye computed the simple correlation coefficients for 212 metropolitan areas in 1962 between the number of governments within the areas and per capita expenditures. They found that fragmentation did "*not* appear to increase or decrease government spending for municipal services" (499). They interpret their findings to mean that the "dollar consequences of metropolitan governmental fragmentation have probably been over-emphasized in the reform literature."

Some recent studies by Aiken and Alford and by Clark provide empirical evidence regarding the relation between centralization of authority (or hierarchy as an organizing principle) and the output of public agencies. Both studies are related to Proposition P_6 and Alternative P_{6A}. Aiken and Alford examined three types of police outputs (public housing, urban renewal, and the War on Poverty) for approximately 600 cities with a population of 25,000 or more in 1960 (Aiken and Alford 1970a). In the course of their study, they tested a number of alternative hypotheses for explaining the variance in levels of output (measured in number of units constructed per 100,000 population since 1933 for public housing and per capita expenditure figures for the other two policy areas). One set of hypotheses related to the concentration of formal political structure. Aiken and Alford's data lead them to conclude that communities with high outputs are not the most centralized and hierarchically organized communities. Rather, communities with exactly the opposite characteristics from those of centralization and integration seem to have the highest levels of output (103). Consequently, they pose the need for a different theory of community output from that frequently presented. The beginning proposition in such a theory, they argue, should be that "successful performance in such programs is more frequently attained in decentralized, heterogeneous and probably fragmented community systems." They pose a further hypothesis that "the greater the number of centers of power in a community and the (more) pervasive and encompassing are the interfaces in the community system, the higher the probability that a community innovation in a given issue will occur" (105). They reason that the "more choice among units in the system . . . and the greater the state of information about organizational actors, the higher the probability that a coalition sufficient to make a decision will occur."[17] The number of cities included in their study and the methodological rigor of their analysis seriously challenge the warrantability of the relationship between reliance on hierarchy and higher output posited in P_6.

An intensive study of 51 communities recently undertaken by Clark provides further evidence related to P_6 (Clark 1968b). Clark's indicators of output were general municipal expenditure figures and urban renewal expenditure figures in the cities studied. One of the hypotheses examined was "the more centralized the decision-making structure, the higher the levels of output" (306). Clark measured the centralization or decentralization of the decision-making structure by asking a small group of key respondents for the names of those who had been involved in policymaking related to four specific policy areas. Cities in which a large number of names were mentioned were coded as having a more decentralized decision-making structure than those in which a few names were mentioned. Using these indicators, Clark's findings were similar to Aiken and Alford's and, thus, "were precisely the opposite of those predicted by this proposition" (ibid.; see also Clark 1968a). Since earlier empirical work had provided some support for the proposition relating centralization of decision-making structure to higher output (Hawley and Zimmer 1970; Rosenthal and Crain 1966), Clark argued that the type of decision being made may affect whether the proposition is empirically true or not—a working hypothesis that is somewhat related to Alternative P_{6A}. Clark characterized decision areas as "fragile" versus "non-fragile"—a distinction that appears somewhat ambiguous. However, in a recent article Clark introduces the concept of public goods as an intervening variable between the centralization of decision-making structures and the level of outputs (see Clark 1972). Given these findings, P_6 would seem to have been seriously challenged.

Conclusion

Two theoretical structures have been derived that postulate relationships among independent variables including the size of governmental units and their multiplicity in a metropolitan area and the dependent variables of output, efficiency, responsibility of local officials and citizen participation. Recommendations for reforming the organization of governmental units in metropolitan areas would vary dramatically depending upon which theoretical structure provided the foundations for analysis.

Recent empirical evidence challenges several of the propositions derived from the metropolitan reform movement and tends to increase the warrantability of several of the propositions derived from the political economy tradition. However, considerable further research is needed before a firm explanation for the relationships among these variables can be established. It is to be expected that a warrantable explanation may be a far more complex structure than the alternative structures posed in this essay.

NOTES

1. See E. Ostrom 1971. Vincent Ostrom also raises questions whether reforms have not in some instances done more harm than good (V. Ostrom 1989).

2. The term *explanation* is being used here to mean "an instrument that generates anticipations about the environment, and makes possible control over events in the environment, by linking changes in the values of two or more variables according to the rules" (Meehan 1971).

3. Committee for Economic Development 1970 (10). See also the earlier report of the CED 1966; National Commission on Urban Problems 1968; Bollens and Schmandt 1970, esp. chap. 11.

4. An early advocate of this tradition was Richard S. Childs. The leading advocate in more recent times has been "the Committee for Economic Development composed of 200 prominent businessmen and educators, which maintains there is a great need for a revolutionary restructuring of what is labeled as an anachronistic system of local government" (Zimmerman 1970, 532).

5. Anderson and Weidner 1950 (609–10, their emphasis). While this summary comes from a textbook written originally in 1925, the basic recommendations of metropolitan reformers have remained amazingly stable. Chapter 1 of Hawley and Zimmer's book, *The Metropolitan Community,* is entitled "The Metropolitan Problem" and restates most of the recommendations made by Anderson and Weidner. See also Grant 1965 (38–56); Marvel 1967 (125–30); Adrian 1967 (454–69).

6. See Advisory Commission on Intergovernmental Relations 1962 for a description of the difficulties encountered in attempts at governmental reorganization in 18 metropolitan areas. Lineberry (1970, 716) presents a list of major reorganization referendums from 1946–1968.

7. However, a number of studies have focused on propositions relating to the socioeconomic correlates of the adoption of reform proposals within particular cities or the correlates of the presence of "reform" institutions within a city and tax and expenditure levels. Indicators of reformed institutions have usually included the council-manager form of government, at-large elections, and nonpartisan elections. See

Banfield and Wilson 1963; Wilson and Banfield 1964 (876–87); Wolfinger and Field 1966 (306–26); Froman 1967 (94–108); Lineberry and Fowler 1967 (701–16); Clark 1968b (576–93); Alford and Scoble 1965; see also Hennessy 1970 (537–64).

8. It is, of course, assumed that some limits exist on the postulated relationship stated in this series. Such limits would need to be ascertained empirically if the propositions appeared warrantable within some range. Metropolitan reformers had an implicit concept of a limit for some of their variables; that is, the a priori upper limit on size implied in their work was the size of the metropolitan area involved; the a priori limit on multiplicity was a single unit for the entire metropolitan area. Richard Childs argued that the "ideal" number of local officials to be elected in an area was five. Limits of professionalization are hard to conceptualize. The a priori limit on reliance on hierarchy would be the development in institutional arrangements within a metropolitan area of a perfect pyramid in shape with no overlap between superordinate positions for any subordinate position. See Alexander 1965 (58–61) for a good analytical description of hierarchy and semilattices as alternative forms of organization.

9. It is hard to know exactly what the underlying assumptions are of the metropolitan reform school of thought. While statements concerning the consequences that are predicted to flow from specified reforms are frequently made, the underlying reasons are infrequently given. If one relies on (A) the work of Richard Childs and the other early reformers who were somewhat more apt to state their underlying logic; and (B) the development of a set of assumptions from which the preceding propositions can logically be derived, then a possible set of underlying assumptions of the reform tradition would be the following: (1) The metropolitan area as a whole is the basic unit of analysis. Actions are judged in light of how they affect the area as a whole; (2) Individual citizens are presumed to be primarily occupied with their own livelihood and have little information about common problems; (3) Urban residents make wise decisions only when they are presented with limited and simplified alternatives; (4) Most urban problems are metropolitan wide in scope; and (5) Individuals can be trained to be superior public servants.

10. For an excellent discussion of the effect of externalities on the provision of urban public or "quasi-" public goods see Davies 1965. See also Breton 1966; Davis and Whinston 1967; Buchanan and Stubblebine 1962.

11. Ibid. Scale economies refers to enterprises in which the larger the scale of production, the lower the costs of production. If scale diseconomies exist, the larger the scale of production, the higher the cost of production.

12. For a review of the basic literature in the political economy tradition and its relevance for the study of administration see V. Ostrom and E. Ostrom 1971.

13. Tullock 1965; see also Williamson 1967 for a more formal statement of the same propositions.

14. A very similar proposition is posited by Dahl 1967 (957).

15. The simultaneous existence of two or more underlying models for analyzing social problems is not unique only to variables associated with the organization of government in metropolitan areas. Alternative theoretical structures underlie many areas of social science. Peter Rossi has noted that the existence of more than one model means "that policy making ought to seek to test out the relative worths of al-

ternative models" (Rossi 1969, 447).

    16. Adapted from table 2 in Hirsch 1968 (508).

    17. Ibid. See also Aiken and Alford 1970b. Laura L. Morlock comes to similar conclusions in her study of 91 cities (Morlock 1971).

REFERENCES

Adrian, Charles R. 1967. "Public Attitudes and Metropolitan Decision Making." In *Politics in the Metropolis,* ed. Charles E. Miller, 454–69. Columbus, OH: Charles E. Merrill.

Advisory Commission on Intergovernmental Relations. 1962. *Factors Affecting Voter Reactions to Governmental Reorganization in Metropolitan Areas.* Washington, DC: Advisory Commission on Intergovernmental Relations.

———. 1966. *Metropolitan America: Challenge to Federalism.* Washington, DC: Advisory Commission on Inter-Governmental Relations.

———. 1970. *Information Bulletin No. 70–8.* Washington, DC: Advisory Commission on Intergovernmental Relations, September 16.

Aiken, Michael, and Robert R. Alford. 1970a. "Comparative Urban Research and Community Decision-Making." *New Atlantis* 2 (winter): 85–110.

———. 1970b. "Community Structure and Innovation: The Case of Urban Renewal." *American Sociological Review* 35 (August): 650–65.

Alexander, Christopher. 1965. "A City Is Not a Tree." *Architectural Forum* 122 (May): 58–62.

Alford, Robert R., and Harry M. Scoble. 1965. "Political and Socioeconomic Characteristics of American Cities." *Municipal Yearbook 1965.* International City Managers Association.

Anderson, William, and Edward W. Weidner. 1950. *American City Government.* New York: Henry Holt.

Banfield, Edward C., and James Q. Wilson. 1963. *City Politics.* Cambridge, MA: Harvard University Press.

Bish, Robert. 1971. *The Public Economy of Metropolitan Areas.* Chicago: Markham Press.

Bollens, John C., and Henry J. Schmandt. 1970. *The Metropolis. Its People, Politics and Economic Life.* 2d ed. New York: Harper & Row.

Breton, Albert. 1966. "A Theory of the Demand for Public Goods." *Canadian Journal of Economics and Politics* 32 (November): 455–67.

Buchanan, James M., and W. Craig Stubblebine. 1962. "Externality." *Economica* 29 (November): 371–84.

Clark, Terry N. 1968a. "Community Structure and Decision Making." In *Community Structure and Decision Making: Comparative Analysis,* ed. Terry N. Clark, 91–128. San Francisco: Chandler.

———. 1968b. "Community Structure, Decision-Making, Budget Expenditures, and Urban Renewal in 51 American Communities." *American Sociological Review* 33 (August): 576–93. (In *Community Politics: A Behavioral Approach,* ed.

Charles M. Bonjean, Terry N. Clark, and Robert L. Lineberry, 293–314. New York: The Free Press, 1971).

———. 1972. "The Structure of Community Influence." In *People and Politics in Urban Society*, 283–314. Urban Affairs Annual Review, vol. 6. Beverly Hills, CA: Sage.

Coase, R. H. 1960. "The Problem of Social Cost." *The Journal of Law and Economics* 3 (October): 1–44.

Committee for Economic Development. 1966. *Modernizing Local Government.* New York: Committee for Economic Development.

———. 1970. *Reshaping Government in Metropolitan Areas.* New York: Committee for Economic Development.

Dahl, Robert A. 1967. "The City in the Future of Democracy." *American Political Science Review* 61 (December): 953–70.

Davies, David. 1965. "Financing Urban Functions." *Law and Contemporary Problems* 30: 127–61.

Davis, Otto, and Andrew Whinston. 1967. "On the Distribution between Public and Private Goods." *American Economic Review* 57 (May): 360–73.

Ellickson, Bryan. 1971. "Jurisdiction Fragmentation and Residential Choice." *American Economic Review* 61 (May): 334–39.

Friesema, H. Paul. 1966. "The Metropolis and the Maze of Local Government." *Urban Affairs Quarterly* 2 (Dec.): 68–90.

Froman, Jr., Lewis A. 1967. "An Analysis of Public Policies in Cities." *Journal of Politics* 29 (February): 94–108.

Gastil, Raymond. 1970. "Social Indicators and the Quality of Life." *Public Administration Review* 30 (November/December): 596–601.

Grant, Daniel B. 1965. "Trends in Urban Government and Administration." *Journal of Law and Contemporary Problems* 30 (winter): 38–56.

Greer, Scott. 1961. "Dilemmas of Action Research on the Metropolitan Problem." In *Community Political Systems*, ed. Morris Janowitz. Glencoe, IL: Free Press.

Hawkins, Brett W., and Thomas R. Dye. 1971. "Metropolitan 'Fragmentation': A Research Note." In *Politics in the Metropolis*, ed. Thomas R. Dye and Brett W. Hawkins. 2d ed. Columbus, OH: Charles E. Merrill.

Hawley, Amos H., and Basil C. Zimmer. 1970. *The Metropolitan Community. Its People and Government.* Beverly Hills, CA: Sage.

Hennessy, Timothy M. 1970. "Problems in Concept Formation: The Ethos 'Theory' and the Comparative Study of Urban Politics." *Midwest Journal of Political Science* 14 (November): 537–64.

Hirsch, Werner Z. 1964. "Local versus Areawide Urban Government Services." *National Tax Journal* 17 (December): 331–39.

———. 1968. "The Supply of Urban Public Services." In *Issues in Urban Economics*, ed. Harry S. Perloff and Lowden Wingo, Jr. Baltimore: Johns Hopkins University Press.

Institute for Local Self Government. 1970. *Special Districts or Special Dynasties? Democracy Diminished.* Berkeley, CA: Institute for Local Self Government.

Kirkpatrick, Samuel A., and David R. Morgan. 1971. "Policy Support and Orientations toward Metropolitan Political Integration among Urban Officials." *Social Science Quarterly* 52 (December): 656–71.

Lineberry, Robert L. 1970. "Reforming Metropolitan Governance: Requiem or Reality." *The Georgetown Law Journal* 58 (March/May): 675–718.

Lineberry, Robert L., and Edmund P. Fowler. 1967. "Reformism and Public Policies in American Cities." *American Political Science Review* 61 (September): 701–16.

Marvel, Allen D. 1967. "Interlocal Relations." *Municipal Finance* 39 (February): 125–30.

McKean, Roland N., and Melvin Anshen. 1965. "Limitations, Risks, and Problems." In *Program Budgeting*, ed. David Novic. Boston: Harvard University Press.

Meehan, Eugene J. 1971. *The Foundations of Political Analysis: Empirical and Normative*. Homewood, IL: Dorsey Press.

Morlock, Laura L. 1971. "Business Interests, Countervailing Groups and the Balance of Influence in 91 Cities." Paper presented at the annual meeting of the Society for the Study of Social Problems, Denver, August.

National Commission on Urban Problems. 1968. *Final Report Part IV*. Washington, DC: U.S. Government Printing Office.

Netzer, Dick. 1968. "Federal, State and Local Finance." In *Issues in Urban Economics*, ed. Harvey S. Perloff and Lowden Wingo, Jr., 435–76. Baltimore: Johns Hopkins University Press.

Niskanen, William A., Jr. 1971. *Bureaucracy and Representative Government*. Chicago: Aldine-Atherton.

Oates, Wallace E. 1969. "The Effects of Property Taxes and Local Spending on Property Values: An Empirical Study of Tax Capitalization and the Tiebout Hypothesis." *Journal of Political Economy* 77 (December): 957–71.

Olson, Mancur. 1969. "The Optimal Allocation of Jurisdictional Responsibility: The Principle of 'Fiscal Equivalence.'" Vol. 1, *The Analysis and Evaluation of Public Expenditures: The PPB System* 321–31. Washington, DC: U.S. Congress, Joint Economic Committee.

Ostrom, Elinor. 1971. "Institutional Arrangements and the Measurement of Policy Consequences in Urban Areas." *Urban Affairs Quarterly* 6 (June): 447–76.

Ostrom, Vincent. 1989. *The Intellectual Crisis in American Public Administration*. 2nd ed. Tuscaloosa: University of Alabama Press.

Ostrom, Vincent, and Elinor Ostrom. 1965. "A Behavioral Approach to the Study of Intergovernmental Relations." *The Annals of the American Academy of Political and Social Science* 359 (May): 137–46. (Chapter 4 in this volume.)

———. 1971. "Public Choice: A Different Approach to the Study of Public Administration." *Public Administration Review* 31 (March/April): 203–16. (Reprinted in Michael D. McGinnis, ed., *Polycentric Games and Institutions* [Ann Arbor: University of Michigan Press, 1999].)

Ostrom, Vincent, Charles M. Tiebout, and Robert Warren. 1961. "The Organization of Government in Metropolitan Areas: A Theoretical Inquiry." *American Political Science Review* 55 (December): 831–42. (Chapter 1 in this volume.)

Press, Charles. 1963. "The Cities within a Great City: A Decentralist Approach to Centralization." *Centennial Review* 7 (winter): 113–30.

Rosenthal, Donald, and Robert L. Crain. 1966. "Structure and Values in Local Political Systems: The Case of Fluoridation Decisions." *Journal of Politics* 28 (February): 169–96.

Rossi, Peter. 1969. "No Good Idea Goes Unpunished: Moynihan's Misunderstanding and the Proper Role of Social Science in Policy Making." *Social Science Quarterly* 50 (December): 469–79.

Schlesinger, James. 1966. *Organizational Structures and Planning*. Santa Monica: RAND Corporation.

Simon, Herbert. 1957. *Administrative Behavior*. 2d ed. New York: Free Press.

Stigler, George J. 1962. "The Tenable Range of Functions of Local Government." In *Private Wants and Public Needs*, ed. Edmund S. Phelps, 167–76. New York: W. W. Norton.

Tiebout, Charles. 1956. "A Pure Theory of Local Expenditures." *Journal of Political Economy* 64 (October): 416–35.

Tullock, Gordon. 1965. *The Politics of Bureaucracy*. Washington, DC: Public Affairs Press.

Williamson, Oliver G. 1967. "Hierarchical Control and Optimum Firm Size." *Journal of Political Economy* 75 (April): 123–38.

Wilson, James Q., and Edward C. Banfield. 1964. "Public-Regardingness as a Value Premise in Voting Behavior." *American Political Science Review* 58 (December): 876–87.

Wolfinger, Raymond, and Osgood Field. 1966. "Political Ethos and the Structure of City Government." *American Political Science Review* 60 (June): 306–26.

Zimmerman, Joseph F. 1970. "Metropolitan Reform in the U.S.: An Overview." *Public Administration Review* 30 (September/October): 531–43.

Part III
Empirical Research
on Police Services

CHAPTER 7

Why Do We Need Multiple Indicators of Public Service Outputs?

Elinor Ostrom

The problem of measuring the output of local public agencies is closely tied to the problem of increasing the productivity of local public agencies. If productivity is defined as the quantity of output derived from a quantity of input, then both the output and input sides need to be measured if one is to compute this difference. The input side is *relatively* easy to compute. Labor, capital equipment, land, and other input resources come in relatively discrete units. Most of these units can be computed in terms of dollar costs so the aggregate effect of different combinations of input units can be determined.

The real crunch comes on the output side. What is the output of a police department, a welfare agency, a school system? Is there only one kind of output produced by such agencies? How do we measure what is produced by such agencies? These are the difficult questions around which this conference has been organized.

The Problem of Measuring Public Goods

My own interest in this question arose several years ago from a theoretical problem. Most local government services can be characterized in theory as being public goods (Breton 1966; Davies 1965; Davis and Whinston 1967; Samuelson 1954). As such, once they are produced by an agency, they are simultaneously available to at least some group of people. The producing agency cannot exclude some individuals from benefiting from the service—

Originally published in *National Conference on Nonmetropolitan Community Services Research* (Washington, DC: U.S. Government Printing Office, 1977), 277–86. Reprinted by permission of the author.

Author's note: Paper presented at the National Conference on Nonmetropolitan Community Services Research sponsored by the Economic Development Division, Economic Research Service, U.S. Department of Agriculture; Farm Foundation; North Central Regional Center for Rural Development; and Northeast Regional Center for Rural Development held at Ohio State University, January 11–13, 1977. Prepared for the Committee on Agriculture, Nutrition, and Forestry—United States Senate, 95th Congress, 1st Session (July 12, 1977).

The research on multimode approaches to measuring the output of local public agencies has been supported by the Research Applied to National Needs Division of the National Science Foundation (Grant No. GI 38535).

even if they are unwilling to pay for receiving the benefit. This characteristic of local governmental services is what most frequently places such services in the public sector. Few private entrepreneurs are tempted to enter and produce goods and services for which they cannot receive payment from potential beneficiaries.

No Regular Information about Output

Given that the producer of such services does not engage in quid pro quo—something for something—relationships with beneficiaries, the producer has limited information about

1. How much has been produced;
2. How much value consumers place on the goods and services produced; and
3. The preferences of consumers for more or different mixes of services.

This lack of information about the nature of any agency's own output means that local governmental agencies are operating at a severe handicap when compared to private agencies producing and selling goods in the market (E. Ostrom 1971). There are no *routine* transactions between producer and consumer that provide constant feedback of information to the producer about productivity or the demand for a product. Any transactions between public officials and citizen-consumers are either unrecorded or no consistent way exists for interpreting the meaning of these transactions.

Police interact, for example, with citizens in many unrecorded manners. While out on patrol, police are hailed by citizens to obtain information or to respond to potentially disruptive interpersonal situations. Unless requests for services are received by telephone, police-citizen transactions are infrequently recorded in any manner. Most "stop and frisk" operations leave no records of who was stopped and what was done. Even when records are made of interactions between police and citizens, it is impossible to give uniform interpretations to the meaning of the records as maintained. How do you measure the "output" of a call for service involving the request to help quiet a neighborhood fight?—to help a motorist get into his locked car?—to get a cat out of a tree?

Such records do provide the basis for "activity analysis." But, activity analysis goes back to the input side of the productivity equation. By careful use of internal records, one can gain some insight—and some quantitative measures of—the range, type, and extent of activities engaged in by local public service agencies such as police, education, and welfare.[1] But, these measures are *not* measures of output—they do not provide information about the impact of the activities on citizens served or the value that citizens give to their performance. Activities can be "counterproductive." In that case, the more that is done, the worse things get (E. Ostrom 1971).

Reliance on Activity Records

Given that activity records are all the top executive of a local public service agency usually has to gain insight about an agency's productivity, managers place heavy emphasis on activity records for establishing their productivity reports to local governing boards. Police annual reports are filled with data about number of miles patrolled, number of calls for service, number of arrests made, number of traffic tickets issued, number of fingerprints processed, and so on. Such reports leave to the city manager or mayor, the city council, and the citizenry at large the necessity of translating these activities into some form of output and evaluating performance.

Without measures of output to compare with activity records, no one can precisely evaluate the productivity of a local government agency's efforts— neither those at the head of the agency, nor elected officials of a city, nor the citizens. In relatively small communities, officials are *also* citizens of a community. As citizens they receive the services of their own agency. They can thus evaluate service levels in their own community on a firsthand basis. If all local governments were relatively small, some of our problems of measuring the output of local public service agencies would be less severe. While the detail of public reports is frequently less in smaller communities, operating heads, local public officials, and citizens can all gain considerable information from their own experience about service levels in the community. However, in very large cities, no official can gain firsthand information about how services are being performed in different neighborhoods in the city. Officials are dependent to a much larger degree on the *reports* provided them about productivity. If these reports contain no measures of output, then they know *only* about inputs. Decisions can be made that increase nonproductive activities.

Empirical Efforts to Measure Output

This theoretical interest in the problems of measuring output—particularly in large cities—led members of the Workshop in Political Theory and Policy Analysis at Indiana University to undertake a series of studies that have attempted to measure the output of local public agencies.

Police

Our first studies compared levels of service outputs for large and small police departments serving relatively similar neighborhoods within a single metropolitan area (IsHak 1972; E. Ostrom 1976; E. Ostrom et al. 1973; E. Ostrom, Parks, and Whitaker 1973; E. Ostrom and Whitaker 1974; Parks 1975; Rogers and McCurdy Lipsey 1974). Our substantive interest in this resulted from the repeated assertions that small-scale police agencies were less effective than large-scale police agencies. These assertions underlie the recommended standards adopted by national and state standards and goals commissions (National Advisory Commission on Criminal Justice Standards and Goals 1973). The Michigan Advisory Commission on Criminal Justice has, for example, just adopted the following standard

> Local government should be encouraged to maintain, through consolidation if necessary, law enforcement agencies containing no fewer than 20 sworn officers who are involved in the delivery of police services. (Michigan Advisory Commission on Criminal Justice 1975, 192)

While asserting that the levels of productivity among small police departments are inadequate, none of the commissions recommending the elimination of these small departments have cited evidence to support the assertion that productivity will increase by following their recommendations.

Types of Measures Used

In our attempt to examine these assertions empirically, we utilized a series of measures derived from citizen surveys. The first type of measure was that of citizen experiences with crime and with police. These included

1. Whether anyone in the household had been the victim of criminal activity.
2. If a victimization incident had occurred, were the police notified?
3. If notified, how fast the police had responded.
4. If the police responded, what level of activity was undertaken?
5. Whether anyone in the household had called upon the police for assistance to deal with a noncriminal but emergency problem.
6. If assistance were requested, how fast did the police respond?
7. If assistance were provided, what level of activity was undertaken?
8. Whether respondents had been stopped by police serving their neighborhood.
9. Whether respondents knew anyone who had been mistreated by police serving their neighborhood.

Second, we utilized a series of indicators of citizen *evaluations* of service levels. These included:

1. How fast respondents thought police serving their neighborhood

responded.
2. Whether respondents thought crime in the neighborhood was rising, about the same, or decreasing.
3. Whether respondents thought that police-community relations were outstanding, good, fair, or inadequate.
4. Whether respondents thought that the job performed by police serving their neighborhood was outstanding, good, fair, or inadequate.
5. Whether respondents thought that police services were equally available to all in their community.

We expanded this list of measures derived from random samples of citizens being served by varying sized departments with further measures derived from interviews with police and from other agency records (Bloch 1974; Hatry 1975). These included

1. The evaluation given by officers to the performance of their own police department.
2. The ratings given to the departments in the area by a pool of police officers serving a metropolitan area.
3. The proportion of warrants issued by the prosecutor to warrants applied for.

Findings

Using these multiple measures of output in a series of studies conducted in Indianapolis, Chicago, and St. Louis and replicated in Grand Rapids and Nashville–Davidson County, we found a consistent pattern *across* indicators of output (IsHak 1972; E. Ostrom 1976; E. Ostrom et al. 1973; E. Ostrom Parks, and Whitaker 1973; E. Ostrom and Whitaker 1974; Parks 1975; Rogers and McCurdy Lipsey 1974). Increases in size of police agencies serving similar neighborhoods did not increase productivity. Small departments performed either at equal or higher levels across the range of all indicators used. Having used the series of different indicators, we can make much more confident statements about the relative productivity of large and small police departments than if we had used a *single* measure of output.

Primary Reliance on One Mode of Data Collection

However, many of our individual measures of output were derived from one *mode* of data collection—that of individual interviews with respondents selected by a random process. Many scholars and public officials are uneasy about *any* reliance upon data collected about public agency performance from a survey of citizens. Citizens are thought by some to be uninformed and unable to give reliable perceptions and/or evaluations of service levels.

This challenge to a particular mode of data collection about the output of public agencies led us to design a study in which multiple measures of output were obtained from multiple *modes* of data collection (Greene et al. 1976; E. Ostrom 1973). We wanted to compare the similarity of data collected from three modes: citizen interviews, physical measurement devices, and agency records. The latter two modes of data collection are considered by many as "objective" data while interview data is considered "subjective." With such comparisons we could ask, for example, whether the pattern of service delivery as perceived by citizens was similar to that measured by some form of physical device or by agency records. We sought to determine whether "subjective" measures are related to "objective" measures.

Road Repair and Street Lighting

While one can talk about "physical" measures of output for local public services, there are few services for which one can "dream up" a way of physically measuring it, let alone having a measurement device already available. We finally selected two service areas—road repair and street lighting—where we thought we could develop physical measures, gain information from a random sample of citizens, and obtain information from agency records concerning levels of output. The Urban Institute had already undertaken some work in the area of measuring road roughness using a "roughometer" and the idea of measuring street lighting by a light meter seemed feasible.

Types of Measures Used

This project took us far astray from social science into the realm of physics, optics, and mechanics. We learned that developing valid and reliable physical measures of output—even for such relatively simple and clear cut services as road repair and street lighting—is not easy. For street lighting, we developed a method to utilize a precision light meter to record the level of night lighting on sidewalks and streets facing a particular blockface (Rich 1978b). For street repair, we developed a mechanical device, called the residential street roughness indicator, to measure the roughness of residential streets (Rich 1978a). In addition, we also developed an observation form and procedure that can be used by trained observers to record specific data about various aspects of street conditions. The procedure includes measuring all potholes on a block face with a "yardstick pothole measurer."

A survey represented our second mode of data collection. Our survey instrument was administered to respondents living in seven neighborhoods in Indianapolis during 1974. A total of 326 respondents were interviewed in this test. Citizens were asked a series of questions to elicit their *perceptions* of street lighting and road repair, their *evaluations* of the same, and their *preferences* for different levels of these services.

Agency records were to be our third mode of data collection. Unfortunately, we found this mode of data collection to be the most difficult of all. Agency records were so fragmentary that few consistent indicators could be developed. For road repair we were able to code the frequency of complaints directed to the Indianapolis Department of Transportation concerning the roads facing the respondents in our survey. For street lighting, we were not able to code much more than the frequency and pattern of street lights shown on agency maps.

Preliminary Findings

Preliminary data analysis has been initiated. One of the first questions we have addressed is, "What is the relationship between citizen perceptions of service levels and our physical measures of service levels?" This is a particularly important question since many policy analysts are hesitant to rely upon citizen-reported evaluation of output due to the assumed inaccuracy of citizen perceptions of service levels. Early analysis does not provide a completely uniform picture of accurate perception across all indicators. However, the more specific and concrete the referent to which our questions were addressed, the more likely a high level of association exists between physical measures and citizen perceptions of service levels.

For example, citizens generally were quite accurate in their perceptions of specific aspects of road repair on their block. Citizens accurately reported the type of street surface, the presence or absence of curbs, the condition of their curbs, the presence of surface disintegration, and the presence of potholes (Carroll 1978).

Sue Carroll of the Workshop staff developed a roughness scale composed of individual items derived from our observation procedures (Carroll 1978). The scale was developed for each quadrant of a block face and for an entire block face. The scale included the observer's coding of the amount of surface disintegration, the number and size of potholes, the presence or absence of bumps, and the presence or absence of utility cuts. Each observer was also asked to rate each block face as being "very rough," "fairly rough," "fairly smooth," and "very smooth." These observer ratings were strongly related to the physical "roughness scale" for both a quadrant (gamma = 0.94) and for the block face as a whole (gamma = 0.97). Given these high coefficients, the roughness scale derived from individual items coded by observers would appear to have at least some validity.

When respondents' perceptions of the roughness of the street on their block were then associated with the quadrant and block face roughness scale, the measure of association between them is fairly strong (gamma = 0.76 for both scales). As shown in table 7.1, some variation occurred across various control variables. Those persons with more than a high school diploma, those over 45, those who lived on a block more than 5 years, and those living on medium to short blocks tended to be more "accurate" in their perceptions of road roughness. Initial data analysis with scores produced by the residential street roughness indicator device is consistent with these findings. A high association exists among all these individual modes of data collection concerning the level of road roughness. The perceptions of citizens, the output from a mechanical device for measuring road roughness, and the coded observations of trained fieldworkers are positively associated.

Although the levels of association are not, in general, as high as in the case of street repair, statistically significant correlations between citizen perceived streetlight brightness levels on their block face and data from a precision photoelectric meter were found. Further, a distinct pattern emerged be-

TABLE 7.1. Measures of Association between Citizen Perceptions of Roughness and Scores on Both the Quadrant and the Block Face Roughness Scales

	Sex		Education			Age	
	Females	Males	Less than high school graduate	High school graduate	More than high school graduate	Less than 30 years old	30–45 years old
Entire sample							
Quadrant							
Gamma = 0.76	0.74	0.78	0.73	0.69	0.85	0.68	0.61
N = (247)	(142)	(102)	(82)	(77)	(80)	(80)	(66)
Block Face							
Gamma = 0.76	0.71	0.81	0.72	0.71	0.80	0.67[a]	
N = (319)	(183)	(132)	(99)	(106)	(106)	(190)	

	Age		Length of Residence		Length of Block Face		
	46–60 years old	More than 60 years old	Less than 1 year/1–5 years	More than 5 years	Short (650 ft)	Medium (650–900 ft)	Long (900 ft)
Quadrant							
Gamma = 0.76	0.87	0.93	0.66[a]	0.89	0.81	0.85	0.44
N = (247)	(57)	(44)	(126)	(121)	(74)	(79)	(74)
Block Face							
Gamma = 0.76	0.89[a]		0.67[a]	0.87	0.91[b]	0.69[b]	0.69[b]
N = (319)	(129)		(160)	(159)	(100)	(101)	(118)

Source: Carroll 1978 (28).

[a]Because of the nature of the distributions, there were too few respondents to compute gamma for these categories separately. Therefore, two categories have been combined.

[b]Even by combining these two categories, there were so few respondents with scale scores in the "very rough" or "fairly rough" categories that gamma could not be computed. Therefore, the scale was dichotomized into "rough" and "smooth" and Yule's quotient was computed.

tween the strength of association and the distance on either side of a respondent's house over which light meter readings were averaged. Correlations reach a maximum when meter readings are averaged over intervals relatively proximate to a respondent's home and decline as the meter readings are averaged over widening intervals.

The lowest correlation is between citizen perceptions of streetlight brightness and light meter readings averaged for an entire block face. For some subsets of the sample, this correlation was not statistically significant. Citizens, thus, appear to show a pronounced tendency to perceive block face streetlight brightness conditions in terms of the brightness levels relatively proximate to their own homes. When asked specifically about conditions near to their homes, citizens are more accurate. We found that citizens who had lived on their block for more than 10 years, who had a high school or better education, or who lived on relatively short blocks showed a higher than average degree of accuracy.

Significance of Findings for Other Service Areas

Ascertaining the Least Expensive and Valid Measure of Output

The finding that measures derived from interviews with citizens and measures derived from physical devices or field observation forms are positively related for two service areas has considerable importance for those interested in measuring the productivity of local public service agencies. In the first place, given the close association between the diverse modes of data collection regarding road repair, public officials or public interest groups concerned in ascertaining the relative productivity of agencies engaged in road repair activities can select the mode of data collection that is least expensive. The results obtained will correlate highly with results obtained from more expensive modes of data collection. Thus, we can increase the productivity of measuring productivity! Of the three modes of data collection compared— the residential street roughness indicator, the field observation form, and the citizen survey—the field observation form is the least expensive mode of data collection. . . .

Citizen Perceptions of Specific Service Attributes are Relatively Accurate

The findings from these studies are important also for those areas where no physical measures of output are possible. Given that citizens seem to be fairly accurate in their perception of specific and clear-cut attributes of road repair and street lighting, one can have somewhat more confidence that citizens will be fairly accurate in their perception of specific attributes of other services. To the extent that questions can be phrased about specific aspects of services for which there are no physical measures of output, it would appear that one can obtain fairly accurate perceptions from citizens.

This means that considerable attention must be paid to the construction of questions on citizen surveys. We found, for example, in our early pretesting of our police-services instrument that asking the question: How fast did the police arrive? (to a person who had been a victim of crime and had called upon the police) was not specific enough. Many respondents indicated only "very fast" or "slow." We then found that some people thought "slow" was 10 minutes while others thought "slow" was 30 minutes. Given this information from our pretests, we obtained data about response time in terms of minutes elapsed between call and response.

The focus of this essay has been on the measurement of the output side of the productivity equation. It is indeed the most difficult problem in determining the relative productivity of different public agencies. Many scholars have "thrown up their hands in despair" and assumed that measuring outputs of public services was impossible. This has, at times, led them to utilize expenditure data as measures of output. The relative productivity of different agencies can *never* be determined if input measures are used as output measures. While the problem of measuring output is indeed difficult, the development of multiple measures of output derived from one or more modes of data collection seems our only route in understanding productivity.

However, to assess productivity, we do indeed need to measure the input side and relate inputs to outputs. Empirical examination of productivity should be related to theory in the sense of identifying the factors we presume to make a difference in affecting productivity. Some of these factors relate to organizational variables such as the size of a jurisdiction, degree of overlap, level of cooperation, etc.[2] Other factors relate to money, personnel, and technologies used in particular production processes. As we examine the comparative productivity of different types of public agencies, we should derive hypotheses about what different factors are expected to make a difference in the productivity of public agencies. Then, our research efforts can secure evidence to reject hypotheses that are not supported and to increase the warrantability of those that are supported.

Most of our presumptions about the factors likely to increase productivity of public agencies have *not* been subjected to empirical test. They are accepted as part of the conventional wisdom. However, many of the findings in our current research about comparative levels of productivity run contrary to conventional wisdom. A surprising number of studies indicate either no significant economies or substantial diseconomies to be associated with increased size of public service agencies (Bish and Ostrom 1973). Yet these findings are often ignored as though we should not be confused by the facts. When presumptions that are assumed to be true are not supported by empirical evidence, we are confronted with the serious task of rethinking our presumptions and of developing alternative explanations for why we get the results we do (E. Ostrom, Parks, and Whitaker 1973). The crisis of confidence that pervades much of U.S. public life calls for more than productivity measures. But productivity measures are key elements in our efforts to explain why we often get such poor results with such lavish efforts.

NOTES

1. Many agencies do not even make full use of the activity records that could easily be converted into important internal reports. For a discussion of the loss of information about the large volume of service calls and activity level resulting from a police department's primary reliance upon the F.B.I. Index Crimes, see Parks 1971.

2. It is these factors that have been the focus of our own studies. These are the "institutional" variables that are frequently the subject of change by policymakers who wish to improve the productivity of operations by local government agencies.

REFERENCES

Bish, Robert L., and Vincent Ostrom. 1973. *Understanding Urban Government. Metropolitan Reform Reconsidered.* Washington, DC: American Enterprise Institute.

Bloch, Peter B. 1974. *Equality of Distribution of Police Services—A Case Study of Washington, D.C.* Washington, DC: Urban Institute.

Breton, Albert. 1966. "A Theory of the Demand for Public Goods." *Canadian Journal of Economics and Politics* 32 (November): 455–67.

Carroll, Sue. 1978. "An Analysis of the Relationship between Citizen Perceptions and Unobtrusive Measures of Street Conditions." Measures Technical Report No. 10. Bloomington: Indiana University, Workshop in Political Theory and Policy Analysis.

Davies, David. 1965. "Financing Urban Functions." *Law Contemporary Problems* 30: 127–61.

Davis, Otto, and Andrew Whinston. 1967. "On the Distribution between Public and Private Goods." *American Economic Review* 57 (May): 360–73.

Greene, Vernon, Elinor Ostrom, Roger B. Parks, and Richard Rich. 1976. "The Measures Project—A Theoretical and Methodological Overview." Measures Technical Report No. 1. Bloomington: Indiana University, Workshop in Political Theory and Policy Analysis.

Hatry, Harry P. 1975. "Wrestling with Police Crime Control Productivity Measurement." In *Readings on Productivity in Policing,* Joan L. Wifle and John F. Heaphy, eds., 86–128. Washington, DC: Police Foundation.

IsHak, S. T. 1972. "Consumers' Perception of Police Performance: Consolidation vs. Deconcentration: The Case of Grand Rapids, Michigan Metropolitan Area." Ph.D. diss., Indiana University.

Michigan Advisory Commission on Criminal Justice. 1975. Criminal Justice Goals and Standards for the State of Michigan. Lansing: Michigan Advisory Commission on Criminal Justice.

National Advisory Commission on Criminal Justice Standards and Goals. 1973. *Report on Police.* Washington, DC: U.S. Government Printing Office.

Ostrom, Elinor. 1971. "Institutional Arrangements and the Measurement of Policy Consequences: Applications to Evaluating Police Performance." *Urban Affairs Quarterly* 4 (June): 447–75.

———. 1973. "The Need for Multiple Indicators in Measuring the Output of Public Agencies." *Policy Studies Journal* 2 (winter): 85–92.

———. 1976. "Size and Performance in a Federal System." *Publius* 6 (spring): 33–73. (Chapter 10 in this volume.)

Ostrom, Elinor, William H. Baugh, Richard Guarasci, Roger B. Parks, and Gordon P. Whitaker. 1973. *Community Organization and the Provision of Police Services,* Sage Professional Papers in Administrative and Policy Studies 03–001. Beverly Hills: Sage.

Ostrom, Elinor, Roger B. Parks, and Gordon P. Whitaker. 1973. "Do We Really Want to Consolidate Urban Police Forces? A Reappraisal of Some Old Assertions." *Public Administration Review* 33 (September/October): 423–33.

Ostrom, Elinor, and Gordon P. Whitaker. 1974. "Community Control and Government Responsiveness: The Case of Police in Black Communities." In *Improving the Quality of Urban Management,* ed. David Rogers and Willis Hawley, 303–34. Urban Affairs Annual Reviews, vol. 8. Beverly Hills: Sage. (Chapter 9 in this volume.)

Parks, Roger B. 1971. *Measurement of Performance in the Public Sector: A Case Study of the Indianapolis Police Department.* Bloomington: Indiana University, Workshop in Political Theory and Policy Analysis.

———. 1975. "Complementary Measures of Police Performance." In *Public Policy and Evaluation,* ed. Kenneth M. Dolbeare, 185–218. Sage Yearbook in Politics and Public Policy, vol. 2. Beverly Hills: Sage.

Rich, Richard. 1978a. "The Development of the Residential Street Roughness Indicator as a Mode of Measurement of the Study of Municipal Services." Measures Technical Report No. 6. Bloomington: Indiana University, Workshop in Political Theory and Policy Analysis.

Rich, Richard. 1978b. "The Development of a Technique for the Physical Measurement of Residential Street Lighting." Measures Technical Report No. 5. Bloomington: Indiana University, Workshop in Political Theory and Policy Analysis.

Rogers, Bruce D., and C. McCurdy Lipsey. 1974. "Metropolitan Reform: Citizen Evaluations of Performances in Nashville–Davidson County, Tennessee." *Publius* 4 (fall): 19–34.

Samuelson, Paul A. 1954. "The Pure Theory of Public Expenditure." *The Review of Economics and Statistics* 36 (November): 387–89.

Smith, Dennis, and Elinor Ostrom. 1974. "The Effects of Training and Education on Police Attitudes and Performance." In *The Potential for Reform of Criminal Justice,* ed. Herbert Jacob, 45–81. Beverly Hills: Sage.

CHAPTER 8

Does Local Community Control of Police Make a Difference? Some Preliminary Findings

Elinor Ostrom and Gordon P. Whitaker

Proponents of community control of police services argue that the differing preferences of individuals living in different neighborhoods should affect the type of services they receive.[1] The argument is made that opportunities for citizen control and participation are enhanced in smaller jurisdictions (see Warren 1970; Nie, Powell, and Prewitt 1969; Indik 1965; Dahl 1967; Citizens' League Committee on Minority Representation in Local Government 1970).[2] Officials chosen by a smaller community are more likely to live in the local community and thus be aware of the needs and interests of that particular community as well as be more open to formal requests for service. It is further argued that the distance between the highest and lowest levels of a smaller department is less than that of a large department. Consequently, formal communication and control within a small department can more easily be accomplished. The likelihood of greater internal control coupled with the opportunity of greater citizen-official interaction might be expected to improve the transformation of citizen demands into police services. However, many proponents of community control do not recommend the elimination of all citywide services. Neighborhood services such as patrol, minor investigation, and emergency aid might be placed under community control while communications and records systems, laboratories, and special investigation units could be maintained on a broader scale (Waskow 1970, 39).

Originally published in *American Journal of Political Science* 17, no. 1 (February 1973): 48–76. Copyright © 1973. Reprinted by permission of the University of Wisconsin Press and the authors.

Authors' note: This essay is based upon a paper presented at the Western Political Science Association meetings in Albuquerque, New Mexico, April 8–10, 1971. The authors gratefully acknowledge support from the Office of Research and Advanced Studies, Indiana University, and from National Science Foundation Grant No. GS-27383. William Baugh, Richard Guarasci, and Roger Parks played an important role in the design of the study and in the field. We also want to thank Richard Hofstetter, Vincent Ostrom, and Dennis Smith for their helpful comments and criticism and Susan Thomas for her reliable work as a research assistant.

While there has been a wide variety of proposals calling for some form of decentralization or neighborhood control over aspects of police services, there are still those who feel strongly that such reforms would *not* lead to, increased police performance. James Q. Wilson, for example, believes that the issue of order maintenance and law enforcement in the central city are "of such emotional and political significance" that police are always under political pressure from a variety of sources: "Allowing them to be governed by neighborhoods could only intensify that pressure, putting the police at the mercy of the rawest emotions, the most demagogic spokesmen, and the most provincial concerns" (Wilson 1968, 289).

General agreement is lacking on the consequences that are produced by different scales of urban police jurisdictions and forms of community organization in metropolitan areas. This lack of agreement calls for evaluative research that attempts to ascertain the warrantability of the implicit propositions contained in arguments for or against community control. Before further "reforms" are recommended, we should attempt to ascertain whether predicted consequences will flow from the changes being recommended.

While the proponents of community control do not yet share a consistent overall theory, a series of interrelated propositions can be derived from the literature cited previously. Such propositions can then form the foundation for evaluative research (Suchman 1967; see also E. Ostrom 1972). Many of the arguments for community control relate to the following nine propositions.

P_1 Police officers and police administrators working in small-sized police agencies will have more information about the areas they serve and conditions in the field than will their counterparts in larger agencies.

P_2 Citizens living in community-controlled jurisdictions will have more capacity to articulate demands for service and will have better knowledge about their police than will citizens living in citywide-controlled jurisdictions.

P_3 An increase in the capacity of citizens to articulate demands for service more effectively and an increase in their knowledge about police will be associated with an increase in the knowledge that police officers and police administrators have of citizen preferences.

P_4 An increase in the citizens' knowledge about police will be associated with an increase in their support of police.

P_5 An increase in citizens' support of police will be associated with an increase in the levels of police output.

P_6 An increase in the knowledge of police officers about the area they are serving and about citizen preferences will be associated with an increase in the levels of police output.

P_7 An increase in the knowledge of police administrators of field conditions in their area will be associated with an increase in their effective control over actions of their department.

P_8 An increase in the effective control of police administrators over actions of their department will be associated with an increase in the levels of police output.

P_9 An increase in the levels of police output will be associated with an increase in citizen support for the police.

The posited interrelationships among the variables are shown schematically in figure 8.1. From this set of propositions, the following working hypotheses can be derived

When smaller, community-controlled police agencies are compared to larger, citywide-controlled police agencies serving similar neighborhoods, the following observations should be found within the jurisdiction of the smaller agencies

H_1 Citizens with more capacity to articulate demands for services,
H_2 Citizens with more knowledge about their police,
H_3 Citizens with higher levels of support for their police,
H_4 Police officers with more knowledge of the area served and citizen preferences,
H_5 Police administrators with more knowledge of field conditions and citizen preferences,
H_6 Police administrators with more effective control over actions taken within their department,
H_7 Higher levels of police output.

The design of a study to examine all of the posited relations involved in the arguments for community control would be a complex and costly endeavor. We have, as a first step, focused primarily on the seventh working hypothesis, that is, that smaller and community-controlled police agencies will have higher levels of output when compared with larger, citywide police agencies serving similar neighborhoods. If evidence supporting this hypothesis is obtained, then more extended research and analysis would be merited. Extended studies could then examine all of the links from size of police agencies and community control through to higher levels of police output. A preliminary study focusing primarily on H_7 was initiated in the spring of 1970. The findings of this study are reported in a later section. However, prior to discussing the findings of this study several questions concerning the methodology of the study will first be discussed.

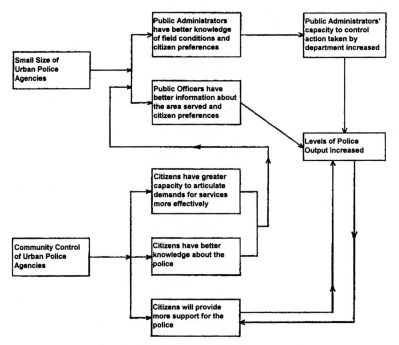

Fig. 8.1. Posited relations of small size and community control with intervening and dependent variables

Measurement and Design

Any attempt to measure the consequences of different organizational arrangements for providing urban police services is handicapped by the general lack of agreement about appropriate methods for measuring police output (see U.S. Department of Health, Education and Welfare 1969; see also Gardiner 1968, 152). For years, the FBI Crime Index has been utilized as a crude indicator of how "poorly" a department was performing. However, the FBI Crime Index is now widely regarded as an extremely unreliable indicator (Price 1966; Wolfgang 1963; Biderman 1966; Beattie 1955; Wilson 1966).[3]

The problem of measuring the output of police agencies is a general problem that pervades the analysis of the output of most public agencies. Services provided by police vary in the extent to which they are nonpackageable, but the provision of public safety and order is certainly the provision of public goods.[4] Public police departments characteristically provide all services without consumer charges, even though some similar services are provided privately. Thus, the market value of police output cannot be obtained.

None of the records that are routinely maintained by police departments themselves enable an analyst to compute easily the effectiveness of a particular police force. The internal records of most police departments consist mainly of workload data: rates of reported crime, traffic citations, and clearance of reported cases, for example. The indeterminacies involved in the production of police services have led some top police officials to place special emphasis on improving performance as measured by such indicators.[5] Thus, police-maintained indicators of output may be inflated due to internal pressures within a police department to produce the "right" data. Moreover, police data are entirely production oriented. Consumers' evaluations of the services they are receiving are not recorded at any point in routine police records (E. Ostrom 1971). As Hatry has cogently argued: "What is needed for evaluation are criteria that come as close as possible to reflecting the basic, underlying objectives of the government—the effects upon people" (see Hatry 1970).[6]

Because of the lack of reliability and validity of police records as a source of data for evaluation of the performance of police agencies, a number of scholars have recently relied upon sample surveys of citizens to obtain information about victimization rates as well as general evaluations of the services received. Studies such as those for the President's Commission on Law Enforcement and Administration of Justice have concluded that citizen surveys are a reliable means for ascertaining the extent of victimization of citizens and give a more complete assessment of crime rates against individuals than police records (see Biderman 1966; Ennis 1967; Reiss 1967; Costner et al. 1970). Other studies have utilized surveys to obtain measures of citizens' general evaluations of the services they were receiving from police and other public agencies (see Aberbach and Walker 1970; Richard 1969; Devine 1970; Rossi and Berk 1970; Jacob 1970).

The problem of measuring police output was met in this study by designing a survey instrument to obtain two types of information about police output. First, respondents reported their experience with police and criminal victimization. Second, they were asked for their general evaluations of police service. The questions relating to *experience* variables concerned whether anyone in the family unit had been a victim of criminal activity, whether the police had been of assistance to the family, whether the respondent had been stopped by a policeman, and whether the respondent knew any policemen who worked in his neighborhood. Follow-up questions were asked of those who were victimized, had been assisted or had been stopped by the police. Follow-up questions were designed to ascertain what the police had done in each instance and how rapidly they had offered assistance.

A second series of questions concerned citizens' general *evaluation* of the output of police serving their respective neighborhoods. They included the following: (1) how rapidly respondents thought police responded to calls in their neighborhood; (2) whether they thought crime in their neighborhood was increasing; (3) their evaluation of neighborhood police-citizen relationships; (4) whether they thought police serving their neighborhood accepted bribes; and, (5) a general evaluation of the job police in their neighborhood were doing.

Any attempt to measure police output, by survey or other methods, must attempt to control for as many as possible of the other variables, in addition to the police themselves, that may affect police performance within the community. Such control can be achieved through the use of a most similar systems research design (see Przeworski and Teune 1970).[7] Such a design requires the location of several communities where most relevant population characteristics are quite similar except for the size of the police force. Given very similar areas, located ideally within one county to reduce the variation of other institutional arrangements, one can make inferences about the output of different police agencies. Such a comparative analysis is as close as we come in the social sciences to the establishment of laboratory conditions in which one variable at a time is manipulated while all other variables are held constant.

Research Site

The location of this study is the Indianapolis metropolitan area. The widely heralded city-county consolidation of the city of Indianapolis with Marion County (most frequently called Unigov in the press) did not in any way affect the organization of police forces in Marion County (Lawrence and Turnbull 1969). Nor did the provisions of this legislation affect the three relatively small separately incorporated communities of Beech Grove, Lawrence, and Speedway, which were excluded from most of the legislation. The location of these independent communities, each having its own small, locally controlled police force immediately adjacent to the territory served by the Indianapolis Police Department, provides a very appropriate research site for a comparative study of the relationship of the size of police agencies to levels of police output. Three neighborhoods inside Indianapolis were matched with the three independent communities in terms of social, economic, and physical characteristics.

The three independent communities vary in population from approximately 12,000 to 16,000. All three are predominantly populated by white, middle-income families with similar educational backgrounds, who are employed in a similar range of occupations and live in owner-occupied residences. One community is organized as a town (Speedway) and the other two as cities.[8] Three adjoining Indianapolis neighborhoods were selected as sample areas. Each was matched to be as similar as possible to the adjacent independent community. The entire city of Indianapolis was *not* selected for comparative study with the three independent communities because of the great variation in population characteristics and neighborhoods within the city as a whole. Many of the factors that may affect the performance of the police are thus present in relatively similar degrees in all six neighborhoods studied. All six are nearly equidistant from the center of Indianapolis.

The most pertinent difference between the three independent communities and the three Indianapolis neighborhoods for this study is the form of their local community organization and the attendant variation in the scale of local police organization. The independent communities each have their own police forces. These are relatively small, ranging in size from 18 to 26 full-time officers. Each force provides on-the-job training for its recruits and utilizes external training facilities to some extent. Some specialization is present in small detective, traffic, and juvenile divisions. All three police forces call upon the Indiana State Crime Laboratory in Indianapolis when specialized laboratory facilities are needed. Cooperative arrangements have been established between the three independent community police forces, the Indianapolis City Police, and the Marion County Sheriff's Office to deal with emergency conditions occurring in each cooperating jurisdiction.

The Indianapolis Police Department consists of approximately 1,100 officers of whom approximately 60 percent are in the Operations Division responsible for traffic patrol and nonspecialized police activities. The entire Indianapolis area is divided into seven sectors. There are no precinct houses in Indianapolis. Until late in 1969, roll calls were held in the City-County Building downtown for all beats. Now roll calls are held at schools located within each sector. The Indianapolis department has been quite innovative in a number of ways and would certainly rank as one of the more modern police departments in the country.[9]

The per capita cost of the police departments in the three small communities is *less* than the per capita cost of the Indianapolis department. However, when one examines the cost of the services being provided to the residents of the three Indianapolis neighborhoods (rather than the city as a whole) the amount expended per capita in all six neighborhoods is similar though slightly higher in the towns (see E. Ostrom et al. 1973).

Data and Methods

The data for this study were collected in a survey conducted during April 1970. An area probability sample was drawn for each of the six neighborhoods from Marion County zoning maps, within sampling frames selected with the aid of information from the 1960 census and a physical examination of the neighborhoods themselves. A total of 722 respondents was interviewed (373 from the independent communities and 349 from the Indianapolis communities) from a total sample of 940 households: a response rate of 76 percent. The effort to match the neighborhoods in regard to socioeconomic characteristics appears to have been relatively successful. Table 8.1 presents a comparison of socioeconomic characteristics of the two groups of households surveyed. In general, very little difference exists between the respondents in the independent communities and respondents in the Indianapolis neighborhoods in regard to such factors as home ownership, length of residence, occupation of head of household, age, and family type. The greatest difference among the respondents on these characteristics is related to the length of residence in the neighborhood. Each respondent was also asked

TABLE 8.1. Personal Background Characteristics of Respondents in the Two Types of Neighborhoods (in percentages)

Community Characteristics	Independent Communities	Indianapolis Neighborhoods
Ownership of housing		
Buying home	85	89
Renting home	8	9
Renting apartment	8	2
Number of cases	369	347
Length of residence		
Less than 2 years	21	21
2 to 5 years	23	25
6 to 10 years	19	35
More than 10 years	36	20
Number of cases	373	349
Occupation of head of household		
Professional-managerial	19	20
Clerical-sales	17	21
Craftsmen-foremen	21	15
Semiskilled	18	20
Unskilled	7	9
Retired	8	3
Housewife	6	6
Number of cases	356	346
Age of respondent		
16–30	27	31
31–40	24	34
41–50	21	21
Over 50	28	14
Number of cases	339	321
Sex of respondent		
Male	42	49
Female	58	51
Number of cases	404	384
Participation in community organizations		
Members of some community organization	39	41
Not members of any community organization	61	59
Number of cases	366	349

about membership in community organizations. Even in regard to this variable, which could not be controlled by sampling and field methods, respondents in both groups of neighborhoods are very similar.

We operationalize the concepts of H_7 by comparing the services provided by small-sized, community-controlled police agencies and large-sized, citywide-controlled police departments serving very similar areas. The dependent variable, levels of police output, is measured by a series of indicators derived from a survey of citizens living in both types of jurisdictions. Since no agreed-upon method exists for weighting the dimensions of output measured by different indicators, we do not collapse them into a single scale. Rather we expect to find the following patterns of responses.

A significantly larger proportion of citizens living in the small, independent communities should

1. Report not being a victim of crime;
2. Receive assistance from the police;
3. Rate the police as responding rapidly;
4. Think that crime is not increasing in their neighborhood;
5. Rate police-citizen relations as good;
6. Indicate that police do not accept bribes; and
7. Rate the job being done by police in their neighborhood as generally good or outstanding.

We do find a general pattern of higher levels of police output in the independent communities when compared to the Indianapolis neighborhoods. In the sections that follow, we will discuss the findings for each type of measure in detail. In the first place, individuals' responses will be aggregated by neighborhoods to determine if the general pattern of higher performance levels in independent communities is consistent throughout the areas studied. Second, for the evaluation variables at the individual level we will also examine the levels of association between the type of community in which individuals live and their evaluations of the police. Experience variables will be introduced as controls to ascertain whether individual responses reflect general community-wide differences or are related to respondents' direct experiences with victimization and police.[10]

Police Output as Measured by Direct Experiences

Victimization

Residents of the Indianapolis neighborhoods surveyed were victims of criminal activity more often than residents of the three towns.[11] One household out of four among the Indianapolis neighborhoods reported victimization during the preceding two years. Households in the independent communities averaged a victimization rate of 18 percent—less than one in five for the same period. Except for one Indianapolis neighborhood, this pattern was consistent in each of the areas studied (see table 8.2). Members of households in the Indianapolis neighborhoods were also more likely to have been victimized twice during the two-year period even though second victimizations were infrequent. Unfortunately, information on the specific location of the crime is not available. The data include crimes against a member of the household whether at home or somewhere else.[12] It appears probable, however, that a citizen's vulnerability to crime in the three Indianapolis neighborhoods is higher than in the independent communities.

In addition to the finding that household members living in the independent communities were victimized less than household members living in the Indianapolis neighborhoods, we also found that residents of the independent communities were more likely to report victimizations to their local police. While only 10 percent of the victimizations of town residents were not reported to police, 18 percent of the victimizations of Indianapolis residents were unreported. Each of the areas fit this pattern with one exception.[13]

One interpretation of a higher rate of reporting victimizations to police is that citizens are more likely to report such events when their expectation of police follow-up is greater. If this interpretation is warranted, we should expect to find citizens in the independent communities receiving a higher level of police follow-up to reports of victimizations than citizens of the Indianapolis neighborhoods. This indeed is what we found. Respondents who had reported victimizations to their local police were asked about the extent of police activity on their behalf. Cases in which the police did nothing, spoke to the victim only by phone, or made only a single trip were classified as involving a low level of follow-up. Reports of more extensive investigation efforts, the "identification of a culprit" or the "solving of the crime," were coded as involving a high level of police follow-up. As shown in table 8.2, independent town residents received high levels of follow-up from their local police in about one out of two cases. Indianapolis police provided a high level of service in only one out of three cases reported. The number of cases is relatively small, but the pattern is consistent for all six areas.

Thus, in regard to victimization, we found that citizens living in the independent communities were victimized less than citizens living in the Indianapolis neighborhoods. Of those who were victimized in both types of communities, residents of the independent towns reported victimizations at a higher rate than residents of the Indianapolis neighborhoods and received a higher level of follow-up from the police serving their areas.

Assistance

Residents of the three towns received assistance from police at a higher rate than did similar residents of Indianapolis neighborhoods.[14] According to our findings, approximately one out of every four households in the towns was given some special service or emergency aid by the local police during the preceding two years. For households in the three Indianapolis neighborhoods, the rate for assistance by city police was about one in six for the same period. Although the rate varied slightly, the pattern was maintained in all six areas (see table 8.2). The services rendered included administering first aid, calming family quarrels, locating lost children, and watching the homes of vacationers (the last only in the independent communities).

While the proportion of residents receiving assistance can easily be ascertained, the value of each separate service to its recipient household is not directly measurable. Likewise, the quality of the service rendered is difficult to assess. The survey did include two follow-up questions designed to elicit some aspects of the quality of police assistance. Those who had called upon the police for assistance were asked how rapidly the police responded. Police serving the independent communities responded within five minutes to approximately 80 percent of their calls for assistance while the Indianapolis Police responded to only some 60 percent of their calls for assistance in five minutes or less. In the second question, respondents receiving assistance were asked to describe what the police did. Responses were coded as either dealing with the problem in a satisfactory or unsatisfactory manner. A similarly high proportion of respondents in all sample areas rated police as responding to calls in a satisfactory manner. Thus, more town residents received assistance from their police, assistance came more rapidly but was of generally similar quality when compared to that provided to residents of the Indianapolis neighborhoods by their police force.

Stopped as Suspected Offenders

The third experience variable relates to whether citizens have been stopped by police for any reason.[15] As shown in table 8.2, the rate at which citizens in all six neighborhoods were stopped by police is very similar. Approximately 25 percent of the residents in both the independent communities and the Indianapolis neighborhoods were stopped by police. The most frequent reasons given for being stopped related to traffic infractions of one type or another. Most of those stopped reported polite treatment from the police. The similarity of citizens' experiences with police in regard to their being stopped as suspected offenders implies a relatively uniform enforcement of the law in the two areas at least in regard to traffic law. The finding that law enforcement activities are relatively uniform in both types of communities eliminates an alternative explanation for the consistently better evaluation given by citizens in the independent communities. The higher ratings of their police by those citizens cannot be explained as being the result of lax traffic law enforcement in the independent communities as compared with the Indianapolis neighborhoods.

Knowing Policemen

The last experience variable, whether citizens know policemen, has a unique position in our analysis.[16] While in and of itself, a higher proportion of citizens knowing police cannot be thought of as a measure of output, we would expect police performance to increase in communities where higher proportions of citizens knew members of the police force due to the increased opportunity for communication between police and citizens. Further, one would expect individuals in smaller political jurisdictions to know more policemen than citizens living in much larger political jurisdictions. One would also expect those who personally knew more policemen to rate police performance more highly than those who knew fewer policemen or no policemen. We did find a higher proportion of individuals in the independent communities who knew policemen (52 percent in the independent communities to 40 percent in the Indianapolis neighborhoods).[17] Residents of the independent communities were also more likely to know more than two policemen (see table 8.2). Knowing policemen is very weakly associated to favorable ratings of police for two evaluation variables and not associated for the others. However, it will be introduced as a control variable to assess further its impact on citizen ratings since it constitutes a potentially relevant difference between the experiences of citizens in the independent communities and Indianapolis.

Police Output as Measured by Citizen Evaluation

Evaluation of Promptness

One important aspect of police performance is the rate at which calls are answered. Whether a call involves a request for emergency aid or a report of a suspicious incident or a crime in progress, speed is often a necessary condition for the success of the police response. Police records often do not include information about response time. Even when such records are maintained, problems involved in reporting and recording such information contaminate the data. Citizens' perceptions of the speed of response in their neighborhood may be even less accurate. However, the past failure to respond quickly enough in an emergency situation, and the resultant lack of police protection, may be remembered by a number of individuals and be a

TABLE 8.2. Police Output as Measured by Direct Experiences (in percentages)

	Independent Communities				Indianapolis Neighborhoods			
Experience Variables	Beech Grove	Lawrence	Speedway	Total	Near Beech Grove	Near Lawrence	Near Speedway	Total
Criminal victimization, crime not reported, and follow-up of local police to reported crime								
Households victimized								
First victimization	23	22	13	18	15	31	31	26
Second victimization	3	1	—	1	3	5	2	3
Number of cases	102	127	144	373	101	124	124	349
Victimizations not reported to police	12	7	11	10	33	22	7	18
Number of victimizations	26	29	18	73	18	45	40	103
Level of follow-up by local police department								
High	40	47	55	47	27	36	38	36
Number of cases	15	17	11	43	11	27	29	67
Citizens assisted, promptness of local departments, and quality of assistance								
Citizens assisted by local police department	23	24	29	26	20	16	16	17
Number of cases	90	119	127	336	92	105	114	311

(continued)

TABLE 8.2.— Continued

Experience Variables	Independent Communities				Indianapolis Neighborhoods			
	Beech Grove	Lawrence	Speedway	Total	Near Beech Grove	Near Lawrence	Near Speedway	Total
Promptness of local department's responses to calls for assistance								
1–5 minutes	71	73	89	79	62	64	53	60
6–10 minutes	17	19	4	13	12	8	33	18
11–15 minutes	6	4	4	4	6	8	7	7
Over 16 minutes	6	4	4	4	19	20	7	16
Number of cases	17	26	28	71	16	14	15	45
Quality of assistance								
Satisfactory	79	73	82	77	81	75	73	77
Number of cases	19	26	27	72	16	12	11	39
Citizens stopped by police								
Stopped	18	31	21	24	23	24	27	25
Number of cases	91	121	113	325	92	106	117	315
Number of policemen known								
None	43	49	51	48	62	66	54	60
One	24	28	19	24	17	17	21	19
Two	13	6	11	10	11	7	12	10
More than two	20	17	19	19	10	10	13	11
Number of cases	89	117	130	336	92	106	117	318

topic of neighborhood conversation. By asking citizens how fast police in their neighborhood respond to calls, one obtains information about citizens' perceptions of the pattern established by the police *and* an evaluation of that pattern in light of citizen preferences about the speed of police response.[18] Such data indicate how well police are meeting citizen demands for prompt availability of police service.

As shown in table 8.3, local police were evaluated as more prompt by residents of the three towns than by residents of the Indianapolis neighborhoods. The pattern is quite consistent for the six areas. At the individual level, the simple relationship between type of community organization and evaluation of police promptness is moderately strong (see table 8.4). The level of association between community organization and evaluation of police promptness is appreciably affected by two of the experience variables. Since those who have been assisted by police in all areas tend to evaluate police promptness more favorably, the level of association between community organization and evaluation of police promptness is weaker for this group than for those who have not been assisted. For those assisted, the relationship between their evaluation of police response rate and the response time they reported for the police assisting them is moderately strong. Thus, the speed with which police respond in specific instances affects the evaluation of how quickly they respond in general. It would appear that those who have not been assisted in the independent communities have heard about the more rapid response time that their police forces are able to sustain when called upon for assistance.

The second experience variable that affects the association between type of community organization and evaluation of police promptness is personal acquaintance with police. Those who know three or more police in both types of areas are apt to evaluate police promptness relatively the same. Thus, the strength of association between community organization and evaluation of police promptness is strongest for those who do not know any police, falls somewhat for those who know one or two policemen, and almost disappears for the higher category. Neither victimization nor stopped as a control variable has much effect on the strength of association between community organization and evaluation of police promptness.

Thus the tendency of town residents to indicate that their police respond very rapidly seems to reflect an evaluation based on indirect knowledge of the general level of police responsiveness in the neighborhood which, as mentioned previously, would appear to be higher in the independent communities. Despite the fact that the relationship is affected by introducing control variables, the most pervasive tendency remains for citizens of the towns to evaluate their police as being more prompt than citizens of the Indianapolis neighborhoods rate response of their police.

Evaluation of Neighborhood Crime Trend

By asking respondents whether they thought crime in their neighborhood was increasing, about the same, or decreasing, we sought to obtain an indirect measure of the effectiveness of crime prevention as perceived by citizens.[19] As shown in table 8.3, a smaller percentage of respondents in the three independent towns thought that crime was increasing in their neighborhoods than did respondents in the Indianapolis neighborhoods, although the rate varies.

At the individual level the strength of relationship between community organization and neighborhood crime trends is considerably stronger for those individuals who have been victimized than for those who have not been victimized (see table 8.4). Fifty-seven percent of the Indianapolis respondents who were victimized responded that crime in their neighborhood was increasing while only 18 percent of the respondents living in the independent communities who had been victimized made the same evaluation of neighborhood crime trend. While the relationship is thus very strong for victims, the level of association between community organization and evaluation of neighborhood crime trends almost disappears for nonvictims. Controlling for the other experience variables does not affect the association between community organization and neighborhood crime trends.

Little systematic difference exists in the responses given by residents of the independent communities and those of the Indianapolis neighborhoods to this question *except for those who were victims.* This is a somewhat puzzling finding. The tendency for Indianapolis victims to believe that crime is increasing in their neighborhoods may reflect an actual increase in crime in those areas that is not yet generally recognized to have occurred by other residents of the same neighborhoods. Town residents, on the other hand, may have a more realistic view of their vulnerability to crime and thus accept a somewhat lower rate of victimization as part of an expected pattern.

Evaluation of Bribe Taking by Police

Little difference is found between residents of the towns and those of three Indianapolis neighborhoods regarding their evaluation of police bribe taking (see table 8.3).[20] At the individual level, those who have been stopped by police are more likely to indicate that police take bribes than those who have *not* been stopped. In general, as shown in table 8.4, experience variables have little effect on the low association between community organization and evaluation of potential bribe taking by police. Since citizens living in each type of community are similarly confident that the police serving their neighborhoods do not take bribes, we conclude for this indicator of performance the two types of areas should be equally ranked.

TABLE 8.3. Police Output as Measured by Citizen Evaluation (in percentages)

Evaluation Variables	Independent Communities				Indianapolis Neighborhoods			
	Beech Grove	Lawrence	Speedway	Total	Near Beech Grove	Near Lawrence	Near Speedway	Total
Evaluation of response rate of neighborhood police								
Very rapidly	62	63	72	66	44	42	46	43
Quickly enough	33	33	28	31	39	41	42	41
Slowly	4	4	—	2	17	18	12	16
Number of cases	90	108	125	323	75	101	100	276
Evaluation of neighborhood crime trend								
Increasing	22	9	35	23	48	35	38	40
About the same	71	87	63	73	48	59	57	55
Decreasing	7	4	2	4	4	6	5	5
Number of cases	91	101	123	315	90	116	109	314
Do the police in this neighborhood accept bribes?								
Yes	21	17	5	14	12	12	20	15
Don't know	26	35	23	28	34	31	31	32
No	53	48	72	58	54	58	49	53
Number of cases	89	115	130	334	91	104	120	315

(continued)

TABLE 8.3.—*Continued*

Evaluation Variables	Independent Communities				Indianapolis Neighborhoods			
	Beech Grove	Lawrence	Speedway	Total	Near Beech Grove	Near Lawrence	Near Speedway	Total
Citizens' evaluations of police-citizen relations								
Good	89	95	97	94	80	85	81	82
Poor or nonexistent	10	5	3	6	20	15	19	18
Number of cases	86	113	122	321	80	93	100	273
I think the police in this neighborhood are doing								
Outstanding job	28	36	29	31	15	11	12	12
Good job	37	39	53	44	42	40	44	42
Adequate job	33	21	17	23	34	43	34	37
Inadequate job	3	3	2	2	10	6	11	9
Number of cases	98	127	144	369	89	122	119	330

TABLE 8.4. Association between Type of Community Organization and Citizen Evaluation Controlling for Experience Variables

Experience Variables Used as Controls	Police Response Rate		Neighborhood Crime Trends		Potential Bribe-Taking by Neighborhood Police		Police-Citizen Relations		Job Done by Police	
	tau_β	N	tau_β	N	tau_β	N	tau_β	N	tau_β	N
Victimized	.26	145	-.34	145	.06	146	.21	135	.18	157
Not victimized	.24	450	-.09	480	-.06	502	.18	455	.27	538
Assisted	.16	160	-.21	155	.01	173	.28	161	.20	173
Not assisted	.28	375	-.12	412	-.05	464	.16	422	.28	454
Stopped	.28	127	-.12	132	-.09	156	.26	143	.26	151
Not stopped	.22	399	-.16	438	-.01	475	.16	431	.26	469
Know no policemen	.33	278	-.15	302	-.08	350	.22	309	.34	337
Know 1 or 2 policemen	.20	175	-.16	179	-.02	197	.15	186	.11	201
Know 3 or more policemen	.08	91	-.09	90	.06	98	.08	93	.28	95
Simple	.25	599	-.15	629	-.04	651	.19	594	.26	699

Evaluation of Police-Citizen Relationships

The respondents in each of the six areas studied generally rated police-citizen relationships as good.[21] However, 94 percent of the residents of the independent communities rated police-citizen relationships as good compared with 82 percent for the residents of the Indianapolis neighborhoods (see table 8.3). The pattern is consistent for all areas studied. At the individual level, the preponderance of "good" ratings among all those who responded leads to a weak association between type of community organization and evaluation of police-citizen relations. When controlling for experience variables, direct experience with police in an official capacity increases the strength of that relationship. A larger proportion of citizens from the independent communities who were victims, assisted by the police, or stopped by the police indicates the police-citizen relations are good when compared with victims, those assisted by the police, or those stopped by the police living in Indianapolis (see table 8.4).

Since those who know three or more policemen generally rate police-citizen relations as good, personal acquaintance with police as a control variable reduces the strength of association between community organization and evaluation of police-citizen relations for that category. Among those who know no police, the relationship is stronger. Thus, direct contact with police in their official capacity appears to create more unfavorable evaluations of police-citizen relations among Indianapolis residents than among town residents.

Evaluation of the Job Being Done by Police

Residents of the independent communities were consistently more willing to rate the job the police in their neighborhood are doing as either outstanding or good when compared to residents of the Indianapolis neighborhoods (see table 8.3).[22] Seventy-five percent of the respondents living in the independent communities rated the job being done by police serving their neighborhood as good or excellent while only 54 percent of the residents living in the Indianapolis neighborhoods made a similar ranking.[23] At the individual level (see table 8.4), the general evaluation of the job being done by local police is associated more strongly with the type of community organization than with any of the experience variables. However, those who have been victims of crime tend overall to rate the job police are doing in their neighborhood lower than nonvictims. Thus, controlling for victimization reduces the strength of the association for victims and increases it for nonvictims. Those who have been assisted tend overall to rate the job police are doing as higher than those who have not been assisted.

Those who know one or two policemen tend in all areas to rate police performance in the middle range. About 75 percent of these respondents evaluated their police as doing a "good" or "adequate" job wherever they lived. Those who know three or more policemen are not as moderate in their evaluations. Town residents who knew three or more policemen were more willing to rate the performance of the police serving their neighborhoods as "excellent" than were residents of the Indianapolis neighborhoods who also knew three or more policemen. The association between community organization and evaluation of the job being done by police is therefore somewhat stronger for this group. While some kinds of direct experience tend to lower the association, the evaluation of the job being done by police in the neighborhood is generally associated with the type of community organization providing police services.

Conclusion

This study was designed to examine the working hypothesis that when smaller, community-controlled police agencies are compared to larger, city-wide-controlled police agencies, higher levels of police output should be found within the smaller jurisdiction. Utilizing a most similar systems research design, we asked citizens living in three small independent communities and three matched neighborhoods located within the city of Indianapolis to tell us about their *experiences* with police and their *evaluations* of police performance.

The survey data indicate a consistent pattern of higher levels of police output in the independent communities when compared to the Indianapolis neighborhoods. As shown in table 8.5, output of police in the independent communities is higher than that of the citywide police for nine out of twelve indicators. Levels of output for the remaining measures were similar in all six sample areas. Residents of the Indianapolis neighborhoods did *not* receive higher levels of police output as measured by *any* indicator. Our findings strongly suggest that in the area studied, small police forces under local community control are more effective than a large, citywide-controlled police department in meeting citizen demands for police protection. It should be stressed that in the areas studied, the economic resources of the six neighborhoods were very similar and that extensive cooperative arrangements have been developed among the agencies studied.

The pattern for *both* the experience reported by citizens and their evaluations of police performance is so consistent across a variety of indicators that a strong commitment to suburban government as a value in and of itself is not a sufficient explanation for these findings. For example, the evaluation made that, in general, police respond very rapidly in the independent communities is consistent with the reported experiences of those residents living in these communities who had to call upon the police.

TABLE 8.5. Comparative Output Levels

Variables	Independent Communities	Indianapolis Neighborhoods
Experience Variables		
Victimization	+	−
Willingness to Report Victimization	+	−
Extent of Police Follow-up	+	−
Assistance	+	−
Promptness of Response	+	−
Quality of Assistance	=	=
Stopped as Suspected Offender	=	=
Evaluation Variables		
Evaluation of Promptness	+	−
Evaluation of Crime Trend	+	−
Evaluation of Potential Bribe Taking	=	=
Evaluation of Police-Citizen Relations	+	−
General Evaluation of Job Being Done	+	−

Note:
+ indicates a higher level of police performance.
− indicates a lower level of police performance.
= indicates similar levels of police performance.

A generalization that community-controlled police are more effective requires further research on the relationships between types of political organization for provision of police services and levels of police output. A series of related studies in the Chicago, Grand Rapids, and St. Louis metropolitan areas habeen initiated since the completion of the Indianapolis study (see E. Ostrom and Whitaker 1971; IsHak 1972; Parks 1973; Smith 1973). A further examination of this relationship in over 200 urban areas has also been initiated (see E. Ostrom and Parks 1973). Findings from these related studies would appear to be consistent with those reported on in the preceding. Consequently, we are beginning to gain a little more confidence in our affirmative answer to the question: Does local community control of the police make a difference?

NOTES

1. For a review of some of the more general proposals for community control and decentralization, see Altshuler 1970; Clark 1970; Center for Governmental Studies 1970; Goodwin 1969; and Kotler 1969.
2. For a different view, see Prewitt and Eulau 1969.

3. See President's Commission on Law Enforcement and Administration of Justice 1968 (108–13) for a discussion of the effect that differences in local reporting have on crime rates.

4. For a discussion of the concept of "packageability of public goods," see V. Ostrom, Tiebout, and Warren 1961. For an overview of the concept of public goods and citations to the extended literature related to this concept, see V. Ostrom and E. Ostrom 1971.

5. Jerome Skolnick (1966, 164–81) has described one large police force on the West Coast in which detectives bargained with suspected criminals to motivate the suspect to confess to more than one crime at a time. Such multiple confessions improve the detective's clearance rate while not increasing the liability of the suspect to more than one prosecution. John Gardiner (1968, 156–57) has found that the creation of a separate traffic division within a department increases the volume of traffic tickets written since officers assigned to such a division can easily prove they have been "on the job" by turning in a raft of tickets each day.

6. Neenan (1970, 119) has also argued in a similar way: "The benefits stemming from any governmental expenditure can, in the last analysis, be measured only by the beneficiaries themselves. Neither governmental agencies, social critic, priest, pope nor party chairman can judge with infallibility when a course of action benefits any citizen."

7. The similarity between our design and that characterized as "most similar systems" by Przeworski and Teune (1970) was called to our attention by an anonymous reviewer whose comments were most useful and appreciated.

8. We will, however, refer to these three separately incorporated municipalities as "towns" from time to time for the sake of brevity and to distinguish them from the three Indianapolis neighborhoods.

9. For a description of the analysis of one of the innovative programs adopted by the Indianapolis Police Department, see Fisk 1970.

10. In addition, background characteristics were measured for each respondent. These included personal attributes usually considered important to attitude formation: sex, age, race, and occupation of head of household. Because of the sampling frame, fewer than 10 of the respondents were nonwhite. Two additional variables were obtained that concerned the respondent's lifestyle: membership in community organizations and upkeep of the household.

The background characteristics of respondents are not discussed or controlled for in this essay since their relation to citizen evaluations is generally very weak. With the exception of age, none of these variables is related to citizen evaluations of police to any appreciable degree. Respondents under 30 years of age tend to rate police performance lower on most items regardless of their place of residence. This has the effect of weakening the association between type of community organization and most evaluation variables for those under 30. The relationships between background variables and evaluation variables is reported in detail in Whitaker 1971.

11. The rate of criminal victimization for members of households in each of the six neighborhoods is much lower than citywide rates in some other major urban areas. Victimization rates from July 1965 to July 1966 were 43 percent for a predominantly poor white precinct in Chicago (Town Hall) and 55 percent for a working-

class white neighborhood in Boston (Dorchester). See Reiss 1967 (159).

12. The specific wording of the question was: "During the past two years has anyone in your family been the *victim* of any kind of criminal activity?"

13. The rate of unreported victimizations in the six Marion County areas studied is quite small when compared to the rates found in studies of other urban areas. Some 57 percent of the white respondents in northern central cities surveyed in 1966 did not report criminal victimizations. Similarly, police were not notified of 54 percent of the victimizations in northern, white suburban areas. See Block 1971. In Seattle, 54 percent of the victimizations described in the survey were not reported to the police (Costner et al. 1970). The rates of nonreporting were 68 percent and 63 percent respectively for respondents in Town Hall and Dorchester (Reiss 1967).

14. The question regarding assistance was phrased in the following way: "Do you remember any occasion in the past two years when the police have assisted you?"

15. The question asked was, "Have you been stopped by a policeman during the last two years while you were on the street or driving a car?"

16. The question was worded: "Do you know any policemen who work in this neighborhood?"

17. This experience variable can be thought of as an indicator for the variable discussed in the introduction related to increased knowledge by citizens of the police serving their area. Thus the finding that citizens living in the independent communities know more police is supportive of P_2 stated above.

18. The question was worded: "When the police are called in your neighborhood, in your opinion, do they respond very rapidly, quickly enough, or slowly?"

19. The item was worded as follows: "Some people are concerned tha. crime is increasing in their neighborhoods. In your opinion, do you think crime in your neighborhood is increasing, about the same, or decreasing?"

20. The question was, "Do you think that some police in this neighborhood accept bribes?"

21. The question asked was, "Some individuals are concerned about police-citizen relations in their neighborhoods. In this neighborhood do you feel that police-citizen relationships are relatively good or bad?" The responses "bad" or "we never see them" were collapsed into one category "poor."

22. The question was worded: "Which of the following statements most closely reflects your own opinion? I think the police in this neighborhood are doing an outstanding job, a good job, an adequate job, or an inadequate job?"

23. In a nationwide Harris poll taken in 1966, 57 percent of the residents of cities rated the job done by local police as good or excellent while 72 percent of those living in suburbs made a similar rating. See Louis Harris, survey reported in *Washington Post* (July 3, 1966), p. 14.

REFERENCES

Aberbach, Joel D., and Jack L. Walker. 1970. "The Attitudes of Blacks and Whites toward City Services: Implications for Public Policy." In *Financing the Me-*

tropolis: Public Policy in Urban Economies, ed. John P. Crecine, 519–38. Urban Affairs Annual Reviews, vol. 4. Beverly Hills, CA: Sage.

Altshuler, Alan A. 1970. *Community Control: The Black Demand for Participation in Large American Cities.* New York: Pegasus Books.

Beattie, Ronald H. 1955. "Problems of Criminal Statistics in the United States." *Journal of Criminal Law, Criminology and Police Science* 46 (July/August): 178–86.

Biderman, Albert D. 1966. "Social Indicators and Goals." In *Social Indicators,* ed. Raymond A. Bauer, 68–153. Cambridge: The MIT Press.

Block, Richard L. 1971. "Fear of Crime and Fear of the Police." Mimeo. Chicago, IL: Loyola University of Chicago.

Center for Governmental Studies. 1970. *Conference on Public Administration and Neighborhood Control, May 6–8, 1970.* Washington, DC: Center for Governmental Studies.

Citizens' League Committee on Minority Representation in Local Government. 1970. *Suburbs in the City.* Minneapolis: Citizens' League.

Clark, Terry N. 1970. "On Decentralization." *Polity* 2 (December): 508–14.

Costner, Herbert L., Richard O. Hawkins, Paul E. Smith, and Garland F. White III. 1970. *Crime, the Public and the Police.* Mimeo. Seattle, WA: University of Washington.

Dahl, Robert A. 1967. "The City in the Future of Democracy." *American Political Science Review* 61 (December): 953–70.

Devine, Richard P. 1970. "Citizen Attitudes toward Their Cities." In *Micro City,* ed. Edward L. Henry, 40–47. Collegeville, MN: St. John's University, Center for the Study of Local Government.

Ennis, Phillip H. 1967. *Criminal Victimization in the United States: A Report of a National Survey.* Field Surveys II, President's Commission on Law Enforcement and Administration of Justice. Washington, DC: U.S. Government Printing Office.

Fisk, Donald M. 1970. *The Indianapolis Police Fleet Plan. An Example of the Program Evaluation for Local Government.* Washington, DC: Urban Institute.

Gardiner, John A. 1968. "Police Enforcement of Traffic Laws: A Comparative Analysis." In *City Politics and Public Policy,* ed. James Q. Wilson. New York: John Wiley and Sons.

Goodwin, Richard N. 1969. "Reflections: Sources of the Public Unhappiness." *New Yorker* (January 4): 38–58.

Hatry, Harry P. 1970. "Measuring the Effectiveness of Nondefense Public Programs." *Operations Research* 18 (September/October): 772–84.

Indik, B. P. 1965. "Organization Size and Member Participation: Some Empirical Tests of Alternative Explanations." *Human Relations* 18 (November): 339–50.

IsHak, Samir Twefik. 1972. "Consumers' Perception of Police Performance. Consolidation vs. Deconcentration: The Case of Grand Rapids, Michigan Metropolitan Area." Ph.D. diss., Indiana University.

Jacob, Herbert. 1970. "Black and White Perceptions of Justice in the City." Paper presented at the American Political Science Association meeting, Los Angeles, California, September 8–12.

Kotler, Milton. 1969. *Neighborhood Government.* Indianapolis, IN: Bobbs-Merrill.

Lawrence, David M., and H. Rutherford Turnbull III. 1969. "Unigov: City-County Consolidation in Indianapolis." *Popular Government* 36 (November): 18–26.

Neenan, William B. 1970. "Suburban-Central City Exploitation Thesis: One City's Tale." *National Tax Journal* 23 (June): 117–39.

Nie, Norman H., G. Bingham Powell, Jr., and Kenneth Prewitt. 1969. "Social Structure and Political Participation: Developmental Relationships." *American Political Science Review* 62 (June): 361–78.

Ostrom, Elinor. 1971. "Institutional Arrangements and the Measurement of Policy Consequences in Urban Areas." *Urban Affairs Quarterly* 6 (June): 447–75.

———. 1972. "Metropolitan Reform: Propositions Derived from Two Traditions." *Social Science Quarterly* 53 (December): 474–93. (Chapter 6 in this volume.)

Ostrom, Elinor, William Baugh, Richard Guarasci, Roger B. Parks, and Gordon P. Whitaker. 1973. *Community Organization and the Provision of Police Services.* Beverly Hills, CA: Sage.

Ostrom, Elinor, and Roger B. Parks. 1973. "Suburban Police Departments: Too Many and Too Small." In *The Urbanization of the Suburbs,* ed. Louis H. Masotti and Jeffrey K. Hadden, 367–402. Urban Affairs Annual Review, vol. 7. Beverly Hills, CA: Sage.

Ostrom, Elinor, and Gordon P. Whitaker. 1971."Black Citizens and the Police: Some Effects of Community Control." Paper presented at the American Political Science Association meetings, Chicago, Illinois, September 7–11.

Ostrom, Vincent, and Elinor Ostrom. 1971. "Public Choice: A Different Approach to the Study of Public Administration." *Public Administration Review* 31 (March/April): 203–16. (Reprinted in Michael D. McGinnis, ed., *Polycentric Games and Institutions* [Ann Arbor: University of Michigan Press, 1999].)

Ostrom, Vincent, Charles M. Tiebout, and Robert Warren. 1961. "The Organization of Government in Metropolitan Areas: A Theoretical Inquiry." *American Political Science Review* 55 (December): 831–42. (Chapter 1 in this volume.)

Parks, Roger B. 1973. "An Analysis of the Production of Police Services in the St. Louis Metropolitan Area." Ph.D. diss., Indiana University.

President's Commission on Law Enforcement and Administration of Justice. 1968. *The Challenge of Crime in a Free Society.* Report. New York: E. P. Dutton.

Prewitt, Kenneth, and Heinz Eulau. 1969. "Political Matrix and Political Representation: Prolegomenon to a New Departure from an Old Problem." *American Political Science Review* 62 (June): 427–41.

Price, James E. 1966. "A Test of the Accuracy of Crime Statistics." *Social Problems* 14 (fall): 214–21.

Przeworski, Adam, and Henry Teune. 1970. *The Logic of Comparative Social Inquiry.* New York: Wiley.

Reiss, Albert J., Jr. 1967. *Studies in Crime and Law Enforcement in Major Metropolitan Areas.* Field Surveys III, President's Commission on Law Enforcement and Administration of Justice. Washington, DC: U.S. Government Printing Office.

Richard, Robert. 1969. *Subjective Social Indicators.* Chicago, IL: University of Chicago, National Opinion Research Center.

Rossi, Peter H., and Richard A. Berk. 1970. "Local Political Leadership and Popular Discontent in the Ghetto." *Annals of the American Academy of Political and Social Sciences* 391 (September): 111–27.

Skolnick, Jerome H. 1966. *Justice without Trial: Law Enforcement in Democratic Society.* New York: Wiley.

Smith, Dennis C. 1973. "Political Implications of Police Professionalism." Ph.D. diss., Indiana University.

Suchman, Edward A. 1967. *Evaluative Research.* New York: Russell Sage Foundation.

U.S. Department of Health, Education and Welfare. 1969. *Toward a Social Report.* Washington, DC: U.S. Government Printing Office.

Warren, Robert. 1970. "Federal-Local Development Planning: Scale Effects in Representation and Policy Making." *Public Administration Review* 30 (November/December): 584–95.

Waskow, Arthur I. 1970. *Running Riot.* New York: Herder and Herder.

Whitaker, Gordon P. 1971. "Urban Police Forces: The Effect of Scale on Neighborhood Services." Ph.D. diss., Indiana University.

Wilson, James Q. 1966. "Crime in the Streets." *Public Interest* 5 (fall): 26–35.

———. 1968. *Varieties of Police Behavior: Management of Law and Order in Eight Communities.* Cambridge: Harvard University Press.

Wolfgang, Marvin E. 1963. "Uniform Crime Reports: A Critical Appraisal." *University of Pennsylvania Law Review* 3 (April): 708–38.

CHAPTER 9

Community Control and Governmental Responsiveness: The Case of Police in Black Neighborhoods

Elinor Ostrom and Gordon P. Whitaker

Creation of neighborhood-sized governments within large U.S. cities has been proposed as a way to increase the responsiveness of municipal officials to their local constituents. Police are among those officials often thought to be least responsive to citizens. Black citizens are among those constituents cited as least satisfied with the performance of local police and other public officials. Because of the controversy surrounding neighborhood police service to urban black Americans, this area is particularly appropriate for inquiry into the effects of community control.

This study compares one big-city- and two neighborhood-sized departments in terms of the police services they provide to residents of similar areas. Since community control experiments have not yet been instituted, it is not possible to examine directly the consequences of reducing the scale of large police jurisdictions. Similar neighborhoods served by different-scale jurisdictions within a single metropolitan area do provide the opportunity to assess comparatively some of the probable effects of community control.

Neighborhood police service is only one of the municipal activities for which community control has been proposed. Additional research on the effects of size of jurisdiction on the quality of other urban public services is also needed. This study investigates two questions: (1) Is community control

Originally published in D. Rogers and W. Halley, eds. *Improving the Quality of Urban Management.* Urban Affairs Annual Reviews, vol. 8 (1974): 303–34. Copyright © 1974 by Sage Publications, Inc. Reprinted by permission of Sage Publications, Inc. and the authors.

Authors' note: The authors are appreciative of the financial support provided by the Center for Studies of Metropolitan Problems of the National Institute of Mental Health in the form of Grant 5 RO1 M1 19911-02, by the National Science Foundation, Grant GS-27383, and by the Afro-American Studies Program at Indiana University. We want to thank Shelley Venick and Susan Thomas for their conscientious work as research assistants and Dennis Smith for his considerable help and criticism. A portion of this essay was presented at the 1971 Annual Meeting of the American Political Science Association in Chicago, September 7–11.

204   Polycentricity and Local Public Economies

conducive to greater governmental responsiveness? (2) Does community control create obstacles to the effective provision of public services? The study examines some specific problems that have been suggested as arising due to community control. It evaluates the extent to which those problems have developed in the small communities studied. It also assesses the relative responsiveness of the small-scale and the large-scale governments. The evidence presented here deals with police services in five neighborhoods of a single metropolitan area, but the findings can, with caution, suggest parallels in other places and for other urban public services.

The Need for More Responsive Police Agencies

Protection of property and person is more desperately needed by the poor than by the rich. While the poor have less to lose, they feel the consequences of loss more acutely. The respect police accord those of high social status is likewise important to those who have suffered the indignities of lower status in an affluent society. However, black Americans charge that they continue to receive inferior police protection and suffer more abuse from the police than do the majority of Americans. The stance of many black citizens toward the police has shifted from "resentment to confrontation" (Fogelson 1968). The resentment has been based on many charges related to the unresponsiveness of the police—police brutality, police corruption, lack of police protection in the ghetto, and the lack of effective mechanisms for protest and remedy (National Advisory Commission on Civil Disorders 1968; Hahn 1971; Campbell and Schuman 1968).

In many instances, the resentment appears to be widespread. In a recent comparative study, for example, TenHouten and others found that two-thirds of the respondents living in ghettos agreed with the statement that "police rough up people unnecessarily when they are arresting them or afterwards" (TenHouten, Stein, and TenHouten 1971, 236). Resentment against police also appears to be based on experience. In a study of 15 cities, using data obtained from four different sources, Rossi and Berk found that ghetto residents' grievances concerning police reflect the reality with which they live. Police brutality as a salient local issue was related to the existence of more abusive police practices, less responsiveness on the part of a local police chief to black grievances, less knowledge by the police of local black residents, and more personal experience by blacks of police abuse (Rossi and Berk 1970, 122–25; see also Lieberson and Silverman 1965). Aberbach and Walker (1970b, 1212) found that among the blacks they interviewed in Detroit during 1967, personal experiences of police mistreatment were negatively associated with political trust and that individuals with low levels of political trust were more likely to be able to imagine a situation in which they would riot. In general, they found that attitudes of political trust were not mere reflections of an individual's basic personality or of background factors. Their most important explanatory variables were "those which arise from the workings of the social or political system" (Aberbach and Walker 1970b, 1214).

Police responsiveness varies by neighborhood. In their study of the large Denver police force, Bayley and Mendelsohn (1969, 114) found that

> Ethnicity is a primary determinant of the amount and kind of contact people have with the police. Within ethnic groups there is by and large no association between age, sex, and class and whether an individual has been stopped and arrested or has called the police for help or talked over difficulties with them.

The differences in contact that Bayley and Mendelsohn find related to ethnicity are largely related to the neighborhood in which individuals live. Denver, like most large U.S. cities, is residentially segregated. Bayley and Mendelsohn learned from their surveys of officers that "police do carry certain predispositions into their contacts with minority people, especially in minority neighborhoods, that can produce a double standard in enforcement behavior" (Bayley and Mendelsohn 1969, 166). A similar dynamic may also be at work in Milwaukee, Seattle, and Detroit where blacks also report more unfavorable contact than whites with police and where neighborhoods are generally racially homogeneous.

Jacob, in his study of black and white Milwaukee neighborhoods, found that "the general reputation of the police in black ghettos has become so bad that good experiences do not bring correspondingly good evaluations" (Jacob 1970, 72). He identified this phenomenon as "neighborhood culture" and considered it "one of the intervening variables between experiences and perceptions." Similar findings in Seattle were explained as a "contextual effect" whereby "persons in sub-communities subject to relatively high probabilities of arrest develop less positive attitudes toward police whether they themselves have been arrested or not" (Costner et al. 1970, 46). The phenomenon which these authors identify as "neighborhood culture" and "contextual effect" appears to be a reflection of the lower levels and poorer quality of service provided to citizens living in black neighborhoods. That is, the low evaluations black citizens make of their police reflect the unresponsiveness of the police serving their neighborhoods.

Trends found in specific large cities have also been established nationwide. In a survey conducted for the President's Commission on Law Enforcement and Administration of Justice in 1966, the National Opinion Research Center administered a nationwide survey including several questions asking respondents to rate their police services. Analysis of the data from that survey shows that black residents of large center cities consistently rated police services lower than white residents of either center cities or incorporated suburbs. As shown in table 9.1, black center-city respondents were less likely than white respondents at all income levels to rate their police as respectful, as paying attention to complaints, as giving protection to the people in their neighborhood, or as being prompt. Wealthier white respondents living in center cities tended uniformly to rate the police higher than did poorer white respondents. White respondents living in independently incorporated suburbs tended to rate the police higher at all but the lowest income level than did white center-city residents. The ratings of police services by black respondents were *not* positively associated with income levels as were the ratings by white respondents. In fact, black respondents of higher income levels tended to be less likely to give high ratings to police than black respondents of lower income levels. Thus, the criticisms of police by black citizens are not restricted to the poor but are shared by all segments of the black urban population.

TABLE 9.1. Rating of Police Services by Black Center-City Respondents, White Center-City Respondents, and White Incorporated Suburb Respondents Controlling for Income

| Percentage Giving Highest Rating to Police for: | Income Levels of Respondents | | | | |
	Less than $3,000	$3,000 to $5,999	$6,000 to $9,999	$10,000 & Higher	*n*
Being respectful to people like themselves					
Black—Center City	40	28	33	25	256
White—Center City	69	59	67	74	877
White—Incorporated Suburbs	62	65	78	77	430
Paying attention to complaints					
Black—Center City	36	18	18	8	242
White—Center City	47	49	54	64	823
White—Incorporated Suburbs	50	56	57	70	387
Giving protection to the people in the neighborhood					
Black—Center City	23	17	22	9	241
White—Center City	50	42	53	55	829
White—Incorporated Suburbs	50	58	60	72	412
Promptness					
Black—Center City	30	16	24	8	249
White—Center City	50	42	53	55	803
White—Incorporated Suburbs	47	56	63	73	379

Note: Data obtained from the National Opinion Research Center, Study N-506. Our thanks to Patrick Bova for assisting us in working with these data. Only respondents living in separately incorporated municipalities are included in the category "White-Suburban" reported in the table.

Complaints related to police brutality and harassment coupled with complaints of insufficient police protection have seemed somewhat paradoxical to some observers. However, it would appear that the practice of "preventive patrolling" utilized by some police forces simultaneously increases the resentment of residents and diverts police manpower from other activities such as answering calls and investigating the many crimes that do occur in the ghetto (Hahn and Feagin 1970). Across the country, victimization rates for blacks are higher than for whites at all levels of income for serious crimes against the person (Ennis 1967, 30). Black residents living in cities of over 100,000 population were considerably more likely to cite a need for self-defense when asked: "Do you think that people like yourself have to be prepared to defend their homes against crime and violence, or can the police take care of that?" (Feagin 1970, 799). Thus, the simultaneous criticism of too much and too little policing may be valid. Police seem to be failing to serve the residents of many black neighborhoods in U.S. cities.

Increasing attitudes of confrontation have become all too obvious. While some confrontations between black citizens and police have occurred within the institutional settings provided by elections, courts, and review boards, many have occurred in the streets. Street confrontations have occurred particularly in larger cities in which the proportion of black citizens has increased significantly. Riots, assaults on officers, and the stony hostility or taunting jibes that often greet policemen are all reflections of hostility between black citizens and their police. Confrontations on the street reflect the absence of opportunities for confrontation through the regular institutions of government. The failure of established governmental institutions to be responsive to black citizens' demands for effective and impartial police services represents a serious threat to domestic peace and order.

Alternative Strategies for Enhancing Responsiveness

Professionalization as a Remedy

Two remedies are frequently recommended for reducing the overt antagonism, mistrust, and hostility toward the police by many black citizens. These are similar to those often suggested as strategies for enhancing the responsiveness of government generally. One remedy involves increasing the "professionalization" of public servants. According to James Q. Wilson (1968a, 175), a "professional" police department is one "governed by values derived from general, impersonal rules which bind all members of the organization and whose relevance is independent of circumstances of time, place or personality." Professional departments are said to have attributes that include the following:

1. Recruitment on the basis of achievement;
2. Equal treatment of citizens;
3. Negative attitudes toward graft both within the force and in the community;
4. Commitment to training of generally applicable standards; and
5. Bureaucratic distribution of authority.

In communities served by professionalized departments, law enforcement may be stricter, but it is thought to be more equally applied to all groups than in communities served by nonprofessional departments (Wilson 1968a). Reliance upon brutality as a means of social control is thought to be less within such departments than in nonprofessional departments.

However, tensions between black citizens and the police have not lessened in the cities with police departments described as highly professionalized. Two of the departments most frequently characterized as "professional," Oakland and Los Angeles, have also been observed to take strong punitive actions against blacks (Skolnick 1967; Jacobs 1966). More "professional" recruitment, training, and authority structure does not necessarily entail equal treatment of citizens. Even advocates of professionalization recognize the "limitations of professionalization especially when it is used to rationalize the employment of preventive patrolling and the other extraordinary tactics which transform the Negro ghettos into occupied territories" (Fogelson 1968, 247). Police professionalization may have served more to insulate the police against external criticism than to reduce the level of discrimination by police against black citizens.[1] James Q. Wilson (1963, 201)—a firm advocate of police professionalism—has argued that "professionalism among policemen will differ from professionalism in other occupations in that the primary function of the professional code will be to protect the practitioner from the client rather than the client from the practitioner." Thus, "professionalization" may in fact decrease rather than increase a police department's responsiveness to citizen needs and preferences.

Paul Jacobs vividly describes resistance to any meaningful review procedures by the Los Angeles Police Department prior to the Watts riot. One of its basic strategies was to demean civil rights groups and others calling for outside review. In the department's 1964 *Annual Report*, for example, the charge was made that

> the detractors of law enforcement stepped up their pervading accusations of police misconduct and pleas for an independent review of police practices in an attempt to create an atmosphere of apprehension, predicting that the streets of this city would also become an arena in which the issues of the civil rights movement would be settled. (cited in Jacobs 1966, 99)

During the same year, 121 complaints were lodged with the police department concerning the excessive use of force. Only 21 were sustained. However, in none of the 21 cases where charges were sustained did the officer charged receive the penalty associated with the use of excessive force. Officers were allowed either to resign without penalty or to receive a lesser penalty (Jacobs 1966, 98–99).

At least one early champion of the "professionalization" remedy has recently reversed his position. Burton Levy, after a two-year period of intensive observation of police departments across the country for the U.S. Department of Justice, concluded that recruitment, training, and community relations efforts did not seem to have a significant impact on police practice.

> The problem is not one of a few 'bad eggs' in a police department of 1,000 or 10,000 men, but rather of a police system that recruits a significant number of bigots, reinforces the bigotry through the department's value system and socialization with older officers, and then takes the worst of the officers and puts them on duty in the ghetto, where the opportunity to act out their prejudice is always available. (Levy 1968, 348)

Professionalism as a remedy for the problems of resentment and hostility toward the police among black citizens would appear to have serious limitations. It provides no leverage for blacks to demand improved service and is thus an inadequate device for institutionalizing confrontation.

Community Control as a Remedy

A second general proposal to alleviate the growing tension between black citizens and government is community control (for the best in-depth overview of the issues involved, see Altshuler 1970; see also Shalala 1971). In the case of police services, proponents argue that reducing the size of local police jurisdictions and bringing the jurisdiction under the control of the citizens living in the community served will increase responsiveness of police to the preferences of citizens. Under a more responsive institutional structure, police would be expected to provide services needed by community residents, thus increasing citizens' satisfaction with police services.

However, community control has been strongly questioned as an effective reform strategy. Sherry Arnstein (1969, 224) has summarized some of the most frequently articulated arguments against community control in the following overview.

> Among the arguments against community control are: it supports separatism; it creates balkanization; it enables minority group 'hustlers' to be

just as opportunistic and disdainful of the have-nots as their white predecessors; it is incompatible with merit systems and professionalism; and
ironically enough, it can turn out to be a new Mickey Mouse game for
the have-nots by allowing them to gain control but not allowing them
sufficient dollar resources to succeed.

Let us briefly examine these arguments against community control and the
responses in favor of such a system.

Separatism

The first argument is that community control supports racial separatism.
Given existing patterns of residential segregation, the population of local
communities would be more racially homogeneous than the population of
citywide areas. Once boundaries were drawn, it is argued, the tendency toward
homogeneity of communities would increase as citizens scurried to move out of
areas where they were in a minority. The result might be that police forces in
each type of community would be much more oriented to abusing members of
the minority race in that community than now occurs in the big city.

Proponents of community control reply that segregation is a fact imposed on black citizens by the unwillingness of white citizens to allow integration in any meaningful form (Spear 1967; Tauber 1968). Community control would not appreciably increase the amount of segregation and racism
currently in existence—it would give to those who had been denied open access to housing a greater opportunity to control what happens in their own
neighborhood. There is no evidence that blacks controlling their own areas
would be more racist in orientation. Aberbach and Walker (1970a) found
that 88 percent of the black residents of Detroit interviewed in 1967 preferred to have the "best trained police, no matter what their race" patrolling
in Negro neighborhoods rather than "Negro police only." Interestingly
enough, of the whites interviewed, 22 percent (as compared to 12 percent for
blacks) thought that "Negro police only" should patrol in black areas.

Balkanization and Economies of Scale

The second argument is that community control creates balkanization of public services and is more costly and less efficient. This is an old argument repeatedly presented by advocates of metropolitan-wide governments. Advocates of metropolitan government recommended the *elimination* of most of
the currently established units of local government in metropolitan areas
(Zimmerman 1970).[2] Metropolitan reformers assume that large economies of
scale exist for all public services and thus urge the creation of one or a few
large-scale public jurisdictions to serve an entire metropolitan area. Those
associated with this movement argue that decreasing the size of police agen-

cies and increasing their number within a particular metropolitan area would increase the costs of service and lead to grave problems of coordination among diverse agencies. The sheer presence of a large number of local units is frequently cited as evidence in and of itself that coordination of efforts among such a multiplicity of jurisdictions cannot be accomplished. Coordination within a single large jurisdiction is presumed to be more easily accomplished than cooperation among many jurisdictions.

Proponents of community control have argued that economies of scale do not exist for such services as police and education and that, consequently, community control may not lead to an increase in the cost of local services. Large-scale agencies could continue to provide such services (which do benefit from large scale) as transportation, water, sewage and to help provide some of the financing for smaller units within the larger unit (Meltzer 1968; Mayer 1971). Just as large units may be more effective and efficient in the provision of certain services, smaller units may also be more advantageous for other services. Police services such as neighborhood patrols and emergency aid appear to be of this type. Furthermore, in many situations in the United States, a number of disparate public jurisdictions are able to coordinate efforts through joint agreements, contracting, and distinct distribution of authority (V. Ostrom, Tiebout, and Warren 1961; Bish 1971; Warren 1966; Bish and Warren 1972). Community control would enable blacks in the center city to have the personalized, small-scale service provided today to whites in the suburbs (Ferry 1968). Suburban residents have vigorously fought against being included within large, metropolitan-wide governmental jurisdictions. Why should residents of the center city be the only ones who cannot have small-scale public agencies responsive to the particular needs of their communities (Rubenstein 1970; Babcock and Bosselman 1967; Press 1963)?

Lack of Participation
The third argument against community control is that local decision making within small communities is more "undemocratic" than that within larger units (Kristol 1968; Perlmutter 1968). Critics point to the low turnout of voters and the ineffective bickering among "poverty representatives" in many of the early community action programs. Because of the relative homogeneity of an individual community, they also argue that there would be less challenge to local leaders who may be more demagogic than leaders of large, heterogeneous city governments. The intimacy of the local community, furthermore, may lead to corruption and lack of uniform enforcement practice (Wilson 1968b; Prewitt and Eulau 1969; for a different argument, see Rossi 1963, 12).

If black citizens have genuine control concerning local affairs, however, participation levels may be expected to increase (Gittell 1968). While participation in many programs in the past has been low, it is unreasonable to expect high participation in newly organized arrangements whose potential benefits may be quite nebulous. Many programs have used "participation" as therapy rather than as a means to enable local people to exercise substantial control over events affecting them (Mogulof 1969; Arnstein 1969). People do not learn to participate actively or constructively in a short time period. If meaningful control were placed in the community, individuals would begin to learn that it was worthwhile to participate and how to participate more constructively.[3] Once community control was established, the effect of having local public officials sympathetic to the needs and aspirations of local citizens would decrease the general level of alienation among black citizens living within the ghetto of a typical large U.S. city.[4]

Amateur Public Servants

The fourth argument is that small, community-controlled police departments would be less professional. It is assumed that a relatively large department is needed to be able to afford adequate salaries, good training facilities, and sufficient levels in the bureaucracy to achieve meaningful advancement for ambitious young personnel (Altshuler 1970, 39). It is frequently argued that small departments cannot attract as qualified employees as can large departments. Such personnel, employed in specialized, hierarchically controlled departments, are seen as necessary to improved police service.

Proponents of community control argue that many of the consequences of "professionalization" have been to keep blacks from obtaining jobs due to irrelevant educational requirements or middle-class, biased examinations (see also Baron 1968).[5] The establishment of less-bureaucratized forces with police officers living in the community they serve and sympathetic to the lifestyle of the residents is seen as a benefit rather than a cost.[6] Career opportunities can be pursued among small jurisdictions by lateral movement as occurs in many school districts rather than relying on vertical movement in a single bureaucracy. Neighborhood agencies can be expected to be less effective in providing specialized units for criminal investigation but more effective in providing police patrol services to the neighborhood (E. Ostrom, Parks, and Whitaker 1973). A centralized police force could continue to provide specialized police services for the entire city.

Lack of Financial Resources

Finally, it is argued that community control may be a futile strategy if significant reallocation of resources is not also accomplished at the same time. Impoverished areas would remain just that—impoverished areas. Once separated from the rest of the city, black citizens would find it difficult to obtain from white citizens living in separate jurisdictions the resources needed for effective programs. Community control might prove to be a cruel joke.

Those in "control" would not have sufficient resources to be able to accomplish their goals (see Altshuler 1970, 53–54). Consequently, the long-run consequences of community control might be further bitterness, disillusionment, and alienation among black citizens (Aberbach and Walker 1970a, 1218).

There is, however, considerable doubt that extensive redistribution in favor of the poor does occur in larger political units. In a study of U.S. cities that had adopted one of the reform measures leading toward greater consolidation, Erie, Kirlin, and Rabinovitz (1972) found no tendency toward redistribution of wealth among elements of the populations within reformed metropolitan institutions. Moreover, many of the needs of poor areas are not solved by the mere infusion of more economic resources. Even if more funds are available, the services provided by the larger government may not suit the affected community. More effective service depends upon fitting public services to the particular needs of a community. Milton Kotler describes the deliberation of a community corporation in a poor neighborhood of Columbus, Ohio, concerning medical services. Doctors were proposing "fancy new clinics with interns rotating the work day by day." However, the people in the neighborhood corporation "said no, they didn't need anything as elaborate as a big clinic. What they needed was a night doctor. . . . Neighborhoods like this need doctors who work on a different schedule" (Kotler et al. 1968, 16). If the views of the professionals had prevailed, more money would have been spent, but the people living in the neighborhood would not have been as satisfied with the type of medical service provided. Many (but, of course, not all) of the problems of the ghetto relate to the need for services tailored to residents' own needs (Itzkoff 1969).

Finally, the financing of services in a public jurisdiction does not always have to come entirely from the area itself (V. Ostrom, Tiebout, and Warren 1961). Redistribution formulas by which larger units provide some of the funds for smaller units are used by both state and federal governments. Effective organization of the local community may enable sufficient pressure to be brought at metropolitan, state, or federal levels to achieve further redistribution of resources. Such resources could then be utilized in a way responsive to the preferences of local residents in various types of areas rather than as a result of decisions made by a single set of officials for all areas.

An Evaluation of the Arguments Related to Community Control

Several studies have been undertaken to evaluate the warrantability of the arguments for and against community control. Most of these studies have focused on white, middle-class neighborhoods. When the performance of relatively small police jurisdictions (serving under 20,000 people) is compared to the performance of relatively large forces (serving 200,000 to 450,000 people) serving similar white, middle-class neighborhoods, the smaller jurisdictions were found to produce higher levels of output at similar or lesser costs (see E. Ostrom and Whitaker 1973; E. Ostrom, Parks, and Whitaker 1973; E. Ostrom et al. 1973; IsHak 1972). An additional study examined a range of police departments located throughout the United States. The 102 departments included in this study served jurisdictions ranging in size from 10,000 to 8 million. When the levels of output of these police departments are compared, smaller departments are found to produce equal or higher levels of service for similar or lower expenditure levels (E. Ostrom and Parks 1973). Thus, contrary to the arguments against community control, larger departments do not appear to provide higher levels of service. Therefore, the small scale implied by community control does not necessarily entail loss of effectiveness or efficiency.

Local control of the police has not been a salient issue for most middle-class, white citizens. Several reasons can be stated for this lack of saliency.

1. Wealthier white citizens are often well served by large-scale police jurisdictions and thus tend to be more satisfied with large-scale jurisdiction than black citizens or poorer white citizens living in the same city (see table 9.1).
2. White citizens—living in large cities—who are dissatisfied with the services provided by their police, or for that matter with any other aspect of local government, can move to a different jurisdiction relatively easily (Tiebout 1956).
3. White citizens at all income levels except those under $3,000 income, living in separately incorporated suburban jurisdictions, appear to be receiving higher levels of service than either white or black citizens living in center cities (see table 9.1).

White citizens appear to have the opportunity to receive the kinds of urban public services they desire either by moving to a jurisdiction that will provide them or by exercising a greater voice in the articulation of their demands for service (Orbell and Uno 1972).

However, most black citizens and members of other minority groups are excluded from these options. They are prevented from moving to smaller, suburban jurisdictions where public services are subject to more direct control by residents. Black citizens can find housing primarily in the most crowded sections of central cities and rarely in suburban jurisdictions. They rarely have effective channels for articulating their service demands to big-city governments (Parenti 1970). Neither are black citizens able to compete effectively for control of police policy in large cities. Consequently, many black demands have been focused on "decentralization" of large-scale police forces already serving central cities.

Given the concentration of black citizens in most large cities and the low percentage of blacks in most suburban cities, it is extremely difficult to locate adequate research sites to examine the consequences of increased levels of local control for black citizens. There are, however, several independently incorporated black communities located in the Chicago metropolitan area. A small study was recently undertaken to evaluate the consequences of community control for the residents living in two separately incorporated black communities by comparing the police service they receive with that provided to residents of matched neighborhoods within the city of Chicago.

The Areas Studied

The villages of Phoenix and East Chicago Heights, Illinois, are both small and poor. The population of Phoenix in 1970, according to official census figures, was 3,596, while village officials feel that the population was closer to 5,000. The official census figure for East Chicago Heights was 5,000. Village officials feel that at least 2,000 East Chicago Heights residents were missed in the official census. In 1970, the median family income in Phoenix was $7,600 while that of East Chicago Heights was $6,750. The median value of homes in Phoenix in 1970 was $15,900 and in East Chicago Heights was $16,000 (Illinois Regional Medical Program 1971). Whenever socioeconomic rankings of the municipalities surrounding Chicago have been published, these two villages have always been among the lowest five municipalities (see De Vise 1967; Illinois Regional Medical Program 1971; *Chicago Sun Times* 1972).

Each village is governed by a six-person Board of Trustees and an independently elected mayor and village clerk. All village officials are black. The ratio of village residents to members of the Board of Trustees is less than 1,000 to 1. Other than the full-time village clerk, all other elected officials serve in a part-time capacity. The mayor and village trustees all hold other jobs and attend to village affairs during the evenings and weekends. However, village officials spend almost all their "free" hours working for the village. The level of volunteerism is high in the villages. Tasks such as clearing snow and salting roads are performed by the trustees along with village citizens who have volunteered to help. Community projects such as painting or repairing a public building are frequently organized on a voluntary basis with a community cookout scheduled for relaxation after the work is completed. Both communities are served by volunteer fire departments.

The police forces in the villages are quite small. The size of each force fluctuates considerably. At the time of the study, however, Phoenix employed four full-time and 15 part-time officers. East Chicago Heights had six full-time and five part-time officers. Part-time police officers were paid at the rate of $1.60 per hour. Full-time officers received approximately $400 per month. Policemen in the villages received little formal training. Both chiefs and some officers have received training at police institutes run by the State of Illinois. Training within each department is provided by the more experienced officers.

The villages face a perplexing problem with regard to training. When they have provided funds to send a regular patrolman to a police training program, they have frequently lost the patrolmen within a short time to one of the surrounding municipalities that pays higher salaries to police officers. Both villages find that their best police officers are frequently lured away after they gain experience on the village force. Consequently, there is a high level of turnover on both police forces. Inexperienced individuals who gain experience in a small police force and demonstrate proficiency in police work are able to follow better career opportunities by seeking employment in other jurisdictions.

Each village has two or three radio-dispatched cars. However, police cars are out of operation for relatively long periods of time due to the high costs of repair. The lieutenant in one of the villages usually drives his personal car (which he has equipped with a radio at his own expense) in order to reduce the operating expenses of the village department.

Both villages cooperate with neighboring villages when extra help is needed in any of the south suburban municipalities. They rely upon the Cook County sheriff for investigative services and laboratory work when needed.[7]

Financially, both departments have extremely limited resources. The police department budget for each community is approximately $40,000 per year. One of the villages has had a long-standing reputation as a speed trap and, until recently, traffic fines provided most of the financing for its police department.

The sample areas within the city of Chicago were selected to match as closely as possible the socioeconomic characteristics of the independent villages. Some factors that affect police service were thus controlled through the use of a most similar systems research design (see Przeworski and Teune 1970). A comparison of respondents in the Chicago neighborhoods to those in the independent communities is shown on table 9.2. A major socioeconomic difference between the two types of sample areas relates to housing patterns. Thirty-seven percent of the respondents living in the independent villages reside in public housing. All these respondents live in East Chicago Heights in two-story, low-density public housing units. It was not possible to find within Chicago, with similar public housing units, a neighborhood that was not greatly dissimilar to the independent communities on most of the other socioeconomic factors. One Chicago neighborhood chosen did have a large low-rent apartment complex within it. Residents of public housing may generally rate public services less favorably than nonpublic housing resi-

TABLE 9.2. Background Characteristics of Respondents in the Two Types of Neighborhoods (in percentages)

	Two Independent Communities	Three Chicago Neighborhoods
Age of Respondent		
16–20	10	16
21–30	16	18
31–40	32	30
41–50	20	15
51–65	10	12
Over 65	11	10
(n)	(213)	(294)
Sex of Respondent		
Female	62	64
Male	38	36
(n)	(213)	(294)
Husband's Occupation		
Professional-Managerial	13	12
Clerical-Sales	9	14
Craftsmen-Foremen	14	18
Semiskilled	26	25
Unskilled	14	14
Retired	14	12
Unemployed	10	5
(n)	(118)	(156)
Ownership of Housing		
Buying home	48	73
Renting	15	27
Public housing	37	0
(n)	(201)	(280)
Length of Residence		
Less than 2 years	16	20
2–5 years	13	27
6–10 years	17	23
More than 10 years	54	37
(n)	(209)	(290)
Education		
8 years or less	33	18
Some high school	26	27
High school graduate	29	32
Some college	9	15
College graduate	2	6
(n)	(198)	(274)
Number of Dependent Children		
No dependent children	16	25
1 or 2 dependent children	26	32
3 or 4 dependent children	26	22
5 or 6 dependent children	18	13
More than 6 dependent children	14	8
(n)	(198)	(274)

dents. Consequently, the presence in our sample for the independent communities of a large number of public housing residents biases that portion of our sample downward with regard to citizens' evaluations of services received.

Chicago is governed by a strong, independently elected mayor and a city council of 50 members. The mayor of Chicago dominates the city council as well as the executive departments, including the police. The ratio of Chicago residents to members of the Chicago City Council is more than 65,000 to 1.

The Chicago Police Department is one of the most modern, best trained, and best financed departments in the country. The force had over 12,500 men at the time of this study. Patrolmen received from $9,600 to $12,000 per year, depending on years of service. The department conducted extensive training programs, including in-service instruction and a 31-week cadet program for recruits. The proportion of blacks serving on the Chicago police force was substantially less than the proportion of black residents in the population of Chicago. While blacks made up approximately 40 percent of the Chicago population, approximately 20 percent of the patrolmen were black; 8 percent of the detectives were black; and 4 percent of the lieutenants were black (Jackson 1970; see also Baron 1968).

Chicago is divided into 21 police districts, each with its own station. The Englewood station is located within one of the neighborhood areas included in this study. Thus, residents of that neighborhood have somewhat more immediate access to police than those of the other two study areas inside Chicago. However, all radio cars in Chicago are controlled by a central dispatch office. In terms of telephone access to police, all three Chicago neighborhoods are quite similar due to this central dispatching. The Chicago Police Department has highly specialized units to handle a variety of investigative and support activities. The total budget for the Chicago Police Department during 1970 was $190,922,514. Expenditures for police services in the three Chicago neighborhoods have been estimated at $1,720,000 (Whitaker 1971). Thus, over 14 times as much was spent on policing each of the three Chicago neighborhoods as was spent by the villages for local police services there.

Given the relative similarity of the sample areas but large difference in financial resources allocated to police and the differences in the training of the personnel employed by the different types of police departments, one would expect the Chicago Police Department to provide a much higher level of service to residents than would the village police departments.

Levels of Police Service Provided

In general, citizens living in the independent communities received equal or higher levels of service than residents of similar neighborhoods in Chicago. As we have discussed elsewhere, there are no generally agreed upon methods for measuring police output (E. Ostrom and Whitaker 1973; E. Ostrom 1971). Because of our interest in services provided to citizens, we have utilized survey methods to obtain two types of indicators of police output. The first type of indicator is the police-related experiences that respondents have had. Levels of criminal victimization and the quality of a variety of police actions are assessed in this way. The second type of indicator consists of citizens' evaluations of service levels. In eight items, citizens were requested to evaluate various aspects of police service. Five additional items were included to obtain respondents' evaluations of local government in general. Citizens' reports of the police services they have received are summarized in table 9.3. For four of the indicators, service levels are reported to be quite similar (tau less than .10). For the other three indicators, village respondents are more likely to indicate higher levels of service (tau greater than .10). A similar pattern is seen for citizens' evaluations of the quality of police services provided by their local forces. As shown in table 9.4, police services are judged similarly by respondents on four of the indicators. On the other four indicators, village respondents are more likely to give high ratings than are Chicago respondents. The service levels reported in this study are much lower than those reported in white neighborhoods of Indianapolis and Grand Rapids. The pattern is the same, however; residents of independent communities report services of similar or higher levels across a large number of indicators when compared to residents of similar central-city neighborhoods. In no case do residents served by large police departments report higher levels of service on any indicator. This finding is particularly surprising in the Chicago area because of the substantially smaller amount of funds devoted to the village police forces. The experiences of these five neighborhoods cannot be generalized to all black neighborhoods, but the study does provide evidence that bears upon arguments for and against community control.

Separatism
The first objection raised to community control is that it would encourage racial separatism in U.S. cities. If community control were to encourage racial separation, one would expect residents of the two independent black villages to have a *stronger* preference for black officials than respondents of the three Chicago neighborhoods. However, residents of the independent black villages were neither more nor less likely to prefer black officials. Twenty percent of the black respondents preferred black officials whether or not they lived in a separately incorporated community served by black officials.

Nor did a higher proportion of respondents in the independent communities express strong racial identity (Mitchell 1973). Strong racial identifiers living in the Chicago neighborhoods were, however, extremely negative in their views toward the legitimacy of local institutions. On the other hand, strong racial identifiers living in the independent communities were more positive in their support of local institutions than were medium or weak racial identifiers (ibid.). Given an opportunity to live in a separately incorporated black community, those with strong racial identification appear to become supporters of regular political institutions rather than antagonists.

TABLE 9.3. Comparison of Service Levels Received (in percentages)

Indicators of Police Services Received	Independent Communities	Chicago Neighborhoods	Tau for Complete Table
Percentage of respondents:			
Reporting that they were not victimized during preceding 12 months	75	74	.01
(n)	(195)	(276)	
Reporting that they do not stay at home because of fear of crime	58	45	.13[a]
(n)	(205)	(276)	
Receiving high levels of police follow-up to reported crime[c]	59	46	.13[b]
(n)	(32)	(48)	
Calling on the police for assistance not related to victimization	19	24	-.05[b]
(n)	(193)	(269)	
Reporting police arrival in less than 5 minutes	60	48	.11
(n)	(30)	(44)	
Reporting effective police assistance[c]	95	94	.01
(n)	(36)	(62)	
Reporting fair treatment when stopped by own police force[d]	77	70	.06
(n)	(35)	(97)	

[a] $p < .001$
[b] $p < .05$
[c] Coded "effective" when respondent indicated that police handled the matter; police gave emergency aid; or police solved problem.
[d] Includes respondents indicating that they were treated nicely or in a fair manner.

Balkanization and Economies of Scale

Opponents of community control frequently assert that small units of government are most costly due to their failure to realize supposed economies of scale in the provision of public services. In the Chicago study, however, the independent communities did not spend more for police protection than was spent by the city of Chicago in policing the neighborhoods studied. In fact, expenditures in the independent communities were much lower. Each inde-

TABLE 9.4. Comparison of Citizen Evaluations of Police Services
(in percentages)

Evaluation Indicators	Independent Communities	Chicago Neighborhoods	Tau for Complete Table
Percentage of Respondents:			
Evaluating local police-community relations good	46	44	.01
(n)	(181)	(254)	
Evaluating local police response time very rapid	26	25	.01
(n)	(144)	(197)	
Believing local police do not accept bribes	37	21	.18[a]
(n)	(110)	(157)	
Agreeing they have some say about what police do	49	47	.01
(n)	(196)	(264)	
Agreeing that local police have the right to take any action necessary	61	38	.24[a]
(n)	(192)	(270)	
Agreeing that redress is possible for police mistreatment	67	66	.01
(n)	(176)	(270)	
Agreeing that local police treat all equally according to the law	46	18	.31[a]
(n)	(105)	(181)	
Agreeing that local police look out for the needs of the average citizen	56	36	.21[a]
(n)	(180)	(264)	

[a]$p < .001$

pendent community spent approximately $40,000 in support of its local police department in 1969. During the same year, the Chicago Police Department, according to our estimates, incurred expenditures averaging over $500,000 for each of the neighborhoods investigated. Similar or better services appear to have been provided by the smaller communities for about 7 percent of the cost of the service provided by the larger police department.

Further, with regard to cooperation and coordination, there is considerable evidence of cooperative efforts between the smaller police departments and other local police agencies. Emergency mutual aid arrangements exist between the small black communities and some of the neighboring white communities. The Cook County Sheriff's Department, a large-scale agency with overlapping jurisdiction, provides a number of backup and technical facilities for the two villages and many of the other small Cook County municipalities.

Lack of Participation

The third objection to community control relates to a fear that small communities will be more undemocratic and their officials less responsive to the preferences of citizens than leaders in larger communities. Our findings indicate the opposite in the area studied. As shown in table 9.5, village residents were more likely than Chicago residents to agree that citizens can get satisfaction from local officials. Village residents also were more likely to believe that local officials were interested in their neighborhoods. These findings are consistent with our findings that more village residents rated their police as responsive than did residents of the city of Chicago. Residents of villages are somewhat less likely to believe that local elections make a difference. Some might argue that this finding indicates a lack of willingness to participate in local elections and thus demonstrates that small-scale governments are less democratic. On the other hand, this finding may reflect the higher level of homogeneity in the villages and a belief that village government will be responsive regardless of electoral outcome.

Amateur Public Servants

With regard to the argument concerning professionalism, we did find that, by most standards, the village police would not be called professional. Because of their limited resources, the villages paid policemen very poorly. The average salary of patrolmen was under $2.00 an hour. Many of the police officers were part-time policemen and held full-time jobs elsewhere. The chief of police in each village was paid approximately two-thirds the salary of an *entering* patrolman in the Chicago Police Department. Officers were poorly trained and equipped. However, despite the obvious handicaps under which the village police pursued their duties, the citizens that they served rated police services as good as or better than similar citizens being served by the highly professional Chicago Police Department. Rates of criminal victimization and quality of police activity followed the same pattern. One would hardly argue that police service in the two villages could not be improved by increased training and higher salaries paid to officers. However, "professional" police without some means of relating to the people they serve do not seem to be more effective than even very "nonprofessional" police who are subject to community control.

Lack of Financial Resources

The final argument raised by opponents of community control relates to redistribution of resources. The two villages studied are very poor and are forced to rely very heavily on their own limited tax base. One of them has found it necessary to enforce traffic laws aggressively on a national highway within its jurisdiction to augment the funds available to the police depart-

TABLE 9.5. Comparison of Citizen Evaluations of Local Government
(in percentages)

	Independent Communities	Chicago Neighborhoods	Tau for Complete Table
Percentage of respondents agreeing that:			
Citizens can get satisfaction from talking with local public officials	53	33	.21[a]
(n)	(170)	(256)	
Who gets elected to local office makes a difference	66	76	-.15[b]
(n)	(195)	(279)	
Citizens can do something to prevent local corruption	37	39	-.03
(n)	(186)	(264)	
Citizens can influence the way the town is run	60	54	.04
(n)	(178)	(261)	
Local government is interested in their neighborhood	46	31	.13[c]
(n)	(182)	(265)	

[a] $p < .001$
[b] $p < .005$
[c] $p < .05$

ment. Limited redistribution does occur as a result of the services provided by the Cook County sheriff, but it does not appear to be very great.

A potentially more important source of redistribution is the revenues that the villages receive under a recently enacted Illinois statute that returns a small percentage of the state income tax to incorporated communities. In personal interviews, both village mayors stressed the importance of the small additional source of revenue from this state source to the operation of the village government. If greater financial support were available from county, state, or federal funds, the villages could improve police pay levels, training of patrolmen and equipment.

At the time of this study, the village governments found themselves in the strange position of not qualifying for most state and federal aid. They are both too small and too poor. Most grants offered by the Law Enforcement Assistance Administration, for example, are directed to police departments of medium and large cities whose budget exceeds a certain minimum level. The *only* federally controlled grant available through LEAA funds to the villages of Phoenix and East Chicago Heights in 1970 would support studies leading toward consolidation of their police forces with neighboring communities. While these police forces have been able to work out cooperative mutual aid arrangements with their white neighbors, consolidation with a neighboring police force is not a politically viable solution. The two villages are physically separate, and joint grant proposals have been refused due to lack of contiguity. Considerable redistribution could be accomplished with only minor changes in state and federal policies to open up opportunities for grants and other funds to small, very poor communities.

However, redistribution of resources, itself, is not sufficient to bring about responsive police services. It appears that considerable resource redistribution is currently occurring within the city of Chicago. More resources are probably being devoted to policing in the black neighborhoods studied than are derived in revenue for such purposes from these areas. Residents of these neighborhoods, however, find police services no better and police somewhat less responsive than do village residents *despite* the much greater difference in resources devoted to policing.

A Policy Recommendation

Police effectiveness depends, in part, on police understanding the nature of the community being served and police openness to suggestions, criticism, and complaints. This is particularly true of the kind of police services citizens receive in their own neighborhoods. Community control appears to be one way of enhancing the possibilities of citizen-police communication, thereby increasing both citizen support of police and police responsiveness to citizen preferences.

This policy alternative has already been adopted by those living in independently incorporated small communities. Perhaps some of the problems of our largest cities might be more effectively dealt with by employing a similar remedy within their jurisdictions. There is no need for the elimination of the large city or its police department. Many police problems are city-, state-, or nationwide. Such police problems require a diversity of relatively large-scale jurisdictions. Moreover, some specialized police services can be provided better by larger-scale units. Communications and records, laboratory facilities, and specialized investigatory details may be more economically provided by larger, citywide units.

Locally controlled police agencies could be established within the boundaries of a larger police jurisdiction to serve the particular needs of the large city's diverse neighborhoods. While many observers have assumed that overlap of jurisdictions was in and of itself wasteful and to be avoided, overlap of jurisdictions may be necessary to deal simultaneously with problems of varying scale (V. Ostrom 1989). The United States has a number of federal agencies existing concurrently with a number of state and local agencies. Just as some police problems are only city- or statewide in scope, others extend only to a single neighborhood. Furthermore, the FBI and other police agencies with broad jurisdictions must rely on local agencies for specific and detailed knowledge of particular areas if their efforts in specific places are to be effective. Those at the top of many large-city police departments may have grave difficulties in getting an accurate picture of local conditions within their districts. Few patrolmen in our largest cities live in the districts that they serve. Many large departments rotate personnel among precincts on a regular and short-term basis. Often the familiarity of officers with a specific area and the residents being served is viewed as something to be avoided. Rotation is frequently justified as a means to avoid corruption. Interestingly, we found that citizens of the small black villages were less apt to indicate that their police took bribes than were black residents of the Chicago neighborhoods where patrolmen are frequently rotated.

The problems in obtaining an adequate knowledge about local situations have led several large-scale police departments to experiment with local commander systems and other arrangements to decentralize administrative control of neighborhood patrol forces. While this reform may increase direct supervision of patrolmen in the field and may lead to more effective coordination of their efforts within neighborhoods, it may be expected to decrease the responsiveness to citizens of patrolmen serving these areas. Beat commander systems further isolate the patrolmen from formal accountability to the general public through regularly established channels. Local control of the police would involve the establishment of formal structures of accountability to the public being served as well as direct internal supervision of patrolmen on the job.

An effective means of establishing local control of the police in large cities might be to set up neighborhood districts to handle a variety of locally confined public problems. Such units would require some means for public selection of officials and the authority to levy local taxes and establish local ordinances. Such districts, of course, would function within the context of larger city, state, and federal governments and be subject to the laws of the larger jurisdictions. Officials and ordinances in the smaller jurisdictions would be submitted to the scrutiny of the courts at all levels. With regard to the police in particular, citywide regulations could enable a local patrolman to pursue a fleeing suspect anywhere within a broad jurisdiction. The large police department serving the city as a whole would be available for technical assistance and specialized investigation in all areas of the city. Citywide forces could also be utilized to supplement the needs of any local area in times of emergency. Redistribution to the poorer neighborhood districts within the large city could be provided from citywide as well as state and federal sources.

Community control of police may, thus, provide an institutional framework for the effective expression of black citizen demands for impartial police service. Calls for protection and respect cannot be expected to disappear. Black citizens have come to regard equal governmental treatment as a right. Professionalism alone does not appear to provide sufficient controls so that police will be responsive to their needs for protection and respect. Community control places that responsibility on the people themselves and provides them with mechanisms by which to exercise it.

NOTES

1. Harlan Hahn (1971, 385), in reviewing the effects of police professionalism, indicated that "the trend toward professionalization also has been occasioned by an increased sense of expertise and self-esteem among police officers and by a corresponding deprecation of external influences. The intense opposition of police forces to proposals for civilian review boards during the 1960s, therefore, appeared to be consistent with some of the major tenets of professionalism. . . . Basic to the impetus for professionalization was a prevalent belief among police officers that they should be freed from outside interference and that they should be allowed to pursue their central mission—the prevention and control of crime—using their own methods and judged by their own criteria."

2. See E. Ostrom 1972 for a description of the theoretical structure implicit in the metropolitan reform movement. See Piven and Cloward 1967 for a discussion of the effect of metropolitan-wide governmental units for black citizens.

3. See Marshall 1971 for a review of the findings from several studies on the amount and type of participation in poverty programs during the late 1960s. She argues that those among the poor who have participated in the programs studied "exhibit increases in political education, information about how the system works, and in organizational skills and feelings of political efficacy" (Marshall 1971, 473).

4. Anthony Orum (1966) argues that lower-class blacks are more likely to belong to organizations than lower-class whites and that voting rates for blacks of all classes have risen since 1952. Marvin Olson (1970) has also found that, when socioeconomic status is controlled, the rates of participation of black citizens are higher than those for white citizens and the rates of participation have been increasing between 1957 and 1968.

5. In a survey of police serving predominantly black areas in 13 U.S. cities, Groves and Rossi found black policemen to perceive the people in the area they are serving to be less hostile than did white policemen serving the same areas (Groves and Rossi 1970, 732). They conclude that "most of what a white policeman anticipates from black citizens is determined by factors other than the actual level of hostility in a city. A good deal of the perceived antagonism appears to be a projection of the policeman's own fears and prejudices—although a high level of acquaintance with community residents, leaders and other individuals tends somewhat to mitigate a highly prejudiced policeman's projection of his hostility" (Groves and Rossi 1970, 741).

6. James Q. Wilson (1968a, 190) describes the officers of a highly professionalized police department serving "Western City" in the following manner: "The city in which they now serve has a particular meaning for only a very few. Many live outside it in the suburbs and know the city's neighborhoods almost solely from their police work. Since there are no precinct stations but only radio car routes, and since these are frequently changed, there is little opportunity to build up an intimate familiarity, much less an identification with any neighborhood. The Western City police are, in a real sense, an army of occupation organized along paramilitary lines."

7. After this study was completed, the informal cooperation between villages was formalized through the establishment of the Suburban Mayors' Planning Group, involving the seven communities of Harvey, Markham, East Chicago Heights, Dixmoor, Chicago Heights, Phoenix, and Robbins. The first project undertaken by this group was a joint proposal by the seven communities to the Illinois Law Enforcement Association to establish a cooperative crime prevention program. (The proposal was, incidentally, turned down after extended negotiations because none of the communities involved had sufficient financial resources to meet the matching requirements of the program.)

REFERENCES

Aberbach, J. D., and J. L. Walker. 1970a. "The Attitudes of Blacks and Whites toward City Services: Implications for Public Policy." In *Financing the Metropolis: Public Policy in Urban Economies,* ed. J. P. Crecine. Beverly Hills: Sage.
———. 1970b. "Political Trust and Racial Ideology." *American Political Science Review* 64: 1199–219.
Altshuler, A. A. 1970. *Community Control: The Black Demand for Participation in Large American Cities.* New York: Pegasus.
Arnstein, S. R. 1969. "A Ladder of Citizen Participation." *Journal of American Institute of Planners* 35:216–32.
Babcock, R. F., and F. Bosselman. 1967. "Citizen Participation: A Suburban Suggestion for the Central City." *Journal of Law and Contemporary Problems* 32:220–31.
Baron, H. M. 1968. "Black Powerlessness in Chicago." *Transaction* 6:27–33.
Bayley, D. H., and H. Mendelsohn. 1969. *Minorities and the Police.* New York: Free Press.
Berger, C. J. 1968. "Law, Justice and the Poor." In *Urban Riots: Violence and Social Change,* ed. R. H. Connery. New York: Random House.
Bish, R. L. 1971. *The Public Economy of Metropolitan Areas.* Chicago: Markham.
Bish, R. L., and R. Warren. 1972. "Scale and Monopoly Problems in Urban Government Services." *Urban Affairs Quarterly* 8:97–122.
Campbell, A., and H. Schuman. 1968. "Racial Attitudes in Fifteen American Cities." In *Supplemental Studies for the National Advisory Commission on Civil Disorders.* Washington, DC: Government Printing Office.
Center for Governmental Studies. 1970. *Public Administration and Neighborhood Control.* Washington, DC.

Chicago Sun Times. 1972. "The Ranking of 200 Suburbs in Status List." August 15, 12.

Clark, T. M. 1970. "On Decentralization." *Polity* 2:508–14.

Costner, H. L., R. O. Hawkins, P. E. Smith, and G. F. White, III. 1970. "Crime, the Public and the Police." Mimeo. University of Washington.

De Vise, P. 1967. *Chicago's Widening Color Gap.* Chicago: Interuniversity Social Research Committee.

Ennis, P. H. 1967. *Criminal Victimization in the United States: A Report of a National Survey.* Washington, DC: U.S. Government Printing Office.

Erie, S. P., J. J. Kirlin, and F. E. Rabinovitz. 1972. "Can Something Be Done? Propositions on the Performance of Metropolitan Institutions." In *Reform of Metropolitan Governments,* ed. L. Wingo. Washington, DC: Resources for the Future.

Feagin, J. R. 1970. "Home Defense and the Police: Black and White Perspectives." *American Behavioral Scientist* 13:797–814.

Ferry, W. H. 1968. "The Case for a New Federalism." *Saturday Review* 30 (June 15): 15.

Fogelson, R. M. 1968. "From Resentment to Confrontation: The Police, the Negroes and the Outbreak of the Nineteen-sixties Riots." *Political Science Quarterly* 83:217–47.

Gittell, M. 1968. "Community Control of Education." In *Urban Riots: Violence and Social Change,* ed. R. A. Connery. New York: Random House.

Groves, W. E., and P. H. Rossi. 1970. "Police Perceptions of a Hostile Ghetto: Realism or Projections." *American Behavioral Scientist* 13 (May/June): 727–44.

Hahn, H. 1971. "Local Variations in Urban Law Enforcement." In *Race, Change and Urban Society,* ed. P. Orleans and W. R. Ellis. Beverly Hills: Sage.

Hahn, H., and J. R. Feagin. 1970. "Riot Precipitating Police Practices: Attitudes in Urban Ghettos." *Phylon* 31:183–93.

Hallman, H. W. 1971. *Administrative Decentralization and Citizen Control.* Washington, DC: Center for Governmental Studies.

Illinois Regional Medical Program. 1971. *Chicago Regional Hospital Study.* Chicago: Chicago Association of Commerce and Industry.

IsHak, S. T. 1972. "Consumers' Perceptions of Police Performance: Consolidation vs. Deconcentration; the Case of Grand Rapids, Michigan, Metropolitan Area." Ph.D. diss., Indiana University.

Itzkoff, S. W. 1969. "Decentralization: Dialectic and Dilemma." *Education Forum* 34:63–69.

Jackson, J. 1970. "On the Case." *Chicago Daily Defender* 4 (weekend edition for August): 22–28.

Jacob, H. 1970. "Black and White Perceptions of Justice in the City." *Law and Society Review* 6:69–90.

Jacobs, P. 1966. "The Los Angeles Police." *Atlantic Monthly* 218 (December): 95–101.

Kotler, M. et al. 1968. "Table Talk/Finding the City." *Center Magazine* 1 (May): 14–17.

Kristol, I. 1968. "Decentralization for What?" *Public Interest* 11 (spring): 17–25.

Levy, B. 1968. "Cops in the Ghetto: A Problem of the Police System." In *Riots and Rebellion: Civil Violence in the Urban Community,* ed. L. H. Masotti and D. R. Bowen, 347–58. Beverly Hills: Sage.

Lieberson, A., and A. R. Silverman. 1965. "The Precipitants and Underlying Conditions of Race Riots." *American Sociological Review* 31 (December): 887–98.

Marshall, D. R. 1971. "Public Participation and the Politics of Poverty." In *Race, Change and Urban Society,* ed. P. Orleans and W. R. Ellis, 451-83. Beverly Hills: Sage.

Mayer, A. 1971. "A New Level of Local Government is Struggling to be Born." *City* (March/April): 60–64.

Meltzer, J. 1968. "A New Look at the Urban Revolt." *Journal of American Institute of Planners* 34 (December): 255–59.

Mitchell, M. 1973. "Racial Identification and Public Order in Black Communities." Bloomington: Indiana University, Department of Political Science, Studies in Political Theory and Policy Analysis.

Mogulof, M. 1969. "Coalition to Adversary: Citizen Participation in Three Federal Programs." *Journal of American Institute of Planners* 35: 225–32.

National Advisory Commission on Civil Disorders. 1968. Report. Washington, DC: U.S. Government Printing Office.

Nie, N. H., G. B. Powell, Jr., and K. Prewitt. 1969. "Social Structure and Political Participation: Developmental Relationships." *American Political Science Review* 62:361–78.

Olson, M. E. 1970. "Social and Political Participation of Blacks." *American Sociological Review* 35:682–97.

Orbell, J. M., and T. Uno. 1972. "A Theory of Neighborhood Problem Solving: Political Actions vs. Residential Mobility." *American Political Science Review* 66:471–89.

Orum, A. M. 1966. "A Reappraisal of the Social and Political Participation of Negroes." *American Journal of Sociology* 72:32–46.

Ostrom, E. 1971. "Institutional Arrangements and the Measurement of Policy Consequences in Urban Areas." *Urban Affairs Quarterly* 6:447–75.

———. 1972. "Metropolitan Reform: Propositions Derived from Two Traditions." *Social Science Quarterly* 53 (December): 474–93. (Chapter 6 in this volume.)

Ostrom, E., W. Baugh, R. Guarasci, R. Parks, and G. Whitaker. 1973. "Community Organization and the Provision of Police Services." Sage Professional Paper in Administrative and Policy Studies 03–001. Beverly Hills: Sage.

Ostrom, E., and R. Parks. 1973. "Suburban Police Departments: Too Many and Too Small?" In *The Urbanization of the Suburbs,* ed. L. H. Masotti and J. K. Hadden, 367–402. Urban Affairs Annual Reviews, vol. 7. Beverly Hills: Sage.

Ostrom, E., R. Parks, and G. Whitaker. 1973. "Do We Really Want to Consolidate Urban Police Forces? A Reappraisal of Some Old Assertions." *Public Administration Review* 33 (September/October): 423–32.

Ostrom, E., and G. Whitaker. 1973. "Does Local Community Control of Police Make a Difference? Some Preliminary Findings." *American Journal of Political Science* 17 (February): 48–76. (Chapter 8 in this volume.)

Ostrom, Vincent. 1987. *The Political Theory of a Compound Republic: Designing the American Experiment.* 2d rev. ed. San Francisco, CA: ICS Press.
———. 1989. *The Intellectual Crisis in American Public Administration.* 2nd ed. Tuscaloosa: University of Alabama Press.
Ostrom, V., C. M. Tiebout, and R. Warren. 1961. "The Organization of Government in Metropolitan Areas: A Theoretical Inquiry." *American Political Science Review* 55:831–42. (Chapter 1 in this volume.)
Parenti, M. 1970. "Power and Pluralism: A View from the Bottom." *Journal of Politics* 32:501–30.
Perlmutter, N. 1968. "We Don't Help Blacks by Hurting Whites." *New York Times Magazine* (October 6): 31.
Piven, F. F., and R. A. Cloward. 1967. "Black Control of the Cities: Heading It Off by Metropolitan Government." *New Republic* (September 30): 19–21; (October 7): 15–19.
Press, C. 1963. "The Cities within a Great City: A Decentralist Approach to Centralization." *Centennial Review* 7:113–30.
Prewitt, K., and H. Eulau. 1969. "Political Matrix and Political Representation: Prolegomenon to a New Departure from an Old Problem." *American Political Science Review* 62:427–41.
Przeworski, A., and H. Teune. 1970. *The Logic of Comparative Social Inquiry.* New York: John Wiley.
Rossi, P. H. 1963. "The Middle-Sized American City at Mid-century." *Library Quarterly* 33:3–13.
Rossi, P. H., and R. A. Berk. 1970. "Local Political Leadership and Popular Discontent in the Ghetto." *Annals of American Academy of Political and Social Science* 391:111–27.
Rubenstein, R. E. 1970. *Rebels in Eden.* Boston: Little, Brown.
Shalala, D. E. 1971. "Neighborhood Governments: Rationale, Functions, Size and Governmental Framework." Prepared for the National Consultation on Neighborhood Government, Institute of Human Relations, New York.
Skolnick, J. 1967. *Justice Without Trial: Law Enforcement in Democratic Society.* New York: John Wiley.
Spear, A. H. 1967. *Black Chicago: The Making of a Negro Ghetto, 1890–1920.* Chicago: University of Chicago Press.
Tauber, K. E. 1968. "The Problem of Residential Segregation." In *Urban Riots: Violence and Social Change,* ed. R. H. Connery. New York: Random House.
TenHouten, W., J. Stern, and D. TenHouten. 1971. "Political Leadership in Poor Communities: Applications of Two Sampling Methodologies." In *Race, Change and Urban Society,* ed. P. Orleans and W. R. Ellis, 215–54. Beverly Hills: Sage.
Tiebout, C. M. 1956. "Pure Theory of Local Expenditures." *Journal of Political Economy* 64:416–24.
Warren, R. 1966. *Government in Metropolitan Regions.* Davis: University of California, Davis, Institute of Governmental Affairs.
Whitaker, G. P. 1971. "Urban Police Forces: Size and Scale in Relation to Service." Ph.D. diss., Indiana University.

Wilson, J. Q. 1963. "The Police and Their Problems: A Theory." *Public Policy* 12:189–216.

———. 1968a. "The Police and the Delinquent in Two Cities." In *City Politics and Public Policy,* ed. J. Q. Wilson, 173–96. New York: John Wiley.

———. 1968b. *Varieties of Police Behavior.* Boston: Harvard University Press.

Zimmerman, J. F. 1970. "Metropolitan Reform in the U.S.: An Overview." *Public Administration Review* 30:531–43.

CHAPTER 10

Size and Performance in a Federal System

Elinor Ostrom

Consolidation and Its Alternate in Simplified Form

Underlying the repeated calls for consolidation of urban police forces is an assumption that larger police forces will provide higher levels of police services more effectively than will smaller police departments. Such an assumption can be presented as a simple theoretical model of predicted relationships as in figure 10.1.

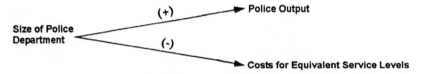

Fig. 10.1. The theoretical consolidation model (simplified form)

This simple model could be examined directly if there were an accepted method for *measuring* police outputs and if all police outputs were the same. However, such is not the case.[1]

The problem of measuring police output was met operationally in our series of studies by first narrowing the range of police services examined to those provided to a neighborhood. These include all direct responses to calls for assistance, criminal investigation, general patrol, and related supportive services such as dispatching. Services such as metropolitan traffic patrol were excluded because the appropriate level of measurement differs signi-

Originally published in *Publius: The Journal of Federalism* 6, no. 2 (1976): 33–73. Reprinted by permission of *Publius* and the authors.

Research reported on in this essay has been supported by the Center for Studies of Metropolitan Problems, National Institute of Mental Health, Grant No. 5 RO1 MH 19911, and the National Science Foundation, Grant No. GS-27383.

James McDavid, Vincent Ostrom, Roger Parks, and Gordon Whitaker commented extensively on the first draft of this essay and their help was extremely valuable. Jnana Hodson's editorial skills have contributed greatly to the rewriting of this essay.

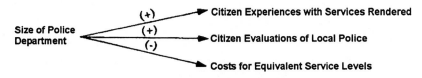

Fig. 10.2. The operational consolidation model (simplified form)

cantly from that of neighborhood-level police services. Given this range of services, survey instruments were designed to obtain two types of information about police output. First, respondents were asked about their direct experiences with police and with criminal victimization. Second, respondents were asked to evaluate their local police on a number of attributes. Thus, the theoretical model presented in figure 10.1 can be translated into an operational model for testing as in figure 10.2.

Given such a model, one would expect to find the following types of relationships in regard to *citizen experiences* with services rendered.

> H_1 Citizens living in neighborhoods served by large police departments should
> a. report fewer victimizations;
> b. report victimizations at a higher rate to the police if they occur;
> c. receive higher levels of police follow-up to a victimization;
> d. call upon the police for assistance more often;
> e. receive more rapid response to their calls for assistance; and
> f. receive more satisfactory levels of police assistance.

In regard to *citizen evaluations* of local police, one would expect to find the following types of relationships.

> H_2 Citizens living in neighborhoods served by large police departments should more frequently
> a. rate the job being done by the police as outstanding;
> b. rate police-community relationships as good;
> c. indicate that police do not take bribes;
> d. indicate that crime is about the same or decreasing;
> e. indicate that police respond very rapidly; and
> f. agree that local police treat all equally.

In regard to costs, the following relationship would be expected.

> H_3 The costs of providing similar levels of police service should be lower in larger jurisdictions than in smaller jurisdictions.

All *dependent variables* in H_1, H_2 and H_3 are jointly referred to as *performance variables.*

This simple model was selected for study for two reasons. First, the posited relationships in the simple model must be supported empirically if the consolidation of police agencies is warranted. If larger police departments do not perform better or more efficiently, the prime argument for police consolidation is not empirically sound.

Second, alternative theoretical formulations predict that the size of police departments is negatively related to citizen experiences and evaluations. An alternative theoretical approach further predicts that size of police departments is positively related to the costs of providing police services at least over a large range of existing departments.[2]

Consequently, empirical examination of this set of relationships would provide simultaneous evidence concerning the warrantability of two models—the simplified consolidation model posited in figure 10.2 as well as an alternative model presented in figure 10.3.

Fig. 10.3. The alternative operational model

An alternative set of hypotheses to those stated here obviously exists. The set is not presented here to avoid repetition. For each of the three hypotheses, the alternative hypotheses posit the opposite.[3]

The First Series of Empirical Studies

The theoretical and operational models examined in our studies take the size of a police department serving a neighborhood as the independent variable. Other variables, however, also affect citizen experiences, citizen evaluations, and the costs of equivalent service levels. In particular, research efforts have identified a number of socioeconomic variables such as the patterns of wealth, density, education, race, and age among neighborhood residents as affecting costs, experiences, and evaluations (see Aberbach and Walker 1970; U.S. Department of Health, Education, and Welfare 1969). Any research that attempts to examine the effect of the size of police departments on performance variables must take into account the potential effect of these socioeconomic variables on the performance variables examined. Research designs that ignore the potential effects of such socioeconomic variables would be seriously vulnerable to criticism that variations in neighborhood socioeconomic status, not size of the police department serving a neighborhood, are affecting citizen experiences, citizen evaluations, and costs of services. In essence, a rival methodological model exists that posits that any effect of size upon performance variables results from variation in socioeconomic status of the neighborhoods included in the study rather than variation in size.[4] Such a rival methodological model is shown in figure 10.4.

Fig. 10.4. A rival methodological model

To take this rival methodological model into account, research on the effects of size must control for the socioeconomic variables by either (1) the careful selection of research sites which minimize the differences in socioeconomic status among the sample areas selected; or (2) inclusion of sufficient areas in the study where the potential effects of socioeconomic status can be handled at the data analysis stage through statistical controls.

The first four studies reported on in this section utilized a "most similar systems" research design to control for the potential effect of socioeconomic variables upon performance variables (see Przeworski and Teune 1970). A most similar systems research design requires that all *other* factors affecting dependent variables be neutralized by selecting study areas that are matched on all relevant factors beyond the independent variables under examination. Thus, in the four studies utilizing the "most similar system" design, neighborhoods are matched in terms of socioeconomic variables such as racial characteristics, density, age distributions, and wealth. In each study, some of the matched neighborhoods were served by relatively small-scale, independent police departments while others were served by larger departments.

The first study was conducted in Indianapolis in three small independent communities immediately adjacent to the jurisdiction of the Indianapolis Police District. (See chap. 8 in this volume.) The independent communities were Speedway, Beech Grove, and Lawrence and had populations of 12,000 to 16,000. They were served by police forces of 18 to 25 sworn officers. Each of the three Indianapolis neighborhoods was immediately adjacent to one of the independent communities. The socioeconomic characteristics, housing patterns, and living conditions of all six neighborhoods were closely matched. They were predominantly white, middle-class residential districts with single-family residences. The Indianapolis neighborhoods were served by a highly professionalized city police force composed of some 1,100 sworn officers serving a total population of nearly 500,000. The Indianapolis Police Department had an excellent reputation as a competent, efficient, and innovative police agency.

The data from the Indianapolis study did not support H_1 or H_2 from the simplified consolidation model. As shown in table 10.1, citizen reports of experiences indicated that the performance of the larger department did not exceed that of the smaller. Citizens in matched neighborhoods served by the larger department did not rank the performance of their department better on any evaluation indicator than did citizens served by the smaller departments. Where differences in output level appear, the consistent pattern is that the small police department serving the independent communities produced at a higher level than did the larger department. Thus, the alternative hypotheses H_1 and H_2 were supported.

The findings on H_3 were somewhat ambiguous. While the per capita expenditures of the city of Indianapolis averaged \$21.33 for the city as a whole, resources worth approximately \$10.72 per capita were devoted to the provision of police services within the Indianapolis Police District neighborhoods included in our study. Police expenditures in the independent communities averaged \$12.76 per capita. Thus, the per capita cost of resources devoted to police services in the sample Indianapolis neighborhoods was less than the per capita cost in the independent communities. This finding does not provide adequate evidence for any conclusions about the relative efficiency of the two types of departments, since the residents of the smaller communities—while effectively allocating more to police services—were also receiving higher levels of service. Without an interval measure of output, no efficiency conclusion can be reached in this case.

Analysis of the expenditure patterns of the two types of police departments did indicate some important differences in resource allocation. The smaller police departments allocated proportionately more of their police budget to patrol services, while the Indianapolis department allocated proportionately more to detective and supervisory services. It would appear that the smaller communities were devoting proportionately more effort to crime prevention and immediate response activities and that the larger department was devoting more resources to investigation of crime after it had occurred.

A replication of this study was undertaken in the spring of 1971 by Samir IsHak in the Grand Rapids, Michigan, metropolitan area (IsHak 1972). The independently incorporated cities of East Grand Rapids, Kentwood, and Walker are located immediately adjacent to the city of Grand Rapids. Three neighborhoods within the city of Grand Rapids, immediately adjacent to the independent communities, were selected for comparative study. The popula-

TABLE 10.1. Comparison of Citizen Experiences and Citizen Evaluations in Indianapolis, Grand Rapids, Nashville, and Chicago

	Indianapolis (white residents)		Grand Rapids (white residents)		Nashville (white residents)		Chicago (black residents)	
	Independent Community	City Neighborhood	Independent Community	City Neighborhood	Independent Community	City Neighborhood	Independent Community	City Neighborhood
Experiences								
% not victimized	80% (373)	70% (349)	90% (516)	86% (563)	83% (106)	64% (98)	75% (195)	74% (276)
% who reported victimizations	86% (73)	82% (103)	93% (74)	85% (57)	67% (18)	46% (35)	—	—
% who received high follow-up	47% (43)	36% (37)	80% (74)	66% (57)	—	—	59% (32)	46% (48)
% who called for assistance	26% (336)	17% (311)	25% (568)	26% (554)	26% (106)	12% (98)	19% (193)	24% (269)
% who received assistance in 5 minutes	79% (71)	60% (45)	56% (142)	45% (122)	—	—	60% (30)	48% (44)
% stopped	24% (325)	25% (325)	27% (557)	26% (559)	17% (105)	15% (98)	—	—
Evaluations								
% rating job done—outstanding	31% (369)	12% (330)	23% (557)	15% (559)	42% (106)	6% (98)	—	—
% rating PCR—good	94% (321)	82% (273)	97% (557)	93% (559)	67% (106)	43% (98)	46% (181)	44% (254)
% police do not take bribes	86% (334)	85% (315)	95% (557)	92% (559)	—	—	37% (110)	21% (157)
% crime about same or decreasing	77% (315)	60% (314)	79% (557)	57% (559)	57% (106)	62% (98)	—	—
% rating police response very rapid	66% (323)	43% (276)	38% (557)	23% (559)	60% (106)	62% (98)	26% (144)	25% (197)
% agree police treat all equally	—	—	88% (557)	65% (559)	82% (106)	64% (98)	46% (105)	18% (181)

tion of Grand Rapids was approximately 200,000, while that of the independent communities ranged from approximately 12,000 to 20,000. The police departments serving these communities varied from 9 to 17 sworn officers, while Grand Rapids employed 313 sworn officers. The Grand Rapids neighborhoods were very similar to each other and to those studied in Indianapolis.

The data from this replication did not support either H_1 or H_2 of the consolidation model. The pattern in the two studies is very similar as shown in table 10.1. Based on both the experiences of citizens and their evaluations, one would have to conclude that the larger department was *not* providing higher service levels.

The findings in regard to H_3, moreover, were more clear-cut than those in Indianapolis. The per capita expenditure of the city of Grand Rapids was $20.00, and the per capita expenditures for police within the three separately incorporated communities ranged from $5.81 to $16.13. When one examines the resources devoted by the Grand Rapids Police Department to providing police services in the neighborhoods under study, the average for the three neighborhoods is $16.88 per capita, while the average for the three independent communities is $10.67. The larger department thus provided lower levels of services at higher costs. Production strategies found in Grand Rapids were similar to those in Indianapolis.

A second replication of the Indianapolis study was undertaken by Bruce D. Rogers and C. McCurdy Lipsey in the spring of 1973 in the Nashville–Davidson County metropolitan area (Rogers and McCurdy Lipsey 1974). Within Davidson County are six incorporated communities that voted in 1962 not to consolidate their governments with the urban services district of Nashville's metropolitan government. They are, however, part of the general services district and thus pay for such countywide services as the Nashville Metropolitan Police Department. One of these communities, Berry Hill, is located immediately adjacent to the Urban Services District and to a closely matched neighborhood called Woodbine, which is served by the Nashville–Davidson County Metropolitan Police Department. Berry Hill provides its own police and park services and contracts for other municipal services even though its total 1970 population was only 1,651. Both Berry Hill and Woodbine are working-class neighborhoods composed predominantly of white residents living in single-family residences.

The Nashville–Davidson County study did not support H_1 or H_2 in the consolidation model. In fact, the findings against H_1 and H_2 are even stronger in this study than in the Indianapolis and Grand Rapids studies. Information regarding H_3 is not yet available. Bruce Rogers and Barbara Greene are currently in the planning stages for a much larger study to take 12 to 18 matched neighborhoods in Nashville–Davidson County and examine their varying arrangements for the provision of police and other urban services. In this study, the question of resource allocation and costs will be thoroughly examined.

A study related to the three previously described was conducted in Illinois. Two poor, black communities in south suburban Cook County, each served by its own police department, were compared with three relatively similar black neighborhoods within the city of Chicago (E. Ostrom and Whitaker 1974 [chap. 9 in this volume]). In this instance, the differences in resources allocated to the different types of neighborhoods were extreme. More than 14 times as much was devoted to police services in the Chicago neighborhoods than in either Phoenix or East Chicago Heights. For all the difference in resources, however, the service levels, as shown in table 10.1, did not differ significantly. Thus, there is again no support for H_1 or H_2. Given the same levels of output and the drastically different levels of costs, the evidence is strongly contrary to H_3.

We have also reanalyzed data gathered by the National Opinion Research Center (NORC) for the President's Commission on Law Enforcement and Administration of Justice in 1966 (E. Ostrom and Parks 1973). This database of approximately 2,000 respondents residing in 109 cities of more than 10,000 population provided data on citizen evaluations of their police, citizen feelings of safety, and their confidence in their police. We added information from the *Municipal Year Book* on city size and expenditure levels.

In general, examining the full set of respondents, we found consistent but weak relationships between size of jurisdiction and general evaluations of police services. All significant relationships run counter to those predicted in the simplified consolidation model. Feelings of safety decrease with size; fear of break-in and attack increase with size; the rating of police honesty decreases with size. In regard to the cost of police services, we found a positive relationship between city size and per capita costs. We then controlled for the quality of services provided. If differences in quality of service were the explanation for the positive relationship between size and cost, the relationship would disappear or would change signs. There was virtually no change in the coefficients when quality levels were controlled. Thus, there was no support for H_3 of the simplified consolidation model.

In this study of 109 cities we were also able to examine in an exploratory manner whether the negative relationship between city size and evaluation of police services was more curvilinear than linear. We did find that the relationship between size and evaluation levels was positive for suburban respondents living in cities under 20,000 and for central-city respondents living in cities under 100,000. Above these cutoff points, the direction of the relationship reversed. Thus, performance levels may be higher in medium-sized departments than in either small or large departments.

In summary, a comparison of levels of services provided by large departments with small- to medium-sized departments for similar neighborhoods in each of the four separate studies shows a consistent finding that larger departments do *not* provide higher levels of services as measured by citizen experiences or evaluations. These findings are also substantiated in a nationwide study of police services in 109 cities ranging in size from 10,000 to 7 million population. Two of the within-metropolitan area studies established that the costs of police services to similar neighborhoods was higher in the larger jurisdiction. The Indianapolis study had ambiguous findings in regard to costs and the Nashville–Davidson County study did not examine H_3. But, the nationwide study found higher per capita costs for providing constant levels of police services in larger police jurisdictions.

These cumulative studies should lead to serious questioning of the empirical warrantability of assumptions underlying the traditional metropolitan reform proposals relating to the provisions of urban police services. Each of the studies, however, was designed to begin exploration of the relationships between costs and benefits of police services under varying jurisdictional arrangements. In these studies, only the simplified consolidation model and its alternate could be empirically examined. But with the consistent lack of empirical support for the simplified consolidation model, it then became essential to delve more deeply into potentially more complex relationships between the size of police departments and performance variables.

For example, how do training and education affect police services? Proponents of consolidation often argue that only larger departments can afford to provide extensive training for police personnel and to employ officers with college education. They assume that higher levels of formal police training and education lead to higher levels of performance. Given the lack of empirical evidence for these assumptions, it becomes important to trace the effect of police department size on levels of formal police training and college education. It is also important to examine the effects of formal police training and college education on the performance of police departments. These more complex relationships could not be examined in the earlier studies but were a major research question in a much larger study.

The St. Louis Comparative Study of Police Performance

The St. Louis metropolitan area was chosen for this study because of the wide variety of relevant organizational arrangements within one area.[5] The St. Louis City Police Department, with 2,200 officers, provides an example of a large force recommended by traditional reformers. The St. Louis County Police Department of 436 officers exemplifies a large countywide department capable of supplying a full complement of police services, supplementary services, or contract services to independent communities. Within St.

Louis County are 93 independently incorporated communities, 63 of which have their own police departments ranging in size from zero full-time officers (they employ only part-time officers) to 76 full-time officers. The remaining jurisdictions contract for police services with either the County Police Department or other municipal departments. This variety of jurisdictional arrangements enabled us to examine effects of the size of police departments upon performance as well as many of the intervening variables that may affect police performance.

Research Design

Again, we utilized a "most similar systems" research design in the selection of neighborhoods within the St. Louis situation. However, we included more than one strata of similar neighborhoods. For this study, a neighborhood is defined as consisting of either

1. an independently incorporated community in St. Louis County with a population in 1970 less than or equal to 28,900;
2. a census tract *within* an independently incorporated community in St. Louis County with a population in 1970 of greater than 28,900;
3. an urban place as designated by the 1970 census within the unincorporated portion of St. Louis County; or
4. a Planning Neighborhood (as designated by the St. Louis City Planning Commission) within the city of St. Louis.

Under these criteria, more than 170 neighborhoods existed in the City of St. Louis—St. Louis County field. Neighborhoods were eliminated from the sample frame where

1. the percentage of population over 65 years of age exceeded 20 percent;
2. the percentage of population under 21 years of age exceeded 45 percent;
3. the median value of owner-occupied housing was $25,000 or more; or
4. less than 60 percent of the dwelling units were owner occupied (this criterion was relaxed slightly in two cases to allow inclusion of two predominantly black communities).

The remaining relatively homogeneous neighborhoods were then stratified along dimensions of neighborhood wealth, as well as by size of police department, where size of community initially stood as a proxy for size of department. The three strata of neighborhood wealth and the seven strata for size of police department produced a matrix with 21 cells. For seven of these logically possible cells there were no existing cases, given the criteria for inclusion stated previously. From the remaining cells, we chose 45 sample areas. In choosing potential neighborhoods for each cell, we first dichotomized these into neighborhoods with greater than 30 percent black population in 1970 and those with less than or equal to 30 percent black population. Sensitivity to this dichotomy ensured—to the extent allowed by the existence of appropriate neighborhoods—that we would include a significant black sample.

Having determined those neighborhoods that were of interest through use of the described criteria, we proceeded to choose among them on the basis of contiguity into clusters of neighborhoods. These considerations allowed us to choose sample areas so that variation existed along the dimensions of both size and organization for provision of police service, of individual wealth within the community, and of the presence or absence of a sizable black population. Variation in other factors affecting police performance was controlled by matching. For each neighborhood in our sample frame, we obtained data from five types of sources: (1) interviews with citizens residing in the neighborhoods; (2) interviews with police officers serving the neighborhoods; (3) internal police records and published reports on police services pertaining to the neighborhoods; (4) published and unpublished data relating to the neighborhoods from agencies external to the communities studied; and (5) unobtrusive observation of neighborhood conditions.[6]

For the analysis presented here we draw upon data gathered from the citizen survey, from the survey of police officers serving the neighborhoods included in the study, and from census data. All data has been aggregated or disaggregated to the specific neighborhoods included within the study. A complete data set is available for 43 neighborhoods, and all analyses in this essay examine relationships within these. One question considered will use a database of 44 neighborhoods.

Research Questions

Given the larger and more diverse database of the St. Louis study, a number of more complex questions can be asked about relationships between the scale of production and police performance. The first question is whether the simple relationships found in earlier studies between the size of police departments serving a neighborhood and citizen experiences, citizen evaluations, and per capita costs remain the same.

The second question is whether the introduction of neighborhood-level socioeconomic variables seriously affect the relationships between size and citizen experiences and evaluations.

The third is whether there are positive relationships between the size of a police department and the level of formal police training and/or college education of its officers.

Further questions ask whether formal police training and/or college education for officers on a police force have an independent effect on citizen experience and/or citizen evaluations. Other questions explore whether citizen experiences operate as intervening variables affecting citizen evaluations. Given answers to these, we can then examine whether empirical data support a more complex model of the relationships between size of police department and citizen evaluation of police performance.

The final question is whether police departments of 10 or fewer full-time officers are less effective than larger departments.

Question One: Are There Bivariate Relationships between Size of Police Departments Serving a Neighborhood and Citizen Experiences, Citizen Evaluations, and per Capita Costs of Providing Police Services?
As shown in table 10.2, a significant relationship exists between the size of the police department serving a neighborhood and many of the indicators of citizen experiences and evaluation used in this and earlier studies. Size here is measured by the number of full-time officers employed by the police department serving a neighborhood. Size is positively related to the victimization rate in a neighborhood and to citizens' indication that crime is increasing. Size is negatively related to: (1) the percentage of citizens assisted; (2) the percentage of citizens indicating that police respond "very rapidly" in their neighborhood; (3) the percentage of citizens rating the job being done by their police as "outstanding"; (4) the percentage of citizens rating police-community relations as "outstanding"; (5) the percentage of citizens strongly agreeing with the statement that police are "honest"; and (6) the percentage of citizens strongly agreeing that "police treat all citizens equally."[7] Size is positively related to the per capita expenditures for police services in the neighborhoods.[8]

Question Two: Do the Relationships between Size of the Police Department Serving a Neighborhood and Citizen Experiences, Citizen Evaluations, and Costs Continue When Socioeconomic Variables are Introduced?
Since the St. Louis study used a *multistrata* research design allowing variations in neighborhood wealth and the proportion of black residents in the neighborhoods, it is necessary to ascertain the independent effect of these socioeconomic variations on citizen experiences and evaluation. The statistical technique utilized is multiple regression. Table 10.3 presents the standardized regression coefficients (betas) for each of three independent variables:

X_1 = the number of full-time officers employed by the police department serving the neighborhood.
X_2 = the median value of owner-occupied housing in the neighborhood.

X_3 = the percentage of black residents living in the neighborhood.

The R^2 for each dependent variable is also reported in table 10.3.[9]

TABLE 10.2. The Correlation between Size of Police Department and Experiences, Evaluations, and Costs

	X_1 Size of Police Department r
Experiences	
X_6 % victimized	.43[b]
X_7 % assisted	-.35[b]
X_8 % stopped	—
X_9 % know someone mistreated by police	—
X_{10} % know one or more policemen	—
Evaluations	
X_{11} % indicating crime increasing	.51[a]
X_{12} % indicating that police response is very rapid	-.64[a]
X_{13} % rating job of police outstanding	-.49[a]
X_{14} % rating police-community relations outstanding	-.25[c]
X_{15} % strongly agreeing that police are honest	-.38[b]
X_{16} % strongly agreeing that police treat all citizens equally	—
Costs	
X_{17} per capita costs of police services in neighborhood	.77[a]

[a] $p = .001$
[b] $p = .01$
[c] $p = .05$

As can be seen through comparison of tables 10.2 and 10.3, the signs of all relationships between size and the dependent variables remain the same even though the two additional independent variables in some cases reduce the size of the coefficient. The socioeconomic variables also have some interesting relationships with citizen experiences and evaluations. The median value of owner-occupied housing in a neighborhood is negatively related to being victimized, knowing someone mistreated, knowing one or more policemen, and perceiving that crime is increasing; it is positively associated with rating the police as outstanding, rating police-community relationships as outstanding, agreeing that police are honest, and agreeing that police treat all equally. The percentage of black residents living in a neighborhood is positively related to victimization rates, to being stopped by police, to knowing one or more policemen, to perceiving that crime is increasing, and to the per capita costs of providing police services; it is negatively related to agreeing that police treat all equally.

TABLE 10.3. **Standardized Regression Coefficients and Variance Explained for Relationships between Size, Socioeconomic Variables, and Experiences, Evaluations, and Costs**

	X_1 Size	X_2 Median Value Owner-Occupied Housing	X_3 % Black Residents	R_2
Experiences				
X_6 % victimized	$.29^b$	$-.30^b$	$.49^a$	.63
X_7 % assisted	$-.35^c$	—	—	.12
X_8 % stopped	—	—	$.31^c$	.10
X_9 % know someone mistreated	—	$.34^b$	$.49^a$	.49
X_{10} % know one or more policemen	—	$-.48^a$	—	.23
Evaluations				
X_{11} % indicate crime increasing	$.42^a$	.20	$.28^c$	.42
X_{12} % police respond very rapidly	$-.64^a$	—	—	.42
X_{13} % rate job outstanding	$-.16$	$.47^a$	—	.27
X_{14} % agree police honest	$-.30^c$	$.43^b$	—	.33
X_{15} % agree police treat all equally	—	$.35^b$	$-.16$	.20
Costs				
X_{16} per capita costs of police in neighborhood	$.72^a$	—	$.33^c$	.68

[a] $p=.001$
[b] $p=.01$
[c] $p=.05$

In no instance does the sign of the relationship between the size of a police department serving a neighborhood and citizen experiences, citizen evaluations, and per capita costs correspond to the predicted direction derived from the original consolidation model (figure 10.2). Thus, the findings from this study are completely consistent with the findings from the earlier studies; they support the alternative model, which predicts a negative relation. In most instances, a negative relation has been found.

Question Three: What are the Relationships between the Size of Police Departments and the Levels of Formal Police Training and College Education among Sworn Personnel?

One of the reasons cited for recommending consolidation of police into larger units is that larger police departments can afford to train their personnel more effectively and to hire college educated personnel. The simple relationship between the size of police departments and median weeks of training of sworn personnel is positive ($r = .45$), while the simple relationship between size and the proportion of officers who have had some college education is negative ($r = -.44$). When size, percentage of black residents, and median value of owner-occupied housing are combined in a multiple regression equation, only size has a significant effect on the levels of training (beta = .45). When combined with size and percentage black residents, median value of owner-occupied housing is most important in explaining the proportion of officers having some college education (beta = .47), size of police department is next (beta = –.39), and the percentage of black residents is third (beta = .26).

Thus, a definite and positive relation between the size of police departments and the level of formal training among sworn personnel on a force is found. In the St. Louis area, the two largest departments have for many years required their officers to attend a 16-week training program at a joint city-county police academy. A recent state law now requires all new police officers in St. Louis County to attend the same city-county academy. At the time of our study, however, the new legislation had been in effect only a few months and the level of training in most departments had not yet been affected by the legislation. Over time, personnel in the smaller departments will have a level of training similar to those in the two larger departments.

The level of college training among sworn personnel, however, is negatively related to the size of police departments. Many of the smaller and medium-size departments employ a higher percentage of officers with some college education than do the larger departments.

Question Four: What are the Independent Effects of the Levels of Formal Police Training and College Education among Police Personnel Serving a Neighborhood upon Citizen Experiences?
Despite all the interest in increasing the levels of training and education among police personnel, few studies have examined what effects these have on police performance. In a preliminary analysis of this question, using data from our St. Louis study, Smith and E. Ostrom found that training was *not* positively associated with either more "professional" attitudes on the part of individual officers or more favorable citizen experiences or evaluations.[10] The level of college education was weakly associated in a positive direction with more "professional" attitudes but had little impact on citizen experiences or evaluations (Smith and E. Ostrom 1974). This analysis, however, was bivariate in nature and did not explore the independent effects of training and college education when other factors were controlled.

When the median weeks of formal training among officers in a department is added to each of the multiple regression equations for experiences shown in table 10.3, it has an independent effect (beta = –.22) in only one equation—the percentage of citizens knowing one or more policemen. The level of training is thus negatively related to the likelihood that citizens will know one or more policemen. Median value of owner-occupied housing is still the most important variable explaining the percentage of citizens knowing police (beta = –.47). The R^2 value for the equation is raised from .23 to .28 by the addition of median weeks of training to the equation.

The percentage of sworn personnel having some college education has an independent effect only in the equation for the percentage of household victimizations in the year prior to our survey. Four variables have an independent effect on victimization rates: (1) percentage of black residents (beta = .44); (2) median value of owner-occupied housing (beta = -.40); (3) size of police department serving the neighborhood (beta = .37); and (4) percentage of officers having some college education (beta = .20). The addition of this variable to the equation increases R^2 from .63 to .65. The relationship between victimization rates and level of college education among police serving a neighborhood is thus weakly positive.

Question Five: What is the Independent Effect of the Level of Formal Police Training and College Education among Police Serving a Neighborhood upon Citizen Evaluations?

When variable X_4—median weeks of training of police personnel serving a neighborhood—is introduced as an intervening variable with X_1—size of police department serving a neighborhood, X_2—median value of owner-occupied housing units in neighborhood, and X_3—percentage of black residents in neighborhood—its independent effect on the six evaluation variables is negative in five equations and of no effect in the sixth. The negative coefficients vary from weak to moderate, as shown on figure 10.5. Median weeks of formal police training is most strongly (and negatively) related to the percentage of citizens likely to rate police community relations as outstanding (beta = -.33). Thus, controlling for size of police department and the socioeconomic status of a neighborhood, the median level of formal police training among sworn officers serving a neighborhood is inversely related to citizens' evaluations of police performance. While the size of a police department serving a neighborhood is positively related to median levels of training, this intervening variable does not have a positive effect on citizen evaluations of police performance.

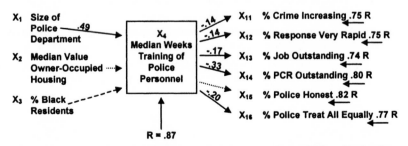

Fig. 10.5. The Independent Effects of Training Levels on Citizen Evaluations Controlling for Size of Police Department and Socioeconomic Status of Neighborhood

When variable X_5—percentage of officers having some college experience—is introduced as an intervening variable with the size of the police department and the two background socioeconomic status variables, its independent effect on the evaluation variables is negligible for five of the dependent variables. The percentage of officers having some college is related only to variable X_{14}—the percentage of citizens rating police-community relations as outstanding (beta = $-.19$)—and then in a negative direction. The level of college training of police officers serving a neighborhood does not appear to have any general effect on citizens' evaluations of police performance.

Question Six: What are the Independent Effects of the Level of Citizen Experience in a Neighborhood Combined with Levels of Training, Size of Police Department, and Socioeconomic Variables upon Citizen Evaluations?
A series of multiple regression equations is presented in tables 10.4, 10.5, and 10.6; each experience variable is introduced separately into an equation with median levels of training, the socioeconomic variables, and size of police department and is then regressed against each of the citizen evaluation variables. Several experience variables have an independent effect on citizen evaluations. The percentage of citizens victimized in a neighborhood has a positive effect on citizen response that crime is increasing in their neighborhood, a negative effect on citizen evaluation of the job being done by police, and a negative effect on citizen evaluation of police-community relationships. The percentage of citizens who know at least one policeman has a consistently positive effect on all evaluation variables except whether citizens strongly agree that police treat all equally. The percentage of citizens assisted and the percentage of citizens stopped in a neighborhood do not have independent effect on more than one or two evaluation variables.

Even with the introduction of several additional variables, the size of the police department serving a neighborhood continues to have a consistently negative effect on the evaluations made by citizens of the police serving their neighborhood. The relative wealth of a neighborhood—measured by the median value of owner-occupied housing—also seems to have a consistently positive effect on citizen evaluations. One can surmise that citizens living in relatively wealthier neighborhoods consistently receive better service from police regardless of the size of the department involved.

Question Seven: Is There a More Complex Model of the Relationship between Size of Police Department and Citizen Evaluation of Police Performance That is More Empirically Warrantable than the Simplified Consolidation Model or Its Alternate?
Implicit in the set of questions pursued in this section is an assumption that the evaluation of police performance is explained best by a more complex

Size and Performance in a Federal System   249

TABLE 10.4. Independent Effects of Victimization and Assistance Rates When Combined with Training, Size of Department, and Socioeconomic Status Variables on Evaluation Variables

		X_6 % Victimized	X_4 Median Weeks Training	X_2 Median Value Owner-Occupied Housing	X_3 % Black Residents	X_1 Size of Police Department	R^2
X_{11}	% crime increasing	.47	-.19	—	—	.39	.47
X_{12}	% police respond rapidly	.14	—	—	—	-.71	.43
X_{13}	% police job outstanding	—	-.17	.46	—	-.33	.45
X_{14}	% PCR outstanding	—	-.33	.51	—	—	.35
X_{15}	% police honest	—	—	.43	—	-.30	.33
X_{16}	% police treat all equally	.28	—	.26	—	—	.23

		X_7 % Assisted	X_4 Median Weeks Training	X_2 Median Value Owner-Occupied Housing	X_3 % Black Residents	X_1 Size of Police Department	R^2
X_{11}	% crime increasing	—	-.14	-.18	.29	.49	.44
X_{12}	% police respond rapidly	.29	-.17	—	—	-.47	.50
X_{13}	% police job outstanding	—	-.17	.46	—	-.33	.45
X_{14}	% PCR outstanding	—	-.33	.51	—	—	.35
X_{15}	% police honest	—	—	.43	—	-.30	.33
X_{16}	% police treat all equally	—	-.20	.43	—	—	.22

model of relationships than by the simplified models presented earlier. This complex model would include the size of a police department and the socioeconomic status of a neighborhood as *exogenous* variables. *Endogenous* variables that would operate as intervening variables might include such factors as the production strategies utilized by a department, the resources available to a department to allocate for police services, the college education and formal police training levels of police personnel, and the types of experiences or perceptions citizens had concerning their police. While the St. Louis study provides a very extensive database for the empirical examination of a

TABLE 10.5. Independent Effects of Percentage of Those Stopped in Neighborhood when Combined with Training, Size of Department, and Socioeconomic Status Variables on Evaluation Variables

		X_8 % Stopped	X_4 Median Weeks Training	X_2 Median Value Owner-Occupied Housing	X_3 % Black Residents	X_1 Size of Police Department	R^2
X_{11}	% crime increasing	—	-.14	-.18	.29	.49	.44
X_{12}	% police respond rapidly	.19	—	—	—	-.67	.45
X_{13}	% police job outstanding	—	-.17	.46	—	-.33	.45
X_{14}	% PCR outstanding	—	-.33	.51	—	—	.35
X_{15}	% police honest	—	—	.43	—	-.30	.33
X_{16}	% police treat all equally	-.33	-.22	.39	—	—	.33

complex model, the number of cases involved does not enable one to explore simultaneously the additive effect of all the above variables. . . .

Question Eight: Are Police Departments with 10 or Fewer Full-Time Officers Less Effective than Larger Departments?
While the consistent relationship between police department size and diverse measures of police performance has been negative, it may be the case that a curvilinear relationship exists. If this were the case, very small departments would have lower performance than somewhat larger departments, even though the dominant direction of the relationship would be negative. The presence of a curvilinear relationship would not be exposed with the linear regression techniques utilized in the previous analysis.[11] Some evidence of a curvilinear relationship was found in an earlier study (see E. Ostrom and Parks 1973).

A more detailed analysis of the performance of police departments having 10 or fewer full-time officers is important because of the frequent judgment by study commissions that the *very small agencies are the most ineffective departments*. The National Advisory Commission on Criminal Justice Standards and Goals in its "Standard on Combined Police Services," for example, recommends: "At a minimum, police agencies that employ fewer than 10 sworn employees should consolidate for improved efficiency and effectiveness" (National Advisory Commission 1973, 108). As evidence to support its recommendation for the "recombination and consolidation of police departments with less than 10 full-time sworn officers" (110), it cited an earlier report of the Advisory Commission on Intergovernmental Relations (1970), which contended

TABLE 10.6. Independent Effects of Percentage of Those Who Know Someone Mistreated and Who Know One or More Policemen when Combined with Training, Size of Department, and Socioeconomic Status Variables on Evaluation Variables

		X_9 % Know Someone Mistreated	X_4 Median Weeks Training	X_2 Median Value Owner-Occupied Housing	X_3 % Black Residents	X_1 Size of Police Department	R^2
X_{11}	% crime increasing	—	-.14	-.18	.29	.49	.44
X_{12}	% police respond rapidly	—	-.14	—	—	-.58	.43
X_{13}	% police job outstanding	—	-.17	.46	—	-.33	.45
X_{14}	% PCR outstanding	-.20	-.31	.40	—	—	.38
X_{15}	% police honest	-.20	—	.33	—	-.29	.35
X_{16}	% police treat all equally	-.41	.17	.21	—	—	.34

		X_{10} % Know One or More Policemen	X_4 Median Weeks Training	X_2 Median Value Owner-Occupied Housing	X_3 % Black Residents	X_1 Size of Police Department	R^2
X_{11}	% crime increasing	.23	—	—	.30	.47	.44
X_{12}	% police respond rapidly	.46	—	.26	—	-.58	.58
X_{13}	% police job outstanding	.25	—	.56	—	-.38	.47
X_{14}	% PCR outstanding	.26	-.27	.63	—	—	.40
X_{15}	% police honest	.39	—	.63	—	-.25	.45
X_{16}	% police treat all equally	—	-.20	.43	—	—	.22

Small local police departments, particularly those of 10 or less men, are unable to provide a wide range of patrol and investigative services to local citizens. Moreover, the existence of these small agencies may work a hardship on nearby jurisdictions. (110)

The national commission was sensitive to the problem of creating police departments that are too large but did not specify what size was considered to be in that range. The report stated: "Most police and government adminis-trators recognize the dangers inherent in extremely large police agencies and agree that the very small agencies present *much greater problems* to the ef-fective and efficient delivery of police services" (ibid., my emphasis). Thus, the commission and others argue that the very small agencies have the poor-est performance of all police departments, regardless of size.

The data from the St. Louis study provide at least a preliminary an-swer to the question of whether the very small departments are less effec-tive than all other departments regardless of size and, if so, the degree of seriousness.

Among 44 neighborhoods for which we have performance measures, nine were served by departments that had 10 or fewer full-time officers. On the other extreme, 11 neighborhoods were served by either the county, with 436 officers, or the city, with 2,200 officers. Twenty-four of the sample neighborhoods were served by municipal departments with 11 to 76 full-time officers. Given the small number of cases, each performance variable was dichotomized at or near the mean to produce an even distribution of high and low values. For example, the mean percentage ranking the job being done by a police department as outstanding was 25 percent. Dichotomizing this variable results in 21 neighborhoods that ranked police high and 23 neighborhoods that ranked police low. The dichotomized experience and evaluation variables were then run against a recoded size variable that placed all departments with 10 or fewer men into a "very small" class, departments with 11 to 76 full-time offi-cers into a "medium" class, and the county and city into a "large" class.

Table 10.7 presents the proportion of each size class that ranked either above or below the mean on each experience and evaluation variable. The choice of above or below the mean was made so that along the entire table, a higher ranking would indicate that departments of that size had a "better" performance on each relevant variable. Thus, for victimization, departments having a low rating would place high since *less than the mean victimization rates* would actually indicate *better performance.* On the other hand, for the evaluation variable—citizens rating the job of police as outstanding—the *above the mean ranking* was used since departments receiving the mean or above on that variable would have the better performance.

For the experience variables, the very small departments compare rather favorably with the other size classes. For victimization, seven of the nine de-partments in this class had lower than mean victimization rates, while only 40 to 45 percent of the other size ranges had low victimization rates. For assis-tance, the middle-size range appears more effective than either the very small or large departments. The middle-sized departments also appear to stop a larger proportion of their citizens than do either the very small or the large departments. A curvilinear relationship is thus evident for both assistance and stop rates. As for citizens knowing someone mistreated, the large departments appear to be performing better than either of the two smaller groups. It should be pointed out that four of the six neighborhoods above the mean on this variable are served by the county department. In regard to citizens knowing police officers, a larger proportion of citizens in both the very small and medium-sized departments know police than in the large departments. Thus, for the experience variables, there is some evidence of a curvilinear relationship for two of the five variables. For four of the five variables, the proportion of small departments performing above the mean is greater than or approximately equal to that of the large departments.

TABLE 10.7.   Percentage of Neighborhoods Served by Small, Medium, or Large Police Departments with Higher than Mean Performance Levels

	Neighborhoods Served by 10 Full-Time Officers or Less	Neighborhoods Served by 11 to 76 Full-Time Officers	Neighborhoods Served by 436 or 2,200 Full-Time Officers
Experiences			
X_6 % victimized (below mean)	78	42	45
X_7 % assisted (above mean)	33	67	36
X_8 % stopped (above mean)	33	54	36
X_9 % know someone mistreated (below mean)	44	46	63
X_{10} % know one or more police (above mean)	56	50	27
Evaluations			
X_{11} % indicate crime increasing (below mean)	78	58	27
X_{12} % indicate police respond very rapidly (above mean)	33	79	9
X_{13} % rate police job outstanding (above mean)	44	67	9
X_{14} % rate PCR outstanding (above mean)	67	50	9
X_{15} % strongly agree police honest (above mean)	56	58	9
X_{16} % strongly agree police treat all equally (above mean)	78	46	45
	N = 9	N = 24	N = 11

For the evaluation variables, some evidence exists for a curvilinear relationship concerning two variables—X_{12} and X_{13}. For the other four variables, either the very small departments are most effective, or else the two smaller size classes are about equally effective. In no case does a higher proportion of large departments perform above the mean than do small departments.

Thus, evidence does not support the National Advisory Commission's contention that "the very small agencies present much greater problems to the effective and efficient delivery of police services" than all other sized departments. With victimization rates lower than average in 78 percent of the surveyed neighborhoods served by a department of 10 or fewer full-time officers, these departments do not appear to be creating "spillover" problems for other surrounding departments.

In addition, the per capita costs of small departments are indeed very low. They range from $7.20 to $20.56 per capita. The per capita costs of providing police services to the neighborhood served in the medium-sized departments range from $12.78 to $36.87; and in the large departments, from $19.29 to $52.77. Consequently, given the relative performance levels, it would be difficult to argue that small departments are less efficient. While an efficiency ratio cannot be computed because of the nature of our performance measures, departments spending less per capita and performing as well as or better than departments spending more per capita can definitely be evaluated as more efficient. One cannot determine how much more efficient.

The evidence presented here should not be interpreted to support contentions that all efforts to consolidate police departments are likely to lead to less effective or efficient performance. That some of the relationships appear to be curvilinear suggests that departments in the 10 to 76 range may have higher levels of performance on some variables than either the small or large departments. Consolidation of small departments into a medium-sized department may indeed increase effectiveness. However, the a priori judgment that very small departments are necessarily ineffective and should be eliminated is *not* supported by this evidence. In fact, the evidence finds the severe problems of law enforcement in the large departments. If future study commissions wish to focus on the most ineffective segment of the police industry, they should shift their focus to the large.

What Have We Learned?

We find in the described studies a consistent pattern of evidence that contradicts the assumptions made by proponents of consolidation; we cannot support their belief that consolidation affords "the" solution to "the" urban problem. In both simple bivariate analysis and multivariate analysis, the size of a police department serving a neighborhood has either a negative relationship or no relationship to a diverse set of performance measures. The studies have been undertaken in five metropolitan areas and have included a nationwide study of 109 cities. For consolidation of police departments to result automatically in improved performance, the evidence should indicate the opposite pattern of relationships.

How Should This Evidence Be Interpreted?

The lack of findings concerning a positive effect of size of police departments upon the performance of neighborhood level police services should *not* be interpreted as evidence that all proposed police consolidations should be rejected. But the evidence leads us to be skeptical of automatic acceptance of an assumption that larger scale always leads to improved performance. The data from these studies do not provide evidence one way or another concerning some types of police services, including traffic patrol on major metropolitan thoroughfares or the provision of crime laboratory services. We have stated in earlier reports that the "most appropriately sized unit for providing one type of service may not be the most appropriate for other types of services" (E. Ostrom and Parks 1973, 397).

However, proponents of consolidation rarely make this distinction. While pointing to the possibility of economies of scale in such services as the provision of crime laboratories, they frequently go on to assume that such economies occur across the entire range of services. Or they assume that to gain the potential economies for one service, all services need to be consolidated. Despite making passing reference to contracts between smaller departments and specialized agencies for some services, the main focus has been on consolidation across all or most services for full counties or metropolitan areas. As an example, the range of proposed options that "every local government and every local police agency should study," according to the National Advisory Commission includes

a. Total consolidation of local government services: the merging of two city governments or city-county governments;
b. Total consolidation of police services; the merging of two or more police agencies or of all police agencies (i.e., regional consolidation) in a given geographic area;
c. Partial consolidation of police services: the merging of specific functional units of two or more agencies;
d. Regionalization of specific police services: the combination of personnel and material resources to provide specific police services on a geographic rather than jurisdictional basis;
e. Metropolitanization: the provision of public services (including police) through a single government to the communities within a metropolitan area;
f. Contracting for total police services: the provision of all police services by contract with another government (city with city, city with county, county with city, or city or county with state);
g. Contracting for specific police services: the provision of limited or

special police services by contract with another police or criminal
justice agency; and

h. Services sharing: the sharing of support services by two or more
agencies (National Advisory Commission 1973, 109).

Half of these options—including the first two mentioned—relate to full
merger of all police services. *All* of the options suggest that "every local government and every local police agency" may find improved effectiveness or
efficiency either by increasing the scale of all police services or some specific services. None mentions the possibility that larger units might improve
their effectiveness by decreasing their scale of operation for at least some
services.

The evidence we have presented should support the contention that with
regard to regular patrol, immediate response to reported crimes, criminal investigation, the provision of emergency services, and other neighborhood-
level police services, very small- to medium-sized police departments consistently perform more effectively and frequently at less cost than do large
police departments. In light of these findings, the consistent negative reaction of voters to proposals for total consolidation of all service agencies into
larger units may not be as irrational as supporters of consolidation think.
When very small departments combine to provide neighborhood level police
services in a small- to medium-sized department, the effectiveness of their
performance with regard to neighborhood level services may increase for
some performance indicators. Sufficient evidence to determine at what size
performance may again decrease, however, does not exist. The performance
of even the smallest police departments does not approach the crisis proportions so frequently asserted. The consistently poor performance levels occur
instead in neighborhoods served by the large departments.

Findings from this series of studies on the comparative performance of
differently sized police agencies call into question the assumed positive relationship between size of urban agencies and level or quality of service. Will
this be true of other services? From a public choice perspective one would
predict similar findings for all urban public goods or services that involve
face-to-face delivery. A review of empirical studies in the field of education
has revealed a similar consistent lack of evidence supporting economies of
large scale (see Kirp and Cohen 1972). The findings of the California Task
Force on Local Government Reform also challenge the traditional wisdom by
finding little evidence for economies of large scale across a wide range of
services (Task Force on Local Government Reform 1974). One can only
hope that prior to major reform in restructuring local government in our federal system, that further emphasis will be placed on the empirical warrantability of the assumptions that we use to guide reform (see V. Ostrom 1989;

Bish and V. Ostrom 1973). The theory of federalism that presumes overlapping jurisdiction and fragmentation of authority may be a more useful tool for policy analysis in the U.S. political system than the theory that presumes unitary centers of authority.

NOTES

1. Several recent studies have discussed the problems of measuring police output or police effectiveness and have concluded that most of the currently used measures—that is, reported crime rates or arrest rates—are inadequate. See National Advisory Commission 1973; Advisory Group on Productivity in Law Enforcement, National Commission on Productivity 1973; American Bar Association 1972. These same reports see victimization surveys as a more accurate method of obtaining information about incidence of crime than reported crime rates. Further, there is a more general acceptance of other indicators derived from citizen surveys than was present a few years back. The National Advisory Commission (1973, 153) reports:

> Perhaps the most controversial group of new indicators of police effectiveness are those that are products of citizen feelings toward the police. The extent to which the police are successful in alleviating citizens' fear of crime reflects police productivity. Consequently, the percentage of the population having feelings of insecurity about police protection should be measured, perhaps as part of a victimization survey.
>
> Conversely, public acceptance of the police could enable the agency to be more effective in deterring crime and apprehending criminals. Citizen satisfaction with police services thus should be evaluated. As such surveys are undertaken, it would be desirable to measure attitudes among various population groups, based on age, income, race, sex and other variables. It should also be understood that such citizen perceptions are often swayed by conditions totally unrelated to police behavior, performance or effectiveness.

For an extended discussion of these problems, see E. Ostrom 1971, 1973.

2. In an earlier work, we outlined some of the reasons for expecting a negative relationship between size and citizen experiences and evaluations (E. Ostrom et al. 1973). Specifically, the following propositions were stated.

1. Police officers and police administrators working in small-scale police agencies will have better information about the areas they serve and conditions in the field than will their counterparts in larger agencies.
2. Citizens living in smaller jurisdictions will have more capacity to articulate demands for service and will have better knowledge about their police than will citizens living in larger jurisdictions.
3. An increase in the capacity of citizens to articulate demands for service and

an increase in their knowledge about police will be associated with an increase in the knowledge that police officers and police administrators have of citizen preferences.

4. An increase in the citizens' knowledge about police will be associated with an increase in their support of police.

5. An increase in citizens' support of police will be associated with an increase in the levels of police output.

6. An increase in the knowledge of police officers about the area they are serving and about citizen preferences will be associated with an increase in the levels of police output.

7. An increase in the knowledge of police administrators of field conditions in their area will be associated with an increase in their effective control over actions of their departments.

8. An increase in the effective control of police administrators over actions of their department will be associated with an increase in the levels of police output.

9. An increase in the level of police output will be associated with an increase in citizen support for the police (ibid.: 11–13).

In regard to costs, one would expect at least a minimal level of investment would need to be made in each department for supervisory and supportive services. Very small police departments will have, therefore, a major portion of their budget devoted to such investment. Increases in size away from very small departments reduce the portion of the budget devoted to these investments and should therefore reduce the average cost of production. However, a continuous increase in the size of department begins to add more and more levels of hierarchy to the department as well as more specialization. These additional levels of hierarchy may add to the costs of providing police services in two ways. First, the costs may be increased substantially by just the investment in the supportive services. Second, costs may rise because those in command begin to lose control over performance at the street level. Thus, costs may have some aspects of a curvilinear relationship with size. Movement from very small departments to medium-sized departments may lower average costs while movement to larger departments may again increase average costs.

3. The hypotheses from the alternative perspective have been stated in E. Ostrom et al. 1973 and in E. Ostrom and Whitaker 1973.

4. An additional rival hypothesis could also be posed. It would state that citizen evaluations of police performance are more affected by expectations of performance than by any concrete evidence of performance. Since citizens living in smaller communities might have higher levels of community pride and thus higher expectations, their evaluations might be based more on this "sense of community" than on police behavior. This rival hypothesis cannot be "controlled" by the sample design. However, we have examined reported experience data as well as reported evaluation data. Citizens have consistently evaluated performance in a manner consistent with reported experiences. For example, there is a strong positive relationship between citizens' reported response rate to actual calls for service in a neighborhood with citi-

zens' evaluations of police response rates in a neighborhood. Thus, it would appear that citizens' evaluations are related to experiences occurring in the neighborhood. For a discussion of rival hypotheses, see Campbell 1969; Campbell and Stanley 1966.

5. Roger B. Parks and Dennis C. Smith shared in both the design and execution of this study. We appreciate the participation of many graduate and undergraduate students at Indiana University in making this study possible. We also appreciate the excellent co-operation we were given by the police chiefs, police officers, and citizens in the St. Louis area, as well as the helpful assistance of Norton Long, Eugene Meehan, and the Center of Community and Metropolitan Studies at the University of Missouri–St. Louis campus.

6. For a fuller discussion of the research design, see E. Ostrom, Parks, and Smith 1973; also see Smith and E. Ostrom 1974. For a related analysis, see Parks 1976.

7. [Footnote deleted.]

8. The method utilized for allocating costs of police service provided to a neighborhood by a large department is described in E. Ostrom, Parks, and Whitaker 1973.

9. A stepwise multiple regression program was utilized. The R^2 value represents the variance explained by the total equation.

10. We also found the mean level of college education of officers in a department was weakly and negatively related to success in obtaining warrants, while mean total weeks of training showed an inconsistent pattern in regard to the ratio of warrants applied for (Smith and E. Ostrom 1974).

11. When the variable—number of full-time officers—is squared and entered into multiple regression equations, the size of the coefficient rises slightly, giving some evidence of a curvilinear relationship. The untransformed variable was utilized throughout this essay since it is much more meaningful to those interested in affecting changes in institutional arrangements.

REFERENCES

Aberbach, J. D., and Jack Walker. 1970. "The Attitudes of Blacks and Whites Toward City Services: Implications for Public Policy." In *Financing the Metropolis. Public Policy in Urban Economics,* ed. John P. Crecine. Beverly Hills: Sage.

Advisory Group on Productivity in Law Enforcement, National Commission on Productivity. 1973. *Opportunities for Improving Productivity in Police Services.* Washington, DC: National Commission on Productivity.

Altshuler, Alan A. 1970. *Community Control: The Black Demand for Participation in Large American Cities.* Indianapolis: Bobbs-Merrill.

American Bar Association. 1972. *The Urban Police Function.* Washington, DC: The American Bar Association.

Bahl, R. W. 1969. *Metropolitan City Expenditures. A Comparative Analysis.* Lexington: University of Kentucky Press.

Brazer, Harvey. 1959. *City Expenditures in the United States.* New York: National Bureau of Economic Research.

Bish, Robert L., and Vincent Ostrom. 1973. *Understanding Urban Government.*

Metropolitan Reform Reconsidered. Washington, DC: American Enterprise Institute for Public Policy Research.

Boyle, Richard P. 1966. "Causal Theory and Statistical Measures of Effect: A Convergence." *American Sociological Review* 31 (December): 843–51.

Campbell, Donald T. 1969. "Reforms as Experiments." *American Psychologist* 24 (April): 409–94.

Campbell, Donald T., and Julian C. Stanley. 1966. *Experimental and Quasi-Experimental Designs for Research.* Chicago: Rand McNally.

Committee for Economic Development. 1972. *Reducing Crime and Assuring Justice.* New York: Committee for Economic Development.

Dahl, Robert A. 1967. "The City and the Future of Democracy." *American Political Science Review* 61 (December): 957.

———. 1973. *Size and Democracy.* Stanford: Stanford University Press.

Duncan, Otis Dudley. 1966. "Path Analysis: Sociological Examples." *American Journal of Sociology* 72 (July): 1–16.

Dye, Thomas R., and Neuman F. Pollack. 1973. "Path Analytic Models in Policy Research." *Policy Studies Journal* 2 (winter): 123–30.

Erie, Steven P., John J. Kirlin, and Francine F. Rabinovitz. 1972. "Can Something Be Done? Propositions on the Performance of Metropolitan Institutions." In *Reform of Metropolitan Governments,* ed. Lowden Wingo. Washington, DC: Resources for the Future.

Gabler, L. R. 1969. "Economies and Diseconomies of Scale in Urban Public Sectors." *Land Economics* 45 (November): 425–34.

———. 1971. "Population Size as a Determinant of City Expenditures and Employment—Some Further Evidence." *Land Economics* 47 (May): 130–38.

Garmire, Bernard L. 1972. "The Police Role in an Urban Society." In *The Police and the Community,* ed. Robert Steadman. Baltimore: John Hopkins University Press.

Hirsch, Werner Z. 1959. "Expenditure Implications of Metropolitan Growth and Consolidation." *Review of Economics and Statistics* 41 (August): 232–41.

———. 1968. "The Supply of Urban Public Services." In *Issues in Urban Economics,* ed. Harvey S. Perloff and Lowden Wingo. Baltimore: Johns Hopkins University Press.

IsHak, Samir T. 1972. "Consumers' Perception of Police Performance: Consolidation vs. Deconcentration: The Case of Grand Rapids, Michigan, Metropolitan Area." Ph.D. diss., Indiana University.

Kirp, David L., and David K. Cohen. 1972. "Education and Metropolitanism." In *Metropolitanization and Public Services,* ed. Lowden Wingo, 29–42. Washington, DC: Resources for the Future.

Kotler, Milton. 1969. *Neighborhood Government: The Local Foundations of Political Life.* Indianapolis: Bobbs-Merrill.

National Advisory Commission on Criminal Justice Standards and Goals (National Advisory Commission). 1973. *Report on Police.* Washington, DC: U.S. Government Printing Office.

National Conference of State Criminal Justice Planning Administrators. 1974. *State of the States on Crime and Justice.* Washington, DC: National Conference of State Criminal Justice Planning Administrators.

Ostrom, Elinor. 1971. "Institutional Arrangements and the Measurement of Policy Consequences in Urban Areas." *Urban Affairs Quarterly* 6: 447–75.

———. 1972. "Metropolitan Reform: Propositions Derived from Two Traditions. *Social Science Quarterly* 53 (December): 474–93. (Chapter 6 in this volume.)

———. 1973. "On the Meaning and Measurement of Output and Efficiency in the Provision of Urban Police Services." *Journal of Criminal Justice* 1 (June): 93–111.

Ostrom, Elinor, William Baugh, Richard Guarasci, Roger B. Parks, and Gordon P. Whitaker. 1973. *Community Organization and the Provision of Police Services.* Beverly Hills: Sage.

Ostrom, Elinor, and Roger B. Parks. 1973. "Suburban Police Departments: Too Many and Too Small?" In *The Urbanization of the Suburbs,* ed. Louis H. Masotti and Jeffrey K. Hadden, 367–402. *Urban Affairs Annual Reviews,* Vol. 7. Beverly Hills: Sage.

Ostrom, Elinor, Roger B. Parks, and Dennis C. Smith. 1973. "A Multi-Strata, Similar Systems Design for Measuring Police Performance." Paper presented at the annual meeting of the Midwest Political Science Association, Chicago, Illinois, May 2–5.

Ostrom, Elinor, Roger B. Parks, and Gordon P. Whitaker. 1973. "Do We Really Want to Consolidate Urban Police Forces? A Reappraisal of Some Old Assertions." *Public Administration Review* 33 (September/October): 423–33.

Ostrom, Elinor, and Gordon P. Whitaker. 1973. "Does Local Community Control of Police Make a Difference? Some Preliminary Findings." *American Journal of Political Science* 17 (February): 48–76. (Chapter 8 in this volume.)

———. 1974. "Community Control and Governmental Responsiveness: The Case of Police in Black Neighborhoods." In *Improving the Quality of Urban Management,* ed. David Rogers and Willis Hawley, 303–34. Beverly Hills: Sage. (Chapter 9 in this volume.)

Ostrom, Vincent. 1989. *The Intellectual Crisis in American Public Administration.* 2nd ed. Tuscaloosa: University of Alabama Press.

Ostrom, Vincent, Charles M. Tiebout, and Robert Warren. 1961. "The Organization of Government in Metropolitan Areas: A Theoretical Inquiry." *American Political Science Review* 55 (December): 831–42. (Chapter 1 in this volume.)

Parks, Roger B. 1976. "Complementary Measures of Police Performance." In *Public Policy Evaluation,* ed. Kenneth M. Dolbeare, 185–218. Sage Yearbook in Politics and Public Policy, vol. 2. Beverly Hills: Sage.

Przeworski, A., and Henry Teune. 1970. *The Logic of Comparative Social Inquiry.* New York: John Wiley.

Rogers, Bruce D., and C. McCurdy Lipsey. 1974. "Metropolitan Reform: Citizen Evaluations of Performance in Nashville–Davidson County, Tennessee." *Publius* 4 (fall): 19–34.

Skoler, Daniel L., and June M. Hetler. 1970. "Government Restructuring and Criminal Administration: The Challenge of Consolidation." In *Crisis in Urban Government. A Symposium: Resturucturing Metropolitan Area Government.* Silver Spring, MD: Thomas Jefferson.

Smith, Dennis C., and Elinor Ostrom. 1974. "The Effects of Training and Education on Police Attitudes and Performance: A Preliminary Analysis." In *The Potential for Reform of Criminal Justice,* ed. Herbert Jacob, 45–81. Sage Criminal Justice System Annual, vol. 3. Beverly Hills: Sage.

Swanson, Bert E. 1970. *The Concern for Community in Urban America.* New York: Odyssey Press.

Task Force on Local Government Reform. 1974. *Public Benefits from Public Choice.* Sacramento: State of California, Office of Planning and Research, California Council on Intergovernmental Relations.

Task Force on Police. 1967. *Task Force Report: The Police.* Washington, DC: U.S. Government Printing Office.

U.S. Department of Health, Education, and Welfare. 1969. *Toward a Social Report.* Washington, DC: U.S. Government Printing Office.

VanMeter, Donald S., and Herbert B. Asher. 1973. "Causal Analysis: Its Promise for Policy Studies." *Policy Studies Journal* 2 (winter): 103–09.

Part IV
Implications for Metropolitan Governance

CHAPTER 11

Defining and Measuring Structural Variations in Interorganizational Arrangements

Elinor Ostrom, Roger B. Parks, and Gordon P. Whitaker

Fragmentation of police services is extreme: there are 32,000 separate police departments. . . .Wasted energies and lost motion due to overlapping, duplication, and noncooperation are not the worst consequences of this fragmentation. Large areas of the United States—particularly rural communities and the small jurisdictions in or near metropolitan areas—lack anything resembling modern, professional police protection. (Committee for Economic Development 1972, 30–31)

Fragmentation, multiplicity, and *duplication* are terms that are frequently used in a pejorative sense to describe the relationships among local governmental units in metropolitan areas. Fragmentation, multiplicity, and duplication are repeatedly cited as causes for many of the ills facing police forces in such areas (President's Commission on Law Enforcement and Administration of Justice 1967; McCausland 1972; Skoler and Hetler 1970). The presumptive knowledge accepted by many is that the presence of a large number of small police agencies within a metropolitan area results in inefficient performance and harmful consequences. Many recommendations have been made to decrease the number of police departments operating in a metropolitan area and to eliminate all small departments, where "small" can range from "less than 10" to "less than 50" sworn officers.[1]

However, for all the use of the terms *fragmentation, multiplicity,* and *duplication,* they have rarely been defined with care. How many units need there be for "multiplicity" to exist? If multiplicity results in inefficiency (as is often charged), does this mean that all federal systems must, by definition, be inefficient? What does it mean to say that units of government duplicate each other?

Originally published in *Publius: The Journal of Federalism* 4, no. 4 (fall 1974): 87–108. Reprinted by permission of *Publius* and the authors.

Authors' note: The research discussed herein is funded by the Research Applied to National Needs Division of the National Science Foundation under Grant No. GI-43949. The authors would like to thank Francie Bish, Vernon Greene, John Hamilton, John McIver, Nancy Neubert, Vincent Ostrom, and Martha Vandivort for their helpful comments on earlier drafts of this essay.

Is such duplication harmful? If careful empirical research is to be conducted at a metropolitan level of analysis, utilizing the operating units of government providing services within metropolitan areas as the analytic units, then many of these terms will need to be defined and operationalized carefully.

Research at the metropolitan level that employs such defined and operationalized terms can also be important from a public policy perspective. Many reform proposals are initiated on the basis of an assumed positive relationship between the fragmentation of governmental units in a metropolitan area and increased costs or lowered output. However, little empirical research has been conducted that has specifically examined propositions associated with these reform proposals. In research efforts that have examined propositions derived from the traditional metropolitan reform literature, much of the evidence produced has not supported propositions that are presumed to be true (see E. Ostrom and Parks 1973).

In undertaking an NSF (RANN) sponsored study, "Evaluating the Organization of Service Delivery: Police," we are attempting to examine the relevant effects of the structure of interorganizational arrangements among police agencies serving a common metropolitan area. In designing this research, we have found it necessary to define such terms as *fragmentation, multiplicity,* and *duplication* and to develop empirical operationalizations for them.

In this essay we shall first describe our general approach to the problem of conceptualizing interorganizational arrangements among police agencies in a metropolitan area. This approach is based on the concept of a public service industry.[2] Second, we shall describe the use of service structure matrices to delineate the service by service configurations of a police industry. Third, we shall illustrate the use of service structure matrices to describe the interorganizational arrangements among police agencies within a single metropolitan area. Fourth, we shall define six measures of metropolitan structure to be derived from service structure matrices. These measures are Fragmentation, Multiplicity, Duplication, Independence, Coordination, and Dominance. The use of such measures enables comparisons to be made *across* metropolitan areas. The fifth section of this essay will then utilize these measures to compare the structure of the police industries in three metropolitan areas with respect to four types of police services. The last section will focus on the use of structural measures in public policy analysis.

Police Agencies Viewed as Firms in Public Service Industries

Instead of thinking of each police agency in a metropolitan area as a department or bureau within a general governmental structure, we conceptualize the various police agencies as producers in a public service industry serving a metropolitan area. Each agency is considered in terms of what it does rather than in terms of its relationship to a governmental unit. Our initial step is to identify those agencies that render police services. The agencies may be public or private.

One of the problems in developing the conceptual underpinnings for research of this nature is how to limit the subject at hand. There is no intrinsic feature of an agency that in and of itself places it definitely in one public industry rather than another. A police department, for example, may be considered in the health industry if it provides ambulance service, in the fire prevention industry if it inspects buildings, and in the recreation industry if it sponsors a softball league. Like all taxonomies, our limits and boundaries necessarily have elements of arbitrariness. If consistent limits are established, however, structural comparisons across metropolitan areas can be made and the effects of structural variations assessed.

Since we are interested in answering questions about the effects of different ways of organizing police agencies in metropolitan areas, we consider a metropolitan police industry to consist of those agencies—public or private—that provide a specific set of services. These will include direct services to citizen-consumers in the metropolitan area and intermediate police services to agencies providing direct police services. There are a number of activities undertaken by police agencies that could be classified as direct police services. We will restrict our focus, however. We will include any direct service agency within the bounds of our analysis if that agency supplies one or more of the following services: patrol, criminal investigation, or traffic control—and if its officers can exercise the power of arrest in rendering that service.[3] Similarly, there are a great many intermediate services required by police agencies that produce these three types of direct services. We will, however, limit the intermediate police services examined in this study to the following services: basic training, detention, dispatching, and criminal laboratory facilities.[4] The configuration of the police industry thus may differ from service to service. In one SMSA there may be many producers of patrol and only one producer of criminal investigation services. In another metropolitan area the situation could be reversed. This way of conceptualizing the industry allows us to examine these service by service patterns.[5]

The Use of Service Structure Matrices for Representing Interorganizational Arrangements in a Metropolitan Area

Having bounded the scope of what will be called a police industry within a metropolitan area by defining direct and intermediate police services, we can then delineate the service by service configuration of a police industry by developing service structure matrices for each metropolitan area.[6] All police agencies that produce a given service in a metropolitan area will be arranged as rows in the structural matrix for that service. For the direct services, columns in the matrix will be the organized consumption units within the metropolitan area. For the intermediate services, the matrix columns are those producers of direct services that are now *consumers* of the intermediate service in question. These will include agencies that receive intermediate services from internal units (e.g., a municipal police department with its own dispatcher) as well as agencies receiving the intermediate service from another agency (e.g., a municipal department that relies upon the county sheriff for detention service).

Some police services are provided regularly to consumers. By *regular provision* we mean that the producer makes the service available to individuals within the consumption unit on a routine basis. Other services are provided irregularly. By irregular provision, we mean that the producer makes this service available only in unusual circumstances. A distinction between regular and irregular service provision would arise in cases where the detective squad of a municipal police department investigates all reported crimes in the city, while the state police provide criminal investigation in that same city only upon rare occasions. The former is the regular producer while the latter is the irregular producer. While we will determine the presence of irregular producers, most of our attention will be devoted to regular producers of each service.

Several producers may simultaneously provide the same service on a regular basis to any one consuming unit. There are three types of regular, simultaneous production: alternation, coordination, and duplication. Service flows between producers and consumers will be shown by entries in the service structure matrix. They will be categorized as Irregular, Regular, Coordinated, or Alternative.

Alternation results when each agency serves a restricted clientele or geographic area or provides services only during restricted periods of time. Detention facilities are frequently provided by two agencies alternatively: that is, one agency provides detention for juveniles and another for adults. The attributes of the clientele determine which agency will provide the service. Alternative geographic provision of traffic control occurs where a city police department exclusively patrols all streets within its jurisdiction with the exception of interstate highways where traffic is regulated by the state highway patrol. An alternative provision of service by time exists when a small town police department does all dispatching for itself during the day while relying on the county sheriff for dispatching at night. Alternative producers will be indicated on the service structure matrix by entering A's in the consuming unit column at each alternative producer's row.

Coordinated production occurs when two or more regular producers interact in the planning of the day-to-day operation of service provision for the same consuming unit. Coordinated patrol, for example, exists when several police departments jointly provide organized surveillance within the boundaries of a single consumption unit through the use of a common communications network. Criminal laboratory facilities are used in a coordinated way when their activities are pooled in supporting a single criminal investigation. On the matrix, C's will be entered for each of the producers that coordinate service to a consuming unit.

Duplication occurs when two or more regular producers provide the same service at the same time, in the same places to the same people without joint consideration of the activities. Two producers of patrol services are duplicative when they serve the same consumption unit without consultation on patrol practices and day-to-day maintenance of radio contact. Two producers of adult detention are duplicative when they independently provide jail facilities to the same police department for the same clientele. Duplication will be shown on the matrix by the entry of two or more R's (for regular producer) in a consuming unit column.

Service Structure Matrices for a Metropolitan Area

To illustrate the use of service structure matrices, we will construct police service matrices for the Fayetteville, North Carolina, Standard Metropolitan Statistical Area (SMSA). The Fayetteville SMSA encompasses 654 square miles and had a 1970 population of 212,000. The area has eight organized consumption units for direct police services. Cumberland County is the largest of these. In addition to the city of Fayetteville (population 54,000), there are three small towns within the SMSA (each with fewer than 4,000 inhabitants). The U.S. Army's Fort Bragg and Pope Air Force Base are also organized consumption units. These two installations together have a population equal to that of Fayetteville. They have tended to dominate the entire metropolitan area although industrial expansion has recently been quite extensive in the southern end of Cumberland County. The remaining consumption unit is the Fayetteville State University campus in Fayetteville. For those services that it receives independently, it constitutes an enclave in the city. The resident population on campus is under 1,000. Half of the total SMSA population lives outside the seven smaller consumption units in unincorporated areas of Cumberland County. The map in figure 11.1 shows the geographic arrangement of the organized consumption units.

In this section, we will present the service structure matrices for four police services as they are organized in the Fayetteville SMSA. Table 11.1 depicts the arrangements for patrol. Each of the eight organized consumption units for police service has a distinct legal arrangement with a regular producer of patrol services. The entries in the main diagonal reflect these rela-

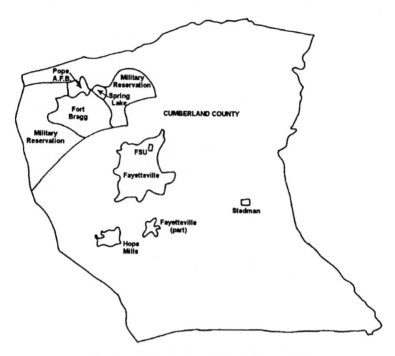

Fig. 11.1. Fayetteville, North Carolina, SMSA

tionships. Military police from Fort Bragg also provide patrol services in areas of Fayetteville frequented by military personnel. Because they have a restricted clientele, they have been classified as alternative producers of patrol services in Fayetteville.

Both Cumberland County and Fayetteville contain organized consumption units that are enclaves. Within Cumberland County are seven organized consuming units served by their own patrol service agencies. The County Sheriff's Department patrols in the remaining areas of the county. The far right-hand column in table 11.1 represents this "remainder." Fayetteville State University is a separately organized consuming enclave for patrol within Fayetteville. For each enclave, special legal arrangements for patrol have been established.

As shown by the double entries in several columns, some areas in Fayetteville have multiple agencies simultaneously providing regular patrol services. Both the sheriff and the Fayetteville Police Department provide regular patrol services to some of the patrol enclaves. Stedman receives regular patrol support from the Sheriff's Department. Fayetteville State University is regularly patrolled by the Fayetteville City Police Department.

TABLE 11.1. Patrol Services Matrix: Fayetteville, North Carolina, SMSA

| | | | Organized Consumption Units/Cumberland County | | | | | |
| | | | Fayetteville | | | | | |
Producers	Fort Bragg	Pope A.F.B.	Fayetteville State University	Remainder of City of Fayetteville	Spring Lake	Hope Mills	Stedman	Remainder of Cumberland County
Fort Bragg provost marshal	R			A				
Pope A.F.B. provost marshal		R						
Fayetteville State University campus police			R					
Fayetteville city police			R	R				
Spring Lake police					R			
Hope Mills police						R		
Stedman police							R	
Cumberland County sheriff					I	I	R	R

Criminal investigation activities in Fayetteville SMSA are organized somewhat differently from patrol as shown in table 11.2. There are only six organized consumption units for criminal investigation because Stedman and Fayetteville State University have no unique legal arrangements with a producer of this service. However, there are nine different producers of criminal investigation serving this SMSA.[7] Only Fayetteville and the Cumberland County "remainder" unit rely regularly on their own investigative services. The military installations each call in specialized criminal investigation units from off base. Spring Lake and Hope Mills regularly coordinate with the Sheriff's Criminal Investigation Unit. The State Bureau of Investigation provides additional services to civilian agencies on request. It is not considered a regular producer of this service.

Turning to intermediate police services provides an opportunity to explore additional facets of the structure of service provision in the police in-

TABLE 11.2.   Criminal Investigation Matrix: Fayetteville, North Carolina, SMSA

Producers	Fort Bragg	Pope A.F.B.	Fayetteville	Spring Lake	Hope Mills	Remainder of Cumberland County
			Organized Consumption Units/Cumberland County			
Fort Bragg provost marshal	C					
U.S. Army criminal investigation	C					
Pope A.F.B. provost marshal		C				
U.S.A.F. criminal investigation		C				
Fayetteville Police Department			R			
Spring Lake Police Department				C		
Hope Mills Police Department					C	
Cumberland County sheriff				C	C	R
N.C. State Bureau of Investigation			I	I	I	I

dustry of the Fayetteville SMSA. Our interest here is in seeing which agencies provide certain intermediate services to those agencies providing direct police services to citizens. The consuming units for intermediate services are police agencies that utilize those services in providing direct police services to citizens. Criminal laboratory services are used to assist criminal investigation. Thus, nine units are listed as consuming these intermediate police services, as nine units are listed in table 11.2 as producing criminal investigation. For adult detention the consuming units are eight police departments which provide patrol services and therefore require adult detention services. As a comparison of tables 11.2 and 11.3 indicates, the number of producers of police services can vary considerably from service to service. For adult detention there are only three producers. The county sheriff provides adult deten-

TABLE 11.3. Adult Detention Matrix: Fayetteville, North Carolina, SMSA

			Organized Consumption Units					
Producers	Fort Bragg	Pope A.F.B.	Fayetteville S.U. Campus	Fayetteville	Spring Lake	Hope Mills	Stedman	Cumberland County Sheriff
Fort Bragg	A		A	A	A	A	A	A
Pope A.F.B.		A	A	A	A	A	A	
Cumberland County sheriff	A	A	A	A	A	A	A	A

tion facilities for all local police units. Each of the two military installations maintains its own detention facility. Military personnel taken into custody by civilian departments are usually remanded to their base for detention. Civilians arrested on one of the military bases would be sent to the county jail for detention. Thus, the three producers can be viewed as providing alternative services restricted by clientele.

There are four producers of crime laboratory services. The Fayetteville Police Department and the Cumberland County sheriff have established a joint crime lab that serves all civilian criminal investigation agencies in the SMSA. The North Carolina State Bureau of Investigation maintains its own crime lab, which is utilized by these same agencies for more sophisticated work. Given the coordination of work between the local and state agencies, the provision of services is coded as coordinated. Each of the military criminal investigation units has its own laboratory facilities, which are used by its investigators.

Direct examination of the matrices themselves provides considerable insight into the difference in the structure of interorganizational arrangements across different services within the same SMSA. However, direct examination of the service structure matrices is not as helpful when one is comparing across metropolitan areas of varying sizes and complexity. One of the advantages of defining measures of metropolitan structure derived from service structure matrices is that such measures allow careful comparison across metropolitan areas.

Measures of Metropolitan Structure

We have defined a series of measures of metropolitan service structure that can be operationalized with the information contained in the service structure matrices. Wherever possible we have attempted to use definitions of terms that are consistent with previous usage, although this has been difficult in

TABLE 11.4. Crime Lab Matrix: Fayetteville, North Carolina, SMSA

	Organized Consumption Units							
Producers	Fort Bragg	Pope A.F.B.	Fayetteville	Spring Lake	Hope Mills	Cumber-land County	N.C. State Bureau of Investiga-tion	U.S. Army Criminal Investiga-tion	U.S.A.F. Criminal Investiga-tion
Fayetteville–Cumberland County Crime Lab			C	C	C	C			
N.C. Bureau of Investiga-tion			C	C	C	C	R		
U.S. Army Criminal Investigation Division	R							R	
U.S.A.F. Criminal Investigation Division		R							R

some cases. At present we have identified six conceptually distinct measures, each of which can be dealt with in either absolute or relative terms. These measures are Fragmentation, Multiplicity, Duplication, Independence, Coordination, and Dominance. Students of metropolitan reform will undoubtedly recognize such terms as ones that are frequently bandied about in the literature but that are rarely defined. It is our intent to provide a series of operational definitions for these terms. We believe they will be useful in our own current research and also provide a consistent basis for discourse about metropolitan organization.

We have operationalized *Fragmentation* as the number of distinct organized consuming units for the service in question. For direct services these units are for the most part governmental jurisdictions, although as noted earlier, we intend to include other organized units wherever appropriate. For the intermediate services, consuming units are themselves producers of direct services. A simple count of the number of such units is then our *absolute* measure of fragmentation. For the direct services a *relative* fragmentation measure is also obtained by dividing the absolute measure by the population of the metropolitan area stated in ten thousands. That is, relative fragmentation for the direct services is the number of organized consumption units per 10,000 metropolitan inhabitants. The absolute and relative measures of fragmentation may vary considerably for the same SMSA. As Thomas M. Scott has pointed out, "The number of local governmental units per capita increases as the total population size of the SMSA decreases"— that is, the largest SMSAs have less relative fragmentation per capita than do the smaller SMSAs (Scott 1973, 215).

Multiplicity is operationalized as the number of service producing units in the metropolitan area. This absolute measure is the same as the lists or counts of police agencies often used by national commissions and others when lamenting the lack of unified law enforcement systems (see President's Commission on Law Enforcement and Administration of Justice 1967; McCausland 1972; and Skoler and Hetler 1970). However, a simple list does not control for the size of the metropolitan area or for the political arrangements in that area. Accordingly, we have defined two relative measures of multiplicity for the direct services and one for the intermediate ones. For both direct and intermediate services, relative multiplicity is measured as the number of producing units for the service divided by the number of consuming units for that service, that is, the average number of producers per consuming unit. For the direct services, relative multiplicity is also defined as the number of producing units for the service per 10,000 residents of the metropolitan area. Our measures of absolute and relative multiplicity are similar to those utilized by Hawkins and Dye in a recent study (Hawkins and Dye 1970, 23). Campbell and Sacks used a measure of multiplicity that was population per government and area per government that they called fragmentation (Campbell and Sacks 1967, 179). Ostrom and Parks used both the absolute and population relative measure of multiplicity (E. Ostrom and Parks 1973). Critics of current police organization have usually argued that multiplicity results in inefficient provision of low quality service. However, the evidence presented in the latter study runs counter to that argument when relative multiplicity is used as the measure. Campbell and Sacks did not find any significant relationship between their measure of population or area per government and expenditure patterns (Campbell and Sacks 1967).

Duplication is operationalized in absolute terms as the number of consuming units in the metropolitan area that regularly receive the service in question from more than one producer. However, those cases in which one producer alternates with another in time, space, or clientele are not counted as service duplication. Similarly, instances where two or more producers co-ordinate in the provision of a service to a consuming unit are not counted as duplication. By our definition, duplication in service provision exists only when two (or more) producing units are regularly providing service to a given consuming unit *and* the producing units do not either alternate or coordinate their activities. While such a definition results in our finding much less service duplication than is commonly claimed, we believe that it sticks more closely to the common meaning of the term. The service duplication seen by most critics is picked up by our other measures. Having defined absolute duplication, we can go on to state relative duplication for direct and intermediate services as the ratio of the number of consuming units receiving duplicate service to the total number of consuming units for that service. Additionally, for the direct services, we define relative duplication as the sum of the population of the consuming units that receive duplicate service divided by the total population of the metropolitan area.

Independence is defined as the number of organized consumption units that receive the service in question regularly and solely from their "own" producing unit, that is, from a producing unit directly under their control (e.g., a municipal police department patrolling all of a municipality). For this measure, irregular service provision by a different producing unit (as e.g., when the State Police cruise through the municipality once or twice a month) is not counted as reducing independence. In general, alternating or coordinated service provision is counted as reducing independence. Relative independence for a metropolitan area on a particular service can then be stated as the ratio of the number of independent consuming units to the total number of such units, and for direct services, as the population in independent units divided by the metropolitan population.

Dominance is defined by the extent to which the consuming units for a particular service are served by the dominant producer of that service. The dominant producer of a direct service is that producer having the largest service population, while for intermediate services, the dominant producer is that producer providing the service to the largest number of consuming units. In both cases, instances of alternate or coordinate service provision are included in the computations. Absolute dominance is measured as the count of consuming units receiving the service from the dominant producer. Relative dominance is then the ratio of this figure to the total number of consuming units. For direct services, relative dominance is also measured by the ratio of the serviced population of the dominant producer to the total population of the metropolitan area.

It should be noted that fragmentation, independence, and dominance taken together tell us additional information about the structure of a metropolitan area. A highly fragmented metropolitan area might show a low degree of independence and a high degree of dominance for a service—say, patrol. This would then indicate that while the metropolitan area is divided into a large number of units providing their own patrol, many of those units also receive patrol service from one major producer, say the county sheriff. High independence together with high dominance (in relative population terms) in a fragmented metropolitan area would indicate that there are many small independent consumption units but that most of the metropolitan population is served by a single producer. But the small independent units are served by their own police force, not the dominant producer.

Our final measure, *Coordination,* is defined as the number of consuming units receiving service from a coordinated arrangement between two or more producers. Such arrangements are often found where, for example, a county sheriff dispatches for both his own patrol car(s) and township police department car(s), both of which patrol a township simultaneously. In such cases the dispatcher coordinates the movement of both producers' vehicles so as to avoid having them play "follow the leader" down Main Street. Arrangements of this nature may tend to result in higher quality service for the same number of units assigned than in the pure duplicative situation. This is a proposition that can be empirically examined. Relative coordination, as with the other measures, can be stated as the ratio of the number of units receiving coordinated service to the total number of consuming units and, for the direct services, as the ratio of the population of units receiving coordinated service to the total population in the area.

Comparing Metropolitan Structures

Now that the measures of metropolitan structure have been defined, we can illustrate their use by comparing the police industries in three metropolitan areas: (1) The Fayetteville SMSA, which was described in some detail in the preceding; (2) The Durham, North Carolina, SMSA; and (3) The Hamilton-Middletown, Ohio, SMSA. All three had a 1970 population of approximately 200,000.

Let us first examine the measures for patrol and criminal investigation services. As shown in table 11.5, these metropolitan areas differ significantly from one another both in absolute fragmentation and in relative fragmentation. The Hamilton SMSA has 20 consuming units for patrol services, while Fayetteville has only eight. Because they have approximately the same populations, an increase from eight to 20 consuming units raises the population relative fragmentation score from .38 to .83. In both the Hamilton and Durham SMSAs there are as many organized consumption units for criminal investigation as for patrol. Therefore, each has the same fragmentation score for both services. The difference in the fragmentation scores in the Fayetteville SMSA reflects the fact that neither Stedman nor Fayetteville State University has unique legal arrangements with a producer of criminal investigation service.

The difference between *fragmentation of consumption units* and *multiplicity of producing units* is also illustrated in the table. Fragmentation refers to consuming units, while multiplicity refers to producing units. The multiplicity score in Fayetteville for criminal investigation is higher than the fragmentation score in the same area for the same service: while there are only six consuming units for criminal investigation in that SMSA, there are nine

units producing for this service (see table 11.2). Where the number of producing units equals the number of consuming units for a particular service,
the multiplicity score relative to consuming units will equal 1.0 as it does in
Hamilton for both patrol and criminal investigation and in Fayetteville for
patrol. Where there are more producing units than consuming units this score
will exceed 1.0. The measure will be lower than 1.0 where there are fewer
producing units than consuming units.

For patrol or criminal investigation, little duplication exists in any of the
three metropolitan areas. Only in the Fayetteville SMSA is there any duplication for either of these services. As shown in table 11.2, two of the columns
of the Fayetteville patrol matrix contain multiple "R" entries indicating regular, nonalternating, noncoordinating producers.

The independence of production units varies considerably in these three
metropolitan areas. While in Durham, all 10 organized consuming units receive patrol regularly and solely from their "own" producing units (a score of

TABLE 11.5. Structural Measures—Direct Services

				SMSA					
	Fayetteville			Durham			Hamilton-Middletown		
		Relative			Relative			Relative	
	Absolute	C.U.	Pop	Absolute	C.U.	Pop	Absolute	C.U.	Pop
Fragmentation									
Patrol	8	—	.38	10	—	.53	20	—	.83
Criminal investigation	6	—	.28	10	—	.53	20	—	.83
Multiplicity									
Patrol	8	1.00	.38	11	1.10	.58	20	1.00	.83
Criminal investigation	9	1.50	.42	11	1.10	.58	20	1.00	.83
Duplication									
Patrol	2	.25	.01	0	—	—	0	—	—
Criminal investigation	0	—	—	0	—	—	0	—	—
Independence									
Patrol	5	.63	.75	10	1.00	1.00	7	.35	.82
Criminal investigation	2	.33	.75	5	.50	.93	6	.30	.80
Dominance									
Patrol	2	.25	.50	1	.10	.48	14	.70	.34
Criminal investigation	3	.50	.53	3	.30	.50	14	.70	.34
Coordination									
Patrol	0	—	—	0	—	—	13	.65	.18
Criminal investigation	4	.67	.25	5	.50	.07	14	.70	.20

1.00 for both relative measures of independence), only five of the eight consuming units (63%) in Fayetteville receive patrol regularly and solely from their own patrol units. However, these four consuming units comprise about 75 percent of the population in the SMSA. While only seven of the 20 consuming units have patrol independence in the Hamilton-Middletown SMSA, these seven constitute about 82 percent of the population.

In regard to dominance, only one of the 10 consuming units in the Durham area receives patrol services from the dominant producer, the Durham City Police. That agency patrols for almost half of the population living in the SMSA. In the Hamilton-Middletown SMSA, 14 of the 20 consuming units receive services from the dominant producer. These consuming units represent only 34 percent of the population, however. The Butler County Sheriff's Department is the dominant patrol agency in the Hamilton-Middletown SMSA, serving 14 organized consuming units. No other producer in the SMSA patrols for a larger population. Thus, the Butler County Sheriff's Department is more dominant than the Durham Police Department in terms of consuming units served, while it is less dominant in terms of total population served.

We have noted that duplication of patrol for the Hamilton-Middletown SMSA is zero and that the dominant producer serves 14 of the 20 consuming units. Is this an inconsistency? We have also noted that only seven of the consuming units in Hamilton have independent patrol service. How are the other 13 to be categorized? As the coordination measure indicates in table 11.5, each of these units is patrolled by multiple agencies that *coordinate* service provision so as to avoid duplication of effort. Neither of our other example SMSAs has coordinated patrol provision. All three SMSAs do have some coordinated criminal investigation, however. In the Fayetteville SMSA, four consuming units receive coordinated criminal investigation. Seventy percent of consuming units in the Hamilton-Middletown SMSA have coordinated criminal investigation, although these are small and include only 20 percent of the area's population. Fifty percent of the consuming units in the Durham SMSA have coordinated criminal investigation, but only 7 percent of the population is included in those units.

Turning to intermediate services in table 11.6, we no longer have two relative measures for each type. Since the consuming units are in this case the producing units of direct services, all relative measures are in terms of the number of consuming units served. For fragmentation, only an absolute measure can be computed for intermediate services. On multiplicity, the number of units producing adult detention and crime laboratory services is much lower than that of patrol and criminal investigation. While there are multiple producers of these services, only in the Hamilton SMSA is there any duplication. Hamilton City Jail and Middletown City Jail are duplicative in

TABLE 11.6. Structural Measures—Intermediate Services

| | SMSA | | | | | |
| | Fayetteville | | Durham | | Hamilton-Middletown | |
	Absolute	Relative	Absolute	Relative	Absolute	Relative
Fragmentation						
Adult detention	8	—	11	—	20	—
Crime lab	9	—	11	—	20	—
Multiplicity						
Adult detention	3	0.38	2	0.18	3	0.15
Crime lab	4	0.44	2	0.18	5	0.25
Duplication						
Adult detention	0	—	0	—	2	0.10
Crime lab	0	—	0	—	0	—
Independence						
Adult detention	0	—	2	0.18	1	0.05
Crime lab	3	0.33	1	0.09	0	—
Dominance						
Adult detention	8	1.00	5	0.45	20	1.00
Crime lab	5	0.56	11	1.00	20	1.00
Coordination						
Adult detention	0	—	0	—	0	—
Crime lab	4	0.44	3	0.27	20	1.00

the sense that the police departments that utilize them also utilize the Butler County Jail.

There is considerably less independence for the intermediate services than for direct services. Few jurisdictions are solely served by their own crime lab or jail facility of adult detention. On the other hand, the dominance measures are much higher for intermediate services than for direct services. In both Fayetteville and Hamilton-Middletown the largest producer of jail services provides for the entire county, while in Durham the largest jail serves about half of the consuming units. The largest crime lab in Durham and Hamilton-Middletown also serves the entire SMSA. There is no coordination in the provision of adult detention in any of the three SMSAs, while coordination of crime lab services ranges from low in Durham to high in Hamilton-Middletown.

Use of these structural measures enables an analyst to be quite specific about the ways in which one metropolitan area is similar to or differs from other metropolitan areas. When many metropolitan areas are simultaneously being considered, the structural measures can be used as variables in statistical analysis to ascertain what other factors are associated with a particular type of structural arrangement among units in a metropolitan area.

The Use of Structural Measures in Public Policy Analysis

Many assertions about the effects of fragmentation and other terms are used to describe the structure of interorganizational arrangements in metropolitan areas [see essays in Part II of this volume].

The defining characteristics of federal systems of government necessarily include fragmentation, multiplicity, and duplication. Coordination, independence, and dominance are additional measures for specifying interorganizational structures. The performance of federal systems as systems of government can be assessed only if we can deal explicitly with different patterns of interorganizational arrangements with such consistent, well-defined, and operational measures.

NOTES

1. See, for example, Garmire 1972 (9).

2. See V. Ostrom and E. Ostrom 1965. See also V. Ostrom 1972; and Bish and V. Ostrom 1973.

3. *Patrol* is defined as organized surveillance of public places within a defined territory and response to reports of suspected criminal acts for the purpose of preventing crime, apprehending offenders, and maintaining public order. *Criminal investigation* is defined as activities undertaken to identify the perpetrators of alleged criminal acts, to gather evidence for criminal proceedings, and to recover stolen goods. *Traffic control* is defined as the monitoring of vehicular traffic, the investigation of traffic accidents, and on-site traffic direction.

4. *Basic training* is defined as the provision of department-required entry level training for a direct police producing unit. (By department-required, we do not mean to exclude state requirements. However, many departments have higher requirements than the state in which they are located.) *Detention* is defined as the holding of an individual up to the time of an arraignment, formal court order, or other dismissal. *Dispatching* is defined as the receipt and processing of calls for police service. *Criminal laboratory facilities* is defined as the maintenance and operation of a technical support facility for the processing of evidence.

5. We will not in this essay attempt to provide a method for measuring the structure of an entire police industry within a metropolitan area.

6. While our use of matrices for representing the structure of interorganizational

arrangements with metropolitan areas is relatively novel, it draws its intellectual base from two traditions. First, this form of representation draws on the work of Wassily M. Leontief in input-output analysis (see Leontief 1951). Input-output analysis arrays producers and consumers of a service as we propose to do but fills in the cells with the amount of goods flowing from one to the other. Our entries will represent presence or absence of certain types of service relationships rather than flows of goods. The second related tradition is the work of sociologists interested in the relationships among individuals in small groups represented by matrices or directed graphs (see, e.g., Harary, Norman, and Cartwright 1965). In a recent article, Paul Craven and Barry Wellman of the University of Toronto discuss the potential use of matrices (or networks) for describing the relationships among communities within a region. "Such matrices can be constructed for any type of relationship between communities. We should then be able to analyze, for example, information exchange among communities, comparing the process to commercial transactions, or to intercommunity friendship links." (See Craven and Wellman 1973.)

7. If one were to include the federal criminal investigation units that serve the area, the number of producers would of course be considerably greater. However, since the operation of the F.B.I., U.S. Postal Service, Internal Revenue Service, and other federal investigative units is relatively invariant *across* SMSAs, they are not being included within the frame of this analysis.

REFERENCES

Bish, Robert L., and Vincent Ostrom. 1973. *Understanding Urban Government. Metropolitan Reform Reconsidered.* Washington, DC: American Enterprise Institute for Public Policy Research.
Campbell, Alan K., and Seymour Sacks. 1967. *Metropolitan America. Fiscal Patterns and Governmental Systems.* New York: Free Press.
Committee for Economic Development. 1972. *Reducing Crime and Assuring Justice.* New York: Committee for Economic Development.
Craven, Paul, and Barry Wellman. 1973. "The Network City." *Sociological Inquiry* 43:57–88.
Garmire, Bernard L. 1972. "The Police Role in an Urban Society." In *The Police and the Community,* ed. Robert F. Steadman. New York: Committee for Economic Development.
Harary, Frank, Robert Z. Norman, and Dorwin Cartwright. 1965. *Structural Models: An Introduction to the Theory of Directed Graphs.* New York: Wiley.
Hawkins, Brett W., and Thomas R. Dye. 1970. "Metropolitan 'Fragmentation': A Research Note." *Midwest Review of Public Administration* 4 (February): 17–24.
Leontief, Wassily M. 1951. *The Structure of American Economy, 1919–1939.* 2d ed. Fair Lawn, NJ: Oxford University Press.
McCausland, J. L. 1972. "Crime in the Suburbs." In *The End of Innocence: A Suburban Reader,* ed. Charles Haar, 61–64. Glenview, IL: Scott, Foresman.
Ostrom, Elinor, and Roger B. Parks. 1973. "Suburban Police Departments: Too

Many and Too Small?" In *The Urbanization of the Suburbs,* ed. Louis H. Masotti and Jeffrey K. Hadden, 367–402. Urban Affairs Annual Reviews, vol. 7. Beverly Hills, CA: Sage.

Ostrom, Vincent. 1972. *Institutional Arrangements for Water Resource Development—With Special Reference to the California Water Industry.* Springfield, VA: National Technical Information Service.

Ostrom, Vincent, and Elinor Ostrom. 1965. "A Behavioral Approach to the Study of Intergovernmental Relations." *Annals of the American Academy of Political and Social Science* 359 (May): 137–46. (Chapter 4 in this volume.)

President's Commission on Law Enforcement and Administration of Justice. 1967. *The Challenge of Crime in a Free Society.* Washington, D.C.: Superintendent of Documents.

Scott, Thomas M. 1973. "Suburban Governmental Structures." In *The Urbanization of the Suburbs,* ed. Louis H. Masotti and Jeffrey K. Hadden, 213–38. Urban Affairs Annual Reviews, vol. 7. Beverly Hills, CA: Sage.

Skoler, Daniel L., and June M. Hetler. 1970. "Governmental Restructuring and Criminal Administration: The Challenge of Consolidation." In *Crisis in Urban Government: A Symposium: Restructuring Metropolitan Area Government,* 53–75. Silver Spring, MD: Thomas Jefferson.

CHAPTER 12

Neither Gargantua nor the Land of Lilliputs: Conjectures on Mixed Systems of Metropolitan Organization

Elinor Ostrom and Roger B. Parks

No matter their field or focus, political scientists study complex systems. Complex systems may involve large numbers of representatives, interacting within the rules, procedures, and folkways of the U.S. Congress; systems of nations interacting at one point in time or over a period of time; and regions within a nation or localities within a metropolitan region interacting on a regular basis. Even though political scientists regularly study complex systems, our predominant modes of explanation draw on models of relatively simple systems. When the experiential world being studied becomes too complex, a frequent reaction has been to presume that the complexity itself is a source of pathology. Calls for political reform are frequently battle cries for imposing simplicity where political systems are found to be complex.

Complex systems lacking domination by a few loci of power are presumed by some to be incapacitated by fragmentation. *Balkanization* is the term used to denigrate not only situations where many small countries interact in a region but also any system composed of many units interacting regularly without clear domination by "major" powers.[1] Congressional scholars have been deeply concerned about the fragmentation of committee structure; administrative scholars have been equally concerned about the fragmentation of administrative agencies (Sundquist 1969). In the field of international relations, considerable debate has been engendered about the fate of systems where no single country plays a hegemonic role (Krasner 1983; Keohane 1984). Among urban scholars, the dominant view has been that fragmentation of authority in metropolitan areas is a major source of the ills facing metropolitan areas (see CED 1970; Harrigan 1985; Hawley and Zimmer 1970; Newton 1975; and Yates 1977).

A quarter of a century ago, Vincent Ostrom, Charles Tiebout, and Robert Warren (1961) (OTW) challenged the presumption that a multiplicity of

Originally presented at the Midwest Political Science Association meetings, Chicago, Illinois, April 9–11, 1987. Published by permission of the authors.

governmental units in a metropolitan area was necessarily a pathological phenomenon. OTW criticized the dominant presumption that some form of "gargantua" or "single metropolitan government" (Wood 1958) was needed to achieve effective governance in metropolitan areas. They coined the term *polycentric political system* as a general term to describe the governance structure in most metropolitan areas.

> 'Polycentric' connotes many centers of decision-making which are formally independent of each other. Whether they actually function independently, or instead constitute an interdependent system of relations, is an empirical question in particular cases. To the extent that they take each other into account in competitive relationships, enter into various contractual and cooperative undertakings or have recourse to central mechanisms to resolve conflicts, the various political jurisdictions in a metropolitan area may function in a coherent manner with consistent and predictable patterns of interacting behavior. (Ostrom, Tiebout, and Warren 1961, 831)

A major thrust of their argument was that scholars should not label as pathological the complex patterns of organization that citizens and public officials evolve simply because the empirical patterns do not match scholarly expectations about efficient, effective, and equitable forms of organization. OTW pointed to the diversity of urban public goods and services found in metropolitan areas and speculated that no single form of organization could be optimal for the provision and production of all goods in every metropolitan area.

OTW stressed the importance of conducting empirical research on the production, provision, and conflict resolution processes occurring within existing institutional arrangements before recommending sweeping reforms to simplify these institutional arrangements. They expected diverse structural aspects of polycentric systems, in combination with various attributes of public goods, to differentially affect the patterns of cooperation, competition, and conflict that would exist within and across independent political units. A simple list of the number of governmental units and the extent of overlap was entirely insufficient, they argued, for any evaluation of performance. Whether a particular structure of governance performed well or badly depended on the mix of goods and services being produced and consumed and the environmental conditions present in an area. Far more detailed empirical research was needed as the basis for the development of a theory of public sector organization and performance.

Since the late 1960s, many empirical studies have been conducted in the effort to come to a better understanding of the consequences of various forms of organization for the delivery of urban public goods and services.[2] We and our colleagues have undertaken a series of studies of the effect of institutional arrangements on the performance of urban policing in metropolitan areas.[3] We concentrated on this single service area for more than a decade for several reasons. First, so much diversity exists in what is referred to as urban policing that we found a rich variety of problems within this "one" service. Second, the provision of public order is one of the core interests in any political system. Trying to understand the diversity of variables that affect public order has been fascinating in and of itself. Third, our initial findings were perceived by others as so controversial that we felt compelled to repeat aspects of our empirical work in many different circumstances to ascertain how robust they were.

...In this essay we begin to formulate the theoretical conjectures by which we can explain how complex structures of small, medium, and large police departments serving variously organized governmental jurisdictions tend to provide higher levels of performance than simpler structures of any scale. The major portion of this essay is our initial effort to present one part of these conjectures. Before we turn to our conjectures, we provide a brief synopsis of our findings for those who are not familiar with our earlier studies.

A Brief Synopsis of Research Findings

The Effect of Metropolitan Organization on Efficiency

Contrary to the frequent expectation that the presence of a large number of police agencies leads to a decrease in the effectiveness and efficiency of policing, we have found the opposite effect. In a study of 80 metropolitan areas (Parks and E. Ostrom 1981), we selected two outputs for analysis: (1) police response capacity, measured by the average number of police patrol cars on the street,[4] and (2) arrests for serious crimes, measured by the number of Part I crimes cleared by arrest in a year. While police produce many varied outputs (see Goldstein 1977), these two are among the most important to consumers and to the police themselves. A high proportion of police resources are typically devoted to maintaining an on-street presence and response capacity. Commonly recommended measures of police performance usually include response time as a measure of capacity and clearances as a measure of the effectiveness of departmental investigative activities.

We initially use a method for determining efficient production functions from observations on the inputs and outputs of different police agencies developed by M. J. Farrell (1957). In concept, the method is simple. One plots all combinations of inputs leading to a given level of output and then determines the innermost envelope of those points (the set of points closest to the origin on each of the input dimensions) for each of the isoquants of interest (see chap. 16 in this volume). Figure 12.1 presents frontier production possibility estimates to show how the number of patrol producers in a metropolitan area affects performance. These frontiers show the maximum combinations of clearances by arrest and cars on patrol (both standardized by the number of sworn officers) that were obtained by departments in metropolitan areas with differing amounts of multiplicity.[5] The frontier functions show the trade-off possibilities for response capacity and clearances among the most efficient departments, with the normal concave shape that one expects. They also show a significant upward shift in output possibilities as the number of patrol producers in a metropolitan area increases. The most efficient producers supply more output for given inputs in high multiplicity metropolitan areas than do the efficient producers in metropolitan areas with fewer producers. Thus, one aspect of complexity—numbers of agencies serving the same metropolitan area—is systematically related to enhanced performance.

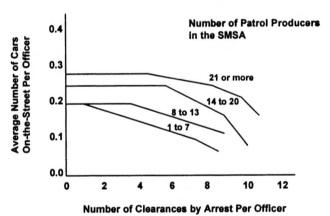

Fig. 12.1. Frontier production possibility curves

Since a diversity of goods and services is produced in metropolitan areas even within one "service," such as policing, one should expect to find diverse scales of production enhancing performance in addition to the positive effects of multiplicity. In our efforts to measure the structure of police service delivery in metropolitan areas, we obtained descriptive data consistent with this expectation (E. Ostrom, Parks, and Whitaker 1978). In 80 metropolitan areas, we identified 1,279 patrol agencies, 860 homicide investigation agencies, 985 radio dispatch agencies, 226 entry-level training agencies, and only 85 crime laboratory agencies. Most of the 80 metropolitan areas are served by one and only one crime lab while the median number of patrol agencies in the same set of metropolitan areas is 13. This simple descriptive data provides some initial evidence that service providers are using different scales of production for different types of police services.

To examine the cumulative effect of several metropolitan structural attributes on efficiency, we treat each SMSA as a unit of analysis. Taking the same measures of performance as in the preceding, we utilized methods developed by Charnes, Cooper, and Rhodes (1978a,b; see also Bessent and Bessent 1980) to identify the most efficient metropolitan areas in our sample and to provide relative ratings of the efficiency of the other metropolitan areas. A graphical representation can provide an initial sense for the method though not the details. Assume that each metropolitan area provides two outputs Y_{1j} and Y_{2j} using only a single input, X_{1j}. On figure 12.2, we have plotted the hypothetical results for five metropolitan areas (labeled M_1 through M_5). Three of the metropolitan areas (M_1, M_2, and M_3) define a production possibility frontier in this example. No metropolitan area obtains a higher ratio of output 1 to the input than does M_1 without some sacrifice in the ratio of output 2 to the input. In this sense, M_1, M_2, and M_3 represent Pareto efficient regions. M_4 and M_5 are not Pareto efficient. M_4 is clearly dominated by M_2. M_2 achieves an equivalent ratio of output 2 to the input factor and a higher ratio of output 1 to the input. M_5 is dominated in turn by a combination of M_2 and M_3. A mixture of their operations, denoted as point E_5, is clearly better than the results obtained by M_5.

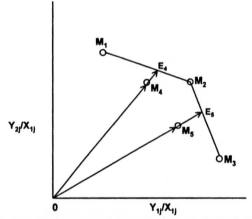

Fig. 12.2. Graphical representation of relative technical efficiency

Using this method, M_1, M_2, and M_3 would be assigned an efficiency rating of 1.0. The relative efficiency of M_4 is measured by the ratio of the length of the line segment from the origin to M_4 to the length of the line segment from the origin to E_4 on the frontier. That is, the relative efficiency of a metropolitan area falling below the production possibility frontier is computed relative to the efficiency of a metropolitan area or a combination of metropolitan areas that produce outputs in the same proportions. The actual computation method uses weighted combinations of inputs and of outputs to compute technical efficiency values rather than single measures, but the basic logic is the same.

The input factors are the total number of sworn officers, the total number of civilians employed, the total number of vehicles available, and the total number of crimes reported in the previous year. The output factors are the number of officers deployed for street duty at 10 P.M. and the number of reported crimes that were cleared by an arrest in the previous year. The production possibility frontier for these two outputs was computed using a version of data envelopment analysis, relating the weighted sum of the inputs to the weighted sum of outputs and maximizing the latter with respect to the former. Having identified those metropolitan areas that defined this frontier, relative efficiencies of the remaining areas were computed by solution of a linear programming problem analogous to the graphical presentation in figure 12.2. The relative efficiencies derived from these computations can then be used as performance measures for the study of structural effects.

The relative technical efficiencies of the 76 metropolitan areas for which full data were available ranged from 40 to 100 percent. Table 12.1 shows the full distribution. Fourteen of the 76 areas defined the production possibility frontier. The median efficiency rating across the 76 areas was 77 percent. The wide range of relative efficiencies found is consistent with what one would expect from public sector organization. Unlike ideal competitive market structures, public service industry structures are not compelled toward high levels of efficient production.

TABLE 12.1. Relative Technical Efficiencies of Metropolitan Service Delivery Structures

Efficiency Rating	Number of SMSAs with this Rating
40–50	3
51–60	6
61–70	19
71–80	16
81–90	9
91–99	9
100	14

Structural Relationships with Relative Technical Efficiency

To examine the relationship of structural measures of public service industries to their technical efficiencies, metropolitan areas were categorized according to the values of structural measures that enable us to examine the effect of multiplicity and diverse scales of production. We focused our analysis on metropolitan structures related to the supply of three police service components—general area patrol, the investigation of serious crimes, and radio communications. The structure of police patrol service was measured by *relative multiplicity,* the number of patrol service producers per 100,000 metropolitan residents, and by *autonomy,* the proportion of jurisdictions in each metropolitan area which received patrol service exclusively from a locally organized producer. The structures of investigative services and of radio communication were indexed by *dominance,* the proportion of service recipients in each metropolitan area that received these services from the supplier with the largest number of such recipients.[6]

In our analysis of structural effects, patrol service structure was categorized by dichotomizing relative multiplicity and autonomy at their median values. Investigation and radio communications structures were categorized by dichotomizing dominance in these services at their respective medians. Table 12.2 shows some clear structural relationships for the relative efficiencies of the metropolitan areas. Those areas with higher multiplicity and autonomy in their service delivery structures for patrol achieve higher technical efficiency measured by the weighted combination of patrol and clearance activities. Those metropolitan areas with greater dominance in homicide investigation and radio communication structures also exhibit higher efficiencies for this weighted combination.

Table 12.3 shows a further breakdown by structural measures that reflect patrol, criminal investigation, and radio communication organization. Although the number of SMSAs in each cell is small in some combinations, the same patterns are found. Relative technical efficiency is higher in SMSAs where patrol services are supplied by relatively higher numbers of autonomous patrol producers and where homicide investigations and radio communications are supplied in a more concentrated manner. Regression analysis of the effects of a larger set of service delivery structure measures on technical efficiency confirms these patterns (data not shown). The strongest coefficients were found for relative multiplicity and autonomy in patrol and for dominance in homicide investigations and radio communications. No other structural measures exhibit significant coefficients in the regression with relative technical efficiency. In total, these four structural measures explained approximately 30 percent of variation in relative technical efficiency across the 76 SMSAs.

The Effect of Size of a Police Department on Performance

In addition to our studies of metropolitan structure and efficiency, we have conducted a large number of studies of police departments in particular metropolitan areas (see citations in endnote 3). Since so many variables affect

TABLE 12.2. Relative Efficiency and Industry Structure

		Patrol Structure Effects	
		Relative Multiplicity	
		≤6.01	>6.01
Autonomy	≤0.54	71[a] (18)[b]	75 (18)
	>0.54	80 (19)	86 (21)
		Investigation Structure Effects	
		Dominance–Homicide Investigation	
		≤0.64	>0.64
Dominance–Radio Communications	≤0.25	70 (26)	74 (9)
	>0.25	83 (28)	88 (21)

[a]Mean relative technical efficiency.
[b]Number of SMSAs (total = 76).

TABLE 12.3. Relative Efficiency and Industry Structure

			Relative Multiplicity–Patrol			
			≤6.01		>6.01	
			Dominance–Homicide Investigation		Dominance–Homicide Investigation	
			≤0.64	>0.64	≤0.64	>0.64
Autonomy–Patrol ≤0.54	Dominance–Radio Communications	≤0.25	63[a] (7)[b]	53 (2)	69 (6)	73 (3)
		>0.25	81 (7)	82 (2)	81 (6)	75 (3)
Autonomy–Patrol >0.54	Dominance–Radio Communications	≤0.25	72 (9)	87 (2)	75 (4)	82 (2)
		>0.25	85 (5)	88 (3)	85 (10)	99 (5)

[a]Mean relative technical efficiency.
[b]Number of SMSAs (total = 76).

police performance, we have consistently studied relatively similar neighborhoods (in terms of type of housing, social homogeneity, and level of family income) being served by police departments of varying sizes. Our studies have included departments that have only part-time officers up to departments with over 2,000 officers. The measures of performance we have used include victimization rates, whether citizens called upon police when victimized, speed of response when victimized, and general evaluations of police performance. In the full array of studies, we have yet to find a large police department (over 350 officers) that has performed more effectively in delivering direct services to citizens in similar neighborhoods than the smaller departments we have studied. Perhaps our most dramatic findings occurred in the Chicago metropolitan area where we compared the performance of two extremely poor, black police forces serving Phoenix and East Chicago Heights with the performance of the Chicago Police Department serving similar black neighborhoods inside the city of Chicago. While the Chicago department allocated 14 times the resources to policing the black neighborhoods included within our study inside the city of Chicago, this modern, professional department was not able to keep victimization rates lower, respond faster, or perform more effectively on any of the indicators included in our study than the extremely poor, small, independent Phoenix and East Chicago Heights Departments.

What our empirical studies have shown repeatedly is that the efficiency and effectiveness (and even, to a major extent, the equity) of the provision and production of police services are enhanced in metropolitan areas characterized by higher levels of complexity. In terms of immediate response to citizens' calls for service, the existence of a fairly large number of autonomous, small- to medium-sized police departments is associated with lower victimization rates, faster response, and higher response capability in the neighborhoods served by those agencies. In terms of providing enhanced investigation of rare events, such as homicides, the presence of fewer agencies serving a larger population (even though the actual production team of investigative specialists may be relatively small) is associated with higher performance. Neither a single layer of small production bureaus nor a single, large bureau appears to have as high a performance potential as a complex, mixed system with many smaller agencies producing some services and some intermediate and large agencies producing others.

Having shown that the structure of institutional arrangements makes a difference in performance, we are not, however, prepared to argue that structure *causes* outcomes in a simplistic cause-effect manner. Rather, years of direct interaction with local public officials, of riding in police cars, of interviewing citizens in their living rooms, of listening and coding calls for service plus the analysis of the data we have collected have led us to view institutions as channeling devices created and changed by human actions over time. Sometimes institutions channel human action in extraordinarily creative ways; at other times, individuals find themselves trapped in institutional settings that channel them toward ever more unproductive results for all involved.

The creation and change of some aspects of institutional structure are the result of conscious choice, while some structural patterns evolve without any one person or persons consciously designing the structure. Aspects of the institutional structure existing in the 14 metropolitan areas rated as most efficient in our sample, for example, were self-consciously designed by specific persons. The overall institutional structure in these areas, however, was *not* designed by one person or groups of persons. Nor is it likely that any key actor in the police service delivery systems in these metropolitan areas fully understands all aspects of the metropolitan structure. Rather, as individuals face a succession of problems over time, they are encouraged or discouraged by the opportunities and/or constraints built into the institutions existing at any particular period of time, and the resulting patterns of human relationships, to explore new options for productive growth and new institutional arrangements. Understanding the capabilities and limits of a particular set of institutional arrangements occurs as individuals attempt to solve problems within the context of that set of institutional arrangements.

Our most general explanation for why complex, multitiered metropolitan service delivery systems enhance performance is that such systems possess a rich array of differently scaled and related problem-solving arenas. If individuals fail to solve a problem in one institutional arrangement, the prior existence of a rich array of other arenas enhances the probability that they can somewhere find an effective institutional mechanism or create still new arrangements building on elements that are already there. In a sparse institutional landscape, particularly one dominated by actors who hold monopoly powers, failure in one arena may mean final failure.

Our development of this general explanation is, like many metropolitan phenomena, still emerging. In the remainder of this essay we focus on one part, the options for organizing the production of police services in differently constituted metropolitan areas. We will contrast the options open for such organization in two "ideal type" metropoli, one fully consolidated and one fully fragmented. Our discussion of the options available in these ideal types is based upon our understanding of organizational factors in the production of policing, particularly those factors related to the scale of effects of various service components and related economies (or diseconomies) of scale. Before turning to that discussion, we briefly review these scale considerations.

Scale Effects in the Production of Police Service Components

Policing involves the production and supply of a complex bundle of service components. Some of these service components, among them general area patrol and immediate response to citizen requests for aid, traffic patrol and accident investigation, and the investigation of specific criminal incidents,

are supplied directly to citizens. Other components, including radio communications, access to specialized information banks, officer training, and laboratory analyses, are not supplied directly to citizens but rather comprise auxiliary services that producers of direct service components draw upon as
needed when producing services for citizens.

When policing is disaggregated into its service components, it becomes
clear that these components differ significantly in their scale of effects and in
the ways that they are produced. The patrol and immediate response component is quite local in its scale of effects and is organized around basic building blocks of individual patrol units with one or two officers. The nature of
this service component, particularly the necessity of specific time and place
information for its effective production, suggests that a close match between
patrol units and the areas they serve is likely to be beneficial and that such
matches should be maintained over significant periods of time.

Traffic patrol and accident investigation has both localized and more
widespread scales of effects. A portion of this component, focused on local
flow control, can be organized around the basic patrol unit building blocks
used for general area patrol. On the other hand, control of the movement over
longer distances of heavy volumes of vehicular traffic requires the coordination of efforts of many production units to ensure a smooth flow. Criminal
investigation, too, has both localized and wider scales of effects. The investigation of many crimes can be organized around the same building blocks as
general area patrol and local traffic control, with perhaps a few more specialized personnel to supplement the efforts of patrol officers. In other cases,
however, particularly those involving the investigation of more serious
crimes or the activities of organized groups of criminals, production units
capable of wider scale efforts will be needed.

Auxiliary service components, too, differ in their scale of effects. A single radio communications center can produce this component for a number
of basic patrol units. It is, however, subject to congestion beyond some number of such units. Information access and officer training components can be
quite extensive in scale. In a sense, the broader the scale of information access, the more useful is the information bank that supports it. Officer training
on a broad scale can be beneficial too, as officers learn common techniques
and develop bonds that carry over into their later interactions. The scale of
training production is limited, however, by the extent to which the common
techniques are appropriate to the areas in which the officers will work. Laboratory analysis can be produced by a single lab facility for many producers of
direct services.

Considering policing as a bundle of components with differing scales of
effects and organization of production leads one to recognize the division of
labor inherent in the production of policing. This division of labor can be

accommodated in many different ways. One can conceive of a system where separate organizations specialize in the production of each component. Their interdependencies would be mediated through a variety of cooperative agreements and contracts. Alternatively, the division of labor can be organized within a single, large organization, with interdependencies among subunits mediated through a bureaucratic command structure. Intermediate alternatives can be conceived as well. There are no obvious a priori grounds for selecting a single, "best" alternative. Indeed one might expect to find different organizational alternatives working more or less well in differing circumstances.

The Emergence of Complex Systems

One commonality that can be safely asserted about the metropolitan areas we have studied, and that we conjecture to be true of the many we have not, is that their institutional structures are *not* the result of some grand design. That is, no single designer or planner, nor any identifiable group of such individuals, sat down to develop the complex of organizational and interorganizational systems found in any metropolitan area. Rather, these patterns emerged as individual decision makers made choices in particular circumstances. To fully understand the pattern found in any particular metropolitan area would require understanding of the circumstances confronting many different decision makers at many different points in the history of that area, an understanding that is unlikely to be obtained for a single area, much less the many different ones found in the United States.

Fortunately, our explanation of complex systems need not (as it cannot) explain all of the details. Rather, we attempt to explain how complex systems of organization of the types we have found to be associated with higher levels of performance *could* emerge, recognizing that the details will be at least in part inapplicable to any given case. We do so by posing two archetypical metropolitan areas having very different organizational structures. Within these structures, we contemplate the dilemmas confronting a decision maker or a set of decision makers who are in the business of producing police services. If their concerns are, at least in part, questions of how to organize production in relation to the scale considerations discussed previously, how might they move?

Hypothetical Case I: Pure Fragmentation

Let us posit an imaginary metropolitan area with a population of 500,000 people. Ignoring political boundaries for a moment and concentrating simply on economic activities and population demographics, we can imagine that individual firms and families as they have moved into, around, and out of the metropolitan area have selected those neighborhoods that they find most appropriate for their own purposes. Firms that desire to be near related firms in order to reduce time and transactions costs have clustered together. Commercial enterprises that benefit from proximity to one another in terms of attracting customers have also clustered near to one another. Families who move into the area because of employment or decide to move within the area due to increased family size or other changes in lifestyle or needs move into neighborhoods with other families having somewhat similar socioeconomic backgrounds and family compositions. Regardless of how political jurisdictions or production boundaries are fixed, a stylized "fact" of all urban areas is the continuous sorting and re-sorting of urban populations into evolving clusters of neighborhoods with greater internal homogeneity on many socioeconomic variables than the heterogeneity on these same variables across neighborhoods in the metropolitan area.

Now let us posit that this metropolitan area is jurisdictionally organized into one set of horizontal jurisdictional boundaries, say 10 cities each containing 50,000 population. Further, let us posit that each of these cities has created its own police department with 50 officers in each department. What opportunities and constraints would face the 10 police chiefs in this hypothetical metropolitan area given the diverse scale effects of various service components related to urban policing?

In regard to neighborhood patrol and immediate response to calls for service, the police chiefs would each be able to serve their neighborhoods relatively well. Officers could become well acquainted with the physical layout of their jurisdiction, the individuals living in the neighborhood and their desires concerning a preferred style of public order. The chiefs themselves would have a relatively good "feel" for what was going on in the community. The chiefs could personally know each of the officers working in the department and all of the major decision makers in the local community. If the chiefs lived in the communities they served, they would be observing routine interactions between citizens and their officers as they went about the community pursuing their official duties as well as when they were relaxing or shopping with their own families. They would likely hear about problem officers or problem areas from several different sources.

In regard to investigatory services, the 10 police chiefs could be relatively satisfied with the capacities of their department to solve many types of crimes committed in their jurisdiction by residents living in the jurisdiction or nearby. The closeness of their officers to the local scene would enable officers to pick up information about juveniles having problems or other information valuable to solving crimes of this sort. However, each of the chiefs would be relatively dissatisfied with their capacities to cope with organized bad-check rings operating throughout the area or other forms of criminal activity requiring either extensive and widespread information nets or access to expensive auxiliary equipment.

If each department had its own radio dispatch unit, each chief would be allocating about one-tenth of his personnel to answering calls for service and dispatching officers. (One needs to allocate about four and one-half officers to keep a dispatch position open 24 hours a day, 365 days of the year.) If each department tried to maintain its own full-time jail, another one-tenth of the departmental personnel would be allocated to the position of jail keeper. Without any joint arrangements, contracts, or overlapping jurisdictions, the police chiefs of the 10 departments would find it even more difficult to provide fully equipped crime labs.

The problem facing police chiefs and municipal officials in a perfectly fragmented metropolitan area would be how to work out joint agreements or contracts to enable several or all of the departments in the area to share in the production of some services while each continued to serve as the patrol and immediate response service supplier in each of the 10 municipalities. If the general institutional infrastructure of the state in which our hypothetical metropolitan area were located allowed a diversity of joint agreements, special districts, and contracts, one could expect that the chiefs would be motivated by budgetary pressures to seek out some forms of supraorganization.

Two or three neighboring jurisdictions with complementary demand patterns who are able to work out compatible policies and priorities for dispatching could each save from the creation of a joint dispatching center. The creation of a specialized investigation unit drawing on personnel from all of the jurisdictions might enable all jurisdictions to share information about some types of criminal activities (such as bad checks and drugs). If a major hospital were located in the metropolitan area, which already had extensive laboratory equipment, the 10 jurisdictions might contract with it to perform specialized forensic analyses at much lower cost than setting up an independent, specialized crime lab even for the entire metropolitan area. An entrepreneurial head of a local city college might see an opportunity in offering a criminal justice program that could serve as the entry level training program for the officers serving the departments in the area. One of the departments might build a jail able to serve the entire metropolitan area and charge each of the other nine departments for inmates sent to this jail.

Without an institutional infrastructure to allow a diversity of arrangements above the level of the individual police departments, police chiefs in a perfectly fragmented metropolitan area would face major problems in organizing effective police services for their communities. The availability of such institutional capabilities is in no way a guarantee that departments will be led to work out the most efficient methods for providing and producing these services. But as budgetary crunches came along within any particular community, one would expect police chiefs and the elected officials serving these communities to try to search out various ways of producing services at lower costs.

If interjurisdictional agreements were worked out to provide various sized and shaped overlapping arrangements, the major problems facing participants in such arrangements would be related to the costs of arriving at and maintaining joint arrangements. Considerable time and energy may be needed to set up the initial plans. The continual negotiations involved when independent agencies must agree on joint policies could involve major disputes. Fragile arrangements may come apart if recalcitrant or unreasonable persons are assigned responsibilities to make them work. On the other hand, while conflict takes time and may lead to a breakup of arrangements if not coped with effectively, conflict also generates information about problems. If conflict resolution mechanisms are effective, multijurisdictional arrangements may also work well for long periods of time.

Hypothetical Case II: Pure Consolidation

Now let us assume this same metropolitan area starting off initially with only one large police department and examine the opportunities and constraints facing the solitary police chief for the metropolitan area. We can imagine such a department being a "full service" department in the first place. It has its own crime lab, jail, and dispatch center and trains its own personnel. The key problem for the chief in this case relates to the organizing of patrol, immediate response, and investigation of neighborhood related criminal activities. Assuming a department of 500 officers, the chief cannot know most of the individual officers serving the department, nor can the chief know the diverse range of neighborhoods being served by this department. By necessity, the chief must rely on information summarized for him by staff preparing statistical reports on patterns of activities across neighborhoods.

A frequent way of organizing the patrol aspects of such a department is to divide the area into a series of districts and patrol beats within districts. Officers are assigned first to a district and then to a beat within a district but are rotated through the districts over time. (Rotation is thought to be a primary device to avoid corruption in urban police departments.) An effort is made to develop standard policies and priorities for response that are uniform across the entire jurisdiction.

This system can result in some rather major problems. A standard set of priorities may not fit the needs of any of the diverse neighborhoods within the jurisdiction. Nor, does anyone in the department acquire a really deep familiarity with any of the neighborhoods being served and the particular needs and problems of citizens living there. Citizens may come to view the police as total strangers not to be trusted, and police may come to view all citizens in a suspicious manner.

A chief trying to combat this problem may try some forms of decentralization within his department. He might, for example, experiment with a form of "team policing" by assigning officers and district captains on a more permanent basis to particular neighborhoods and assigning control to the district captain as to how personnel shall be allocated within each district. To do this, he and other top ranking officials in the department have to forego a considerable amount of control over the day-to-day events in the department. But, when things go wrong, it is the chief and his top aides who will take the heat rather than the district captain. Soon after an effort to decentralize, the same chief or his top aides may be motivated to again take charge. Decentralization is dangerous for those at the top when they cannot find effective mechanisms to reward and punish those heading subunits in a manner directly related to the performance of the subunit. Organizing large private corporations around profit centers has proved a far more successful method of decentralization than any of the experiments that have been tried to achieve administrative decentralization within large public bureaus. (Virtually all of the recent experiments in team or neighborhood policing in recent years have foundered on this point—middle and upper managers have been reluctant to allow sufficient decentralized discretion, and, where granted, central control has been quickly reasserted.)

The Emergence of Complexity

No matter whether one starts from a perfectly fragmented or a perfectly consolidated metropolitan area, one would expect that decision makers in either system would face problems that could not be effectively handled by simple organizational designs. Those starting with a horizontally fragmented system would be searching for ways to create larger scale enterprises to handle those services better produced at a larger scale. Those starting with a horizontally consolidated system would be searching for ways to create smaller scale enterprises to handle those services where time and place information is valuable in producing effective policing. There is no guarantee that decision makers starting from either a relatively consolidated or a relatively fragmented metropolitan area would find feasible, let alone optimal, solutions.

Complex arrangements put together by independent organizations will tend to be mediated through bargaining and negotiation processes. These will tend to work well when most of the participants agree on general policies and continue to see a mutual benefit from their continuance. Bargaining among participants who may have blocking or veto capabilities can produce lots of information about disagreements and are susceptible to breakdown if recalcitrant participants are involved. Arrangements to decentralize authority within a large enterprise will tend to be mediated through hierarchy and command. These will tend to work well when performance of subunits can be easily identified and responsibility can be assigned to those at the lower levels. Such arrangements will tend to break down if major problems occur because of failure in the smaller units, and those assigned general coordinating functions must bear the brunt of the costs of failure.

It is our speculation that starting from smaller units and building upward is more likely to lead to better solutions than trying to create effective smaller scale units within already constituted large units. This is enhanced, we think, when metropolitan areas are located in institutional environments that facilitate the working out of joint arrangements and provide effective conflict resolution arenas for when things go wrong. A set of smaller police departments is a more stable building block than a decentralized patrol division. A police chief of a small community cannot avoid taking responsibility for what goes wrong in his jurisdiction in the way that a district captain can evade that responsibility. What is created by administrative decentralization can be as easily destroyed through administrative recentralization. When services that are more economically produced at a larger scale are produced by independent agencies who themselves need "customers," a mutually productive arena is established that is less likely to fall apart through recalcitrance and divisiveness. Mutually productive arrangements tend to be self-reinforcing.

The major point is that the full array of problems involved in urban policing (and most other aspects of political life) is diverse enough that decision makers trying to solve these problems will be pressed to seek out complex organizational arrangements no matter from what "initial" organizational position they start. Whether or not police chiefs and locally elected officials are able to work out effective operational arrangements depends on many factors—one of the most important of which is their own entrepreneurial creativity. Human decision makers can certainly get themselves stuck in perverse situations that get worse and worse. The more social scientists preach the need for simple solutions to complex problems, the more harm we can potentially cause in the world (or the more irrelevant we will become to the analysis of difficult problems). There is much to understand about the processes of building complex organizational arrangements given the diverse problems that decision makers are facing. We need to try to understand rather than to condemn these processes.

NOTES

1. There are even allusions to "warfare" resulting from "fragmented" or "balkanized" metropolitan areas (see, e.g., Vernon 1964, 101; Newton 1975, 35).
2. See Savas 1977a,b; Ahlbrandt 1973; Kirp and Cohen 1972; Sher 1977;

Sproule-Jones 1978; Benton and Rigos 1985; Nivola 1979; V. Ostrom and Bish 1977; Hawkins 1976; Bish and V. Ostrom 1973.

3. See McDavid 1979; E. Ostrom, Parks, and Whitaker 1973, 1977, 1978; Sharp 1981; Whitaker 1980; Mclver 1978; E. Ostrom and Smith 1976; Rogers and Lipsey 1974; E. Ostrom and Whitaker 1973, 1974; E. Ostrom and Parks 1973.

4. Response capacity is actually a more complex function of the number of cars available, the volume and distribution of service requests, and the time to service each. The number of response units deployed is but a proxy for response capacity.

5. In reality, there are "nearly maximum" combinations. In examining the plots for these relationships, some points appeared aberrant in that they were far removed from any similar points. Such aberrant points were excluded in drawing the frontiers.

6. In our 80 metropolitan area study we developed a large number of well-defined measures of metropolitan structure (E. Ostrom, Parks, and Whitaker 1978). These measures were based upon a matrix analysis similar to that of input-output analysis, requiring the identification of all organized units for the consumption of ten distinct police services in each metropolitan area, all producers of those services, and the relationships among them. For brevity, we define only those used in the present analysis.

REFERENCES

Ahlbrandt, Roger S. 1973. *Municipal Fire Protection Services: Comparison of Alternative Organization Forms.* Beverly Hills: Sage.

Alchian, Armen, and Harold Demsetz. 1972. "Production, Information Costs, and Economic Organization." *American Economic Review* 62 (December): 777-95.

Anderson, William, and Edward W. Weidner. 1950. *American City Government.* Rev. ed. New York: Henry Holt.

Becker, Gary S. 1976. *The Economic Approach to Human Behavior.* Chicago: University of Chicago Press.

Bendor, Jonathon B. 1985. *Para'lel Systems. Redundancy in Government.* Berkeley: University of California Pre· s.

Benton, J. Edwin, and Platon ї ⁄. Rigos. 1985. "Patterns of Metropolitan Service Dominance. Central City and Central County Service Roles Compared." *Urban Affairs Quarterly* 20, no. 3 (March): 371-79.

Bessent, Authella M., and E. Wailand Bessent. 1980. "Determining the Comparative Efficiency of Schools through Data Envelopment Analysis." *Educational Administrative Quarterly* 16 (spring): 57-75.

Bish, Robert L., and Vincent Ostrom. 1973. *Understanding Urban Government: Metropolitan Reform Reconsidered.* Washington, DC: American Enterprise Institute for Public Policy Research.

Boyle, John, and David Jacobs. 1982. "The Intra-City Distribution of Services: A Multivariate Analysis." *American Political Science Review* 76, no. 2 (June): 371-79.

Breton, A., and R. Wintrobe. 1975. "The Equilibrium Size of a Budget-Maximizing Bureau: A Note on Niskanen's Theory of Bureaucracy." *Journal of Political*

Economy 83, no. 1:195–207.

Charnes, A., W. W. Cooper, and E. Rhodes. 1978a. "Measuring the Efficiency of Decision Making Units." *European Journal of Operational Research* 2 (September): 429–44.

———. 1978b. "A Data Envelopment Analysis Approach to Evaluation of the Program Follow Through Experiment in U.S. Public School Education." Research Report 331. Austin: University of Texas at Austin Center for Cybernetic Studies.

Committee for Economic Development (CED). 1970. *Reshaping Government in Metropolitan Areas*. New York: Committee for Economic Development.

Dahl, Robert A. 1967. "The City in the Future of Democracy." *American Political Science Review* 61 (December): 953–70.

Downs, Anthony. 1967. *Inside Bureaucracy*. Boston: Little, Brown.

Farrell, M. J. 1957. "The Measurement of Productive Efficiency." Part 3. *Journal of the Royal Statistical Society,* series A, 120:253–81.

Fuchs, Victor R. 1968. *The Service Economy*. New York: National Bureau of Economic Research.

Goldstein, Herman. 1977. *Policing a Free Society*. Cambridge, MA: Ballinger.

Harrigan, John J. 1985. *Political Change in the Metropolis*. Boston: Little, Brown.

Hawkins, Robert B., Jr. 1976. *Self-Government by District. Myth and Reality*. Stanford, CA: Hoover Institution Press.

Hawley, Amos H., and Basil C. Zimmer. 1970. *The Metropolitan Community. Its People and Government*. Beverly Hills: Sage.

Hirshman, Albert O. 1970. *Exit, Voice and Loyalty*. Cambridge, MA: Harvard University Press.

Jacobs, Paul. 1966. "The Los Angeles Police." *Atlantic Monthly* 218 (December): 95–101.

Keohane, Robert O. 1984. *After Hegemony. Cooperation and Discord in the World Political Economy*. Princeton: Princeton University Press.

Kirp, David L., and David K. Cohen. 1972. "Education and Metropolitanism." In *Metropolitanization and Public Services*, ed. Lowden Wingo. Washington, DC: Resources for the Future.

Krasner, Stephen D. 1979. *International Regimes*. Ithaca, New York: Cornell University Press.

Lancaster, Kelvin J. 1966. *Consumer Demand: A New Approach*. New York: Columbia University Press.

Langbein, Laura I. 1980. "Production or Prerequisites in Public Bureaus." Paper prepared for delivery at the Public Choice Society meetings, San Francisco.

———. 1981. "The Section 8–Existing Housing Program's Administrative Fee Structure: A Formal Model of Bureau Behavior with Empirical Evidence." Paper presented at the Midwest Political Science Association meetings, April.

Lucas, Robert E., Jr. 1986. "Adaptive Behavior and Economic Theory." Part 2. *Journal of Business* 59, no. 4 (October): 401–26.

Lyons, William E., and David Lowery. 1986. "The Organization of Political Space and Citizen Responses to Dissatisfaction in Urban Communities: An Integrative Model." *Journal of Political Science* 48 (May): 321–46.

MacKay, Robert J., and Carol L. Weaver. 1978. "Monopoly Bureaus and Fiscal Outcomes: Deductive Models and Implications for Reform." In *Issues in Urban Economics*, ed. Harvey S. Perloff and Lowden Wingo, 527–65. Baltimore, MD: Johns Hopkins University Press.

McDavid, James C. 1979. *Police Cooperation and Performance: The Greater St. Louis Interlocal Experience.* University Park, PA: Pennsylvania State University.

McIver, John P. 1978. "The Relationship between Metropolitan Police Industry Structure and Inter-Agency Assistance: A Preliminary Assessment." *Policy Studies Journal* 7 (Special Issue): 406–13.

Morgan, David R., and John P. Pelissero. 1980. "Urban Policy: Does Political Structure Matter." *American Political Science Review* 74, no. 4 (December): 999–1,005.

Newton, Kenneth. 1975. "American Urban Policies: Social Class, Political Structure, and Public Goods." *Urban Affairs Quarterly* 1, no. 2 (December): 241–64.

Niskanen, William. 1971. *Bureaucracy and Representative Government.* Chicago: Aldine-Atherton Press.

———. 1975. "Bureaucrats and Politicians." *Journal of Law and Economics* 18 (December): 617–43.

Nivola, Pietro S. 1979. *The Urban Service Problem.* Lexington, MA: Lexington Books.

Ostrom, Elinor. 1985. "Racial Inequalities in Low-Income Central City and Suburban Communities: The Case of Police Services." In *Policy Implementation in Federal and Unitary Systems*, ed. Kenneth Hanf and Theo A. J. Toonen, 235–65. Dordrecht, the Netherlands: Martinus Nijhoff.

Ostrom, Elinor, and Roger B. Parks. 1973. "Suburban Police Departments: Too Many and Too Small?" In *The Urbanization of the Suburbs*, ed. Louis H. Masotti and Jeffrey K. Hadden, 367–402. Urban Affairs Annual Reviews, vol. 7. Beverly Hills: Sage.

Ostrom, Elinor, Roger B. Parks, and Gordon P. Whitaker. 1973. "Do We Really Want to Consolidate Urban Police Forces? A Reappraisal of Some Old Assertions." *Public Administration Review* 33 (September/October): 423–33.

———. 1977. *Policing Metropolitan America.* Washington, DC: U.S. Government Printing Office.

———. 1978. *Patterns of Metropolitan Policing.* Cambridge, MA: Ballinger.

Ostrom, Elinor, and Dennis C. Smith. 1976. "On the Fate of Lilliputs in Metropolitan Policing." *Public Administration Review* 32 (spring): 192–200.

Ostrom, Elinor, and Gordon P. Whitaker. 1973. "Does Local Community Control of Police Make a Difference? Some Preliminary Findings." *American Journal of Political Science* 17, no. 1 (February): 48–76. (Chapter 8 in this volume.)

———. 1974. "Community Control and Governmental Responsiveness: The Case of Police in Black Communities." In *Improving the Quality of Urban Management*, ed. David Rogers and Willis Hawley, 303–34. Urban Affairs Annual Reviews, vol. 8. Beverly Hills: Sage. (Chapter 9 in this volume.)

Ostrom, Vincent, and Frances P. Bish, eds. 1977. *Comparing Urban Service Deliv-*

ery Systems: Structure and Performance. Urban Affairs Annual Reviews, vol. 12. Beverly Hills: Sage.

Ostrom, Vincent, Charles M. Tiebout, and Robert Warren. 1961. "The Organization of Government in Metropolitan Areas: A Theoretical Inquiry." *American Political Science Review* 55: 831–42. (Chapter 1 in this volume.)

Parks, Roger B. 1979. "Assessing the Influence of Organization on Performance: A Study of Police Services in Residential Neighborhoods." Ph.D. diss., Indiana University.

———. 1985. "Metropolitan Structure and Systemic Performance: The Case of Police Service Delivery." In *Policy Implementation in Federal and Unitary States,* ed. Kenneth Hanf and Theo A. J. Toonen, 161–91. Dordrecht, the Netherlands: Martinus Nijhoff.

Parks, Roger B., and Elinor Ostrom. 1981. "Complex Models of Urban Service Systems." In *Urban Policy Analysis: Directions for Future Research,* ed. Terry N. Clark, 171–99. Urban Affairs Annual Reviews, vol. 21. Beverly Hills: Sage. (Chapter 16 in this volume.)

Perrow, Charles. 1965. "Hospitals: Technology, Structure, and Goals." In *Handbook of Organizations,* ed. James G. March, 910–71. Chicago: Rand McNally.

Peterson, Paul E. 1981. *City Limits.* Chicago: University of Chicago Press.

Plott, Charles R. 1986. "Rational Choice in Experimental Markets." Part 2. *Journal of Business* 59, no. 4 (October): 301–27.

Rogers, Bruce D., and C. McCurdy Lipsey. 1974. "Metropolitan Reform: Citizen Evaluations of Performances in Nashville–Davidson County, Tennessee." *Publius* 4, no. 4 (fall): 19–34.

Savas, E. S. 1977a. "An Empirical Study of Competition in Municipal Service Delivery." *Public Administration Review* 37:717–24.

———. 1977b. *The Organization and Efficiency of Solid Waste Collection.* Lexington, MA: Lexington Books.

Sharp, Elaine B. 1981. "Responsiveness in Urban Service Delivery: The Case of Policing." *Administration and Society* 13 (May): 35–58.

Shepsle, Kenneth A., and Barry R. Weingast. 1981. "Political Preferences for the Pork Barrel: A Generalization." *American Journal of Political Science* 25 (February): 96–111.

Sher, Jonathan P. 1977. *Education in Rural America. A Reassessment of Conventional Wisdom.* Boulder, CO: Westview Press.

Simon, Herbert A. 1981. *The Sciences of the Artificial.* 2d ed. Cambridge, MA: MIT Press.

Smith, R. Jeffrey. 1985. "An Omnifarious Data Bank for Biology?" *Science* 228 (June 21): 1,410–11.

Sproule-Jones, Mark. 1978. "Coordination and the Management of Estuarine Water Quality." *Public Choice* 33:41–53.

Sundquist, James L. 1969. *Making Federalism Work.* Washington, DC: Brookings Institution.

Thompson, James D. 1967. *Organizations in Action.* New York: McGraw-Hill.

Tiebout, Charles. 1956. "A Pure Theory of Local Expenditures." *Journal of Political*

Economy 64 (October): 416–24.

Tullock, Gordon. 1965. *The Politics of Bureaucracy.* Washington, DC: Public Affairs Press.

Weingast, Barry R., Kenneth A. Shepsle, and Christopher Johnsen. 1981. "The Political Economy of Benefits and Costs: A Neoclassical Approach to Distributive Politics." *Journal of Political Economy* 89 (August): 642–64.

Whitaker, Gordon P. 1980. "Coproduction: Citizen Participation in Service Delivery." *Public Administration Review* 40, no. 3 (May–June): 240–46.

Williamson, Oliver. 1967. "Hierarchical Control and Optimal Firm Size." *Journal of Political Economy* 75, no. 2:123–38.

————. 1975. *Markets and Hierarchies: Analysis and Antitrust Implications.* New York and London: Free Press.

Wood, Robert C. 1958. "The New Metropolis: Green Belts, Grass Roots on Gargantua." *American Political Science Review* 52 (March): 108–22.

Yates, Douglas. 1977. *The Ungovernable City: The Politics of Urban Problems and Policy Making.* Cambridge, MA: MIT Press.

CHAPTER 13

Citizen Voice and Public Entrepreneurship: The Organizational Dynamic of a Complex Metropolitan County

Ronald J. Oakerson and Roger B. Parks

For many years, local government arrangements in the metropolitan United States have been criticized as being ineffective, inefficient, and even chaotic. Complex metropolitan areas are characterized frequently as *fragmented*. By this term, critics mean both *jurisdictional* fragmentation (i.e., too many separately organized units of government, especially small municipalities) and *functional* fragmentation (i.e., a lack of coordinated planning and administration). More generally, the critique is aimed at complex patterns of metropolitan organization that include, in addition to municipal fragmentation, the use of overlapping jurisdictions and special purpose governments.

At the same time, others have argued that a large number and variety of jurisdictions contribute to a functional metropolitan order that emerges from the choices of citizens and local officials (V. Ostrom, Tiebout, and Warren 1961). Most recently, the U.S. Advisory Commission on Intergovernmental Relations reached this conclusion.

A strong case can be made for local governments that range, in size, from small neighborhood units to areawide units and, in functional scope, from single-purpose to multi-purpose units. To obtain the benefits of large-scale organization, it is unnecessary and unwise to drive out small-scale organization. Large and small, as well as single-purpose and multi-purpose, units of local government, when used concurrently, reflect complementary expressions of public preference, not contradictory principles of organization (U.S. ACIR 1987, 53).[1]

Originally published in *Publius: The Journal of Federalism* 18, no. 4 (fall 1988): 91–112. Reprinted by permission of *Publius* and the authors.

Authors' note: The U.S. Advisory Commission on Intergovernmental Relations (U.S. ACIR) sponsored the case study that we conducted in the St. Louis area. Henry Aaron Bell was also a principal member of the research team. We are grateful to the many local officials and citizens who assisted us in our work.

Recent empirical research on the effects of jurisdictional fragmentation casts doubt on the validity of the traditional critique of metropolitan organization in the United States. New findings include the following.

- More fragmented metropolitan areas have been found to spend less than more consolidated areas in the aggregate. Mark Schneider reported that, after controlling for factors affecting local service demands, growth in local expenditures was slower in metropolitan areas with more rather than fewer local governments (Schneider 1986). Thomas DiLorenzo concluded that more concentrated systems of local government tend to have higher service costs than more fragmented systems (DiLorenzo 1983; see also Wagner and Weber 1975).
- Fragmentation may have greater positive effects when accompanied by overlapping jurisdictions. Roger Parks, using a measure of the technical efficiency with which input resources are converted to outputs in local policing, found that complex local service systems that combine fragmentation with overlap were more efficient than either consolidated systems or fragmented systems lacking overlap (Parks, 1985).
- Differential effects have been observed for service concentration across different services. David Chicoine and Norman Walzer found perceived service quality to be higher for some services (libraries and streets) where service provision was concentrated, but higher for others (education and parks) where service provision was fragmented (Chicoine and Walzer 1985).

What is not clear from this line of research is how (i.e., by what mechanism) complex metropolitan areas generate preferred consequences. To explain these new empirical findings, what is needed is a process theory that can link jurisdictional complexity to efficiency and effectiveness as outcomes. The traditional literature on metropolitan organization suggests a process theory that would lead to opposite results. That is, complex jurisdictional patterns lead to voter confusion and thus to a lack of accountability. At the same time, a large number of jurisdictions is alleged to make metropolitan-wide coordination difficult and costly, leading to functional fragmentation in relation to areawide problems and a failure to control spillover effects among jurisdictions. A large number of small jurisdictions is said to prevent the capture of scale economies in the production of public goods and services. All of this should lead to areawide inefficiency and ineffectiveness, but evidence from empirical research increasingly shows the reverse. Why? What process or mechanism operates in jurisdictionally complex metropolitan areas to account for seemingly counterintuitive results?

Exit and Voice: An Argument

One long-standing account of how fragmented systems of local government induce efficiency is the "Tiebout model," which emphasizes the potential for citizens to "vote with their feet" or to *exit* from a jurisdiction if relatively dissatisfied (Tiebout 1956; see also Hirschman 1970). In this model, a metropolitan area with a large number of small local jurisdictions can possess self-regulating properties similar to those of a market. Individuals are said to select jurisdictions that most closely satisfy their preferences for local public goods and services, including a preference for least-cost service provision at given benefit levels. Local government officials who wish to maintain their communities at some optimal size are then disciplined by the location decisions of individual citizens. Competition among local jurisdictions, analogous to competition among firms in a marketplace, would be greater where there are more jurisdictions and thus produce greater efficiency in more fragmented metropolitan areas.

The question is whether citizen exit alone can engender efficiency in service provision. Consider the situation of a homeowner who dislikes the tax and service bundle supplied by his or her local government and seeks, therefore, to exit. In order to relocate, the homeowner must, usually, sell his home. In order to sell, he must find a buyer. Finding a buyer is equivalent to *replacing* the tax loss from his relocation. A business is constrained by the ability of customers to take their business elsewhere, but a local government is less constrained by this mechanism. A homeowner cannot ordinarily shift his residence to a different community without finding a "new customer" for his present local government. Even if a homeowner must sell at a loss, and is willing to do so, he will attempt to replace as much of the tax loss as possible.

In the ordinary marketplace, consumers send market signals that show up in the cash drawer of a business. More customers mean more dollars; fewer customers, fewer dollars. The entry and exit of consumers produce tangible, direct, immediate effects on private entrepreneurs. Entry and, particularly, exit have no such direct or immediate effects on public officials, however. Consider what "business failure" looks like in the local government context. One possibility is that local officials, out of incompetence or sloth, allow the quality of community services to deteriorate. This is followed, after a time, by a decline in property values and subsequently, after even more time, by a loss of local revenue. Another possibility is that local officials, in an effort to extract a political rent, raise taxes without increasing service quality. Again, property values decline, followed eventually by tax revenues. In either case, there is no immediate cash drawer effect upon local officials. The negative results are long-run effects.

Surprisingly, a market model of local government seems to require farsighted local officials who are committed over the long term to their respective communities. Given officials of such civic character, it is hard to see the necessity of market discipline. If local politicians are not strongly motivated by long-run calculations, the prospect of eventual erosion of the property tax base among homeowners is unlikely to provoke an early response, when doing so would entail significant short-run costs.[2]

Suppose that local officials fail to respond to market signals. A business whose managers did so would soon fail: "market discipline" would prevail. When this happens in local government, market discipline will be borne mainly by "customers" rather than by those minding the municipal store. If local officials allow services to deteriorate, a process of community decline leads to lower property values, and subsequently to lower assessed valuations (which may tend to spur community decline). The effect of market discipline is felt by an entire community, not just by local officials. The big losers are property owners who decide to sell at a loss and those for whom exit is unavailable as an option and who must, therefore, choose loyalty or even resignation. Community decline is a collective bad. Its effects are not selectively imposed on municipal officials. The officials responsible for initiating a period of community decline may no longer be in office, or even in town, once the "market signals" have become strong and obvious.

To summarize, local citizens are unlikely to find exit a sufficient remedy for local government weakness or failure. First, the signals available to local officials from the real estate market are weak—unaccompanied in most cases by an immediate and substantial cash drawer effect.[3] Second, the ultimate effect of the discipline imposed by the real estate market is a collective bad shared by citizens. If local officials fail, for whatever reason, to maintain the collective well-being of a community, citizens suffer the consequences.[4]

It does not follow, however, that the entry and exit decisions of homeowners are without importance in local governance. A large number of jurisdictions within a metropolitan area creates a significant choice set for homebuyers. Jurisdictional fragmentation allows a self-sorting process to operate as individual households choose among diverse communities, locating and relocating in communities more closely matched to their preferences. A self-sorting process, however, does not automatically impose effective market discipline upon local officials. It is here that "voice," recognized by Albert Hirschman (1970) as an alternative to exit, becomes important.

Citizen voice complements the sorting process that occurs in a fragmented metropolitan area. When an individual moves from one community to another, he is choosing a community, not that community's officials. This is a truism, but it is an important one. By choosing a community composed of like individuals, a person is selecting a community whose "collective

voice" is closely matched to his own. Instead of depending solely on the entrepreneurship of public officials, as informed by market signals, individuals
can choose communities where the sum of individual voices is both in accord
with their preferences and likely to be effective in determining the content of
the public goods bundle.

The power of voice is linked more directly to the ballot box than to exit.
The local citizen who comes to a city council meeting and loudly complains
about a municipal service is surely more effective than the citizen who writes
to the mayor threatening to move out of town. If local officials feel un-
constrained by the ballot box, where the potential effect is quite immediate,
they are unlikely to feel constrained by the more remote and uncertain consequences associated with a potential for citizen exit.

The concept of "voting with your feet" can be a somewhat misleading
analogy. Voting can provide ordinary citizens with political leverage in their
present jurisdiction of residence; "voting with your feet" enables a citizen to
choose a new jurisdiction when regular voting fails. Regular voting, however, cannot provide a "way out," and, by the same token, "voting with your
feet" cannot be used as a source of political leverage by citizens who find the
ballot box ineffective. Both voice and exit provide significant citizen capabilities. "Voting with your feet" is an important complement to voice but not
a substitute for it.[5]

Multijurisdictional metropolitan areas, therefore, must not only multi-
ply the opportunities for citizen entry and exit but must also be able to amplify the power of citizen voice. This conclusion suggests that the processes that link jurisdictional fragmentation to efficiency and effectiveness
in service delivery may be considerably more complex than the operations
of a market mechanism.

A Case Study

To explore these questions further, we present the results of a case study of
St. Louis County, Missouri,[6] one of the more complex, jurisdictionally fragmented, metropolitan counties in the nation. A fast growing area of nearly 1
million people, the county has been jurisdictionally separate from the city of
St. Louis—itself a county under Missouri law—since 1876. Sixty percent of
county residents live in 91 municipalities (defined variously under Missouri
law as villages, third and fourth class cities, and home rule cities), but the
other 40 percent live in unincorporated areas.[7] The largest municipality has
approximately 55,000 people. The majority of those who live within municipal limits reside in cities of 10,000 or more population. Still, there are 23
municipalities with fewer than 1,000 residents and 71 with fewer than 10,000
residents. All those who live outside municipal boundaries, and most of those

who live in smaller municipalities, receive fire protection services from 25 independent fire protection districts. Public education is organized through 23 independent school districts and a countywide special district for special and vocational/technical education. Areawide special districts exist for water and sewer services and to support cultural facilities, such as museums and a zoo. There are also an undetermined number of organized subdivisions, both inside and outside municipalities, more than 400 of which provide their residents with local street services.

St. Louis County has been the focus of many reform recommendations, principally for consolidation of local governments.[8] Limited evidence from empirical studies of local service delivery suggests, however, that the county performs well with its present structure. Recent polls regarding resident assessments of services received from local governments found very high levels of satisfaction, with 80 to more than 90 percent favorably rating such key services as police and fire protection (Market Opinion Research 1982; Warren 1985; Research Corporation 1987). Summarizing results of a 1982 poll, a local citizens group stated that "it would be difficult to build a compelling case for governmental reform at the current time based on a need for general improvement of municipal service delivery capability through elimination of governmental fragmentation" (Spitzer 1982). Earlier research on police service effectiveness and responsiveness in the county found citizens there to be well served by their small- and medium-sized departments (E. Ostrom 1976).

For our case study, data were collected through personal interviews and from published and unpublished reports. Interviews, conducted mostly during the summer of 1986, included officials in more than a third of the county's municipalities and school districts (usually mayors and school superintendents) and county government officials. Published data sources included compilations by state and county departments and fiscal reports filed with the state auditor's office. Data were also collected from a sample of 53 organized subdivisions that provide street services in four municipalities.

Citizen Voice in St. Louis County

A number of mechanisms operate in St. Louis County to enhance the power of citizen voice. The most obvious is representation by a large number of elected officials, yielding very low citizen/elected-official ratios in the incorporated (more fragmented) portion of the county. Moreover, most elected officials are not full-time professionals but part-time citizen legislators and citizen mayors. Additional representation for citizen interests throughout the county is afforded by numerous overlying jurisdictions. In addition to representational mechanisms, citizens also participate directly in a number of collective and constitutive choices by means of petition and referendum. All tax and fee increases require citizen approval. Basic structural and jurisdictional choices pertaining to the organization of the county are also reserved to citizens. In this sense, metropolitan governance, conceived as the governance of relationships among multiple jurisdictions in a metropolitan area, is exercised directly by citizens.

Representation

A total of 729 municipal officials and 144 elementary and secondary school board members are separately elected in St. Louis County. This number results in citizen/elected-official ratios that are quite low, though variable by type and size of municipality. In all but two of the 26 villages and in many of the smaller fourth class cities, the ratio is less than 500 citizens for each elected official but never greater than 3,000. Among the larger third class and home rule cities, only two have citizen/elected-official ratios that exceed 5,000. County government presents a sharp contrast. The seven members of the county council must each represent some 140,000 constituents. For the incorporated area, this is additional representation, beyond that obtained from municipal officials, but for the unincorporated area, the difference is striking. Even in the unincorporated area, however, citizens separately elect school board members and fire protection district board members.

Citizens are unlikely to use voice in attempts to persuade or discipline political officials unless they have confidence that their voices will be heard. We posit that the likelihood of a citizen's voice being heard (and, more, carrying weight with public officials) is inversely proportional to the number of other voices to which an official attends. Small municipalities (and small school districts and fire protection districts) provide individual citizens with easily accessible local governments as a point of first recourse when problems arise and with a readily usable method of accountability in small local elections that keep the cost of challenging an incumbent relatively low. For individual citizens, representation and accountability are more costly in larger jurisdictions with higher citizen/elected-official ratios, where independent group organization on the part of constituents may be required to be effective.

Elected officials and bureau chiefs in county municipalities frequently referred to these low ratios during our interviews. They were virtually unanimous in asserting that they were highly constrained to be responsive to their citizenry, indeed to any individual citizen. Principal actors in attempts to incorporate remaining portions of the unincorporated county cited better representation as one of the motivations for their efforts. That is, they said they wanted decisions affecting local matters to be made locally, by officials directly accountable to those directly affected.

Citizen Mayors

A pervasive feature of local government in St. Louis County is reliance on part-time officials whose responsibilities are shouldered as a civic avocation, rather than as a political or professional career. Except for the county's largest city, Florissant, which has a full-time mayor, all of the county's municipalities have citizen mayors or village board chairmen, the majority of whom hold full-time jobs outside of local government or are retired. To be sure, the role of the mayor varies somewhat with the size of the municipality. The larger cities tend to employ a city manager or administrator who has day-to-day responsibility for administration. Smaller cities and villages tend to rely on a clerk for the same purpose.

For the smaller cities and villages, the use of part-time officials is a matter of economic necessity: the scale of operation does not warrant a full-time executive officer. The feasibility of using nonspecialists is enhanced by the tendency of the smallest units to contract out for the production of all, or nearly all, the services provided. The chief executive officer, instead of functioning as a supervisor, is more nearly a procurement officer for what amounts to a neighborhood.

Performance may be enhanced by the qualities that citizens bring to the office. Citizen officials are generally not careerists. Their interests are closer to the interests of an ordinary citizen, even if not identical. The potential gap between principal and agent in the relationship between citizens and officials is narrowed when a citizen rather than a professional is the chief official. In an important sense, however, citizen mayors are specialists. In addition to the fact that many are career professionals in their full-time occupation, citizen mayors are specialists in their own communities. The focus of their specialization is more on specific time-and-place information than on abstract knowledge, but the availability of such information is an important and scarce resource in the provision and production of public services. The close tie between information and responsibility, achieved in the work of citizen mayors, may contribute to the efficiency and effectiveness of local governments in fragmented metropolitan areas.

Part-time officials, we learned, also tend to schedule municipal meetings in evening hours or on weekends, when it is also more convenient for citizens to attend. This further enhances the accessibility of local officials in addition to low citizen/elected-official ratios.

The Use of Overlying Jurisdictions

Overlying or overlapping jurisdictions are often viewed as a source of duplication, confusion, and inefficiency, much like fragmentation. With the addition of jurisdictional overlays, however, a fragmented metropolitan area can address both common and diverse interests simultaneously. The use of a variety of overlying jurisdictions is, in fact, characteristic of highly fragmented metropolitan orders and is an important corrective for many of the deficiencies attributed to jurisdictional fragmentation. Without jurisdictional overlays, highly fragmented metropolitan areas could be more accurately characterized as "balkanized," unable to act jointly to address areawide concerns.

The major overlying jurisdiction in St. Louis County is county government. Two special districts—one for sewerage, another for a zoological park and museums—link St. Louis City and County. A countywide Special School District (overlying the 23 regular school districts in the county) provides for education of handicapped students and for vocational/technical education. The most significant subcounty districts are the 23 school districts and 25 fire protection districts, many of which overlie smaller municipalities but also cover all of the unincorporated area of the county. A number of municipalities also overlie privately organized subdivisions, more than 400 of which provide residential streets and a diverse array of street services.

Streets and highways provide a good illustration of how overlying jurisdictions function as complementary provision units. Residential streets are provided in most instances by subdivisions and small municipalities; collector streets, by municipalities; arterial streets, by county government; and major throughways, by the state. Specialized, not duplicate, provision is the basic feature of this arrangement. Various interests are represented in the process. Subdivisions and small municipalities tend to impose access restrictions that impede the flow of traffic through residential communities. County government, on the other hand, is oriented toward facilitating traffic flow and preempts municipal regulation on a countywide arterial road system.

Jurisdictions that vary in the scale of organization tend to serve somewhat different interests. Larger jurisdictions provide services, such as arterial streets, in response to preferences that reflect a wider community of interest. Smaller jurisdictions address concerns that are smaller in scale and affect a more limited community, such as the control of neighborhood streets. The use of overlying jurisdictions thus facilitates the use of voice to gain representation for a variety of shared interests.

To take another example, the St. Louis County Special School District serves more specialized concerns than do the county's 23 regular school districts. While preferences for general education may aggregate well on the basis of residential location, preferences for special education may not. Because of the considerably higher expenditure per pupil in special education, no school district has much incentive to specialize in this service. Residents therefore cannot expect to secure a response to their demands by relocating to particular school districts. A rational economic response is to discourage entry and encourage exit by neglecting special education. The alternative is to create an overlying jurisdiction that enhances the power of voice in behalf of special education. Provision for special education by a countywide district makes economic sense in a way that countywide provision for general education does not.

The use of overlying jurisdictions in fire services is somewhat different still. In the incorporated area of the county, fire protection districts overlie most smaller municipalities that, separately, could find it difficult to maintain a full-time fire company and station. In the unincorporated area, fire protection districts are a smaller scale alternative to provision by county government. The basic purpose, however, is the same throughout the county: to maintain local, community-based organizations to provide fire protection.

Tax Referenda

Notwithstanding the low citizen/elected-official ratios that characterize much of St. Louis County, the state constitution reserves to citizens the direct authority to approve all tax and fee increases. As an across-the-board requirement, this feature is new—instituted by the Hancock Amendment adopted by statewide initiative and referendum in 1983. Direct citizen participation in property and sales tax increases, however, has been a long-standing feature of Missouri local government, triggered whenever officials sought to increase rates beyond a statutory ceiling. The constitution now requires that all tax rate and fee increases be approved by a simple majority of voters, with state law frequently requiring two-thirds approval for property tax rates beyond the statutory limit.

These fiscal procedures cast local officials in the role of public entrepreneurs who must persuade voters that service levels justify tax and fee increases. Local officials clearly find tax referenda constraining, even though proposed increases are frequently approved. One professional administrator in a county municipality noted that local governments must search for ways to be more efficient in order to justify expenditures to citizens. Citizen voice, when exercised in this direct manner, can be more constraining than the potential for citizen exit.

Direct Citizen Governance

As in fiscal procedures, direct citizen choice is maintained for the fundamental issues that bear upon metropolitan governance. The creation and dissolution of municipalities and special districts, the annexation of new territory and consolidation of jurisdictions, and amendments to the county charter—all require approval by citizens voting in a referendum. In particular, consolidation requires approval by concurrent simple majorities in the jurisdictions affected,[9] and annexation requires approval by a simple majority of voters in the area to be annexed. These rules place the basic responsibility for metropolitan governance directly in the hands of local citizens. Instead of thinking of fragmented metropolitan areas as ungoverned on an areawide basis—because of their not being governed by a single metropolitan government—we propose that metropolitan governance be viewed as a constitutional order, one in which citizens make the basic constitutional choices that create and modify local jurisdictions.

It is the constitutional order that enables local citizens to preserve and maintain the representational mechanisms, including low citizen/elected-official ratios and part-time mayors, that enhance citizen voice in the everyday affairs of local governments. The constitutional order in St. Louis County includes a capability on the part of citizens to say "no" to comprehensive reform proposals that would greatly reduce the total number of locally elected officials and make local accountability more costly to citizens. In this century, county citizens have rejected proposals that would merge St. Louis City and County to establish a single metropolitan government (1926) and, alternatively, to create a two-tier system embracing both city and county (1959).

At the same time, citizens of St. Louis County have said "yes" a number of times to proposals that build upon and extend the basic system in place. These occasions include not only a number of municipal incorporations but also the creation of countywide and wider (including St. Louis City) special purpose districts—for special education, sewers, a zoo, museum, and transportation. These proposals led to a greater concentration of authority to act in limited functional areas, but did not erode the power of citizen voice by consolidating the primary units in which local citizens act.

From 1960 to 1983, municipal incorporation and annexation were largely at a standstill. At the same time, the county continued to grow at a rapid rate, giving rise to a substantial unincorporated population, reaching a high of 40 percent of the county population in the mid-1980s. This pattern was an extreme contrast to the steady pattern of municipal incorporation that occurred in the 1940s and 1950s. Two factors seem to account for the difference. First, municipal incorporation became unnecessary to obtain local public goods and services. Fire protection could be obtained from fire protection districts, water from a private water company, sewers from a metropolitan sewer district, and police services from the county police department, separated from the county sheriff by amendment to the county charter and supported from taxes collected only in the unincorporated area. County roads, other than the countywide arterial system, were also supported from taxes earmarked for the unincorporated area. Planning and zoning were also available from county government. Second, county government exercised what amounted to a veto over proposed municipal annexations in court. County officials were thus able to protect themselves from service competition by existing municipalities.

In 1983, the state supreme court removed the county government's de facto veto power and thereby exposed county officials to potential competition. In an ensuing flurry of annexation proposals, more have been defeated by voters in areas proposed for annexation than have been approved. The rule change, however, coincided with renewed interest in municipal incorporation, driven by mounting citizen concern over the lifestyle effects of rapid commercial development. Two new midsize cities have recently been created in high-growth areas. Citizens continue to voice their preference for the relatively high levels of representation available through municipal organization.

The total number of municipalities in the county reached a high of 98 in 1959. Since then, citizens have approved limited municipal consolidations on nine occasions, principally involving the merger of small villages with somewhat larger neighboring municipalities. Clearly, consolidation rules based on citizen initiative and consent do not preclude consolidation.

Enabling citizens to make constitutional choices by creating (and occasionally abolishing) local governments at their own initiative involves much more than obtaining the "consent of the governed." Such an arrangement directly taps the creative energies of citizens; it allows those most directly affected by local public problems to take constitutive action to address those problems. Instead of petitioning "the government" to take action, citizens can literally create their own government. The radical democratic nature of such a system has been little appreciated.

A Local Government Constitution

The constitutional powers of citizens to create and modify local governments derive from a body of rules provided by enabling legislation found in state law or the state constitution. The constitutional order of a metropolitan area can thus be sorted into two levels of choice: (1) an enabling level that provides a body of rules by which local government units are created with limited authority to act (e.g., procedures for municipal incorporation); and (2) a chartering level at which local citizens use the powers created at the first level to select and form local government units. Both levels perform constitutional functions; both involve a choice of rules for making rules, a means of governing the processes of government.

It is useful to think of the whole body of enabling rules affecting a metropolitan area as a "local government constitution," that is, as an interdependent configuration of rules, even though the elements of the set may be derived from more than one legal source. Each rule is then understood in its relation to other rules that apply to closely related actions. Four principal subsets can be distinguished: (1) *rules of association*, enabling local citizens to create specific types of local units with general or specific powers; (2) *fis-*

cal rules, authorizing local units to raise specific types of revenue; (3) *boundary-adjustment rules*, especially annexation rules, allowing for adjustments in the boundaries of local units; and (4) *interjurisdictional rules*, especially contracting rules, allowing separate jurisdictions to enter into joint agreement and create joint arrangements.

The local government constitution for St. Louis County is unique to the county. Some aspects derive from provisions of the state constitution; others, from statewide provisions of general law. Its uniqueness, however, derives from the use of "special legislation" by the Missouri legislature—legislation that, in effect, applies only to St. Louis County. This device allows the county delegation to the state legislature, composed of seven senators and 31 representatives, all elected from separate districts, to obtain modification of the enabling rules that pertain to local government uniquely for St. Louis County. The members of the local delegation become, in effect, a mechanism of constitutional decision making with respect to the local government constitution. Despite its formal rooting in state law, the local government constitution is primarily a product of local decision-making processes. The county delegation to the legislature mainly implements local agreements reached among local actors. A number of multijurisdictional associations serve as forums for voicing diverse interests and negotiating a local consensus. Members of the local legislative delegation frequently appear as guests before these groups.

Legislative deference to a local delegation tends to work only when the local delegation is in substantial agreement. Substantial agreement among members of the local delegation can only be reached when there is substantial agreement among citizens in respective constituencies. This requirement biases decision making toward reaching consensus, as opposed to putting together a minimum winning coalition. Negotiation organized by voluntary associations of local governments and officials becomes the favored method of conflict resolution.[10]

The St. Louis County Municipal League—representing nearly all cities and villages in the county—is the broadest of these groups. It is supplemented by an organization representing Mayors of Large Cities and a newly organized group, Mayors of Small Cities. Proposed adjustments in the local government constitution are debated intensely within these organizations. Substantial consensus among affected groups, though not unanimity, is the prevailing norm for obtaining a modification in the fundamental rules of local government.

In the realm of public education, the Cooperating School Districts of the Greater St. Louis Area serves a purpose similar to the Municipal League. Professional associations in other functional areas, especially police and fire, also function as forums for the maintenance and adjustment of basic rules in their respective fields. The East-West Gateway Coordinating Council and Bi-State Development Corporation afford forums for discussions of issues extending beyond the boundaries of St. Louis County to include the City of St. Louis and other counties in Missouri and Illinois.

Subcounty forums exist for the purpose of considering issues of more limited joint interest. The mayors of adjacent or nearby municipalities often share information and discuss issues of common concern. One of the most developed groups is the Normandy Municipal Council, composed of a number of small fourth-class cities and villages that lie in close proximity to one another. A small council staff is headed by a director who supplies members with information about county, state, and federal programs and policies and with planning support.

Metropolitan governance in St. Louis County is organized through an elaborate set of arrangements. A multilevel process is used to amplify and sustain the power of voice. A local government constitution consisting of a body of enabling rules is maintained through the work of voluntary associations of local governments and the election of a county delegation to the state legislature. The enabling rules vest authority for creating and modifying units of local government in citizens, who use their authority to preserve a set of local jurisdictions that maintain low citizen/elected-official ratios.

A system that depends so heavily on voice will tend to be "noisy." Conflict is an essential precondition of meaningful consensus. If conflicts cannot be resolved at one level, however, they may be more amenable to settlement at another level. The reference is not to the so-called levels of government but to multiple levels of choice that produce rule sets nested within other rule sets. Having reference to constitutional choice creates a capability to change the basic "rules of the game." In the constitutional order found in St. Louis County, at least three levels of choice are available, two of which are constitutional. Not only does this structural feature enhance the conflict-resolution capabilities of the system, it also enables local citizens within a variety of communities to maintain considerable leverage in relation to local officials.

Public Entrepreneurship

Citizen voice, while a basic feature of complex metropolitan organization, does not tell the whole story. Like exit, voice functions mainly, though not exclusively, as a *constraint* on the conduct of local officials. Missing from the story, thus far, is the exercise of *initiative* by these same local officials. Without continuing sources of initiative from public officials, a local government system could not maintain a position of relative efficiency.

Organizational innovations, especially those that involve multiple jurisdictions, emerge from discussions and negotiation—processes that enable individuals to discern common interests among diverse communities. Innovation is therefore costly, especially in terms of time and effort. Some individuals must be willing to incur those costs if a complex metropolitan area is to function effectively. This is the work of individuals we call "public entrepreneurs" namely, persons who propose ideas and carry the burden of ensuring discussion, compromise, and creative settlement.

The opportunity to exercise initiative is the key to entrepreneurship, which tends to increase, therefore, with the number of possible sources of initiative. Counting the number of elected officials, police chiefs, fire chiefs, school superintendents, directors of public works, and city administrators or managers yields a rough measure of the potential for public entrepreneurship in a metropolitan area.[11] Public entrepreneurship is frequently exercised in the context of a professional association in St. Louis County. Such organizations as the Board of Governors of the Law Enforcement Officials of the Greater St. Louis Area, the Greater St. Louis Fire Chiefs' Association, the Cooperating School Districts of the Greater St. Louis Area, and the county chapter of the American Public Works Association facilitate the work of public entrepreneurs—and thus hold down their cost—by bringing relevant parties together on a regular basis. Local elected officials, working bilaterally and through the auspices of their multijurisdictional forums, also engage in entrepreneurial activities that link their jurisdictions.

Public entrepreneurship can be understood as a response to citizen voice. Public entrepreneurs, like private entrepreneurs, seek to build enterprises that can survive and grow. To do so, a private entrepreneur must relate both to a product market where consumers make the critical decisions and to a factor market where a combination of individual factor owners and firms makes the critical decisions. In a complex metropolitan area, a public entrepreneur is in a similar position. To succeed, he or she must relate both to a set of primary local jurisdictions in which citizens make the critical decisions and to a multijurisdictional environment in which other public agents make the critical decisions. Private entrepreneurship without the constraint of the marketplace is dysfunctional; it leads to monopoly power and the sacrifice of consumer interests. Public entrepreneurship without the effective constraint of citizen voice may be similarly dysfunctional.

With citizen voice as a basic constraint, public entrepreneurship is efficiency enhancing. In order to win voter approval, public entrepreneurs must strive to offer more and better services at lower cost. They seek changes in multiorganizational arrangements that enable them to do more for less. The efficiency-inducing properties of a metropolitan order lead not to a single, most efficient pattern of organization but to a continual search for more efficient ways to perform. This is a dynamic of metropolitan organization that is clearly operative in St. Louis County.

Emergent Properties of Metropolitan Organization

Public entrepreneurship generates emergent properties of metropolitan organization (V. Ostrom 1987), not determined by the jurisdictional structure but allowed as possibilities. Some possibilities tend to be foreclosed. Thus, uniform patterns of service delivery, long sought after by metropolitan reformers, tend to be foreclosed by a metropolitan order based on citizen choice. When allowed to choose, citizens in different communities and circumstances tend to make different trade-offs among competing values and, thus, arrive at different jurisdictional choices that lead, in turn, to different functional arrangements. The overall result of citizen choice is often characterized as an organizational "patchwork" inasmuch as different communities arrange for the delivery of similar services in different ways. These alternative arrangements comprise the emergent properties of complex metropolitan organization.

The configuration of arrangements can be analyzed with the aid of a distinction between the *provision* and *production* of local public services (V. Ostrom, Tiebout, and Warren 1961). Provision refers to taxing and spending decisions, determining appropriate types of service and levels of supply, and arranging for and monitoring production. Production denotes the transformation of inputs into outputs. A political unit organized to provide a public service need not necessarily produce the service. A local provision unit can organize its own production unit—a bureau of the local government, for example—but it can also purchase service from an external producer or enter into a joint service arrangement with other provision units.

Different criteria apply to the organization of provision than to the organization of production. This suggests the possibility that highly interdependent local public economies, composed of an array of provision and production units, may be more efficient than a set of general purpose jurisdictions in the organization of metropolitan areas (see U.S. ACIR 1987). Among the efficiency-enhancing characteristics of a local public economy that we observed in St. Louis County are the use of functional ties and overlays, as well as service contracting—both intergovernmental and private.

Functional Ties and Overlays

Multiple jurisdictions in a metropolitan area tend to create numerous organizational ties and overlays that are useful in the production and delivery of services. Economies of scale for particular components of service production (e.g., communications or training) often make joint production arrangements economically attractive. St. Louis County is the locus of many such cooperative ventures organized in every sector of public service. State law authorizes units of local government to enter into joint agreements and to create joint production units, subject only to the constraint that the jurisdictions involved be separately authorized to provide the service in question. Many of the ties and overlays that link jurisdictions in the county also extend to the city of St. Louis and to jurisdictions in other counties in the larger metropolitan area.

Police services offer a number of examples. An areawide Major Case Squad is a functional overlay that draws investigators from many different police departments to bring personnel and expertise to bear upon serious crimes in any community. A countywide "Code 1000" plan provides rapid mobilization and deployment of officers from multiple jurisdictions in the event of natural or man-made disasters, civil or labor disturbances, or other occurrences requiring a large number of officers. The St. Louis County Police and Fire Training Academy, another functional overlay, supplies recruit training for all police in the county.[12] The Regional Justice Information System maintains a computerized database for police related matters, affording online access to police dispatchers and access to State of Missouri and FBI databases. An areawide 911 system of call-for-service routing and dispatching is operated as a joint venture by municipal departments and the county police. On less than an areawide scale, numerous joint operations are undertaken for police dispatch and sharing of investigative officers. In addition, functional ties involving mutual aid among patrol officers crossing jurisdictional lines are found throughout the county.

Fire protection also exhibits substantial coordinated service production. Mutual aid agreements, linking all of the municipal and fire district departments in the county,[13] ensure needed backup capability to respond in high demand circumstances, such as large or numerous fires. Many of these mutual aid agreements contain "first response" provisions that delimit areas within one jurisdiction where a fire company from an adjoining jurisdiction will respond immediately to a fire call. First response is a particularly valuable functional tie that adds considerable flexibility to service delivery boundaries, minimizing response times. The fire departments, together with county police departments, maintain a joint recruit training program. Joint fire and emergency vehicle dispatch centers serve several departments, enhancing mutual aid capabilities and increasing the deployment of personnel for fire prevention and suppression activities.

In education, a number of functional overlays have been created by consortia of elementary and secondary education producers. The Cooperating School Districts of the Greater St. Louis Area supplies its members with audiovisual services, data processing, and joint purchasing of supplies and equipment, as well as a forum in which to develop and lobby for educational programs that require state action. The Regional Consortium for Education and Technology supplies members with computer technology, software, training, and maintenance. The Special School District of St. Louis County engages in coordinated service delivery for "mainstream" students who require special education. Special District teachers work in the classrooms of each of the county's 23 regular public school districts. Coordination also occurs in the diagnosis and evaluation of students for special education programs. County school districts have joined with the St. Louis City district to create the Voluntary Inter-District Coordinating Council to implement a desegregation plan linking city and county schools.

Highly coordinated activity is less important in some service areas than others. Street services, for example, exhibit more "alternation" than coordination. Alternation refers to a type of mutual adjustment among service providers or producers in which different organizations divide up service responsibility according to area, clientele, or time period. In this way, street responsibilities are divided among county government, municipalities, and organized subdivisions. Private contracting tends to be more important than intergovernmental cooperation in street services, although some equipment sharing does occur, especially among smaller municipalities. The local chapter of the American Public Works Association organizes an annual joint purchase of road salt.

Coordinated service production substantially reduces the "duplication of effort" that is frequently cited as one bane of fragmentation. Although economies of scale in the production of some service components (e.g., the dispatch of emergency units) would indicate wasteful duplication were each governmental unit to attempt to "go it alone," cooperative arrangements have been created to address most such circumstances in St. Louis County. Obvious and significant duplication is hard to find. Coordination and alternation are much more common. Functional ties and overlays are found in precisely those areas of service production where one might expect duplication.[14]

From our examination of St. Louis County, we conclude that highly fragmented systems of local government need not be synonymous with duplication. Moreover, coordinated service production in St. Louis County minimizes duplication while enhancing backup capabilities through redundancy. Duplication is a characteristic of service *delivery* and is rightly considered wasteful and inefficient. Redundancy, on the other hand, is a characteristic of service *capacity* and, within limits, serves to enhance efficiency. Coordinated service production seeks to avoid duplication while it builds redundancy.

Private and Intergovernmental Contracting

Intergovernmental contracts reduce the number of production units for most services in St. Louis County well below the number of provision units.

Ninety-one jurisdictions, including county government, have authority to provide police services, for example, and 90 of these jurisdictions actually make some provision for local police. The total number of police departments—those units that produce policing—however, is substantially smaller. Sixty-three municipalities and the county government have organized full-time police departments. Two more municipalities maintain part-time departments. Twenty-four municipalities that make provision for police services have not organized their own police departments. Seventeen of these 24 enter into contracts with adjoining municipalities, while seven contract with the county police. Ninety provision units are served by 66 production units.

Does this indicate that the number of provision units might just as well be 66 as 90? Not at all, no more than it indicates a need for 90 police departments. Different criteria apply to the organization of provision than to the organization of production. Provision units are based upon the way in which individual preferences for services cluster in neighborhoods. Production units are organized to capture limited economies of scale and utilize a more specialized division of labor. The two sets of criteria need not coincide. Provision units that choose to contract out for production are not inactive. They may be very active as providers. A degree of competition on the production side gives provision units some capacity to choose from among alternative producers. Evidence of this sort of "shopping" is found in St. Louis County policing, as municipalities occasionally shift contracts from one production unit to another. Local officials in a provision-only unit function as procurement officers, representing citizen-consumer interests. Their job is not to supervise a production unit but to evaluate its performance and remain alert to alternative sources of service supply.

In street services, separation of provision and production is also pronounced, but the independent production units tend to be private firms. Virtually all subdivisions and most small municipalities contract out for nearly all street services. Some subdivisions contract with an overlapping municipality for particular street services (e.g., snow removal or sweeping). Although we did not collect data on private producers of local street services, the number of independent provision units and relatively limited economies of scale in most street services would point to the likelihood of a highly competitive market.

An interesting result of the partial separation of provision from production that occurs in St. Louis County is the existence of a number of "pure" (or nearly pure) provision units—small municipalities that organize little or none of their own production activities but instead contract for an array of local services. Street services may be contracted with one or more private suppliers, police with an adjacent municipality, refuse collection with a private firm, and so forth. Orthodox public administration literature has treated such units as nonperforming and nonviable,[15] but this view neglects the distinction between provision and production. Anthony Downs has argued, for example, that pure provision units offer distinct advantages, insofar as the presence of production units organized by a provision unit might distort planning and procurement decisions, introducing a producer's bias that may inhibit the representation of citizen consumer interests (Downs 1976; chap. 12). From this perspective, small local governments enhance citizen voice in three ways: (1) maintaining low citizen/elected-official ratios for the purpose of representation; (2) relying upon part-time citizen mayors or village chairmen; and (3) contracting out for service production, adding further assurance that local officials represent consumer, not producer, interests.

Mayors and village chairmen of small municipalities in St. Louis County reported a high level of provisioning activity, especially in those cases of pure provision. Even in the many provision units that had chosen self-production, with their own bureaus for service production, officials frequently indicated awareness of and appreciation for the alternatives afforded them by a separation of provision and production. Without using these terms, they recognized that the availability of alternative suppliers of local services—adjoining municipalities, the county, and private firms—gave them additional leverage when negotiating budgets and service delivery expectations with their own bureau chiefs. The alternative of contracting out local service production, they said, kept local producers "on their toes."

Conclusion

It seems unlikely that the efficiency effects found in complex metropolitan areas can be attributed primarily to competition among local governments for residents. Constraints on citizen exit are too great to give individual citizens significant leverage with local officials. An alternative possibility is that citizen voice serves as the primary mechanism for translating jurisdictional fragmentation and overlap into relatively efficient outcomes.

The reliance on citizen voice in St. Louis County is pervasive and fundamental. Low citizen/elected-official ratios coupled with the use of part-time citizen mayors enable citizens to gain easy access to local government decision making. A local government constitution, such as that found in St. Louis County, further amplifies the power of citizen voice in local governance. Local citizens can, on their own initiative, create, modify, or abolish local governments; hold the purse strings of local government by exercising a veto over tax rate increases in local referenda; approve or disapprove expansions in the boundaries of local units; and, through their elected local officials, enter into mutually productive relationships with citizens in neighboring and overlapping jurisdictions.

Unlike a private economy, a local public economy depends more upon voice than upon entry and exit to activate and constrain the system. Public entrepreneurs are given both incentive and opportunity in this context to configure and reconfigure productive organizational and interorganizational arrangements. The interaction that occurs between citizen voice and public entrepreneurship can explain the efficiency-inducing properties of complex metropolitan areas and may be essential to the preservation of local democratic governance in an age of complexity.

NOTES

1. Earlier, U.S. ACIR had characterized metropolitan governance as "a jungle of competing, overlapping" jurisdictions. See U.S. ACIR 1976.

2. One practice that would introduce an immediate cash drawer effect is frequent reappraisal of property. This could conceivably create a shadow market for local governments—one that would not depend on exit. Frequent reappraisal, however, is not widespread. One reason may be the large number of factors, other than the value of local government services less the tax-price, that affect real estate prices. Frequent reappraisal may be a device more conducive to frequent increases in revenue, without having to increase rates, than to the disciplining of local government officials.

3. There is at least one exception to the weakness of market discipline induced by homeowner entry and exit. If the supply of housing can be easily expanded within existing jurisdictions, the number of homeowners can be increased, with an immediate impact on local government revenues. When a municipality has undeveloped territory (or enjoys unilateral annexation powers in relation to adjacent undeveloped territory), the entry decisions of housing developers (who act to some extent as agents for future residents) have an immediate cash drawer effect, increasing the total assessed valuation of a local jurisdiction. The prospect of growth, therefore, exerts a competitive pressure directly on local government officials. This special case, however, contains a bias: new development may be favored over the maintenance of existing residential amenities. Exit by property owners whose capital is mobile is another exception in which there is an immediate effect on revenues.

4. The effect of community services on property values may in fact lead individual property owners to act more as "citizens" concerned in general about their community than simply as "consumers" concerned about the delivery of services to themselves alone. The effect of the real estate market is, perhaps paradoxically, to create a community of interests—a pure (though local) public good. The expression of that community of interest, through voice, is the critical link between property values and municipal government.

5. Yet surely, it might be argued, if homeowners can see the long-term importance of maintaining property values, so can officials. If officials and citizens share the same incentives, both are constrained by the local real estate market. However, by itself, the real estate market cannot supply local officials with selective incentives to

serve the long-term interests of their community if individual officers can derive selective benefits, in the short run, from self-serving strategies.

6. For a full discussion of the study see U.S. ACIR 1988.

7. In July 1988 the number of municipalities increased by one with the incorporation of Chesterfield, a new city of approximately 33,000 residents. Our research was conducted in 1986 and 1987, and our discussion in this article refers to local government in the county prior to this incorporation.

8. A Metropolitan Board of Freeholders, constituted under a provision of the state constitution designed to provide the city and county of St. Louis with a way to adjust their relationship, is presently considering reform recommendations for the county developed by the local citizens group, Confluence St. Louis, and St. Louis County's Department of Planning. The proposals, if approved by voters in both the city and the county, would reduce the number of municipalities in the county by more than half.

9. An exception to this requirement is the "reorganization" of school districts, a procedure that requires approval by only a majority of all voters within the proposed new set of boundaries.

10. For an example of this process at work, illustrating the role of the County Municipal League as a forum for reaching local consensus, see the discussion of the county sales tax formula in Brasfield 1987.

11. Not that each one is an entrepreneur, but the greater is the potential to exercise initiative, the more likely entrepreneurship becomes. In a more consolidated system one could expect lesser exercise of public entrepreneurship. Where bureau chiefs in smaller jurisdictions may be in a position to be entrepreneurial, subordinate commanders in larger bureaucracies rarely are. The smaller number of public officials in more consolidated systems, too, reduces the potential for public entrepreneurship.

12. Establishment of this academy in 1987 replaced a previous arrangement, the Greater St. Louis Police Training Academy, that, prior to establishment of the county academy, trained officers from the city of St. Louis as well as all municipal and county police.

13. These agreements extend to include fire companies in surrounding counties and, recently, to include the fire department of the city of St. Louis.

14. Moreover, a statistical search for remaining, uncaptured economies of scale turned up only very slight possible scale economies in police and fire services, and no significant economies for municipal services in general. See the discussion in U.S. ACIR 1988 (chap. 8).

15. See, for example, U.S. ACIR 1982 (446–48). The commission has recently changed its view with respect to viability criteria for local governments, recognizing that pure provision units may have a valid role to play. See U.S. ACIR 1987 (55), where the commission rescinded its earlier recommendation on this topic.

REFERENCES

Brasfield, James M. 1987. "Follow the Money: Fiscal Structure and Metropolitan Reorganization in St. Louis County." Paper presented at the annual meeting of the American Political Science Association, Chicago, August.

Chicoine, David L., and Norman Walzer. 1985. *Governmental Structure and Local Public Finance.* Boston: Oelgeschlager, Gunn & Hain.

DiLorenzo, Thomas J. 1983. "Economic Competition and Political Competition: An Empirical Note." *Public Choice* 40:203–9.

Downs, Anthony. 1976. *Urban Problems and Prospects.* Chicago: Rand McNally.

Hirschman, Albert O. 1970. *Exit, Voice, and Loyalty: Responses to Decline in Firms, Organizations, and States.* Cambridge, MA: Harvard University Press.

Market Opinion Research. 1982. *Public Opinion on Governmental Reorganization Alternatives for St. Louis City and County with Recommendations for Change.* Detroit, MI: Market Opinion Research.

Ostrom, Elinor. 1976. "Size and Performance in a Federal System." *Publius: The Journal of Federalism* 6 (spring): 33–73. (Chapter 10 in this volume.)

Ostrom, Vincent. 1987. "Constitutional Foundations for a Theory of System Comparisons: An Inquiry into Problems of Incommensurabilities, Emergent Properties, and Development." Paper presented at the Radein Research Seminar, Redagon, Italy, February 14–25.

Ostrom, Vincent, Charles M. Tiebout, and Robert Warren. 1961. "The Organization of Government in Metropolitan Areas: A Theoretical Inquiry." *American Political Science Review* 55 (December): 831–42. (Chapter 1 in this volume.)

Parks, Roger B. 1985. "Metropolitan Structure and Systemic Performance: The Case of Police Service Delivery." In *Policy Implementation in Federal and Unitary States*, ed. K. Hanf and T. A. J. Toonen, 161–91. Dordrecht, the Netherlands: Martinus Nijhoff.

Research Corporation. 1987. Poll conducted for the local citizens group, Citizens to Streamline Government. In *St. Louis Post Dispatch*, Friday, November 27.

Schneider, Mark. 1986. "Fragmentation and the Growth of Local Government." *Public Choice* 48:255–63.

Spitzer, Dana L. 1982. *Fostering Development in Metropolitan St. Louis.* St. Louis: City-County Task Force, Civic Progress.

Tiebout, Charles M. 1956. "A Pure Theory of Local Expenditures." *Journal of Political Economy* 64 (October): 416–24.

U.S. Advisory Commission on Intergovernmental Relations (U.S. ACIR). 1976. *Improving Urban America: A Challenge to Federalism.* Washington, DC: ACIR.

———. 1982. *State and Local Roles in the Federal System.* Washington, DC: ACIR.

———. 1987. *The Organization of Local Public Economies, A-109.* Washington, DC: ACIR.

———. 1988. *Metropolitan Organization: The St. Louis Case.* Washington, DC: ACIR.

Wagner, Richard E., and Warren E. Weber. 1975. "Competition, Monopoly, and the Organization of Government in Metropolitan Areas." *Journal of Law and Economics* 18 (December): 661–84.

Warren, Kenneth F. 1985. *KTVIs Survey on Metropolitan Consolidation: A Summary Report.* St. Louis: KTVI.

CHAPTER 14

Fiscal, Service, and Political Impacts
of Indianapolis–Marion County's Unigov

William Blomquist and Roger B. Parks

Urban reformers have long advocated various forms of metropolitan government, including city-county consolidation, to remedy problems faced by central cities in the United States. Contemporary authors, such as David Rusk
and Neal Pierce, recommend merger of central cities with suburbs as the way
to help the cities and enhance the governance and economy of their regions.

What are the implications of city-county consolidation for central cities in
the United States? Our review of the Unigov experience in Indianapolis–
Marion County, Indiana, suggests that the benefits of consolidation—in terms
of urban service delivery, public finance, and citizen participation and especially the distribution of these benefits—depend critically on specific details
of how a consolidation is designed and implemented by policymakers. There
is evidence that central-city Indianapolis has enjoyed few financial or service
delivery advantages, and a considerable loss of political influence, under
Unigov.

Background

Beginning early in this century, urban development extended beyond the city
of Indianapolis into outlying areas of Marion County, Indiana. By the 1940s,
the city was losing residents to suburban communities.

Annexation of these developing areas was possible legally but difficult
practically. In all but a few cases, suburban Marion County residents chose to
incorporate their own communities or to remain unincorporated rather than
be annexed to Indianapolis. Suburbanites did not need annexation in order to
procure direct public services, such as police and fire protection or elementary and secondary education, because they already received these from
county or township government, special districts, or their incorporated mu-

Originally published in *Publius: The Journal of Federalism* 25, no. 4 (fall 1995): 37–54.
Reprinted by permission of *Publius* and the authors.

Authors' note: The authors appreciate comments received on an earlier version of this
manuscript from Richard L. Cole, Daniel J. Elazar, John Kincaid, and an anonymous reviewer.

nicipality. Annexation also offered little advantage for improving capital-intensive services, such as water and sewer systems or road construction and maintenance, because of restrictive state limitations on municipal debt.

Instead, certain urban public services were extended across Marion County through the creation of separate municipal corporations, governed by boards of directors. This option facilitated the production of capital-intensive public services because each municipal corporation could borrow up to its own 2 percent debt limit. Several such corporations were created between the mid-1940s and the mid-1960s by special acts of the Indiana General Assembly.[1] By 1967, the U.S. Census of Governments recorded 60 governments within Marion County: the county, 23 cities and towns, nine townships, 11 school districts, and 16 special-purpose governments.

These special-purpose municipal corporations extended the service and taxing areas for several local government functions. However, each corporation was governed by a different appointed board. Most of the boards had some positions appointed by the mayor of Indianapolis, some by the Indianapolis City Council, and some by the Marion County Council and/or the county commissioners. Board members served staggered terms under vague provisions or no provisions for removal. Local voters could replace their city council members, mayor, county council members, and county commissioners if they wished, but doing so did not necessarily change the governance of the local government services supplied by special-purpose districts. On paper, the city of Indianapolis had a strong mayor-council form of municipal government; in practice, neither the mayor nor the council directed the administration of several key services.

Partisan politics exacerbated the dispersion of authority. The Democratic party usually controlled the Indianapolis city government; Democrats won the mayor's office and council majorities in three of the four municipal elections from 1951 through 1963. Republicans typically controlled the Marion County government; Republicans held majorities of the county council and county commissioner seats in all but one of the elections in even-numbered years from 1950 through 1964. Thus, any proposal to enlarge the control of either city or county government over local government services encountered partisan opposition in addition to the usual inertia characteristic of institutional arrangements.

Local political events from 1966 through 1968 changed the partisan context of local government dramatically. A reform group calling itself the Republican Action Committee, composed largely of young professionals from the private sector, overthrew the Marion County Republican party leadership in the 1966 primary elections and swept all county offices on the ballot in the fall. The Republican Action Committee was committed to contesting the upcoming municipal elections in 1967 more vigorously. One of its leaders, Dr.

Beurt SerVaas, became chairman of the Marion County Council and treasurer of the Marion County Republican party and set to work recruiting a Republican candidate for the mayor's race. Richard Lugar, a young businessman and member of the Indianapolis school board, agreed to run for the office.

An unforeseen split in the Marion County Democratic party in 1967 aided Lugar's cause. The Democratic party county chairman, James Beatty, chose to run against his own party's incumbent mayor, John Barton, for the nomination. The contest divided local Democrats, and a renominated but badly weakened Mayor Barton lost to Lugar by 9,000 votes. At the time, Indianapolis used an at-large system for electing the city council; so, as usual, the party that won the mayor's office carried a majority of the council seats, too.

Early in 1968, SerVaas, Lugar, and Thomas Hasbrook (the Indianapolis City Council president), Republican Action Committee chairman John Burkhardt, Marion County Republican party chairman Keith Bulen, and a few others from the Republican Action Committee began informal and private discussions about the possibility of reorganizing local government along the lines of the city-county consolidations in Nashville–Davidson County, Tennessee, and in Jacksonville–Duval County, Florida. Later in the year, their ideas for government reorganization became public when Lugar created a 40-member Government Reorganization Task Force, with county-council president SerVaas and city-council president Hasbrook as its cochairs. An additional 11-member task force of local attorneys was created to explore means for consolidating city and county government within the confines of Indiana law.

In November 1968, the Republicans swept the rest of the county government offices and also won control of the governor's office and majorities in both chambers of the Indiana legislature. The resulting partisan alignment—Republican control of city, county, and state government—presented an unusual opportunity to reorganize the structure of local government in Marion County without the partisan divisions common to Indiana. The lawyers' task force produced a draft bill to change the Indianapolis city charter, to be introduced in the state legislature when it convened in January 1969.

In the 1969 legislative session, the General Assembly voted essentially along party lines to pass a Republican-sponsored bill consolidating some of the elective offices of the city and county, bringing some of the special-purpose corporations and their functions under the control of those consolidated offices and absorbing several of the separately incorporated suburban communities within Marion County. The new government structure was called "Unigov," short for "unified government."

Unigov consolidated political leadership in Marion County to a considerable degree. A Unigov mayor is elected countywide for renewable four-year terms. A 29-member city-county council replaced the county council and city council. Unigov created six principal departments of city-county government that absorbed the functions of some of the special-purpose corporations.[2]

However, four incorporated municipalities—Beech Grove, Lawrence, Southport, and Speedway—were excluded from the Unigov structure, as were six of the special-purpose corporations and all of the local school districts, township fire departments, township property-assessment and poor-relief functions, the Marion County court system, and the separately elected Marion County offices (which are specified in the Indiana Constitution).

Local Government Structure in Marion County

Although the "Unigov" nickname stands for "unified government," Marion County retains 50 separate local governments (down from 60 in 1967), and the number of separate taxing units in the county has grown since 1970. In some respects, the Unigov structure is more complicated than the structure it replaced in 1969.

The Unigov legislative body is the city-county council. Twenty-five of the city-county councilors represent single-member districts; four more are elected at large. All city-county councilors are elected every four years, during municipal elections held the year before presidential election years. There is no limit on the number of terms city-county councilors may serve.

The Unigov executive branch is headed by the mayor, elected county-wide at the same time as the council. The mayor appoints deputy mayors (with responsibilities for certain policy or programmatic areas), the directors of the Unigov departments, and the heads of some of the divisions within departments, subject to confirmation by the city-county council. The mayor also appoints members of several boards and commissions.

Six special-purpose municipal corporations remain outside the direct governance of the mayor and council: the Capital Improvements Board, the City-County Building Authority, the Health and Hospital Corporation of Marion County, the Indianapolis Airport Authority, the Indianapolis Public Transportation Corporation, and the Indianapolis-Marion County Public Library. These units come under the indirect control of the mayor and council in two ways: their governing boards are appointed according to different formulas by the mayor and council (or county officials), and their budgets are subject to varying degrees of review by the mayor and council.

In addition to the Unigov structure, Marion County government continues to exist, with separately elected offices of assessor, auditor, clerk, coroner, prosecutor, recorder, sheriff, surveyor, and treasurer. The Marion County Board of Voter Registration and the Marion County Election Board also retain separate existence. The Marion County assessor, auditor, and treasurer now serve ex officio (and without additional pay) as the Marion

County commissioners.

The Unigov structure also does not include the Marion County court system. The jurisdictions and judicial selection processes of the Marion County Circuit Court, municipal courts, small claims courts, and superior court were not affected, except that the budget for the court system is subject to review by the city-county council.

Marion County's nine townships (see fig. 14.1) continue as separate governments, with separately elected township assessors, constables, and trustees. The nine township trustees still administer poor relief within their respective jurisdictions. The eight townships around the outside of Marion County (i.e., excluding Center Township) remain the territorial basis for eight volunteer fire departments and for eight of the county's 11 public school districts (the other three being Indianapolis Public Schools and school systems in the city of Beech Grove and the town of Speedway).

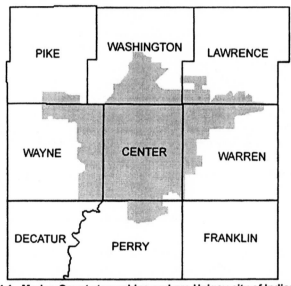

Fig. 14.1. Marion County townships and pre-Unigov city of Indianapolis

The Unigov law also excluded from consolidation any incorporated city other than Indianapolis and any incorporated town with a population over 5,000. This qualification leaves the cities of Beech Grove, Lawrence, and Southport and the town of Speedway as separate jurisdictions. These "excluded cities" retained their previous government structures and provide several serv-ices directly to their residents. Because they pay taxes to the county and receive county services, voters in the excluded cities may vote for the Unigov mayor, a district city-county councilor, and the four at-large city-county councilors.

The other 17 incorporated municipalities within Marion County at the time of the Unigov reorganization are known as "included towns." These communities may maintain governments, levy property taxes, and provide local services in addition to those provided by the city and county. Some included towns still have a town board, but most have not remained actively functioning governments.

Delivery of Local Public Services

The continued existence of the county, the townships, the school districts, the excluded cities, the included towns, and six of the special-purpose municipal corporations means that the consolidated city of Indianapolis is far from being the only provider of local public services in Marion County. Even the services that are provided by the consolidated city cover different territories within the county, much as they did before Unigov. Some local services are provided by city-county government and extend across the territory of the pre-Unigov "old city" of Indianapolis; others extend across the territory of the consolidated city (i.e., Marion County minus the excluded cities); others extend countywide; and still others extend over areas that correspond with none of the above. Most of the services that are provided countywide now (e.g., transportation, parks and recreation, public health, and library services) were already provided countywide before Unigov.

The consolidated city provides some services to different portions of Marion County by using special service districts and special taxing districts. For example, the Indianapolis Police Department (now a division of Unigov's Department of Public Safety) serves the 380,000 residents of the Police Special Service District, an area somewhat larger than the "old city" but not as extensive as the consolidated city. Outside the Police Special Service District, Marion County residents receive police protection from the Marion County Sheriff's Department (390,000 residents) or from the municipal force of an excluded city (60,000 residents combined). By contrast, the Department of Capital Asset Management (formerly the Department of Transportation) is a countywide special taxing district. The boundaries of special service and special taxing districts may be adjusted by the city-county council and the mayor, subject to the provisions of the Unigov Act.

Because of the number of local governments that remain in Marion County, plus the special service and special taxing districts, a resident in a given location in Marion County may receive services from several sources and pay taxes to several entities. The extent to which Unigov simplified local public service delivery is arguable; the territorial reach of some city services has been extended beyond the old city limits, but very few local government services are actually delivered countywide by the consolidated city-county government.

Service Provision and Production

Police protection is provided to different territories within the county by the Indianapolis Police Department (serving the Police Special Service District); by municipal police departments in Beech Grove, Lawrence, Southport, and Speedway; and by the Marion County Sheriff's Department (serving all other areas in the county as well as maintaining countywide corrections facilities). In addition, some included towns maintain supplemental police patrols, and a separate security service protects the campus and properties of Indiana University–Purdue University at Indianapolis (IUPUI).

Fire protection is performed by the Indianapolis Fire Department (serving the Fire Special Service District, which is essentially the pre-Unigov city of Indianapolis), by fire departments in the eight outer townships, and by municipal fire departments in the cities of Beech Grove and Lawrence and in the town of Speedway. Mutual aid agreements exist among all of these units.

Emergency communications, with an enhanced 911 service funded by a charge on local telephone subscribers, are provided countywide by the recently created Metropolitan Emergency Communications Agency (MECA).

Local parks and recreation are provided countywide by the Unigov Department of Parks and Recreation. In addition, some of the excluded cities maintain their own local parks.

Street maintenance and traffic-flow regulation are performed countywide by the Unigov Department of Capital Asset Management (DCAM). Public transportation is performed countywide by the Indianapolis Public Transportation Corporation, which is administered by DCAM. Public airport service is provided countywide by a separate municipal corporation, the Indianapolis Airport Authority, which was in place prior to Unigov.

Public health and hospital services are provided countywide by another pre-Unigov special-purpose municipal corporation, the Health and Hospital Corporation of Marion County. The original 1969 Unigov proposal would have replaced this separate unit of government with a Department of Public Health, but political opposition led the legislature to delete that section, leaving the Health and Hospital Corporation substantially independent.

Local public assistance to the poor, including temporary housing and clothing assistance, is provided only by trustees in each of the nine townships. Federal and state public assistance programs, such as Aid to Families with Dependent Children (AFDC) and Medicaid, are administered by the Marion County office of the Indiana Family and Social Services Administration, for which the county contributes some of the funding.

Public elementary and secondary education are provided by the Indianapolis Public Schools (a separate unit of local government with boundaries roughly coterminous with those of the pre-Unigov city of Indianapolis) and by school districts in the eight outer townships, the city of Beech Grove, and the town of Speedway. Public higher and vocational education services are provided by the state.

Public housing is administered countywide by the Indianapolis Housing Authority within the Unigov Department of Metropolitan Development. The housing authority's activities are supported by a property tax over the "Unigov area" (the county minus the four excluded cities).

Countywide planning, zoning, and land-use regulation are governed by the Metropolitan Development Commission and administered by the Department of Metropolitan Development.

Solid-waste collection is performed by the Sanitary Division of the Department of Capital Asset Management. Crews of DCAM employees perform collection within the pre-Unigov boundaries of Indianapolis. Elsewhere in the county, collection is performed by private companies under DCAM's supervision.

Solid-waste disposal is performed on a countywide basis by private operators supervised by the Sanitary Division of the Department of Capital Asset Management. One private operator manages a waste-to-energy mass-burn incinerator. Another operator manages a sanitary landfill for items not taken to the incinerator.

Sanitary sewers are maintained by the Sanitary Division of the Department of Capital Asset Management. Sewage sludge treatment and disposal are provided and financed countywide through a special taxing district, administered by a section of the Sanitary Division of DCAM. Wastewater treatment is provided by a private operator supervised by DCAM's Sanitary Division but financed countywide through another special taxing district.

Residents' Satisfaction with Public Services

A 1993 survey of households throughout Indianapolis–Marion County offers evidence on the distribution of service satisfaction and the possible effects of service consolidation.[3] Table 14.1 displays citizen ratings of six consolidated services—parks and recreation, street repair, street lighting, storm sewers, and public transportation—and two services that continue to be provided by districts—police and public education. Residents within the pre-Unigov boundaries of Indianapolis rated four of the six countywide services lower than did their coresidents in the remainder of the county, but the differences are not large.[4] For two services that are formally countywide—street lighting and public transportation—ratings in the old city are substantially higher than in the outlying county. Although DCAM and the transit authority have countywide responsibilities, neither lighting nor bus service has been extended very much beyond the pre-Unigov city boundaries.

As noted earlier, two important public services—police and public schools—

TABLE 14.1. Ratings of Local Government Services by Residents of Areas within Marion County, 1993

	Positive Ratings[a] of Services Received in		
	Pre-Unigov City	Pre-Unigov County	Excluded Cities[b]
Countywide services			
Parks and recreation	53	60	82
Street repair	29	38	63
Street lighting	64	52[c]	77
Storm sewers	57	60	66
Trash collection	83	91	96
Public transportation	71	45[c]	58
District-Based services			
Police	62	74	86
Elementary schools	60	90	89

Source: Center for Urban Policy and the Environment, IUPUI, *1993 Indianapolis Community Survey.*
[a]Percentage rating service in their neighborhood "excellent or good."
[b]Excluded cities supplement Unigov parks and recreation, street lighting, and street repair. Each has its own police department. Two of the four excluded cities have their own school districts.
[c]Unigov has not excluded public street lighting or bus service to most of the county.

remained district responsibilities despite the Unigov consolidation. Here the differences in service ratings suggest that residents of the pre-Unigov city are significantly disadvantaged, especially with respect to elementary education.

While some observers might infer that these rating differences show that city-county consolidation should have been more thorough, a comparison of the ratings for police services suggests that the differences are more likely due to a scale effect. Citizens served by the small police departments of the excluded cities rated their police services highest, followed by those served by the somewhat larger sheriff's department, and then by those served by the 900+ officers of the Indianapolis Police Department.[5] The elementary school data show a similar effect, as the township school districts and those of the excluded cities are much smaller than the Indianapolis Public Schools. Thus, it may be that residents of the pre-Unigov city could be better served by a decentralization of their police and public schools than by any merger with surrounding departments and districts.[6]

Local Public Finance

With respect to public finance, the Unigov structure is more complicated in many respects than the one it replaced. In particular, Unigov fell short of extending or consolidating revenue sources for the central city.

The principal local tax in Marion County, as in all of Indiana, is the property tax. Although one set of property-assessment rules applies through-out the county, property tax rates are far from uniform. Not only do Indian-apolis residents still pay different bundles of taxes depending on where they live in the county, but the number of different tax rates in the county has ac-tually increased since Unigov. This is due to the presence of many different taxing units within the county (i.e., the county, the cities and towns, the inde-pendent municipal corporations, the townships, and the school districts), plus the use by the consolidated city of special service districts and special taxing districts to support different services and capital projects (League of Women Voters of Indianapolis 1985, 55).

The 1992 notice of property tax rates in Marion County, published by the county auditor and county treasurer, presented a 3,840-cell matrix of property tax rates. There were 60 applicable property-tax levies and 64 areas representing unique combinations of taxing jurisdictions within the county.[7] Total nominal property tax rates varied from a low of $7.92 per $100 as-sessed valuation in parts of Washington Township (a northern suburban area of the county) to a high of $13.09 per $100 assessed valuation in part of Cen-ter Township inside the pre-Unigov boundaries of Indianapolis.

The Unigov reorganization has had some beneficial financial effects in Marion County. The increase in assessed valuation resulting from the inclu-sion of the out-county suburban areas raised the debt limit available to the city of Indianapolis, which has allowed the city to undertake some capital projects that might otherwise have been difficult to fund. The consolidated city also maintains a beneficial bond rating that keeps interest costs relatively low, while at the same time, the city receives more favorable interest rates on revenues it has available for temporary investment. The consolidated city has been able to acquire greater insurance coverage at lower premiums. Some observers argue also that centralized purchasing and accounting systems have resulted in savings for the city and county; however, it is difficult to verify these claims.

In the years immediately following its passage, Unigov is said to have enhanced Indianapolis's ability to attract federal funds. By fiscal year 1975, federal aid to Indianapolis ($36.2 million) was more than four times the amount received in support from the federal and state governments combined in fiscal year 1970. Whereas federal and state assistance together represented just 11.4 percent of Indianapolis' general revenues at the time of Unigov's implementation in 1969–70, those sources accounted for 42.9 percent of the consolidated city's revenues in 1974–75 and peaked at 52.6 percent in 1980–81. That year, federal funds alone represented one-fourth of the consolidated city's revenues.

The increase in federal support is attributable to three contemporaneous factors. First, the extension of the city's boundaries to the Marion County lines raised the reported population of Indianapolis from about 450,000 to about 750,000 residents, which, by definition, increased Indianapolis's share of federal assistance that is distributed through population-based formulas. Second, Mayors Lugar (1968–76) and William H. Hudnut III (1976–92) actively sought federal assistance, unlike their predecessors (under whom intergovernmental aid had even declined as a percentage of Indianapolis's general revenues during the 1960s). Third, during all but four of the first 20 years after Unigov, Republicans controlled the executive branch of the federal government, and Indianapolis was the largest U.S. city governed by Republicans. Richard Lugar's reputation as "Richard Nixon's favorite mayor" did not hurt the city's ability to attract federal support in the immediate post-Unigov period.

Beyond these benefits, public finance in Indianapolis shows little effect from the Unigov reorganization. In particular, the structure of public finance under Unigov does not reflect significant efforts to use the larger jurisdiction of the city-county government to effect wealth or income redistribution within the metropolitan area. Extensions of the tax base for municipal public services are easier to accomplish procedurally under Unigov, but most extensions that have been implemented have supported capital projects to extend infrastructure improvements to the suburban areas. Even the property tax base for the consolidated city's Department of Administration, whose activities ostensibly benefit all county residents, has not been extended as it could be (Owen and Willbern 1985, 123).

With respect to funding direct public services, the city's operating philosophy has been to attempt to match scale of taxation with scale of benefit (ibid.). This operating philosophy has had two important effects. First, it has led to a proliferation of different tax rates and taxing units within the county, as each new endeavor of the consolidated city tends to be funded through the creation of a new special service or special taxing district. Second, property tax rates are higher in the inner-city Center Township area than elsewhere in the county, because this area pays for all countywide services plus all municipal services for which the tax base has not been extended beyond the old city boundaries.

Supporters of Unigov's adoption in 1969 argued that the consolidation would have a redistributive impact by making the suburban property tax base available for central-city services, but this has not been manifest in practice. The property tax bases for the local public services on which poorer residents arguably rely most heavily—public safety, public elementary and secondary education, and public assistance—remain confined to the inner city.

Public safety is supported by property taxes levied within the police and fire special service districts, which still conform most nearly to the pre-Unigov city boundaries. Furthermore, residents in the "old city" area pay property taxes to support both the Indianapolis Police Department and the Marion County Sheriff's Department, while "out-county" residents pay property taxes only to support the Marion County Sheriff's Department.

Public elementary and secondary education are supported by property taxes levied within the boundaries of the Indianapolis Public Schools (IPS). Furthermore, as part of the implementation of a federal court desegregation order, IPS pays the suburban township school corporations a per-pupil fee for educating the central-city children who are bused out to the townships, while no township children are bused to IPS schools—both the money and the pupils travel from the central city to the outer townships and not vice versa.

Public assistance is funded through the townships within the county. Accordingly, the area of greatest need and weakest property tax base—Center Township—must support its own poor-relief activities through property taxes levied within the township. By 1994, the poor-relief tax rate in Center Township was 10 times larger than the rate in other Marion County townships (Rosentraub and Nunn 1994, 25).

Economic Development

Unigov has often been credited for contributing to economic growth in Indianapolis. C. James Owen and York Willbern, for example, wrote: "We contend that a large portion of community development in Indianapolis–Marion County—whether applauded or criticized—can be attributed in a clear and significant way to the mayor's office restructuring done under the Unigov reform" (Owen and Willbern 1985, 195).

The strengthening of the mayor's administrative and budgetary powers under Unigov enhanced the ability of Mayors Lugar and Hudnut to participate actively in the public-private partnerships for which Indianapolis has become known. When local leaders (including the mayor) agreed on an amateur-sports focus for refurbishing Indianapolis's image, the mayor's new powers to act as a public developer contributed strongly to the success of the effort.

The mayor has been able to use the Department of Metropolitan Development and the Capital Improvements Board to assemble large public development packages for the downtown "Mile Square." City-county participation, with public funds and public authority, was important to such developments as the Market Square Arena, the Merchants Plaza office and hotel facility, the American United Life building, Union Station renovation, the Pan American Plaza, and the Hoosier Dome and Indianapolis Convention Center. The city is an important partner in the financing and construction of Circle Centre Mall, a large downtown shopping development that opened shortly before municipal election day in 1995.

By including all of Marion County within the boundaries of the consolidated city, Unigov contributed definitionally as well as actually to Indianapolis's "Star of the Rust Belt" image. By definition, employment growth in what had been suburbs became employment growth in Indianapolis. Given that much recent employment growth in the United States has been in suburbs, including that growth in Indianapolis's accounts helped the city stand out when compared with nearby cities that could not count their suburbs' employment growth as their own.

Countylevel comparisons of employment growth reveal, however, that Indianapolis's employment growth was not only definitional. Employment in Indianapolis–Marion County grew by 43 percent from 1970 to 1989. Other large central-city-and-county combinations in adjacent states—Columbus–Franklin County, Cincinnati–Hamilton County, and Dayton–Montgomery County in Ohio, plus Louisville–Jefferson County in Kentucky—generally showed smaller employment growth during that period. Employment growth was higher only in Columbus–Franklin County, Ohio (see table 14.2).

TABLE 14.2. Total Percentage Employment Growth, 1970–1989

Columbus–Franklin County	73
Indianapolis–Marion County	43
Cincinnati–Hamilton County	34
Louisville–Jefferson County	19
Dayton–Montgomery County	15

Source: U.S. Department of Commerce, Bureau of the Census, *County Business Patterns,* Report No. CBP-70-27, 1970, and U.S. Department of Commerce, Bureau of the Census, *County Business Patterns,* Report No. CBP-89-27, 1989.

Similar to the experience in the United States more generally, most of the new jobs created in Indianapolis during this period were in the lower paying service sector (Rosentraub et al. 1992). Metropolitan areas throughout the Midwest, including Indianapolis, lost manufacturing jobs during the 1970s and 1980s. Indianapolis–Marion County's manufacturing employment decline of 27 percent fell in the middle of losses experienced by neighboring large Midwestern counties.

Tools commonly used for economic development in the metropolitan United States today include tax abatements, tax-increment financing (TIF), and enterprise zones. All of these tools have been used to stimulate economic development in Indianapolis. They are most common in Center Township, the heart of the pre-Unigov city, where more than one-third of all property valuation benefits from a tax abatement or is located in a TIF or enterprise zone. The township is home to more than one-half of all tax-exempt or deferred property in the county. In 1992, these tax incentives for economic development cost Center Township some $18 million, or roughly $97 per capita in taxes that would have been collected otherwise. This abatement pattern contributes to Center Township's significantly higher property tax rate (Rosentraub and Nunn 1994, 34–38). The abatements' combined effect is, in part, a subsidy of suburban taxpayers by Center Township residents. The abatements created employment and entertainment opportunities enjoyed by suburban residents, opportunities paid for by increased taxes on nonabated properties in Center Township.

Political Power and Citizen Participation

What may be Unigov's clearest and longest lasting impact on central-city residents is that the consolidation solidified Republican party control of city government, which had been controlled most often by the Democratic party during the two decades before Unigov. Politically, the Republican-dominated county took over the marginally Democratic city.

Through the inclusion of the previously separate suburban electorate, Republicans have gained a decided advantage in municipal elections. This prospect did not go unnoticed at the time of Unigov's adoption. When the Unigov bill passed the Indiana General Assembly in 1969, Marion County Republican party chairman Keith Bulen exclaimed, "It's my greatest coup of all time, moving out there and taking in 85,000 Republicans." Unigov raised the number of registered voters who could participate in the election of the mayor and city-county council from 239,371 to 406,155. Just over half of those voters added, the 85,000 to whom Bulen referred, were registered as Republicans. The remaining 80,000 included others who regularly voted Republican in general elections but were not listed on the registration rolls as Republicans because they had not voted in a recent Republican primary.

Indianapolis's pre-Unigov history of relatively close mayoral elections from 1951 through 1967 has shifted to a pattern of Republican mayoral landslides from 1971 through 1995 (see table 14.3). Control of the council majority, which occasionally changed hands during the 1950s and 1960s, has also been solidly in the hands of the Republicans since 1971. In the past two decades, the ratio of Republicans to Democrats on the city-county council has ranged from just below two-to-one to nearly four-to-one. The four-seat gain in Democratic city-county councilors in the 1991 municipal elections was attributable largely to redistricting in the aftermath of a voting-rights lawsuit that forced the redrawing of district lines to create more majority-minority districts.

All 10 of the city-county council districts within the pre-Unigov city limits were held by Democrats. All 15 districts outside the old city limits, plus all four at-large seats, were held by Republicans. In 1991, the Democratic mayoral candidate carried the pre-Unigov Indianapolis precincts but lost the election because the margin was offset by the Republicans' ability to carry the out-county areas. Thus, Unigov's political effects could not be clearer. Without it, the 1991 elections would have resulted in a Democratic mayor and a Democratic council majority; with it, the 1991 elections resulted in a Republican mayor and a Republican council majority.

Regarding voter participation, the first two municipal elections under Unigov, 1971 and 1975, brought increased voter turnout. Turnout as a percentage of the voting-eligible population increased from 42.0 percent in 1951

TABLE 14.3. Municipal Election Outcomes in Indianapolis, 1951–1991

Year	Winning Mayoral Candidate	Number and Percentage of Votes	Losing Mayoral Candidate	Number and Percentage of Votes	City Council Seats	
					R	D
1951	Clark (R)	68,415 (55.6)	Bayt (D)	54,744 (44.4)	6	3
1955	Bayt (D)	74,682 (56.1)	Birr (R)	58,497 (43.9)	3	6
1959	Boswell (D)	70,031 (57.4)	Sharp (R)	51,994 (42.6)	3	6
1963	Barton (D)	68,316 (48.1)	Drayer (R)	63,091 (44.4)	3	6
1967	Lugar (R)	72,278 (53.3)	Barton (D)	63,284 (46.7)	6	3
1971	Lugar (R)	155,164 (60.5)	Neff (D)	101,367 (39.5)	21	8
1975	Hudnut (R)	124,100 (52.2)	Welch (D)	109,761 (46.1)	19	10
1979	Hudnut (R)	124,515 (73.9)	Cantwell (D)	43,955 (26.1)	22	7
1983	Hudnut (R)	134,550 (67.5)	Sullivan (D)	63,242 (31.7)	23	6
1987	Hudnut (R)	109,107 (66.3)	Senden (D)	38,193 (23.2)	22	7
1991	Goldsmith (R)	110,545 (56.2)	Mahern (D)	79,817 (40.6)	18	11
1995	Goldsmith (R)	64,209 (57.9)	Jimison (D)	39,539 (35.6)	19	10

Source: Election reports and Office of the Marion County Clerk, various years.

to 53.8 percent in 1971. Thereafter (see table 14.4), voter turnout in municipal elections declined to 17.5 percent in 1995.

This turnout decline in municipal elections does not match the pattern that has occurred in the United States generally or in Marion County with respect to other elections. Table 14.4 also presents Marion County voter-turnout percentages for general elections in presidential election years from 1952 through 1992. Voter turnout in presidential-election years in Marion County shows the same pattern of gradual decline that can be seen throughout the United States during that period: down about 5 percentage points during the 1950s, another 7 during the 1960s, another 5 during the 1970s, and stabilizing in the 1980s. Voter turnout in municipal elections exhibits a very different pattern: stable during the 1950s, rising in the 1960s and early 1970s, and then dropping by 20 percentage points in the late 1970s before stabilizing at a much lower level through the 1980s.

TABLE 14.4. Voting Turnout in Marion County, Municipal and Presidential Election Years, 1951–91 (percentage of voting-age population casting ballots)

Year	Municipal Election	Year	Presidential Election
1951	42.0	1952	73.0
1955	45.4	1956	61.9
1959	41.1	1960	68.0
1963	47.9	1964	65.9
1967	45.2	1968	61.2
1971	53.8	1972	59.7
1975	52.4	1976	61.9
1979	33.6	1980	54.5
1983	39.3	1984	54.7
1987	29.1	1988	54.0
1991	34.1	1992	54.0
1995	17.5		

Source: Election reports and Office of the Marion County Clerk, various years.

A return to table 14.3 reveals more about that drop in municipal election turnout in the 1970s. The 1975 municipal election was the first post-Unigov election in which the mayor's office was open. In 1971, the popular Richard Lugar had been reelected overwhelmingly, carrying all parts of the county. In 1975, because Indiana law still barred the mayor from seeking reelection to a third term, the mayor's race was between former U.S. representative William Hudnut III and a wealthy and well-known local developer, Robert Welch. Democrat Welch amassed approximately 110,000 votes, carried the pre-

Unigov central city, and undoubtedly aided the Democratic ticket in carrying 10 council districts (their largest share until 1991). Nevertheless, Welch lost the mayor's office to Hudnut, who prevailed in the suburban area.[8]

To many Democratic party activists, and apparently to many Democratic voters, the 1975 elections sent a message that Democrats could not win under Unigov. Turnout in the 1979 municipal elections, and in all municipal elections since, indicates that central-city Democratic voters have adjusted their behavior accordingly. In 1979, 60,000 fewer Marion County residents voted in the mayor's race than had done so in 1975. Yet Hudnut's 1979 vote total was almost identical to that of 1975. In other words, between 1975 and 1979, 60,000 potential Democratic votes disappeared from Indianapolis's municipal elections. Since 1975, Republican votes for mayor have stayed between 110,000 and 135,000, while no Democratic candidate has risen to even 75 percent of Welch's 1975 total.

Thus, the size of the decline in voter turnout in municipal elections in Indianapolis since 1975 corresponded precisely with the loss of Democratic votes. Most of that loss occurred in the precincts of the old central city. These voters did not leave the city, nor did many of them leave the voter registration rolls. Most of them continued to vote in state and national elections. They simply stopped showing up for municipal elections after 1975. To the extent that voter turnout is a measure of citizen participation, Unigov's conversion of Indianapolis government into a single-party (Republican) domain has diminished that participation, and the diminution has occurred primarily among Democratic voters in the central city.

Lessons from Unigov for Central Cities

David Rusk characterizes Indianapolis as an "elastic" city—one that grew by capturing land and population that otherwise would have been separate suburbs (Rusk 1993). However, we think it better to say that pre-Unigov Indianapolis is a city captured by its suburbs. The political leaders who crafted Unigov, and those who have operated Unigov since its inception, were and are suburban Republicans. Democrats represent all districts lying within the pre-Unigov city but stand little chance of winning a majority of council seats or of electing a Democrat as mayor.

The stability of political leadership through the 1970s and 1980s enabled significant change in Indianapolis. Republican leaders from suburban Indianapolis used the strong powers of the city's mayor backed by large council majorities and the authority of the countywide Department of Metropolitan Development to contribute to substantial development of Indianapolis's downtown. That development helped greatly to remake the city's image, "from India-no-place to India-show-place" as former mayor Hudnut describes it (Hudnut 1995). This remaking, however, was not made possible by an inflow of new tax dollars from the suburbs; rather, most of the public costs accrue to residents of the pre-Unigov city, especially those who live in Center Township. The combination of service-delivery financing via special district and TIF-ing downtown has given Center Township residents the highest tax burdens in the consolidated city-county. The Unigov consolidation did not give central-city residents access to a wider tax base. It gave suburban leaders access to the central-city base with which to pursue development projects chosen by them, not by city residents.

Unigov did not significantly alter provision and production arrangements for most local public services. Arrangements for police, fire, and elementary and secondary education remain essentially the same as pre-Unigov, despite occasional calls for further consolidation or, in the case of schools, decentralization. These expensive local services are financed within special districts, ensuring little or no redistribution from suburb to city. Some service departments have gained access to the countywide tax base. These, especially Capital Asset Management and Parks and Recreation, have used their new funds to extend what were principally city services out to the former suburban portions of the county, thus maintaining a rough fiscal equivalence. The fiscal patterns of Indianapolis bear witness to the truth of the Matthew Principle ("to him who has, so shall it be given") and remind us that the poor are rarely able to exploit those better off.

In January 1992, Indianapolis's third Unigov mayor, Stephen Goldsmith, took office. Goldsmith's relationship to the Marion County Republican party has been distant much of the time and occasionally difficult. During his first four years in office, Goldsmith initiated several projects to rearrange certain aspects of city government and service delivery. Major efforts include privatizing the delivery of some services and the management of some city operations, decentralizing service management through the use of township-based management "teams," implementing community policing within the Police Special Service District, and attempting to increase the involvement of neighborhoods in making decisions and setting priorities. Privatizing, including the transfer of the city's wastewater treatment plant, has allowed the city to meet large fiscal obligations for development—the Circle Centre mall and United Airlines maintenance facility—without raising tax rates in Center Township. There seems to be a limit (which has been reached) to resources that can be tapped in this manner, however.

Since its implementation in 1970, no changes have been sought in the Unigov law that would alter the structure of local government and public finance in Indianapolis–Marion County. The partial consolidation achieved by the law has had significant benefits for the city's image, for its dominant political party, and arguably for its economy. However, many of these benefits have accrued less to residents of the pre-Unigov central city and more to their neighbors in the surrounding suburban townships. Such a pattern may not be entirely unexpected but may serve as a caution to those who recommend consolidation with suburbs as the hope for the United States' central cities.

NOTES

1. The city's old sewer and sanitation department was turned into the Indianapolis Sanitary District in 1945 and authorized to exercise jurisdiction beyond the city limits. Legislation adopted in 1947 established the Indianapolis Public Library District—now the Indianapolis–Marion County Public Library—and extended its service and taxing area beyond the city limits. In 1951, legislation created a separate countywide municipal corporation responsible for public health and hospital activities—now the Health and Hospital Corporation of Marion County. In 1953, the City-County Building Authority was organized to finance, construct, and operate a new office building for the use of the city and county governments. In 1955, the Indianapolis Housing Authority was formed, and a Metropolitan Planning Commission was created to assume the authority from the city and the county over land use planning and zoning. In 1961, an Indianapolis Airport Authority and an Indianapolis–Marion County Parks and Recreation District were created, each with a countywide base. A 1963 law authorized a countywide Metropolitan Thoroughfare Authority. In 1965, the Capital Improvements Board was created to finance, construct, and operate a convention and exhibition center. Not all proposals for special-purpose governments were adopted. A 1957 plan to consolidate the school districts within the county, and a 1967 proposal for a countywide police force, were defeated by strong local opposition.

2. The executive-branch departments created under Unigov were Administration, Metropolitan Development, Parks and Recreation, Public Safety, Public Works, and Transportation.

3. The 1993 Indianapolis Community Survey was sponsored by the Center for Urban Policy and the Environment, School of Public and Environmental Affairs, Indiana University at Indianapolis. A total of 3,837 household respondents were asked their perception of the quality of public services in their neighborhoods, among a variety of other questions.

4. A possible explanation of these small differences favoring the area outside the old city is that many homeowners' associations there supplement the public services they receive from city-county departments.

5. The relative ratings of the small excluded-city police departments, versus the large sheriff's and Indianapolis departments, are consistent with those obtained soon after the Unigov consolidation. See Ostrom, Parks, and Whitaker 1973.

6. Indianapolis mayor Stephen Goldsmith recently proposed splitting the Indianapolis Public Schools into five minidistricts as part of a plan to strengthen neighborhood schools. The proposal was strongly opposed by the IPS board and the teachers' union and was withdrawn.

7. Although the total number of taxing units within the county is much greater

than 64, some of those taxing units have overlapping territories and others do not.

8. This "Unigov effect" on municipal elections in Indianapolis was evident again in the next open-seat mayoral race, in 1991. For the first time since 1975, Hudnut was not on the ballot. The Republican nominee, former Marion County prosecutor Stephen Goldsmith, faced an energetic and well-known Democratic opponent in state senator Louis Mahern. Mahern drew the largest vote total of any Democratic mayoral candidate since Welch and beat Goldsmith in the pre-Unigov portion of Indianapolis. Once again, the suburban vote carried the Republican candidate, Goldsmith, into office.

REFERENCES

Hudnut, William H., III. 1995. *The Hudnut Years in Indianapolis, 1976–1991.* Bloomington, IN: Indiana University Press.

League of Women Voters of Indianapolis. 1985. *Unigov Handbook: A Citizens' Guide to Local Government.* 2d ed. Indianapolis, IN: League of Women Voters.

Ostrom, Elinor, Roger B. Parks, and Gordon P. Whitaker. 1973. "Do We Really Want to Consolidate Urban Police Forces? A Reappraisal of Some Old Assertions." *Public Administration Review* 33 (September/October): 423–33.

Owen, C. James, and York Willbern. 1985. *Governing Metropolitan Indianapolis: The Politics of Unigov.* Berkeley, CA: University of California Press.

Rosentraub, Mark S., Michael Przybylski, Dan Mullins, David Swindell, and Krista Perman. 1992. *Partnerships, Economic Development, and Public Policy: Indianapolis and its Future.* Indianapolis, IN: Center for Urban Policy and the Environment.

Rosentraub, Mark S., and Sam Nunn. 1994. *Cities and Suburbs: Linkages, Benefits, and Shared Responsibilities.* Indianapolis, IN: Center for Urban Policy and the Environment.

Rusk, David. 1993. *Cities without Suburbs.* Washington, DC: Johns Hopkins University Press/Woodrow Wilson International Center for Scholars.

CHAPTER 15

Do We Really Want to Consolidate Urban Areas? [It's Like Deja Vu All over Again]

Roger B. Parks

In spring 1970, an intrepid band of graduate and undergraduate students, ably led by Lin Ostrom, set forth on the streets of Indianapolis and its close suburbs. Their task was to collect data relevant to the question of whether police services were better supplied by large, highly professionalized bureaus or by much smaller departments characteristic of most of the suburban United States. In the face of recent [then] and recurring recommendations for consolidation of police forces, other public services, and local governments in urban areas, this venture might seem quixotic, but it was instead quite productive. From it sprang a stream of Workshop research that kept many of our friends employed. This research also, we believe, helped to change the tenor of debates over how to organize policing in urban areas and, more broadly, whether consolidation of local governments in metropolitan areas was the unmixed blessing perceived by its proponents.

SPEA's Center for Urban Policy and the Environment completed a household survey of nearly 4,000 residents of Indianapolis and Marion County in 1993. The survey allows a partial replication of the Ostrom et al. 1970 research. The data supply evidence for the old saw, "The more things change, the more they stay the same" (see table 15.1). More residents of the independent communities that adjoin the Indianapolis Police Services District (approximately the pre-Unigov city) thought their police were doing an outstanding or good job in 1970 than did their neighbors in matched neighborhoods just inside the district. In 1993, more residents of the independent communities thought their police services were excellent or good. The questions are slightly different, but the patterns are essentially the same. The policy explanations for these differences, too, continue to be the same. The independent communities put a high proportion of their sworn personnel on the streets, patrolling and available to respond to service calls. Indianapolis, despite its commitment to community policing, still assigns many officers to specialized

Originally published in *Polycentric Circles* 1, no. 2 (July 1995): 7-8. Reprinted by permission of the author.

TABLE 15.1.   Evaluation of Neighborhood Police, 1970 and 1993

1970: I think police in this neighborhood are doing . . . (%)		An Outstanding Job	A Good Job	An Adequate Job	An Inadequate Job	(n)
Independent communities	Beech Grove	28	37	33	3	(98)
	Lawrence	36	39	21	3	(127)
	Speedway	29	53	17	–	(144)
Indianapolis neighbor-hoods	Near Beech Grove	15	42	34	10	(89)
	Near Lawrence	11	40	43	6	(11)
	Near Speedway	12	44	34	11	(119)

1993: Would you say that police services in your area are . . . (%)		Excellent	Good	Fair	Poor	(n)
Independent communities	Beech Grove	48	40	9	3	(97)
	Lawrence	28	53	16	3	(104)
	Speedway	49	42	7	2	(104)
Indianapolis neighbor-hoods	Near Beech Grove	19	58	19	4	(100)
	Near Lawrence	8	51	33	9	(104)
	Near Speedway	29	47	21	3	(112)

Note: The 1970 data are reported in table 8.3 in this volume.

tasks, thereby lowering its on-street presence. The difference is reflected in citizen knowledge of police who work in their neighborhoods—50 to 60 percent of those who live in the independent communities say they know officers by name or by sight; in Indianapolis, the percentage is 25 to 35.

With apologies to Yogi Berra for the subtitle, I note that most public debates have a tendency to recur. In the last few years, colleagues at the Universities of Kentucky and North Carolina (Bill Lyons and Dave Lowery) have made more than a cottage industry of comparisons between fragmented Louisville and consolidated Lexington, with their results said to favor consolidated metro government. A recent book by Albuquerque's former mayor, David Rusk, is but one of a resurgence of calls for metropolitan consolidation. Neal Peirce is advocating consolidation in several metro areas. Beurt SerVass, one of the architects of the Indianapolis Unigov reform, recently claimed it to be time to move further by consolidating police services there. In 1993, as in 1970, our data show these recommendations are not well grounded—at least not in the context of one important local public service.

Part V
Continuing Challenges
for Research and Policy

CHAPTER 16

Complex Models of Urban Service Systems

Roger B. Parks and Elinor Ostrom

Most conventional analyses of public service delivery employ a unitary model of local governments. In such models, the "government" aggregates consumer preferences, procures and organizes means of service production, and delivers services as a monopoly supplier to constituents. Decisions about output and expenditure levels are assumed to be made by simple referenda or by omniscient and benevolent administrators. But few local government service delivery structures are so simple.

Since the early 1960s, scholars have argued for more complex models of public service delivery (e.g., V. Ostrom, Tiebout, and Warren 1961; Margolis 1964). Noting that the local public sector is most frequently comprised of several layers of enterprises engaging in a wide variety of exchanges, they argued the need to consider the structure of intra- and interjurisdictional arrangements as influences on service delivery. Margolis, for example, argued that the structure of interorganizational arrangements might make it possible to deal with problems that are less amenable to solution at the level of individual organizations or jurisdictions.

A consideration of the structure of governments gives a new perspective to old questions. We might ask whether some of the insoluble problems posed in the theory of public expenditures are worked out through the behavior of the structure. That is, does the structure have some of the characteristics of an industry and market, so that there is an interaction among governments which leads to desirable results? (Margolis 1964, 236).

Originally published in T. N. Clark, ed., *Policy Analysis: Directions for Future Research* Urban Affairs Annual Reviews, vol. 21: 171–99. Copyright © 1981 by Sage Publications, Inc. Reprinted by permission of Sage Publications, Inc. and the authors.

Authors' note: We gratefully acknowledge support for the analysis presented in this essay from the National Science Foundation in the form of Grant No. NSF SES 79-13397; and for the data collection from Grant No. NSF GI 43949. The findings and opinions expressed herein, however, are solely those of the authors and do not necessarily reflect those of the foundation. We also appreciate the helpful comments of Otto Davis, Debra Dean, Vincent Ostrom, and Barry R. Weingast on earlier drafts and the high caliber of professional assistance we have received from the staff of the Workshop in Political Theory and Policy Analysis.

In addition to his concern over the neglect of interorganizational structure, Margolis also criticized analysts of public finance for excessively collapsing the internal organization of governmental units. Rather than being direct democracy or pure hierarchy, most governmental structures are far more complex. As Margolis recognized, these governmental structures may give rise to opportunities for private gain. "Just as the market can be rigged, the government can be manipulated to protect private interests of some constituents. Just as promoters can orient and stimulate the market, there is a government bureaucracy which can gain from government activities" (1964, 236–37). Despite the cogency of Margolis's argument and those of others (such as McKean 1964), few analysts of local service outputs and expenditures have taken into account overtly the ways the structure of intra- and interorganizational arrangements may affect the performance of local public sector economics. In order to examine the question of how internal and external decision-making structures affect performance, we draw on recent theoretical developments related to theories of public bureau behavior and how interorganizational arrangements affect public bureau behavior.

Niskanen (1971) was the first to present a rigorous and well-developed formal model of bureau behavior. Mique and Belanger (1974) criticized the Niskanen model and developed an alternative model. Orzechowski (1977) provides a cogent review of the difference between Niskanen and Mique and Belanger and develops a third model drawing on the theoretical work of Williamson (1964) and the empirical studies by DeAlessi (1969) and Parkinson (1957). Orzechowski predicts that public bureaus, facing demands similar to private firms, will produce output at higher per-unit costs and higher labor-to-capital ratio. Orzechowski reviews several empirical studies, including his own, that compare the unit costs and the relative labor-to-capital ratios for public versus private producers. The consistent finding across a number of different studies is that unit costs of similar output are higher in public than in private firms. Public firms also employ a larger proportion of staff to capital than do private firms (see ciations in Orzechowski 1977; see also Savas 1978; Pondy 1968; Lee 1972).

Work on a theory of interorganizational influences on public bureau behavior has progressed more slowly. V. Ostrom, Tiebout, and Warren (1961) and V. Ostrom and E. Ostrom (1965) argued for the utility of conceptualizing public service delivery structures as "industries." Public service industries, they claimed, might be analyzed using many of the same tools as those employed by economists of the industrial organization persuasion (e.g., Bain 1959). Consideration of service delivery structures in terms of their monopoly, duopoly, oligopoly, or competitive forms might enable behavioral predictions analogous to those made for private firms in market structures. In an early application of industrial organization concepts to the public sector,

Bain, Cavas, and Margolis (1966) studied the water industry in northern California. But little other empirical or theoretical application of industrial organization concepts occurred until the middle 1970s, partly, we believe, because of a lack of conceptual tools for characterizing the structure of service delivery arrangements in the public sector and a consequent lack of theoretically related empirical measures of this structure.

As a result of studies supported by the National Science Foundation of the organization of service delivery in metropolitan areas, two similar conceptualizations of service delivery arrangements in the public sector were developed (E. Ostrom and Whitaker 1974; E. Ostrom, Parks, and Whitaker 1978; Savas 1978). In both conceptualizations, service delivery arrangements are disaggregated by specific type of service (e.g., general area police patrol, investigation of residential burglaries, radio communications, garbage collection, dry trash collection, and newspaper recycling). The participants in the service delivery arrangements are separately classified as *producers* of the service, as *consumers* of the service, or as *providers* or collective decision-making units that link producer and consumer.[1] Once these three types of participants are separated conceptually, they can be identified empirically for any given service in a particular geographic area (a city, a county, an SMSA, and so on). Matrices can be constructed arraying, for example, all of the producers against all of the consumers (or all groups of consumers for services with attributes of public goods). Each cell in the matrix identifies whether a service link exists between a particular producer and a particular consumer (or group) and, if so, the nature of that service link. Matrices can also be constructed for producer and provider linkages, for provider and consumer linkages, and for linkages between producers of one service and producers of other services that are necessary or useful to the former producers. These service structure matrices, together with computations based on their sizes and the patterns and types of entries, can then be used to characterize the structure of service delivery arrangements for each service of interest in many different geographic areas (see E. Ostrom, Parks, and Whitaker 1978).

By analyzing the relationships between service delivery structures and the behavior of participants within structures of very different forms, we hope to improve our understanding of interorganizational influences on public bureau behavior. Does a public bureau that occupies a monopoly supply position with respect to a large population and across several different services behave differently than a set of smaller monopolists serving an equivalent total population or a mixed set of more specialized producers of particular services that, in the aggregate, supply an equivalent population? Does the availability of service supply to a given consumer (or group) from two or more different producers lead to inefficient duplication, as some would argue, or does the presence of potential competition, even if highly oligopolistic, lead to more vigorous supply efforts by all producers?

In this essay, we develop several of the components we believe are necessary to an understanding of intra- and interorganizational influences on public service delivery. We begin by considering an output or production function for a bureau and discuss how such a function, once empirically estimated, could be used to examine bureau behavior. We then examine the technical exigencies of production functions, and consider the psychological factors likely to influence managerial decision-making in public bureaus. In a third theoretical section we discuss how different service delivery structures may affect bureaucratic supply. That is, how might the technical, psychological, and behavioral aspects of a bureaucratic supply model change from one form of service delivery structure to another? Then, in an empirical section, we develop production function estimates for some common police outputs.

Bureau Production Functions

Bureaus, like firms in market situations, are involved in the conversion of inputs into one or more outputs. A number of interesting questions can be raised with respect to the conversion processes adopted by bureaus. Are bureaus technically efficient—do they obtain the maximum amount of output obtainable with a particular set of inputs? Are bureaus allocationally or price efficient—do they purchase the least cost combinations of inputs sufficient to supply a given level of output? Are bureaus scale efficient—do bureaus produce sufficient output to exhaust any scale economies in the conversion process while avoiding scale diseconomies (if any) associated with further increases in production? Finally, are bureaus efficient in a social welfare sense—do they tend to produce the level and mix of outputs preferred by the community or communities for whom their supply is intended? (These questions are raised with respect to educational bureaus by Levin 1976. See also Leibenstein 1976; and Moran 1977.)

We believe that the institutional structure within and among bureaus and linking bureaus to consumer communities will have significant effects on answers to these questions. In the private sector pressures on entrepreneurs and managers resulting from the presence of many competitors are believed to lead those decision makers to choose technically and allocationally efficient production processes and input mixes. The necessity of producing outputs that consumers are willing to purchase is thought to push the levels and mixes of outputs produced toward socially efficient frontiers. We think it important to determine whether analogous pressures on decision makers can be found in public sector bureaus and, if so, how pressures for efficiency in each sense of that term used in the preceding may vary from one form of institutional structure to another. We begin this investigation by developing a bureau production function. The specific example to be used is that of bureaus supplying police services.

Police bureaus are clearly multioutput producers. Wilson's (1968) simple trichotomy of "law enforcement, order maintenance, and service" illustrates this, as do more elaborate typologies, such as Goldstein's (1977) eightfold list of police "objectives." In fact, three- or eightfold typologies cannot do justice to the variety of outputs that are produced by police bureaus. We will be forced to make drastic simplifications when we turn to estimating production functions for police bureaus. Initially, however, we write these functions at a very general level.

We can state an implicit police bureau production function as

$$F (Y, X, S) = 0 \qquad (1)$$

where Y is a vector of police service outputs, X is a vector of police service inputs, and S is a vector of service condition variables. For each output, Y_i, we can write:

$$Y_i = F_i (Y^*_i, X, S) \qquad (2)$$

where Y^*_i is a vector of all outputs other than Yi itself. This formulation explicitly acknowledges that police outputs are jointly produced, one with another. Thus, for example, arrests for automobile theft may be produced simultaneously with a reduction in the number of automobile accidents resulting from excessive speed, both by a policy of having officers stop all speeders and request a license check on all stopped vehicles.

While the variety of police bureau outputs is very large, the variety of inputs used by most police bureaus is much less. Police bureaus are highly labor intensive. Inputs of sworn police officers and civilian employees typically exhaust 80 to 95 percent of police agency budgets. An additional chunk of resources is devoted to the purchase (or lease) of vehicles. For purposes of specifying a production function (and, for later investigation of bureaucratic preferences), we divide sworn police officer inputs into those officers assigned to patrol duties in police agencies and those assigned to other, nonpatrol duties. With this division, we may state the production function[2] for the ith police output as

$$O_i = K_i P^{a_i} NP^{b_i} C^{c_i} A^{d_i} (\prod_{j=1}^{n} S_j^{g_{ij}})(\prod_{\substack{j=1 \\ j \neq i}}^{m} Y_j^{h_{ij}}) \qquad (3)$$

where
O_i = the quantity of output of the ith type produced,

K_i = a scale factor appropriate for output i,

P = the number of sworn police officers assigned to the bureau's patrol division,

NP= the number of sworn police officers assigned to nonpatrol duties in the bureau,

C = the number of civilians employed by the bureau,

A = the number of automobiles used by the department,

S_j = service conditions affecting output of the ith type, and

Y_j = all other outputs of the bureau whose production may affect the quantity of output i that is produced.

If we could assume that police bureaus operated in conditions that forced them toward efficient transformations of inputs to outputs (e.g., competitive markets in local police services), we could examine questions of relative efficiency by focusing on the coefficients of this function. Holding service conditions and all other outputs constant, the coefficients a_i, b_i, c_i, and d_i for a given output would have ready interpretations. They would be the elasticities of output i with respect to their respective inputs. That is, a 1 percent increase in the number of sworn officers assigned to a department's patrol division, P, would be predicated to result in a_i percent increase in the output, O_i. The marginal physical product of a particular input could be stated as the ratio of the amount of output being produced to the amount of that input employed, multiplied by the output elasticity of the input. Thus, for officers assigned to patrol, the marginal physical product could be stated as

$$MPP = a_i O_i / P \qquad (4)$$

By estimating output functions of this form for various police outputs, we could begin to examine the technical, allocational, and scale efficiency of police bureaus.

For a particular police bureau, we could enter its values for P, NP, C, and A, together with the coefficients for the estimated production function, and determine immediately whether the bureau was doing as well as predicted or was producing more or less of a given output than predicted by the function (with other outputs held constant). Thus, we could discuss the technical efficiency of particular bureaus. If we knew the ratio of wage rates (and automobile costs) confronting a particular police bureau, we could determine whether it had chosen a least cost mix of inputs to produce a given output. The total cost function for a particular choice of inputs is

$$TC = w_P P + w_{NP} NP + w_C C + r_A A + \sum_i r_{O_i} O_i + FC, \qquad (5)$$

where

w_j = median wage plus wage related benefits for personnel input j,

r_A = average cost of owning and operating a police vehicle,

r_{O_i} = other variable nonwage and nonvehicle expense per unit of output type i, and

FC = fixed costs of operating a department.

If a given department were operating at the minimum total cost to produce a given mix of outputs, it should employ inputs such that the ratio of their marginal physical products (across all outputs) was just equal to the ratio of their respective wage rates. For officers assigned to patrol and officers assigned to other duties in a department, this would require that

$$\frac{MPP_P}{MPP_{NP}} = \frac{a_i O_i / P}{b_i O_i / NP} = \frac{w_P}{w_{NP}}, \tag{6}$$

or that the ratio of patrol officers to officers with other assignments in the department be

$$\frac{P}{NP} = \frac{a_i w_{NP}}{b_i w_P}. \tag{7}$$

Police departments that employed inputs in ratios other than these could still be operating in a technically efficient manner, but they would not have chosen the least cost combination of inputs to produce a given output.

By examining the estimated output elasticities, still assuming pressures for efficient operation, we could explore questions of scale efficiencies (holding other outputs constant). All of these elasticities are assumed to lie between zero and one. Whether the sum of the output elasticities, $a_i + b_i + c_i + d_i$, is less than, equal to, or greater than 1.0 would indicate whether production is subject to decreasing, constant, or increasing returns to scale of output. With that in mind, we could define a scale efficiency parameter, e_i, as

$$e_i = (a_i + b_i + c_i + d_i) - 1. \tag{8}$$

Where this parameter was positive, increasing the scale of output would be warranted on efficiency grounds. Where it is negative, decreasing the scale of operation would be in order.

Unfortunately, the factors contributing to scale efficiency are likely to be complex. Economists since at least Adam Smith have thought that economies of scale would result from the opportunities for the division of labor and corresponding specialization and mechanization. If such economies are found, then an X percent increase in all inputs should result in a greater than X percent increase in output, and the firm or bureau should expand its output accordingly. Most engineering and process estimates of production technologies indicate that returns to scale are positive over a very wide range (Walters 1963). Thus, unless some other factor intervenes, one would expect firms and bureaus to be ever increasing in scale.

Engineering estimates generally do not include the most commonly discussed limiting factor, however. This factor, control loss, is a managerial factor, not subject to easy engineering specification. Control loss results from the dynamics of the flow of information and control among members of the producing organization, particularly across levels of hierarchy within organizations. The information on actual operating conditions that flows upward to managers of such organizations can become distorted as lower-level personnel choose to report only those data that place their own activities in a favorable light (Tullock 1965; Downs 1967; Williamson 1967). Directions and commands issued by top administrators tend to become distorted and/or treated as irrelevant to actual conditions as they flow down through hierarchical levels. Thus, control loss phenomena, which increase with an increase in the size of an organization, may serve as the limiting factor on scale economies (Coase 1937; Robinson 1958). The interplay, then, of technical factors contributing to economies of larger scale and of managerial factors that lead to diseconomies of larger scale will determine in specific instances whether the scale efficiency parameter, e_i, is found to be positive, negative, or zero.

Other scholars have attempted to estimate police and other public service production functions and to make efficiency comparisons along the lines indicated above (e.g., Votey and Phillips 1972; Walzer 1972). Their findings have been mixed, some indicating the presence of scale economies (as in Walzer 1972); others finding no such economies, or even diseconomies, in police service production. One reason for these mixed findings may be that the assumption of pressures for efficiency in production is unwarranted. In order to explore that possibility, we turn to a behavioral model of bureau supply behavior.

A Model of Bureau Supply

In his formal model of bureau behavior, Niskanen (1971, 15) defines bureaus as those organizations that have both of the following characteristics.

1. The owners and employees of these organizations do not appropriate any part of the difference between revenues and costs as personal income.

2. Some part of the recurring revenues of the organization derives from other than the sale of output at a per-unit rate.

Most public service delivery agencies meet both these defining characteristics, in that neither managers nor employees can legally appropriate as personal income any difference (if one exists) between the lump sum revenues that are the major part of their budget and the costs of operating a department. Considerable disagreement exists about the objective function of bureau managers, but the first condition makes it unlikely that managers are motivated to reduce operating expenditures below the revenue received by a department. Most public bureaus are observed to spend as much money as they receive in appropriations. Little incentive exists to reduce expenditure levels below approved budget levels, as most rewards—status, increased salary, and other perquisites, for example—appear to be associated with larger bureau budgets. One way bureaucrats can increase the probability of larger future budgets is to ensure that all revenue allocated to them in a defined period is spent before the period is over. This line of reasoning leads quickly to assumptions of budget-maximizing and/or output-maximizing bureaus and bureaucrats. While much contemporary observation of bureaucratic behavior seems consistent with such assumptions, we prefer to delve a bit deeper into motivational concerns before stating any single bureaucratic objective.

The Bureaucrat's Maximand

Unless bureau chiefs are totally under the control of providers (or consumers), at least a part of the determination of bureau output and expenditures should be responsive to their preferences. To explore the influence of bureaucratic preferences, we must consider the objective function of a bureau chief. In particular, what are the likely entries in such a function?

A brief digression on private sector enterprises is useful here. In the classical theory of firms operating in competitive markets, entrepreneur-owners are assumed to have profit maximization as their sole objective. This is plausible in light of their position as claimant to all residual profits in such a firm. This motivation is not necessary to the assumption, however. The entrepreneur in the situationally determinate environment of the competitive market (Latsis 1972) either chooses profit maximization or market operations force his firm out of business. As Alchian (1950) demonstrated, it does not matter whether profit maximization is selected consciously or randomly; the result is the same. Only firms that follow profit maximization strategies survive. Not only is the entrepreneur forced to adopt profit maximization, but the analyst of competitive markets is also forced to assume that entrepreneurs in a competitive market are profit maximizers.

As soon as the rigorous conditions of a competitive market are relaxed, neither the entrepreneur nor the manager of a firm is forced to adopt profit maximization. Nor is the analyst forced to adopt this assumption. The theory of the management of the firm has advanced by adopting the utility maximization assumption underlying explanations of consumer behavior, rather than simple profit maximization (Marris 1964; Williamson 1964; Alchian 1965). In the managerial discretion approach to private firm behavior, the manager is assumed to pursue a mixed strategy, including striving for a minimally acceptable level of profits for shareholders. Once a minimum level of profits is achieved, theorists predict the manager will trade off some of any further increments in profits for expenditures that increase the manager's status, income, and leisure. The extent to which a manager is capable of diverting resources for personal rewards "depends on the costs to the stockholders of detecting and policing the manager's behavior and effectiveness, i.e., on the costs of enforcing contracts" (Alchian 1965, 34). These costs vary systematically with the type of ownership arrangements.

It seems reasonable to anticipate that *public sector* managers might also wish to divert some resources for personal rewards. Despite possible training and socialization with respect to "the public interest," public actors should not be thought of as a race apart from normal human beings (McKean 1964). Utility maximization assumptions may be as useful, perhaps more so, in predicting public sector behavior as they have been in analyses of private sector managerial behavior.

Utility-maximizing private sector actors are assumed to have objective functions that include profits as well as perquisites. That is, some level of profits is necessary to the successful enterprise, with both pecuniary and nonpecuniary rewards to managers determined in part by the level of profits. Profits, too, are typically used as a measure of performance in the private sector. Firms that are more profitable than others facing comparable markets are judged more effective, and their managements are likely to receive higher rewards, both in direct salaries and in other benefits (Lewellyn and Huntsman 1970). To develop a public sector analogy, we must define the public sector equivalent of profits.

Possible substitutes include the concept of a fiscal residuum (Orzechowski 1977) or that of a bureau's discretionary budget (Niskanen 1975). Orzechowski defines fiscal residuum as "the difference between tax dollars collected for a public service and the minimum costs of producing that service" (1977, 231). The bureau's discretionary budget is the difference between the maximum budget that the provider would approve for a given output and the minimum total cost of supplying that quantity of output.[3] Both concepts include some attention to the net benefits supplied to a provider's constituents. That is, we assume that no provider would approve a budget and output combination where net benefits to at least a majority of consumers are not greater than (or just equal to) zero. Otherwise, an alternative slate of candidates for provider positions could replace the current provider at the next election (see MacKay and Weaver 1978; and Langbein 1980, for explicit statements of this position). Using the concepts of fiscal residuum or discretionary budget, attention immediately turns to discovering whether the bureau is able to capture this surplus through overproduction or through inefficient (higher unit cost) production of a given quantity.

We prefer a different formulation, one that explicitly puts the benefits to consumers into the model. Consequently, we define a performance measure called a benefits residuum, which is the difference between the total value of a bureau's output to citizens of a providing organization and the total cost of producing that quantity of output. That is,

$$BR = \sum_i v_i O_i - TC, \qquad (9)$$

where
BR = benefits residuum,
v_i = the average per unit valuation of output i across citizens of the providing organization, and
TC = total cost of producing the sum of the O_i's.

Obviously, this formulation requires eventual refinement to include consideration of the distribution of benefits across consumers. We are also aware that, for most public bureaus, it is extremely difficult to obtain reliable and valid measures of outputs, of the values per unit of output, and even for the components of a cost function. The difficulty of measuring costs is not, however, avoided by using the concept of fiscal residuum. While measuring the outputs of some public bureaus is extraordinarily difficult given the public good nature of those outputs, we feel it is essential to develop a conceptual performance measure that captures some aspects of the meaning of the term, the public interest.

Having defined the benefits residuum as an entry in bureaucratic objective functions, we hasten to add that there are likely to be additional entries in those functions as well. Bureau chiefs are assumed capable of diverting some bureau resources to personal rewards, perhaps additional perquisites of office, increased status among his or her peers, or, like some characterizations of private sector managers, an easy life. The extent to which such capabilities are exercised depends on bureaucrats' motivations and the constraints they confront. We turn next to some models of bureaucratic motivation and then to constraints.

Models of Bureaucratic Managers

Two polar models of bureaucratic managers can be advanced. One of these, a "selfless bureaucrat" model, seems implicit in much of the literature of public administration. The second polar model suggests a totally rapacious bureaucrat, who strives to capture all possible surpluses for himself and for those whom he must satisfy to maintain his position. We suspect that neither polar model captures the reality of bureaucratic motivations, but briefly review each before offering an alternative.

The selfless bureaucrat in our terminology is solely interested in maximizing the benefits residuum. The selfless bureaucrat knows citizens' preferences sufficiently well to be able to define "the public interest." He or she pursues that public interest with single-minded devotion. Using this model, one can safely dispense with controls aimed at monitoring or constraining bureau chiefs' exercises of discretion. Thus when one hears of reforms designed to strengthen hierarchical control in public bureaus or, even more, when one hears of reforms designed to reduce political control or "interference" in the operation of public bureaus, one can assume the proponents are employing a selfless bureaucrat model. By eliminating unnecessary impediments, they would argue, bureau chiefs are freed to maximize net benefits to their consumers. This selfless bureaucrat model might be viewed as the equivalent of the pure profit-maximizing model in the private sector. Given that profit maximization is not the sole strategy adopted in the private sector unless heads of firms are driven to it by the rigor of a competitive market, it seems naive to assume complete selflessness in the public sector unless comparable mechanisms exist to force such single-minded bureaucratic pursuit. We see few institutional arrangements in the public sector that carry such force.

On the other hand, total rapaciousness seems naive also. Models of this nature posit budget maximization as the sole strategy, where bureau chiefs attempt to extract the full consumer surplus available to a consuming community by increasing budgets (and output) to the maximum obtainable. We disagree with such a formulation on two different grounds. First, it seems to us to entail too much work on the part of bureaucrats and bureaucratic employees. Increasing output beyond some point, even if it were to lead to subsequently higher budgets, is likely to increase the workload of bureau managers beyond their preferred levels. Second, we perceive bureau chiefs—at least at the local level—as taking some pride in "doing a good job." Part of that good job, we believe, includes supplying net benefits to their consumers.

Because of our reservations about either polar model of bureaucratic managers, we choose to use a utility-maximizing model, with objective function entries drawn from both polar models. Our utility-maximizing model is basically a managerial discretion model, modified from the work of Williamson (1964), Pondy (1968), and Orzechowski (1977). We assume that bureau managers derive utility from the benefits residuum *and* from resources devoted to bureau personnel. The utility derived from a positive benefits residuum comes from the increased probability of job retention and advancement associated with a positive consumer surplus among the constituents of the providing organization and from personal satisfaction with serving the public well. Many local urban service bureau managers live in the community they serve and consume the output of their own bureau. We feel it is reasonable to assume that a local public service bureau chief will want to gain confidence and appreciation from citizens served and from friends, family, and neighbors for creating a positive consumer surplus. We also feel it is reasonable that a bureau chief would be willing to trade off some utility derived from the benefits residuum for increased utility derived from investment in bureau personnel.

In terms of total numbers of employees, a bureau chief's own salary and status are usually a positive monotonic function of the size of the bureau. However, the chief may derive even more satisfaction from investments in specialized personnel and staff assigned to help with the administrative load. In regard to hospitals, Lee (1972, 85) has argued that "inputs are used as status symbol, or, in other words, the pattern of input utilization defines the status group to which a hospital belongs." He also argues that hospital managers participate in a "keep up with the Jones's game" in that the "desired inputs of, say the ith hospital is assumed to be a function of the inputs utilized by other hospitals" (ibid.). If this same game characterizes urban police departments, which we think is the case, departments and their managers derive considerable status and recognition for investing in specialized personnel. Having their own homicide investigation bureau, bad check or arson team, dispatch facility, crime lab, and entry-level training academy adds to the status and, thus, the utility of an urban police chief. The sworn personnel assigned to administration significantly lighten the workload of a chief and also contribute to his utility.

Formally, the model we adopt posits that managers of urban police departments derive utility from both the benefits residuum and the number of staff or specialized personnel. In other words, the manager attempts to

$$\text{Max: } U = (NP, BR) \text{ Subject to } TC < B \tag{10}$$

The constraint is that costs cannot exceed the approved budget. Equation (10) can be rewritten:

$$\text{Max: } U = (NP, \Sigma_i v_i O_i - w_P P - w_{NP} NP - w_C C - r_A A - \sum_i r_{oi} O_i - FC) \tag{11}$$

Figure 16.1 shows the relationships among benefits residuum, bureau output, and specialized bureau personnel. For this graphical presentation, all output variety is collapsed to a single output index. In the figure we construct iso-benefits residuum contours for all staff and output combinations. Along the ridge line (L), the marginal effects on the benefit residuum of an increase in output holding staff constant is zero. Along (D) the marginal effect on the benefits residuum of increasing staff while holding output constant is zero. At (K), where the two ridge lines intersect, the optimum staff-output combination exists in terms of the benefits residuum. By slicing through the iso-benefits residuum contour in figure 16.1 along the ridge line (L), we obtain the possibility curve relating staff to the benefits residuum shown in figure 16.2. Points (K) and (A) are the same in both diagrams. We can use the possibility curve and axes of figure 16.2 to illustrate the difference between a selfless bureaucrat's objective function and preferred staff and benefits combination and the objective function and preferred position of our utility-maximizing bureaucrat.

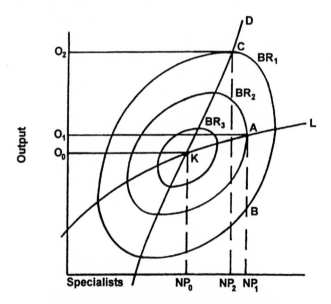

Fig. 16.1. Iso-benefits residuum contours

The selfless bureaucrat would derive no utility from the employment of staff specialists per se. His or her single-minded preference for benefits residuum is illustrated in figure 16.2 by the parallel horizontal lines labeled I_{sb1} and I_{sb2}. The line I_{sb2} represents a higher level of utility for the selfless bureaucrat and is achieved solely through increases in benefits residuum. Thus,

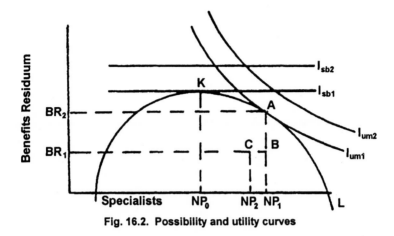

Fig. 16.2. Possibility and utility curves

a selfless (and efficient) bureau manager would select the output-staff combination that produces (K) on the benefits residuum. If the selfless bureaucrat were not efficient, some point below the frontier possibility curve would be chosen. In this case a reduction in the benefits residuum would result from the bureau chief's inefficiency rather than from the objectives sought by the bureau chief.

While the indifference curves of a "selfless" bureaucrat would be horizontal, the indifference curves of a utility-maximizing bureaucrat would tip to the right and be convex to the origin, as shown by the two curves labeled I_{um1} and I_{um2}. Thus, the utility-maximizing and efficient bureau chief would select a staff-output combination at A, with a lower level of net benefits for the community. If the bureau manager were not technically efficient, more staff than NP_0 would be employed but less output would be produced. An inefficient but utility-maximizing bureau chief might end up at point (B) in both figures, where the number of staff personnel is more than NP_0 and the increase beyond optimal levels (for the community) does not even produce the most output for the combination of input resources. Any utilization of staff larger than NP_0 can be considered an investment in excess staff from the perspective of consumers. The amount of excess staff can also be considered a measure of the extent of managerial discretion that can be exercised.

The extent to which utility-maximizing bureaucrats are able to exercise their preferences without constraint is a function of the institutional arrangements in which they operate. Any point along the possibility frontier from (K) to (A), or interior points to that section of the frontier, might result from bargaining between bureaucrats and officials of providing organizations.

Bureau managers must negotiate with providers on a regular but infrequent basis (sometimes once a year) for authorization to spend a lump sum over a defined period of time. Niskanen argues that the nature of the relationship between a bureau and the officials of a providing organization frequently approximates that of a bilateral monopoly. Given that officials of providing organizations frequently have no other potential supplier of bureau services, bureau managers may gain the "same type of bargaining power as a profit-seeking monopoly that discriminates among customers or that presents the market with an all-or-nothing choice" (Niskanen 1971, 25). If officials of the providing organization are unwilling to forego the bureau's services, they may be at a disadvantage in the negotiation over the amount of budget to be approved for a bureau. If the bureau is able to conceal information about its production and cost functions while obtaining substantial information about the demand characteristics of members of the provider's constituency, the bureau chief's capacity to confront providers with a take-it-or-leave-it proposition is enhanced (Stockfisch 1976). This capacity is further enhanced when no competitive or potentially competitive proposals are forthcoming, either from alternative suppliers or from comparative analyses by providers of the proposals offered and accepted in other, similar situations. Of course, institutional arrangements linking the provider and the bureau (and, where applicable, other potential suppliers) will affect the relative bargaining strengths of each. The situation is not fully determinate, as it is in Niskanen's first model (1971), but rather will depend on these relative strengths (Breton and Wintrobe 1975; Niskanen 1975). In addition, the role of constituents or consumers as they constrain provider behavior through elections and other means must be considered in fully developed models (see MacKay and Weaver 1978; and Langbein 1980, for models incorporating consumers as voters).

Interorganizational Arrangements and Bureau Supply

Just as we think that the linkages between managers of a particular bureau, the officials of the providing organization with which bureau officials negotiate, and the citizen-consumers who are the constituents of the providing organization will have significant influences on the bureau's supply, so we believe that the interorganizational structure of service delivery in a particular area will affect the supply by all bureaus in the area. Interorganizational structure for the delivery of police services varies dramatically from area to area across the United States and also from service to service within the broad police service rubric (E. Ostrom, Parks, and Whitaker 1978). These diverse service delivery arrangements for policing in this country afford us fertile ground for empirically testing effects of differing interorganizational structures. In this section we first describe some of the variation in service delivery structures for policing we have found and then suggest how some structural differences might affect bureau supply.

In 1974 and 1975 we conducted a census of all organizations supplying public police services in 85 metropolitan areas (SMSAs) across the country. We found that the number of suppliers of patrol service in the 85 areas ranged from one single supplier in Meriden, Connecticut, to in excess of 90 suppliers in Paterson-Clifton-Passaic, New Jersey. Fewer than half the areas had a single supplier of patrol service for as much as 50 percent of the population. The median number of producers of general area patrol in an SMSA was 13. The existence of multiple producers of this service in the metropolitan areas meant that, at least in theory, providers could obtain comparative data to weigh against the budget and output performance of their current producing bureau and might even replace their current supplier with one or more competitors.

We posit that the number of patrol producers (multiplicity) in an SMSA should affect the level of information that citizens as consumers and officials as providers have concerning the relative benefits residuum produced by a bureau that supplies their jurisdiction with patrol services. In a metropolitan area where there are many different producers (high multiplicity), citizens obtain information about comparative performance in several ways. Simply driving through the metropolitan area provides regular information about patrol density and the extent and style of enforcement in different jurisdictions. If a citizen or a member of his or her immediate family receives a traffic ticket in two different jurisdictions, an opportunity exists to compare directly the fairness, courtesy, and honesty of officers working in different jurisdictions. Most citizens in a metropolitan area with many jurisdictions know residents living in many different jurisdictions. Informal discussions of such personal events as being victimized, calling the police for assistance, or getting a ticket often occur among friends.

Public officials in a metropolitan area with high multiplicity also are likely to be better informed about comparative performance levels in the metropolitan area. Citizens who are unhappy with their own police and who know that their friends and neighbors receive a better level of service are more likely to call their elected officials than are citizens living in a low multiplicity area who have no way to compare the service they receive with that of other jurisdictions. Further, if city managers and/or mayors in the metropolitan area meet regularly, they can exchange relevant input and output information that helps each of them in their bargaining with police chiefs. The relative monopoly over information that Niskanen posits is reduced in a metropolitan area with a large number of producers. Thus, police chiefs operating in metropolitan areas with high levels of multiplicity are more exposed to removal if they increase staff and other input variables beyond the level at

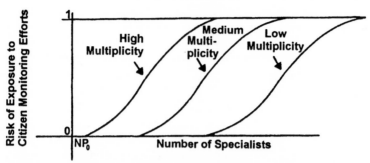

Fig. 16.3. Relationship between risk of exposure to citizen monitoring efforts and multiplicity of industry structure

which more effective departments in the metropolitan areas operate.

We expect that the lower costs of monitoring police department performance in metropolitan areas with high multiplicity will affect the shape of the indifference curves for bureau managers operating in those areas. In figure 16.3 we illustrate how this might operate by examining the relationship between increasing the staff of a producing agency in any particular jurisdiction and the risk of exposure to the monitoring activities of citizens and provider organization officials. As the risk of exposure increases, bureau managers confront such sanctions as severe criticism in the local press or by the city council, or even being fired for the relatively high costs of policing in one jurisdiction when compared to similar jurisdictions in the immediate vicinity. Where the benefits residuum is increased by adding to staff, there is little or no risk of exposure to sponsor monitoring activities. However, the risk of exposure should rise exponentially once the benefits residuum maximum combination of staff and other inputs has been surpassed. We assume that this "risk" curve is affected by the level of multiplicity in the metropolitan area. In areas characterized by large numbers of other producers, the risk is higher at all levels of staff beyond the optimal number for the benefits residuum (NP_0). This contextual effect of multiplicity on the relationship between size of staff and risk of exposure to monitoring activities should be reflected in the size of staff in police departments serving similar populations in metropolitan areas varying from low to high multiplicity. This results from the posited changes in the shape of managers' indifference curves, as shown in figure 16.4.

Using our assumption that police chiefs are utility maximizers, figure 16.4 shows the indifference curves for bureau chiefs in two different types of metropolitan areas (SMSAs). In low multiplicity SMSAs, the information available for monitoring a chief's performance in trading off benefits residuum and staff is low. Therefore, chiefs in such areas may be freer to indulge a preference function with a shift toward increased staff at the expense of some benefits residuum. In high multiplicity SMSAs, we posit that more information for monitoring will be available and, thus, chiefs will be forced to develop preference functions closer to that of the selfless bureaucrat, emphasizing benefits residuum more than their counterparts in areas with less information. One might argue that chiefs learn the risk of exposure and adjust their preference functions accordingly. As an alternative for those who wish to keep any individual chief's preferences constant, one can envision chiefs whose preferences are inappropriate given the level of information available for monitoring being replaced by a new top administrator whose preference function is appropriate to the situation. Police chiefs in the United States typically have quite short tenures (approximately two years on average), so this adjustment process should occur with fair rapidity.

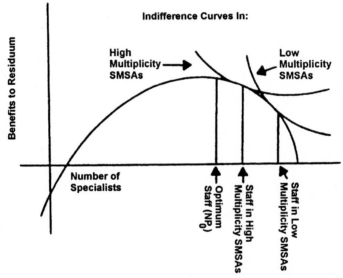

Fig. 16.4. Bureau chiefs' indifference curves in high and low multiplicity SMSAs

The usefulness of utility-maximizing assumptions (as opposed to assuming a single maximand such as budget, output, or benefits residuum) depends on being able to specify the arguments in the utility functions of managers and to identify instances where managers' costs of pursuing different combinations of those entries vary from situation to situation (Alchian 1965). We have specified two entries in such functions for police managers: the benefits residuum or net community benefits supplied by their efforts and the number of specialized personnel employed by the agency. We have also identified variations in interorganizational structure that will, we believe, provide some empirical explanation for differences in the choice of benefits residuum-specialists combinations across police agencies in different structures. We anticipate that police agencies operating in structures that reduce the cost of monitoring by citizens and by officials of provider organizations will choose to employ relatively fewer officers in specialized assignments, thus moving to the left on their benefits-specialists possibility curves.

Estimating Police Service Production Functions

In this section we estimate production functions for two common police outputs. We examine the functions for departments in differently structured SMSAs. We will see if the modes of production differ, as we might expect from our discussion of utility-maximizing bureau chiefs and the differences in their exposure to monitoring in different service delivery structures.

The two outputs we have chosen for analysis are (1) police response capacity, measured here by the average number of police patrol cars on the street;[4] and (2) arrests for serious crimes, measured by the number of Part I crimes cleared by arrest in a year. While police produce many varied outputs (see Goldstein 1977), these two are certainly among the most important to consumers and to the police themselves. A high proportion of police resources is typically devoted to maintaining an on-street presence and response capacity. Commonly recommended measures of police performance usually include response time as a measure of capacity and clearances as a measure of the effectiveness of departmental investigative activities. Thus, we feel comfortable in using these output measures for our initial estimations.

Alternative Estimating Techniques

Use of the Cobb-Douglas specification for modeling the production function for response capacity may be appropriate, in that many estimated production functions have been found to resemble this specification. But using ordinary least squares (OLS) estimation techniques with the logged equation and data from a large sample of departments raises other problems. OLS produces estimates for the coefficients of the model based on data from departments in the data set that may or may not have chosen technically efficient production strategies (efficient in the sense of maximizing output for a given set of inputs). If all departments confronted equal incentives toward production efficiency, this would not be a major problem. However, as one of our major research interests is the factors that contribute to choice of efficient production strategies, the use of average production functions is undesirable on this score.

M. J. Farrell (1957) offers a method for determining efficient production functions from observations on the inputs and outputs of many different firms. In concept the method is simple. One plots all combinations of inputs leading to a given level of output and then determines the innermost envelope of those points (the set of points closest to the origin on each of the input dimensions) for each of the isoquants of interest. Charnes, Cooper, and Rhodes (1978) offer a related method and show how it can be used with readily available linear programming algorithms.

Figure 16.5 shows a graphical representation of the method using only two inputs and one output. This restriction enables the presentation of two-dimensional envelopes. Three such envelopes are shown in the figure, one for departments deploying from 1 to 5 patrol cars, a second for departments deploying 6 to 15 cars, and third for departments deploying 16 to 30 cars. These envelopes were determined by dividing the number of sworn officers assigned to patrol and the number assigned to other duties by the number of patrol cars on the street at 10 P.M., and then plotting these ratios against one another for clusters of departments with given ranges of outputs.[5] The plots were then scanned and the innermost envelopes drawn for each cluster. Within each cluster, those departments that lie to the right of the envelope employ either more sworn officers in patrol for each car on the street, more sworn officers with assignments other than patrol for each car, or a combination of more officers with both patrol and nonpatrol assignments for each car on the street.

Decreasing returns to scale are shown for response capacity output using the frontier function approach. That is, the frontier production functions represent the minimum combinations of inputs that were observed to produce given outputs. The frontiers for higher levels of output lie to the right of the frontiers for lower levels of output, thus showing the need for more than proportional increases in inputs as the scale of this particular output increases. Of course, a portion of the decreasing returns to scale in the production of response capacity shown here must be attributed to the increased likelihood that departments are producing other types of outputs as the scale of their response capacity increases. We will investigate this phenomenon using the frontier function technique (generalized to n inputs and m outputs—see Farrell 1957; Charnes, Cooper, and Rhodes 1978) as our work in this area progresses.

Two average production function estimates are shown in figure 16.5 for comparison purposes.[6] The average estimate for 3 cars shows that approximately 4 sworn officers with patrol assignment are required for each car on the street, a figure close to that developed in various engineering estimates of officer requirements (e.g., by Kapsch 1970; and Misner 1960). The frontier function for 3 cars on the street indicates the possibility of achieving this output with, for example, 2.5 sworn officers per car on the street—1.5 with patrol assignment and 1 with a nonpatrol assignment. Thus, average estimates

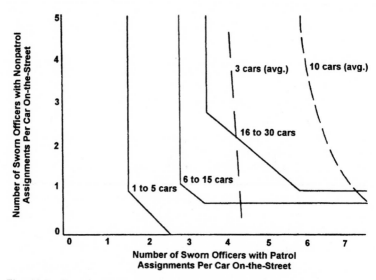

Fig. 16.5. Frontier and average production functions—number of on-street cars

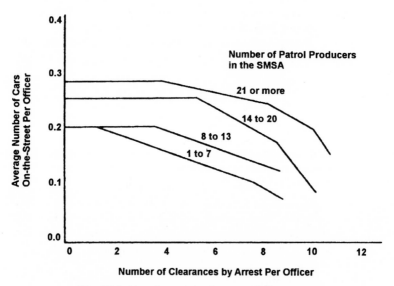

Fig. 16.6. Frontier production possibility curves

Note: This figure is reproduced from figure 12.1 of this volume.

indicate a requirement of at least 12 officers to put 3 cars on the street, while frontier estimates indicate this could be done with as few as 7 to 8 officers. The average estimates for deploying 10 cars indicate a minimum of about 80 officers required, while the frontier estimates show the possibility of deploying 10 cars with approximately 40 officers. These are indeed wide differences in input requirements.

Figure 16.6 (a reproduction of fig. 12.1 in this volume) presents frontier production possibility estimates to show how metropolitan structure may, in fact, make a difference. These frontiers show the maximum combinations of clearances by arrest and cars on patrol (both standardized by the number of sworn officers) that were obtained by departments in metropolitan areas with differing amounts of multiplicity.[7] These frontiers show the trade-off possibilities for response capacity and clearances among the most efficient departments, with the normal concave shape that one expects. They also show a significant upward shift in output possibilities as the number of patrol producers in a metropolitan area increases. The most efficient producers supply more output for given inputs in high multiplicity SMSAs than do the efficient producers in lower multiplicity areas.

We believe that the frontier curves of figures 16.5 and 16.6 are leading us to some interesting insights. It is likely that the shifts shown in figure 16.6 result partly from the presence of more departments of smaller sizes in SMSAs with higher multiplicity. Diseconomies among the fewer (and larger) departments in low multiplicity areas could explain their curve locations. At the same time, it seems reasonable that part of the shifts is attributable to the differences in availability of information in differently structured areas. We are currently working to split these two reinforcing tendencies, attempting to specify better the effects of service delivery structures.

Where Do We Go from Here?

In this essay we have proposed several models that we believe are useful in exploring police and other public agency performance. These models include an output or production function model, a model of bureau supply that suggests utility-maximizing bureau chiefs may trade off increments of net community benefits for status-raising choices of personnel deployment, and a model of some ways that interorganizational structure might influence such trade-offs. . . .

We have presented our models and empirical results to date as work in progress. We hope that our efforts to consider interorganizational influences will encourage other scholars to include consideration of such influences in their own theoretical and empirical work. We welcome suggestions and critiques on our work to this point as well as for further efforts.

NOTES

1. The use of producer, consumer, and provider comes from E. Ostrom and Whitaker 1974; and E. Ostrom, Parks, and Whitaker 1978; and, earlier, from V. Ostrom, Tiebout, and Warren 1961. Savas (1978) uses the terms *provider, consumer,* and *arranger* where we use *producer, consumer,* and *provider.*

2. We have chosen to use a Cobb-Douglas form for this initial statement of a police production function. In recent years many more sophisticated production function specifications have been developed (Intriligator 1978, chap. 8). Most empirical estimation has, however, employed the Cobb-Douglas specification. Most readers will find such a specification more familiar. We intend to explore alternative specifications as our work continues, with particular attention to the general form of translog functions, because of their capacity to fit virtually any form (Christensen, Jörgensen, and Lau 1973).

3. We use our own term, *provider,* here, rather than the term *sponsor,* which is more common in the literature presenting formal models of bureaucratic behavior.

4. Response capacity is actually a more complex function of the number of cars available and the volume and distribution of service requests and the time to service each. We are currently developing queueing theory based estimates of response capacity, including the number of response units and call volume estimates derived from functions representing the service conditions in each police agency's response area.

5. The method of standardization, dividing inputs by outputs, requires the assumption of constant returns to scale. We make such an assumption within somewhat arbitrary classifications of output level, but, by examining several such classifications, we are able to consider variations in scale returns.

6. These average function curves are computed using OLS estimates with equations such as (3).

7. In reality, these are "nearly maximum" combinations. In examining the plots for these relationships, some points appeared aberrant in that they were far removed from any similar points. Such aberrant points were excluded in drawing the frontiers.

REFERENCES

Alchian, A. A. 1950. "Uncertainty, Evolution and Economic Theory." *Journal of Political Economy* 58 (June): 211–21.

———. 1965. "The Basis of Some Recent Advances in the Theory of Management of the Firm." *Journal of Industrial Economics* 14 (November): 30–41.

Bain, J. S. 1959. *Industrial Organization.* New York: John Wiley.

Bain, J. S., R. E. Caves, and J. Margolis. 1966. *Northern California's Water Industry.* Baltimore: Johns Hopkins University Press.

Breton, A., and R. Wintrobe. 1975. "The Equilibrium Size of a Budget-Maximizing Bureau: A Note on Niskanen's Theory of Bureaucracy." *Journal of Political Economy* 83:195–207.

Charnes, A., W. W. Cooper, and E. Rhodes. 1978. "Measuring the Efficiency of Decision Making Units." *European Journal of Operations Research* 2 (September): 429–44.

Christensen, L. R., W. Jörgensen, and L. J. Lau. 1973. "Transcendental Logarithmic Production Frontiers." *Review of Economics and Statistics* 55 (February): 28–45.

Coase, R. H. 1937. "The Nature of the Firm." *Economica* 4 (November): 386–405.

DeAlessi, L. 1969. "Implications of Property Rights for Government Investment Choices." *American Economic Review* (March): 13–24.

Downs, A. 1967. *Inside Bureaucracy.* Boston: Little, Brown.

Farrell, M. J. 1957. "The Measurement of Productive Efficiency." Part 3. *Journal of the Royal Statistical Society,* series A: 253–81.

Goldstein, H. 1977. *Policing a Free Society.* Cambridge, MA: Ballinger.

Intriligator, M. D. 1978. "Applications to Firms: Production Functions and Cost Functions." In *Econometric Models, Techniques, and Applications,* ed. M. D. Intriligator. Englewood Cliffs, NJ: Prentice-Hall.

Kapsch, S. 1970. *Minnesota Police Organization and Community Resource Allocation.* St. Paul: Minnesota State Planning Agency.

Langbein, L. I. 1980. "Production or Perquisites in the Public Bureaus." Paper presented at the 1980 meeting of the Public Choice Society, San Francisco, California, March.

Latsis, S. J. 1972. "Situational Determinism in Economics." *British Journal of Philosophical Science* 23 (August): 207–45.

Lee, M. L. 1972. "Interdependent Behavior and Resource Misallocation in Hospital Care Production." *Review of Social Economy* 30 (March): 84–96.

Leibenstein, H. 1976. *Beyond Economic Man.* Cambridge, MA: Harvard University Press.

Levin, H. M. 1976. "Concepts of Economic Efficiency and Educational Production." In *Education as an Industry,* ed. J. T. Froomkin, D. T. Jamison, and R. Radner, 149–98. Cambridge, MA: Ballinger.

Lewellyn, W. G., and B. Huntsman. 1970. "Managerial Pay and Corporate Performance." *American Economic Review* 60 (September): 710–20.

MacKay, R. J, and C. L. Weaver. 1978. "Monopoly Bureaus and Fiscal Outcomes: Deductive Models and Implications for Reform." In *Policy Analysis and Deductive Reasoning,* ed. G. Tullock and R. E. Wagner, 141–65. Lexington, MA: D. C. Heath.

McKean, R. N. 1964. "Divergences between Individual and Total Costs within Government." *American Economic Review* 54 (May): 243–49.

Margolis, J. 1964. "The Structure of Government and Public Investment." *American Economic Review* 54 (May): 236–42.

Marris, R. 1964. *The Economic Theory of "Managerial" Capitalism.* New York: Basic Books.

Mique, J. L., and G. Belanger. 1974. "Toward a General Theory of Managerial Discretion." *Public Choice* 17 (spring): 24–47.

Misner, G. E. 1960. "Recent Developments in Metropolitan Law Enforcement." *Journal of Criminal Law, Criminology and Police Science* 50 (January/February): 497–508; 51 (July/August): 265–72.

Moran, R. A. 1977. "The Importance of Economic Criteria to Agency Administrators." *Evaluation Quarterly* 1 (February): 173–82.

Niskanen, W. A., Jr. 1971. *Bureaucracy and Representative Government.* Chicago: AVC.

———. 1975. "Bureaucrats and Politicians." *Journal of Law and Economics* 18 (December): 617–43.

Orzechowski, W. 1977. "Economic Models of Bureaucracy: Survey, Extensions, and Evidence." In *Budgets and Bureaucrats. The Sources of Government Growth,* ed. T. E. Borcherding, 229–59. Durham, NC: Duke University Press.

Ostrom, E., R. B. Parks, and G. P. Whitaker. 1978. *Patterns of Metropolitan Policing.* Cambridge, MA: Ballinger.

Ostrom, E., and G. P. Whitaker. 1974. "Community Control and Governmental Responsiveness: The Case of Police in Black Communities." *Improving the Quality of Urban Management,* ed. D. Rogers and W. Hawley, 303–34. Beverly Hills, CA: Sage. (Chapter 9 in this volume.)

Ostrom, V., and E. Ostrom. 1965. "A Behavioral Approach to the Study of Intergovernmental Relations." *The Annals of the American Academy of Political and Social Science* 359 (May): 137–46. (Chapter 4 in this volume.)

Ostrom, V., C. M. Tiebout, and R. Warren. 1961. "The Organization of Government in Metropolitan Areas." *American Political Science Review* 55 (December): 831–42. (Chapter 1 in this volume.)

Parkinson, C. N. 1957. *Parkinson's Law and Other's Studies in Administration.* New York: Ballantine.

Pondy, L. R. 1968. "Effects of Size, Complexity, and Ownership on Administrative Intensity." *Administrative Science Quarterly* 14 (November): 47–60.

Robinson, E. A. G. 1958. *The Structure of Competitive Industry.* Chicago: University of Chicago Press.

Savas, E. S. 1978. "The Institutional Structure of Local Government Services: A Conceptual Model." *Public Administration Review* 5 (September/October): 412–19.

Stockfisch, J. A. 1976. *Analysis of Bureaucratic Behavior: The Ill-Defined Production Process.* RAND P-5591. Santa Monica, CA: Rand Corporation.

Tullock, G. 1965. *The Politics of Bureaucracy.* Washington, DC: Public Affairs Press.

Votey, H, L., and L. Phillips. 1972. "Police Effectiveness and the Production Function for Law Enforcement." *Journal of Legal Studies* 1 (June): 1–15.

Walters, A. A. 1963. "Production and Cost Functions: An Econometric Survey." *Econometrica* 31 (January/April): 1–66.

Walzer, N. 1972. "Size of Operations and Cost of Police Protection: A Note." *Journal of Economics and Business* 54 (spring): 60–63.

Williamson, O. E. 1964. *The Economics of Discretionary Behavior: Managerial Objectives in a Theory of the Firm.* Englewood Cliffs, NJ: Prentice-Hall.

———. 1967. "Hierarchical Control and Optimum Firm Size." *Journal of Political Economy* 75 (2): 123–38.

Wilson, J. Q. 1968. *Varieties of Police Behavior.* Cambridge, MA: Harvard University Press.

CHAPTER 17

Consumers as Coproducers of Public Services: Some Economic and Institutional Considerations

Roger B. Parks, Paula C. Baker, Larry L. Kiser, Ronald J. Oakerson, Elinor Ostrom, Vincent Ostrom, Stephen L. Percy, Martha B. Vandivort, Gordon P. Whitaker, and Rick K. Wilson

In recent years, attention to the productive activities of consumers has increased. This attention is most common for service production (Fuchs 1968; Garn et al. 1976). Garn and his colleagues argue that when services are produced,

> the person being served (the client or consumer) is inevitably part of the production process, if there is to be *any* production whatsoever. Therefore, the resources, motivations, and skills brought to bear by the client or consumer are much more intimately connected with the *level* of achieved output than in the case of goods production. The output is always a jointly produced output. (1976, 14–15)

The role of consumers in producing public services has received particular attention. Partly in response to fiscal pressures and partly due to evidence regarding the inefficacy of their own unaided efforts, some public producers are increasing consumer involvement in service production (e.g., community anticrime efforts such as Neighborhood Watch or solid waste collection agencies' replacement of backyard with curbside trash pickup). In other service areas, consumers are demanding an increased role (e.g., parents and students working with groups like Push for Excellence to improve education

Originally published in "Consumers as Coproducers of Public Services: Some Economic and Institutional Considerations," *Policy Studies Journal* 9 (summer 1981): 1001–11. Reprinted by permission of *Policy Studies Journal* and the authors.

Authors' note: This essay results from regular discussions among the several authors that have extended over the past two years. Parks took responsibility for getting these ideas on paper at this time. The remaining authors are listed in alphabetic order for convenience. Our discussions and the preparation of this essay have been supported in part by grants from the National Science Foundation (NSF GI-43949 and NSF SES-79-13397), the National Institute of Mental Health (5T32-MH-15222-02), and the National Institute of Justice (78-NI-AY-0086). The support of these agencies is gratefully acknowledged.

services or the Wellness movement among health service consumers). Most analysts of public service delivery, however, have focused on the efforts of organized bureaus and firms, ignoring consumer inputs or assigning them only an insignificant, supplementary role. This focus by analysts is generally shared by public administrators and other actors. However, the productive role of consumers as *coproducers* of the services they receive has been a continuing interest for us. (See, e.g., Kiser and Percy 1980; V. Ostrom and E. Ostrom 1977; Percy 1978; and Whitaker 1980).

Coproduction

Robinson Crusoe (ante Friday) was a consumer producer. Crusoe consumed no more than he, himself, could produce or collect. As societies become more complex, however, a division of labor is common. Most individuals or groups of individuals produce goods or services in order to exchange them for money. Individuals and groups in a society who produce for exchange are, in our terms, *regular producers* of those goods and services they supply. These same individuals occupy consumer roles with respect to other goods and services. However, individual consumers or groups of consumers, *acting outside of their regular production roles,* may contribute to the production of some goods and services they consume. In such cases they act as *consumer producers.*[1] In many instances, consumer production is an essential complement to the efforts of regular producers; without the productive activities of consumers nothing of value will result. This appears to be characteristic of much public service production.

Coproduction involves a mixing of the productive efforts of regular and consumer producers. This mixing may occur directly, involving coordinated efforts in the same production process, or indirectly through independent, yet related efforts of regular producers and consumer producers. Coproduction, if it occurs, occurs as a result of technological, economic, and institutional influences. Technology determines whether there are production functions for a service where both regular and consumer producer activities contribute to the output. Economic considerations determine whether it is efficient to mix regular and consumer producer activities to produce the service. Institutional considerations determine whether appropriate mixing is allowed in situations where coproduction is technically feasible and economically efficient and whether mixing is discouraged where it is inefficient.

Technical Feasibility

If the quantity of output obtained from a production process is a function of both regular and consumer producer inputs, at least over some range of values of those inputs, then coproduction is technically feasible. All this means is that some change in the quantity of output obtained is expected if there is a change in regular or consumer producer inputs. The marginal products of regular producer inputs and consumer producer inputs are nonzero over some range of input values.[2] Technical feasibility is a weak constraint. Coproduction is technically infeasible only where no amount of regular producer inputs can affect the output obtained or, alternatively, where no amount of consumer producer inputs can affect the output. Technical production relationships among regular and consumer producer inputs with respect to the output obtained are crucial, however, for determining the economic relevance of coproduction.

Two ideal types of relationships can be stipulated where coproduction is technically feasible. In the first, regular producer inputs (RP) and consumer producer inputs (CP) are *substitutes*. If the production relationship takes the form, $Q = aRP + bCP$, for example, with a and b the respective marginal products of regular and consumer producer inputs, the two types of inputs can be substituted for one another. It is possible to produce output Q_O using only regular producer inputs (in the amount $RP_O = Q_O/a$) or only consumer producer inputs ($CP_O = Q_O/b$). To give a mundane example, municipal trash collectors and citizens may be substituted for each other in transporting refuse to the curbside or to other collection locations. At any point in the production relationship, a one unit reduction in regular producer inputs can be replaced by an a/b unit increase in consumer producer inputs and vice versa. When the relationship is one of substitution, it is unnecessary to know how much of one type of input is being used in order to determine the extra output that will be obtained by adding a unit of the other input. Thus, decisions about adding or reducing regular producer or consumer producer inputs can be made independently, guided only by their marginal impacts on the level of output.

This independence is not possible with the second ideal type, where the inputs are *interdependent*. An interdependent relationship might take the form $Q = cRP^dCP^e$, where c is a scale factor and d and e are the respective output elasticities of each input. With complete interdependence, no output can be obtained without inputs from both regular and consumer producers. The interaction of teacher and student in producing education in the classroom is a ready example of substantial interdependence. The amount of additional output from adding a unit of one of the inputs depends upon how much of the other input is supplied. Thus, decisions about adding (or reducing) regular or consumer producer inputs cannot be guided by independent marginal calculations.

Real world service production relationships probably combine segments where the inputs are substitutes with segments where they are interdependent. Most of the present authors would relax strict interdependence in service production, agreeing that some levels of output can be obtained via consumer production alone, though few of us would entertain the possibility of much service production using only regular producer inputs. Students can supply much of their own education in the absence of teacher inputs, but teachers can supply little education without inputs from students. Police have very little capacity to affect community safety and security without citizen input, yet citizens are able to protect their own homes to a degree in the absence of regular police inputs. Protection from fire loss is more of a result of household precautions than of inputs from regular fire service producers.

Economic Relevance

The particular mix of regular and consumer producer inputs that is efficient depends on the extent of interdependence and substitutability in producing a particular service and upon the relative wages and opportunity costs for regular and consumer producers. Production is always subject to constraint. Simplifying service production by stating all regular and consumer producer inputs as hours of labor, we can characterize economic constraints on service coproduction with a budget function. This function has the form, $B = wRP + oCP$, where w is the wage rate for regular producers and o is the opportunity cost applicable to consumer producer inputs. The budget function states all of the combinations of regular and consumer producer inputs obtainable at a given expenditure. The budget function, together with a production function, determines whether coproduction is economically relevant in a given situation and, if so, the efficient mix of inputs.[3]

Several combinations of budget functions and production relationships are shown in figure 17.1. Panel A demonstrates that the optimal choice of inputs with a substitutive production relationship is either all regular producer inputs or all consumer producer inputs. If the production relationship for Q_O is as shown and the relationship of regular producer wages and consumer producer opportunity costs is that of line B_1, then the least cost combination for producing Q_O is at point P_1, with RP_1 hours of regular producer input and zero hours of consumer producer input. If, on the other hand, consumer producer opportunity costs are much lower than regular producer wages, represented by budget line B_2, then the optimal (least cost) combination is at point P_2, with no regular producer inputs and CP_2 hours of consumer producer input.

In any specific case coproduction is unwarranted, though in the aggregate the output might be produced optimally using both regular and consumer producer inputs. That is, some consumer producers will feel that their opportunity costs are low and wish to supply the service exclusively with their own input. Other consumers will feel that their opportunity costs exceed the regular producer wages and will wish to have all of their service supplied by regular producers. Where both arrangements are possible, the aggregate service is likely to result from inputs of both kinds of producers.

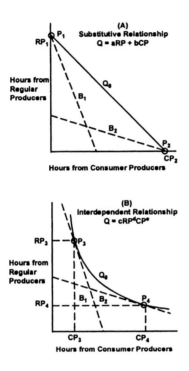

Fig. 17.1. Production relationships and budget functions

Panel B shows the more likely case for service production, interdependency of regular and consumer producer inputs. Neither regular producers nor consumer producers can supply the service alone; inputs from both are required. Still, the mix of inputs for least cost production depends on the wages and opportunity cost ratio. If it were as in line B_1, where regular producer time was cheap relative to that of consumer producers, the least cost for producing Q_O would be found at point P_3, with RP_3 hours from regular producers and only CP_3 hours from consumers. With more expensive regular producer inputs and/or cheaper consumer producer inputs, the budget function represented by B_2 might hold, calling for production at point P_4. Regular producer input would be cut to RP_4 while consumer producer input would increase to CP_4 for least cost production. Where interdependency exists, neither very high wages for regular producers nor high opportunity costs among consumer producers will prevent some mixing of their inputs. Indeed, by the nature of interdependency, some minimum quantity of input from each is required before any output can be obtained.

Institutional Considerations

Where coproduction is technically feasible and economically desirable in the production of a service, institutional considerations may still prevent or limit it. Institutional arrangements that negatively affect the likelihood of coproduction include those that bar or limit the use of particular inputs, those that fail to provide sufficient incentives for the employment of particular inputs, or those that mandate the employment of particular inputs. On the other hand, institutional arrangements may call forth coproductive behavior where it is economically undesirable. Mandated employment of particular inputs or production processes are examples.

Institutional Arrangements and Coproduction

Institutional arrangements are the key to matching coproductive activities to production opportunities where they would be efficient, and to their avoidance in inefficient areas. For some production opportunities, it is possible to rely upon market arrangements to call forth requisite levels of regular and consumer producer activities for efficient production. For other production opportunities, alternative institutional arrangements will be necessary to correctly apportion benefits and costs and thus constrain regular and consumer producer inputs to the correct mixes. An understanding of how institutional arrangements can foster or inhibit coproduction is important for designing efficient service production systems.

Market Arrangements

Where the production relationship of regular and consumer producer inputs is substitutive over some range, pricing mechanisms may be employed to induce an efficient mix of activities or to avoid mixing where it would be inefficient. Solid waste collection is a public service area where market arrangements can work well (Savas 1979). If there are sufficient competing regular producers, consumers can bargain with them to achieve the particular mix of price and service characteristics they prefer. Characteristics include frequency of pickup, location of pickup (e.g., backyard, curbside, or community dumpster), or whether any discounts for consumer separation of waste items are forthcoming. Some public regulation is required to ensure that service contracts meet sanitation and health standards, but details of service arrangements can be left to bargains between regular producers and consumers.

The key to efficiency in market arrangements is the capacity of consumers to choose the price and service mix they prefer. If constraints are imposed beyond those necessary for health and sanitation purposes—requiring, for example, that all consumers carry their own trash to curbside—then inefficiencies will result. Some consumers would be willing to pay the extra cost of backyard pickup. Requiring them to carry their own trash imposes an unnecessary opportunity cost on them. Other consumers might prefer to carry their trash to a community dumpster or even to a permanent disposal site if they could reduce collection costs. Forcing them to use and pay for curbside collection imposes an unnecessary direct cost upon them. Both types of unnecessary costs represent inefficiencies.

Difficulties with Market Arrangements

Market arrangements may be less successful in organizing the supply of services exhibiting interdependent production relationships. With interdependence, the apportioning of benefits and costs to each producer that is necessary to call forth productive efforts in a market arrangement may be impossible to determine. Regular producers and consumer producers may face incentives to shirk in their productive activities if they anticipate that their shirking will go undetected due to the difficulty of monitoring productivity. Where undetected shirking is a possibility, market exchange may fail as producers of either type cannot be sure that others will conform to their sides of bargains.

Interdependent production relationships may be doubly threatened by shirking where the consumer producer activities are collective in nature. Each individual consumer has an interest in seeing that the correct amount of consumer producer activity is forthcoming, yet has a personal preference that others supply the activity (Olson 1965). Consumer producers may shirk against one another as well as in their relationship with a regular producer.

Nonmarket Arrangements

Alchian and Demsetz cite the firm as one means of solving interdependence problems (1972). If input suppliers are joined in a firm, with a monitor observing the activities of each contributor to ensure that shirking is minimized, this substitution of hierarchy for market relationships enables the joint contributors to obtain additional output from use of the interdependent production relationship, while protecting each from exploitation by the others. If the team organization is successful, all members receive more than they might through individual, uncoordinated actions.

Are there public analogies to the organizational arrangement of a firm that can link and monitor the efforts of regular producers and consumer producers? V. Ostrom, Tiebout, and Warren (1961) offered a model of local government as service *provider,* organizing service financing through collective consumption units and purchasing services from the government's own bureaucracies or from alternative public or private suppliers. Providers can monitor the behavior of the hired regular producers. Providers can monitor consumer producer behavior, too, thus filling the role of monitor in the Alchian and Demsetz sense of linking inputs in an interdependent relationship.

Consider a group of potential consumer producers organizing themselves with respect to the consumption of a particular service. By assumption the service is collective in nature, so some coercive organization is necessary to ensure its financing. The individuals involved constitute themselves as a collective consumption unit, adopt rules governing the financing of service supply, and designate some individual(s) with authority to enforce the rules. The latter collect the necessary funds from members of the collectivity, make an arrangement with a regular producer of the service, and monitor the performance of the regular producer. Where collective consumer producer activities are interdependent with regular producer activities, rules governing their supply may also be adopted. Providers may then be in a position to monitor consumer producer performance as well as that of regular producers. The providers who supply this monitoring function could be local government officials as in V. Ostrom, Tiebout, and Warren's model or might be officials of local neighborhood organizations (Rich 1979). If monitoring by providers works well, efficient mixing of inputs by regular and consumer producers may be expected.

Difficulties with Nonmarket Arrangements

In the firm, the monitor occupies a central position in the productive arrangements. He can replace any of the input contributors whom he deems to be shirking, and at the same time, keep the team in operation. Two elements are essential. One, the authority to replace shirking team members and, two, the ready availability of replacements (Alchian and Demsetz 1972). Both elements are missing in public service supply. Consumer producers who shirk cannot be easily replaced. Banishment from a community is not a common practice. Fines can be assessed against members of collective consumption units who are found shirking, but the cost of monitoring is high. The authority to replace regular producers and the availability of replacements are problematic. Many local governments are limited by law to self-supply of public services. Where this is not the case, large local bureaucracies may use their political power to prevent replacement. Indeed, civil service and union agreements make it difficult to replace even one shirking worker in regular production agencies.

A private monitor has ample incentive to monitor vigorously, as his direct reward is derived from surplus generated by interdependent production relationships (Alchian and Demsetz 1972). This is not the case with most collective arrangements, where surpluses cannot be readily appropriated. Since their compensation is divorced from the efficiency of input mixing, public providers find it comfortable to avoid unpleasant or costly monitoring activities. Where inefficient production by regular or consumer producers reduces service output or increases costs, it may be simpler to raise taxes or assessments or seek a federal grant than to attempt to spur either side to more action. As the cost of monitoring input behavior is probably a positive function of the number of input contributors, we would expect inefficiency to increase with the size of the collective consumption unit. Local neighborhood organization providers may be able to control interdependent production efficiently, while officials of larger city organizations may not.

Local government arrangements for service production may often lead to a greater usage of regular producer inputs than is efficient. Organized regular producers may be in a better position to influence service providers than are consumer producers. Bureau heads meet regularly with mayors, city managers, or councilmen. Bureau employees constitute a politically significant minority in many communities. Where their influence is strong, bureau heads and employees can pressure local government providers to overinvest in regular producer inputs, thus increasing bureau budgets. Where monitoring of diverse inputs requires extra efforts to achieve efficient mixes, collective providers may decide to avoid those efforts by relying on regular producers and ignoring consumer inputs.

For all these reasons, collective organization of public service delivery may fall short of the efficiency possible (though not necessarily attained) in interdependent production organized in private firms. The lack of provider incentives to closely monitor input behavior and choose efficient coproductive mixes, together with rigidities that make it difficult to alter the input mix or directly stimulate improved input performance, virtually ensures some inefficiency. But as budget constraints tighten and further investment in regular production is less likely, local government providers may be induced to pay more attention to the possibility of increased consumer production (Rich 1981).

The recognition of consumer production opportunities may be accelerated as neighborhood organizations become more involved with service production (Rich 1979). Local neighborhood coproduction of public services may help to illustrate the efficiency gains that can be made. Neighborhood coproduction is likely to have service distribution implications also. Neighborhoods that are organized to supply and monitor consumer producer inputs in interdependent production situations are likely to obtain considerably better service outcomes. Regular producers may shift their efforts away from neighborhoods that are supplying substantial consumer producer inputs, however. Neighborhoods that supply a substantial amount of their own security through resident patrols or Block Watch groups may find themselves receiving fewer police patrols, for example. If so, the advantages in service outcomes that might be obtained from coproduction may be lost and citizens may become discouraged if their increased efforts are met with decreased efforts by regular producers.

In spite of these difficulties, we anticipate increased attention to and reliance upon coproductive arrangements in public service delivery. Budget constraints, together with a rising consumer awareness of the importance of their own efforts, suggest that a shift in the input mix toward consumer producers may be inevitable. As this occurs, coproduction may come to be recognized as an efficient alternative to increased reliance on regular producers in meeting rising service demands.

NOTES

1. Our use of the term *regular* for those who produce for exchange is not intended to imply that consumer production is not normal. Obviously consumer production antedates regular production for virtually all goods and services. As we argue here, consumer production is essential for most services.

2. The use of the term *nonzero* is intentional. Regular and consumer producer inputs may have negative marginal products in some ranges of production relations. Alternatively, one can consider the supply of inputs in the range of negative marginal products as a failure to refrain from inappropriate behavior, or shirking. We are undecided at present as to how such relationships should be conceived.

3. *Efficient,* as used here, refers to technical efficiency, using the minimum amounts of inputs necessary to achieve a given output; and to allocational efficiency, using the minimum cost combination of these inputs.

REFERENCES

Alchian, A., and H. Demsetz. 1972. "Production, Information Costs, and Economic Organizations." *American Economic Review* 62 (December): 777–95.

Fuchs, V. 1968. *The Service Economy.* New York: National Bureau of Economic Research.

Garn, H., M. Flax, M. Springer, and J. Taylor. 1976. "Models for Indicator Development: A Framework for Policy Analysis." Urban Institute Paper 1206–17. Washington, DC: Urban Institute.

Kiser, L., and S. Percy. 1980. "The Concept of Coproduction and Its Prospects for Public Service Delivery." Working Paper No. W80–6. Bloomington, IN: Indiana University, Workshop in Political Theory and Policy Analysis.

Olson, M., Jr. 1965. *The Logic of Collective Action.* New York: Harvard University Press.

Ostrom, V., and E. Ostrom. 1977. "Public Goods and Public Choices." In *Alternatives for Delivering Public Services. Toward Improved Performance,* ed. E. Savas, 7–49. Boulder, CO: Westview Press. (Chapter 3 in this volume.)

Ostrom, V., C. Tiebout, and R. Warren. 1961. "The Organization of Government in Metropolitan Areas." *American Political Science Review* 55 (December): 831–42. (Chapter 1 in this volume.)

Percy, S. 1978. "Conceptualizing and Measuring Citizen Coproduction of Safety and Security." *Policy Studies Journal* 7 (Special Issue): 486–92.

Rich, R. 1979. "The Roles of Neighborhood Organizations in Urban Service Delivery." *Urban Affairs Papers* 1 (fall): 81–93.

———. 1981. "The Interface of the Voluntary and Governmental Sectors: Toward an Understanding of the Coproduction of Municipal Services." *Administration and Society* 13 (May): 59–76.

Savas, E. 1979. "Public vs. Private Refuse Collection: A Critical Review of the Evidence." *Journal of Urban Analysis* 6: 1–13.

Whitaker, G. 1980. "Coproduction: Citizen Participation in Service Delivery." *Public Administration Review* 40: 240–46.

Suggested Further Readings

The best place to begin is with a report published by the U.S. Advisory Commission on Intergovernmental Relations (ACIR). *The Organization of Local Public Economies* (1987), written by Ronald J. Oakerson, provides a clear and succinct summary of the Workshop approach to understanding local government. A revised version of this report was published in 1999 as *Governing Local Public Economies: Creating the Civic Metropolis* (Institute for Contemporary Studies [ICS] Press). For detailed applications of these analytical concepts to specific cases, see *Metropolitan Organization: The St. Louis Case* (1988); and *Metropolitan Organization: The Allegheny County Case* (1992), both published by ACIR.

Local Government in the United States (ICS Press 1988), by Vincent Ostrom, Robert Bish, and Elinor Ostrom, is a textbook that provides an overview of the Workshop perspective on the study of local government. The authors devote considerable effort to locating local government within the context of the overall structure of U.S. government, because this book was originally prepared for publication in Italian. An earlier monograph that provides a clear discussion of the financing arrangements needed to make polycentric governance work is *Understanding Urban Government: Metropolitan Reform Reconsidered* (American Enterprise Institute for Public Policy Research, *Domestic Affairs Studies*, vol. 20, 1973), by Robert Bish and Vincent Ostrom. For a survey of the basic principles of rational choice theory upon which the Workshop approach to institutional analysis is built, see Robert Bish, *The Public Economy of Metropolitan Areas* (Markham 1971).

Patterns of Metropolitan Policing (Ballinger 1978), by Elinor Ostrom, Roger B. Parks, and Gordon P. Whitaker, covers the full range of research findings from the survey of 80 metropolitan areas. This book provides a considerable amount of detail on how these metropolitan areas line up on the values of several measures of overall governance structure. Descriptive summaries of a good portion of this material are presented in a pamphlet by the same authors, *Policing Metropolitan America* (U.S. Government Printing Office 1977). The contributors to F. X. Kaufmann, G. Majone, and V. Ostrom, eds., *Guidance, Control, and Evaluation in the Public Sector* (de Gruyter 1986), suggest several related approaches toward resolution of the conceptual difficulties involved in modeling large-scale systems.

There is no single book that provides an explicit comparison of the results of the evaluation of police performance in the Indianapolis, Chicago, St. Louis, and other metropolitan areas. Indeed, this lack of a book-length treatment was one of the inspirations behind the current volume. One important monograph is *Community Organization and the Provision of Police Services* (Sage Professional Paper in Administrative and Policy Studies 03-001, 1973), by Elinor Ostrom, William H. Baugh, Richard Guarasci, Roger B. Parks, and Gordon P. Whitaker. This monograph summarizes results from the earlier part of these projects, and it includes a clear statement of the components of the "production strategy" that smaller police forces rely upon to obtain such good results. Essays related to this project were included in *The Delivery of Urban Services: Outcomes of Change* (Urban Affairs Annual Review, vol. 10, 1976), edited by Elinor Ostrom; *Comparing Urban Service Delivery Systems: Structure and Performance* (Urban Affairs Annual Review, vol. 12, 1977), edited by Vincent Ostrom and Frances Pennell Bish; and special issues of *Publius* (4, fall 1974, "The Study of Federalism at Work," edited by Vincent Ostrom); and *Policy Studies Review* (7, 1978, "Symposium on Police and Law Enforcement Policy," edited by Fred A. Meyer, Jr., and Ralph Baker).

The implications of polycentric order for the study of public administration are detailed by Vincent Ostrom in his first major book, *The Intellectual Crisis in American Public Administration* (2d ed., University of Alabama Press 1989; 1st ed. 1973). The field of public administration has been defined as an attempt to realize the aspirations of the reform tradition (as exemplified by the classic work of Woodrow Wilson), even though this mode of thinking was inconsistent with the structure of the U.S. constitutional system as set up by the founders. The underlying principles of design that the founders used to set up a limited constitution are detailed in Vincent Ostrom's *The Political Theory of a Compound Republic* (2d ed., ICS Press 1987; 1st ed. 1971). In his two most recent books, *The Meaning of American Federalism* (ICS Press 1991) and *The Meaning of Democracy and the Vulnerability of Democracies* (University of Michigan Press 1997), Vincent Ostrom further expounds on the continuing relevance of Tocqueville's understanding of self-governance as the foundation of American democracy.

All of the research reported here has dealt with the U.S. context. Mark Sproule-Jones, *Governments at Work: Canadian Parliamentary Federalism and Its Public Policy Effects* (University of Toronto Press 1993); and Robert L. Bish, *Local Government in British Columbia* (Union of British Columbia Municipalities in cooperation with the University of Victoria School of Public Administration 1987), both demonstrate that institutional analysis and self-governance work north of the border as well. The latter book is nicely complemented by Robert L. Bish, *Governing Puget Sound* (University of Washington Press, 1982), which investigates all levels of governance in the neighboring state of Washington, including Native American governments. This same scholar prepared a summary statement on decentralization, *Basic Principles of Political Decentralisation to Local Authorities* (University of Pretoria 1983), as a contribution to constitutional reform in South Africa. Another country in Africa with a federalist governance structure is Nigeria, and Dele Olowu's *Lagos State: Governance, Society, and Economy* (Malthouse Press 1990) provides a comprehensive analysis of local governance in Nigeria. Dele has coedited several volumes dealing with issues of local and national governance in Africa, including *The Failure of the Centralized State: Institutions and Self-Governance in Africa,* 2d ed. (ICS Press 1995), edited by James S. Wunsch and Dele Olowu.

Two books completed by scholars from other institutions while they were visitors at the Workshop are worth careful examination, because they demonstrate how Workshop research can be connected to broader issues of import in literature on urban politics more generally. Robert Stein's *Urban Alternatives: Public and Private Markets in the Provision of Local Services* (University of Pittsburgh Press 1990) evaluates the effects on public policy of the ways in which municipal governments are organized. Mark Schneider's *The Competitive City: The Political Economy of Suburbia* (University of Pittsburgh Press 1989) examines competition among suburban communities as a form of market in public goods. Neither of these scholars adopts the Workshop perspective in toto, but they address many of the same dilemmas of local governance.

The current volume was prepared in conjunction with two other volumes of previously published articles and book chapters by Workshop scholars. Both of these books focus on research conducted by Workshop scholars after the bulk of the research projects summarized in the current volume was completed. *Polycentric Governance and Development* (University of Michigan Press 1999) focuses on the management of common-pool resources by self-governing communities throughout the world. This book also includes early statements of the Workshop perspective, dating back before the initiation of the police studies reported here. Both of the cofounders of the Workshop completed Ph.D. dissertations on resource use in the western United States, and it was only after they moved to Indiana University that they developed an interest in evaluation of police services. *Polycentric Games and Institutions* (University of Michigan Press 1999) includes technical papers that develop formal models and experimental tests of the conditions under which self-governance is likely to be successful. These two volumes complement each other well, because most of the models and experiments developed there are based on a generic representation of the problems associated with managing common-pool resources. It remains to be seen whether simple game models can be equally successful in helping us to understand the foundations of effective public service provision in metropolitan areas as the empirical studies brought together in this volume.

Scholars interested in federalism, citizen participation, and self-governance will find useful bibliographies at <http://www.indiana.edu/~workshop/wsl/bibs.html>. These bibliographies are maintained by Charlotte Hess, Workshop Librarian. Finally, readers are encouraged to check the Workshop's home page <http://www.indiana.edu/~workshop> for recent updates and for links to other reference and teaching materials.

Contributors

Paula C. Baker is currently a senior research associate at the Center for Human Resource Research at Ohio State University. She has an extensive background in the design and implementation of studies of public service delivery, labor market dynamics, fertility, family behavior, child care, and child development. Prior to her experience in survey research, she worked with experimental psychophysical and learning data in a laboratory setting. Since 1981, she has participated in the design, fielding, and analysis of the National Longitudinal Surveys of Youth (NLSY79). She is currently assessing the quality of the most recent NLSY79 data on the socioemotional, physical, and cognitive development of children, as well as coordinating the design of the next wave of data collection.

William Blomquist is associate professor of political science at Indiana University's Indianapolis campus and currently chair of the department. He was a graduate student in the Workshop from 1983 through 1987. He is the author of *Dividing the Waters* and the 1991 U.S. Advisory Commission on Intergovernmental Relations report *Coordinating Water Resources in the Federal System.* His areas of research interest have included water resources policy, theories of the policy process, and the organization of local government in the United States.

Larry L. Kiser is professor of economics and associate vice provost of university studies at Eastern Washington University. He spent a two-year postdoctoral fellowship (1978–80) at the Workshop in Political Theory and Policy Analysis and returned for a sabbatical year in 1983–84. He has published work derived from his Workshop experience in the *Policy Studies Journal, Urban Affairs Quarterly, Constitutional Political Economy,* and the edited volume *Strategies of Political Inquiry.* His current administrative responsibility for interdisciplinary programs also grew directly from his experience at the Workshop.

Michael D. McGinnis is Associate Professor of Political Science and Co-Associate Director of the Workshop in Political Theory and Policy Analysis.

397

After receiving a B.S. degree in Mathematics from Ohio State University and a Ph.D. degree in Political Science from the University of Minnesota, he joined the faculty at Indiana University in 1985. His initial research on arms rivalries and international conflict was published in several articles and in a book manuscript *Compound Dilemmas,* coauthored with John Williams. He became a Workshop Research Associate in 1990 and a Co-Associate Director in 1997. His current research interests concern institutional arrangements for the provision of humanitarian aid to communities displaced by conflict and famine.

Ronald J. Oakerson is currently professor of political science and chair, Department of History and Political Science, Houghton College. He received his Ph.D. from Indiana University in 1978 and served for several years as a senior scholar with the Workshop in Political Theory and Policy Analysis. He also served as a senior analyst for the U.S. Advisory Commission on Intergovernmental Relations. His research interests in institutional analysis have led him to publish on topics as diverse as coal haul roads in the rural United States, the overall structure of local public economies in urban areas in the United States, and the prospects for institutional reform and development in Africa. His most recent book is *Governing Local Public Economies: Creating the Civic Metropolis.*

Elinor Ostrom is Arthur F. Bentley Professor of political science, co-director of the Workshop in Political Theory and Policy Analysis, and co-director of the Center for the Study of Institutions, Population, and Environmental Change, all at Indiana University in Bloomington. She received her Ph.D. from the University of Southern California in 1965 and began teaching at Indiana University that same year. She has served as chair of the Political Science Department and as president of four professional associations: American Political Science Association, International Association for the Study of Common Property, Midwest Political Science Association, and Public Choice Society. She has served as consultant and member of advisory boards for several local and national organizations. She is a fellow of the American Academy of Arts and Sciences and received the Frank E. Seidman Distinguished Award in political economy in 1997. She was a cofounder and coeditor of the *Journal of Theoretical Politics.* Her best-known book is *Governing the Commons,* and she has authored, coauthored, or edited 11 other books as well as numerous journal articles and book chapters.

Vincent Ostrom is Arthur F. Bentley Professor Emeritus of political science and co-director of the Workshop in Political Theory and Policy Analysis. He received his Ph.D. from the University of California at Los Angeles in 1950. After teaching at the Universities of Wyoming and Oregon and at the University of California–Los Angeles, he joined the political science faculty at Indiana University in 1964. Throughout his career he has kept active in resource policy, serving, for example, as consultant for the Wyoming Legislative Interim Committee, the Alaska Constitutional Convention, the Territory of Hawaii, and the National Water Commission. He was editor in chief for *Public Administration Review* (1963–66) and president of the Public Choice Society (1967–69). He is the author of several books and numerous articles and book chapters. Among his principal works are *The Intellectual Crisis in American Public Administration, The Political Theory of a Compound Republic, The Meaning of American Federalism,* and *The Meaning of Democracy and the Vulnerability of Democracies.*

Roger B. Parks joined the Workshop family in the spring of 1970 when he enrolled in Elinor Ostrom's research methods class. This class began the Workshop's series of police studies with a comparative study of police service production in Indianapolis and three of its suburbs. Elinor Ostrom, Gordon Whitaker, and Roger Parks were co–principal investigators of this research project, which culminated in the Police Services Study of 1975–79. He completed his Ph.D. at the Workshop in 1979 and stayed on as associate director until taking a faculty position in Indiana University's School of Public and Environmental Affairs in 1983. He contributed to multiple articles in the mid- to late 1970s that demonstrated the foolishness of recommendations for consolidating police agencies. More recently, he coauthored (with Ronald Oakerson) a series of monographs and articles that serve as foundation pieces for the forthcoming National Academy of Sciences/National Research Council report on metropolitan organization in the United States.

Stephen L. Percy is professor of political science and director of the Master of Public Administration Program and Center for Urban Initiatives and Research at the University of Wisconsin–Milwaukee. He was a research associate at the Workshop from 1976 until 1982, during which time he worked on various components of the urban service delivery projects. In addition to writing the book *Disability Rights, Civil Rights and Public Policy,* he is author and coauthor of academic journal articles in *Payables, Public Administration Review, Urban Affairs Quarterly, Journal of Politics,* and *Social Science Quarterly.* With his colleagues, Steve continues theoretical and empirical assessment of Tiebout's model of local public economies.

Charles M. Tiebout received his Ph.D. in economics from the University of Michigan, as a student of Richard Musgrave. He was a member of the Department of Economics at the University of California–Los Angeles (UCLA) when Vincent Ostrom and Robert Warren were affiliated with the Department of Political Science at UCLA. Tiebout later joined the Department of Economics at the University of Washington. His article "A Pure Theory of Local Expenditures," published in 1956, is widely recognized as the pioneering work in the field of fiscal federalism. He unexpectedly passed away in 1968.

Robert L. Warren received a Ph.D. in political science from the University of California–Los Angeles, as a student of Vincent Ostrom. He has taught at the Universities of Washington and Southern California and is currently a professor in the School of Urban Affairs and Public Policy, University of Delaware. Issues in urban and metropolitan governance have been a primary focus in his research and writings.

Gordon P. Whitaker is professor of public administration and government in the Institute of Government at the University of North Carolina at Chapel Hill, where he has taught since 1973. He earned a Ph.D. in political science from Indiana University in 1972. His research interests include civic education and citizen participation, local government organization and management, alternative public service delivery arrangements (including nonprofit agencies), and professional education for public service. He helped organize North Carolina's Consortium for Civic Education. His books include *Patterns of Metropolitan Policing, Evaluating Performance of Criminal Justice Agencies,* and *Local Government in North Carolina.* In 1997 he received the International City/County Management Association's Award for Local Government Education for his work in civic education.

Rick K. Wilson has been an associate of the Workshop since 1977, when he entered graduate school at Indiana University. He received his Ph.D. in 1982. From 1982 to 1983, he was a postdoctoral fellow at Washington University. In 1983, he joined the faculty of Rice University, where he is currently professor of political science. He was in residence at the Workshop for the academic year 1989–1990 while on sabbatical. During 1996–1998, he served as program officer of political science at the National Science Foundation. He has published many journal articles and is coauthor (with Cal Jillson) of *Congressional Dynamics: Structure, Coordination and Choice in the First American Congress, 1774–1789.*

Index

Accountability, 307, 312
Administration, democratic vs. bureaucratic, 73, 97–98, 141
Advisory Commission on Intergovernmental Relations, 14, 151, 250, 306, 326–27, 393
African-American communities/black neighborhoods, 13–14, 203–27, 239, 242–43
Alternation, 268, 323
Annexation, 317, 329
Aristotle, 76, 81
Austin, John, 65–66

Balkanization, 284, 300n.1, 314
Beech Grove, Indiana, 181–96, 235, 332
Benefits residuum, 20, 365–73
Boundary conditions, 36–39, 109
Budget function, 384–85
Bureaucracy, 130, 148, 356–70, 388
See also Public agency/bureau

Center city, 126, 128, 130, 132, 206, 211, 329, 339, 342, 345–47
Chicago, Illinois, 13, 128, 167, 215–26, 239, 292
Citizen
    evaluation of police, 165–68, 179–81, 187, 190–96, 219, 233, 240, 243–45, 247–48, 258–59n.4
    experiences with police, 165–68, 179–81, 184–87, 188–89, 219, 233, 240, 243
    participation, 22, 141, 144, 149, 154, 176, 211–12, 222, 315, 342–45
    perception vs. physical measures, 168–71

Citizen mayors, 313
Coercion, 81, 83
Collective consumption unit, 3–4, 34–41, 83–96, 269–73, 275–79
Columbus, Ohio, 213
Common-pool resources, 1, 19–20, 78–79
Community
    control, 143–50, 176–78, 203, 209–26. *See also* Polycentricity
    corporation, 213
    organizations, 184, 315. *See also* Voluntary associations/volunteerism
    policing, 22–23, 346, 349
Complex systems, 284, 295, 306, 307, 355–78
Complexity, 120, 284, 287, 292–93, 299–300, 307, 310, 320–21, 325–26, 356, 382
Conflict resolution, 47, 70–72, 96–97
    public economy, 7, 83, 96, 98, 298, 300, 318–19
Congestion, 77, 93, 294
Consolidation, 8, 10, 12, 18, 141, 166, 223, 298–99, 329–47
    See also Metropolitan reform tradition
Constitutional order, 316–17, 319
    See also Polycentricity
Consumption unit. *See* Collective consumption unit
Contract/contracting, 3, 41, 43, 46, 83, 85, 87, 95, 97, 98–99, 114, 148, 211, 255, 295, 297, 313, 321, 323–25
Cook County, Illinois, 13, 239
Cooperative arrangements, 53, 96, 98–

99, 148, 182, 196, 295, 323
Coordination, 277, 307, 323
Coproduction, 7, 21–22, 93–94, 381–90
Corruption, 97, 211
Cumberland County, North Carolina, 270

Decentralization/devolution, 1, 18, 215, 225, 299, 300, 346
Democratic administration. See Administration, democratic vs. bureaucratic
Denver, Colorado, 205
Desegregation, 340
Detroit, Michigan, 204–5, 210
Dewey, John, 32–34, 50n.7
Discretionary budget, 364–65
Discrimination, 208
Distribution of financial resources, 128–29
Dominance, 276
Downs, Anthony, 325
Duplication, 265, 278, 313, 323, 357
    See also Police services, duplication
Durham, North Carolina, 277–80

East Chicago Heights, Illinois, 215, 292
Economic development, 340–42
Education, 80, 91, 93, 109–10, 311, 318, 322, 335, 340, 347n.6
Efficiency, 3, 16, 38, 39, 44, 52–53, 82, 94, 98–99, 124, 143, 145, 150, 155, 214, 265, 286–93, 307, 308, 313, 320, 325, 358, 360–62, 374, 389, 390n.3
Elections. See Mayoral elections
Emergency communications, 335
Empirical research, importance of, 74, 126, 129, 142, 285, 307
Exit (voting with the feet), 2, 148, 308–10, 315, 325, 326n.3
    See also Tiebout
Externalities, 46, 96, 141, 145
    See also Spillover
    internalize, 33, 37, 40, 43, 45, 47

favorable and unfavorable, 33, 47, 145

Fayetteville, North Carolina, 15, 269–80
FBI Crime Index, 11, 179, 225
Federal funds, 338
Federalism, 1, 3, 63–66, 97, 265, 281
Federalist, 8, 57, 63–64
Financing, 5, 7, 89–92, 213
Fire protection, 77, 93, 311, 312, 315, 316, 322, 335
Fiscal equivalence, 91, 99, 141, 146–47
Fiscal residuum, 364–65
Fragmentation, 15, 52–53, 57, 68, 72, 95, 121, 140, 153, 224, 257, 265, 275, 277, 279, 281, 284, 295–98, 306–7, 310, 313–14
    illusion of chaos, 52–53, 119–20, 132, 140
Free-ride, 81

Gargantua, 31, 41–42, 49–50n.1, 284–85
Government failure, 82, 308
Grand Rapids, Michigan, 167, 197, 219, 236, 238

Hamilton-Middletown, Ohio, 279–80
Health care, 93
Hierarchy, 98, 143, 148, 149, 153, 300, 362, 387
Highways, 77, 314
Hobbes, Thomas, 65–66
Holdout, 81, 83–84, 96
Homeowners' associations, 4, 83–84, 347n.4
Home rule, 40, 41, 70, 312
Houston, Texas, 19

Incorporate/incorporation, 17, 40, 43, 47, 142, 316, 329
Independently incorporated communities/suburbs, 181–96, 206, 215–26, 235–36, 238, 241, 349–50
    See also Research design

Indiana Department of Motor Vehicles, 97
Indianapolis, Indiana, 11–13, 23, 167, 168, 181–96, 219, 235–36, 240, 329–47, 349–51
Institutional analysis and development (IAD) framework, 9, 11, 124
Intergovernmental relations, 14, 107, 116, 323
   See also Negotiation
Interorganizational arrangements, 94, 265–81, 355–56, 370–77
   See also Negotiation

Lakewood Plan, 43, 44, 114
Lawrence, Indiana, 181–96, 235, 332
Lexington, Kentucky, 18, 350
Local government structure, 332–34
Local public finance, 337–40
Los Angeles, California, 32, 38, 43–49, 114, 128, 208
Louisville, Kentucky, 18, 350

Madison, James, 66
Majority vote vs. unanimity, 83–84
Managers, 363–64, 366–70, 372
Market failure, 7, 82, 387
Marketlike, 3, 79, 83, 94, 97
   See also Quasi-market
Mayoral elections, Indianapolis, 17, 342–45, 348n.8
Measure(s), 11, 15, 151, 165–69
   See also Police services; Metropolitan structure
Meriden, Connecticut, 371
Metropolitan reform tradition, 10, 12–13, 140–43, 156n.9, 240, 266
   See also Consolidation; Propositions
Metropolitan structure, measures of, 267–81, 295–30
Milwaukee, Wisconsin, 205
Monitoring, 372–74, 387–89
Multiplicity, 15, 21, 31, 73, 143, 154, 211, 265, 275, 277–79, 287, 290, 371–73, 377
Municipal corporation, 330
Municipal water administration, 47–49

Nashville–Davidson County, Tennessee, 167, 238, 240, 331
National Advisory Committee on Criminal Justice Standards and Goals, 250 , 254, 255
National Opinion Research Center, 239
Negotiation, 48–49, 85, 299, 318
Neighborhood/community, 7, 12, 165, 181, 205, 225, 239, 241–42, 296, 298–99, 390
Niskanen, William, 20, 356, 362, 370–71
Nonprofit organizations, 5
   See also Voluntary associations/ volunteerism

Oakland, California, 208
Oklahoma City, Oklahoma, 152

Parks and recreation, 335
Paterson–Clifton–Passaic, New Jersey, 371
Performance, measures of, 18, 79, 81, 86, 99, 115, 124, 154, 165, 180, 184, 256, 287–88, 292–93, 299, 313, 324, 356, 365, 371–72, 374, 377, 389
Phoenix, Illinois, 215, 292
Polanyi, Michael, 6, 57–60, 61, 63
Police services, 1, 11–13, 93, 96, 110, 111–12, 146, 285–99, 322, 324, 335, 349, 359–62, 370–77
   consolidation, 232, 234, 236, 239, 240, 245, 250, 254–55
   cooperative arrangements, 182, 216, 221, 268
   costs, 233, 236, 238, 239, 243–45, 254, 258n.2, 297–98
   direct service, 267, 268, 272, 275–77, 280
   duplication, 268, 275, 279
   intermediate services, 267, 268, 271–72, 275, 279–80
   See also Citizen evaluation of police, Citizen experiences with police
   production function, 374–77

Political economist's approach
    See Polycentricity; Community
    control
Political machine, 67–68, 97
Polycentricity
    competition, 40, 42–46, 72, 95, 97,
    98–99, 148
    conflict resolution, 14, 42, 46–49,
    53
    cooperation, 42, 53, 72, 96, 146
    constitutional rule, 8, 61–64, 306,
    317–19
    definition, vi, 3, 31–32, 50n.2, 55,
    57–60, 71, 73, 285, 306
    judicial decision making, 59–61
    markets, 60–61
    political leadership and coalitions,
    66–68
    public service economy, 39, 69–73
Poor relief, 335, 340
Preferences. *See* Collective consump-
    tion unit; Provision vs. production
Private goods, 78, 81
Privatization, 346
Production function, 358–62, 374–77,
    384
Production units, 4, 82–94, 275, 277–
    78, 294, 322–24
Professionalism, 143, 149, 207–9, 226
    See also Consolidation,
    Metropolitan reform tradition
Propositions
    consolidation/reform tradition, 142–
    43, 155n.7, 207–9, 232–33, 298–
    99
    polycentricity/community control,
    126–29, 148–50, 177–79, 209–
    26, 234, 257–58n.2, 295–98
Provision vs. production, 3, 36, 43, 44,
    45–46, 84, 146, 314, 321, 357
    See also Collective consumption
    units
Public agency/bureau, 163, 165, 172,
    356–58, 365
    See also Bureaucracy
Public choice, 7–8, 10, 99
Public enterprise, 70–71, 72, 112, 113

Public entrepreneurs, 6, 16, 60, 67, 70,
    89, 91, 310, 315, 319–20, 321,
    326, 327n.11
Public firms, 356
Public goods
    boundaries, 33, 37
    definition, 33, 76–80
    exclusion, 34, 98–99
    jointness of use, 77–79, 86
    measurement, 13, 34, 35, 45, 71, 76,
    79, 99, 163–73
    scale, 33, 37–38
Public health, 335
Public housing, 335
Public interest, 364–366
Public service industry/industries, 9,
    50n.3, 69–73, 87–89, 99, 108–13,
    117n.4, 266–67, 321–25
Public-private partnership, 340

Quasi-market, 21, 43, 45, 54, 72–73,
    95, 98, 114, 116, 309
    See also Marketlike

Redistribution, 2, 91, 147, 213, 222,
    339, 346
Reform tradition. *See* Metropolitan
    reform
Regulation, 92–93, 113–16
Representation, 312
    See also Provision vs. production
Research design (most similar sys-
    tems), 181, 216, 235, 241
Road repair, 168–71
Roughometer, 12, 168–71
Rules
    decision rules, 124–25
    enabling, 317–19
    enforcement, 60, 62–64, 69, 84, 92
    formulation and revision, 60

San Francisco, California, 128
Scale economies, 94, 151, 156n.11,
    210–11, 220–21, 255, 256, 293–
    94, 307, 321, 323, 324, 358, 362
    See also Production unit
Scale of organization, 37, 314

Scale of political community, 39–40
See also Collective consumption unit; Provision vs. production
Scale of production, 14, 46, 145, 242, 288
See also Efficiency
Schumpeter, Joseph A., 131
Seattle, Washington, 205
Segregation, 127–28, 210, 219–20
Self-organizing. See Polycentricity; Spontaneous order
Self-regulating mechanisms, 115, 308
Service structure matrices, 15, 267–81, 281–82n.6
Shirking, 387, 388
Size of government unit, 141, 143–44, 149
See also Provision vs. production
Special districts, 142, 311, 314, 323, 330, 334, 338, 346, 347n.1
Speedway, Indiana, 181–96, 235, 332
Spillover, 254, 307
See also Externalities
Spontaneous order, 6, 57–60, 295–300
St. Louis, Missouri, 13, 140, 167, 197, 240–52, 310–25
Stigler, George, 144–46
Street lighting, 12, 168–71
Street services, 323, 324
Subtractability, 77, 89, 99
Suburban, 126, 128, 329, 339, 341, 342, 345

Tax base, 339–40, 346
Tax referenda, 315
Tiebout, Charles, 3, 16, 214, 308
See also Exit (voting with the feet)
Tocqueville, Alexis de, 8, 9, 66–67, 119–20
Toll goods, 78, 87
Tullock, Gordon, 62, 148

Unigov, 17, 181, 329–47, 351
Unincorporated areas, 43, 310, 312, 314–16
Unit of analysis, 83, 123, 125, 144, 266, 288

Unit of government, 83, 121–22
See also Provision vs. production; Collective consumption unit
User charges, 79, 92, 112, 115–16
Veto, 316–17, 325
Voice, 4, 71, 82, 90–91, 130, 140, 214, 308–20, 325
Voluntary associations/volunteerism, 8, 83, 88, 94, 96, 215, 318–19
Voting with the feet. See Exit; Tiebout
Voucher, 80, 87

Water industry, 89, 109–11, 115
Watts riot, 208
Wilson, James Q., 177, 207–8, 227n.6
Wilson, Woodrow, 8, 123